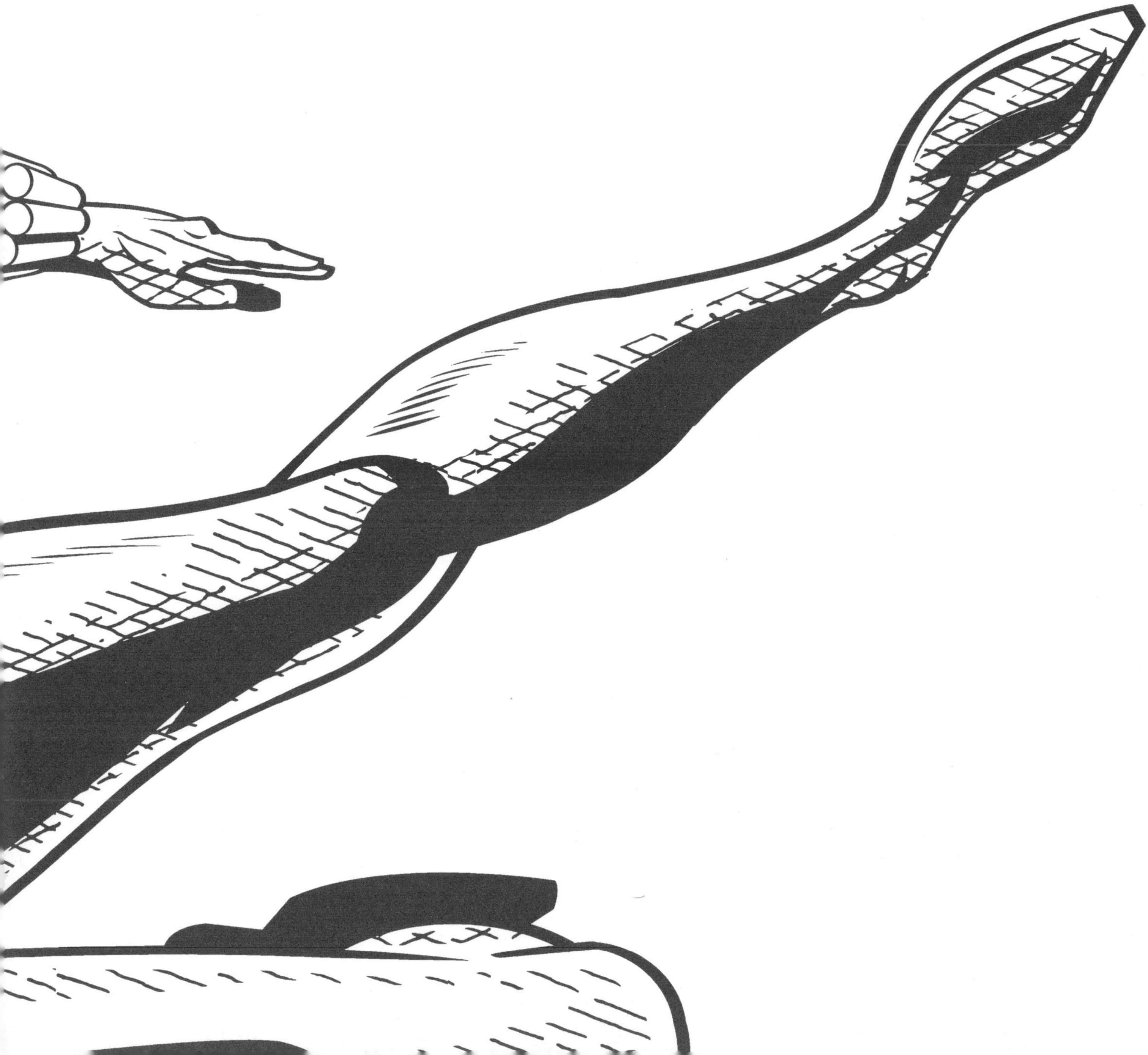

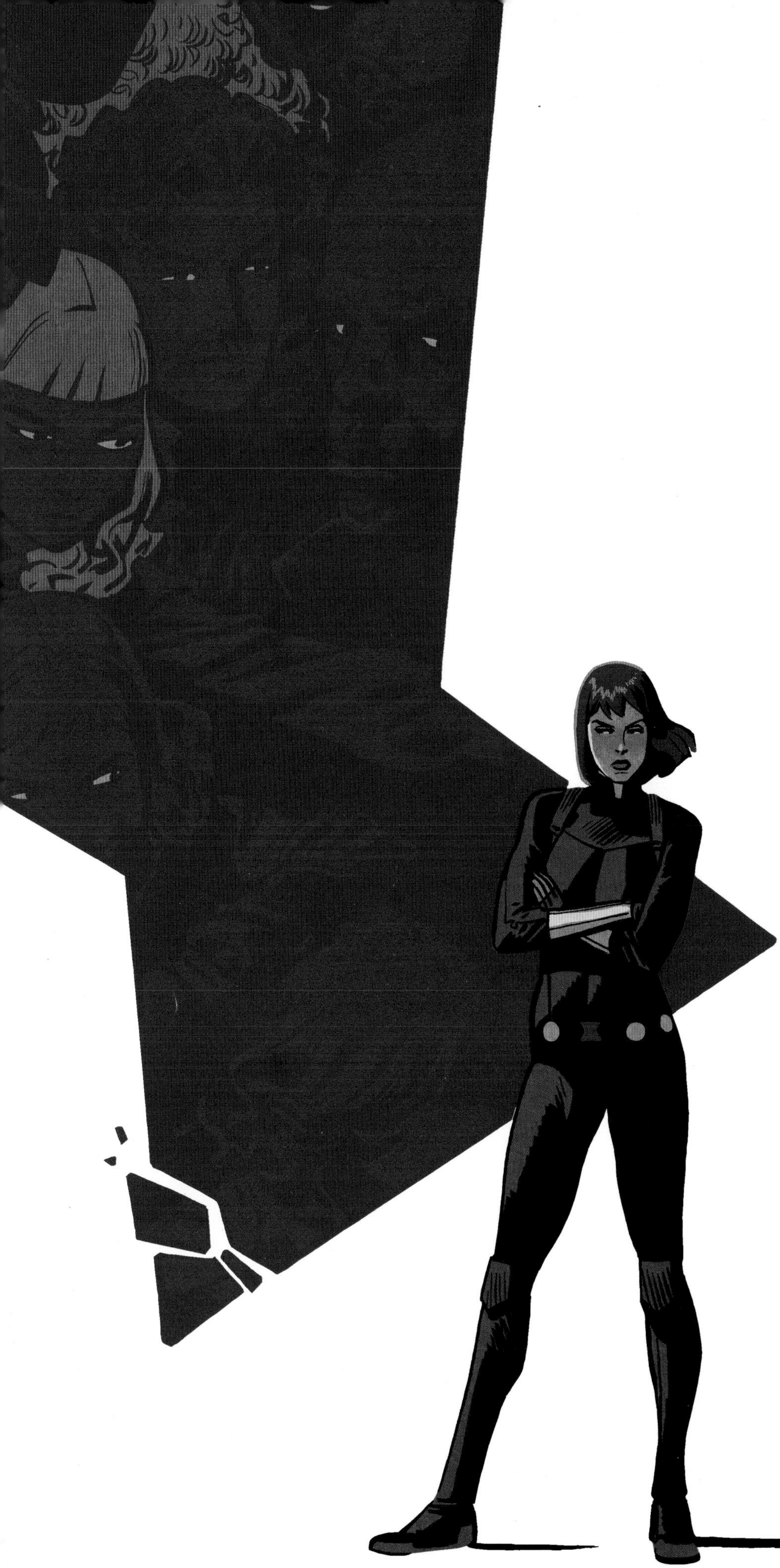

MARVEL

BLACK WIDOW

SECRETS OF A SUPER-SPY

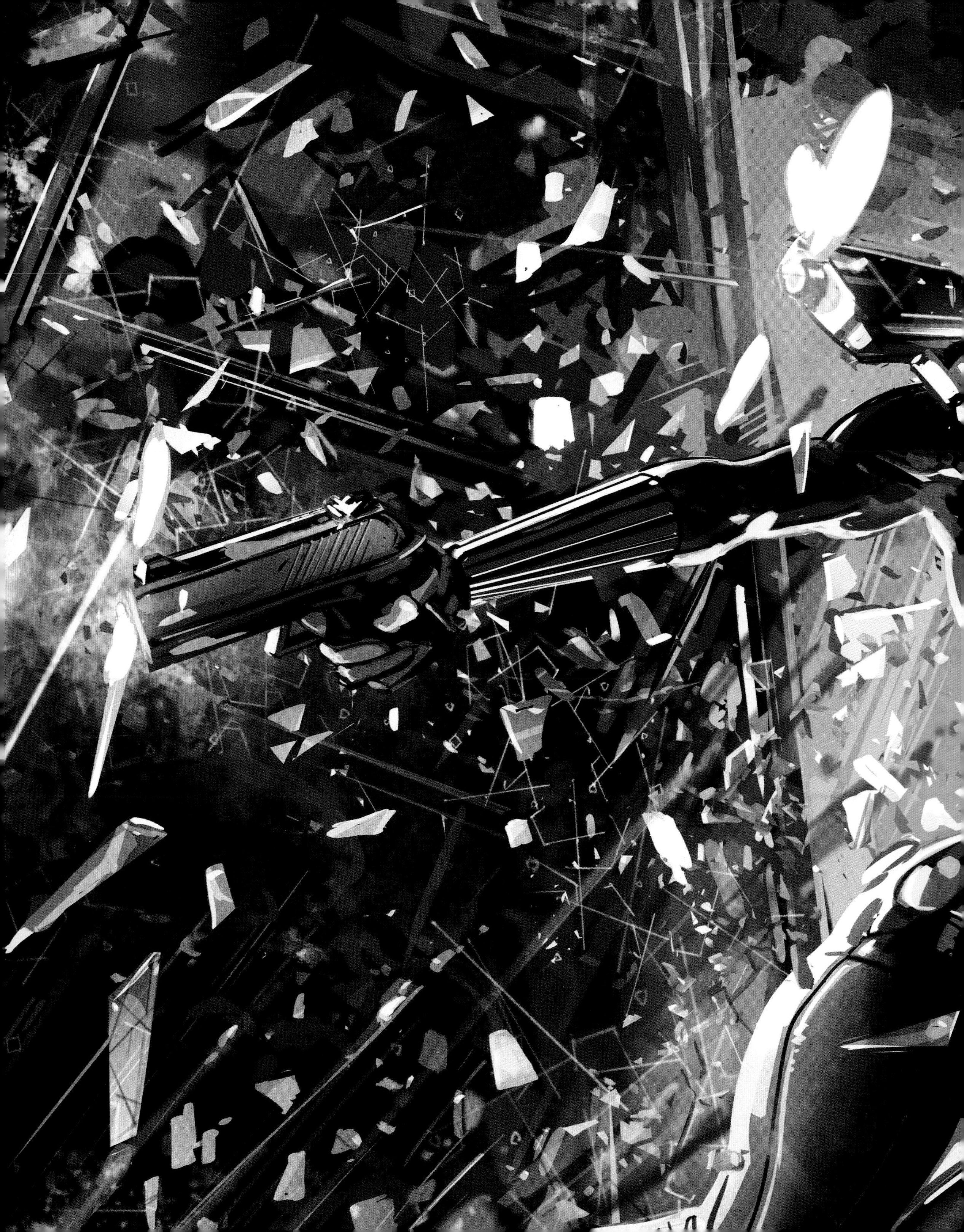

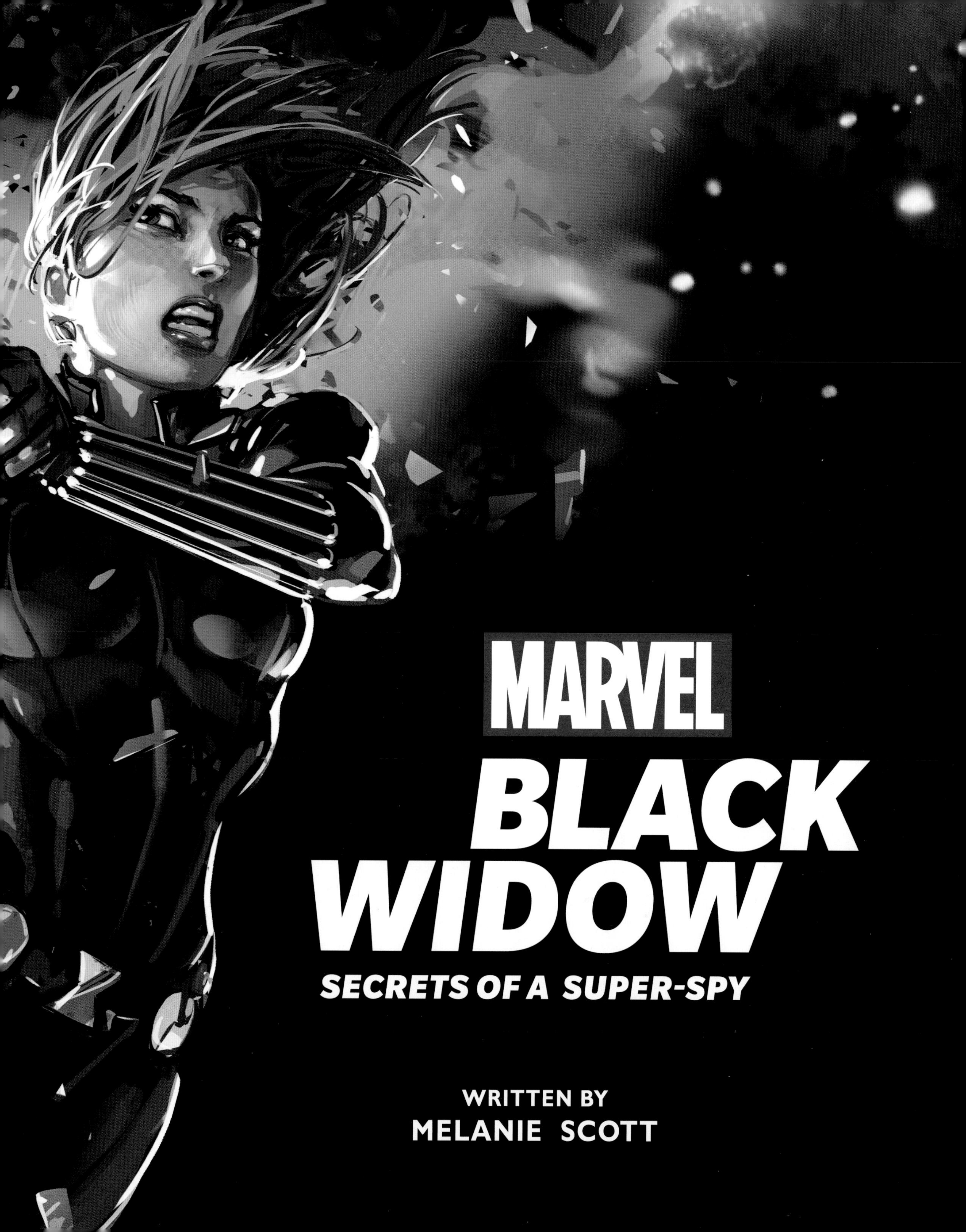

MARVEL

BLACK WIDOW

SECRETS OF A SUPER-SPY

WRITTEN BY
MELANIE SCOTT

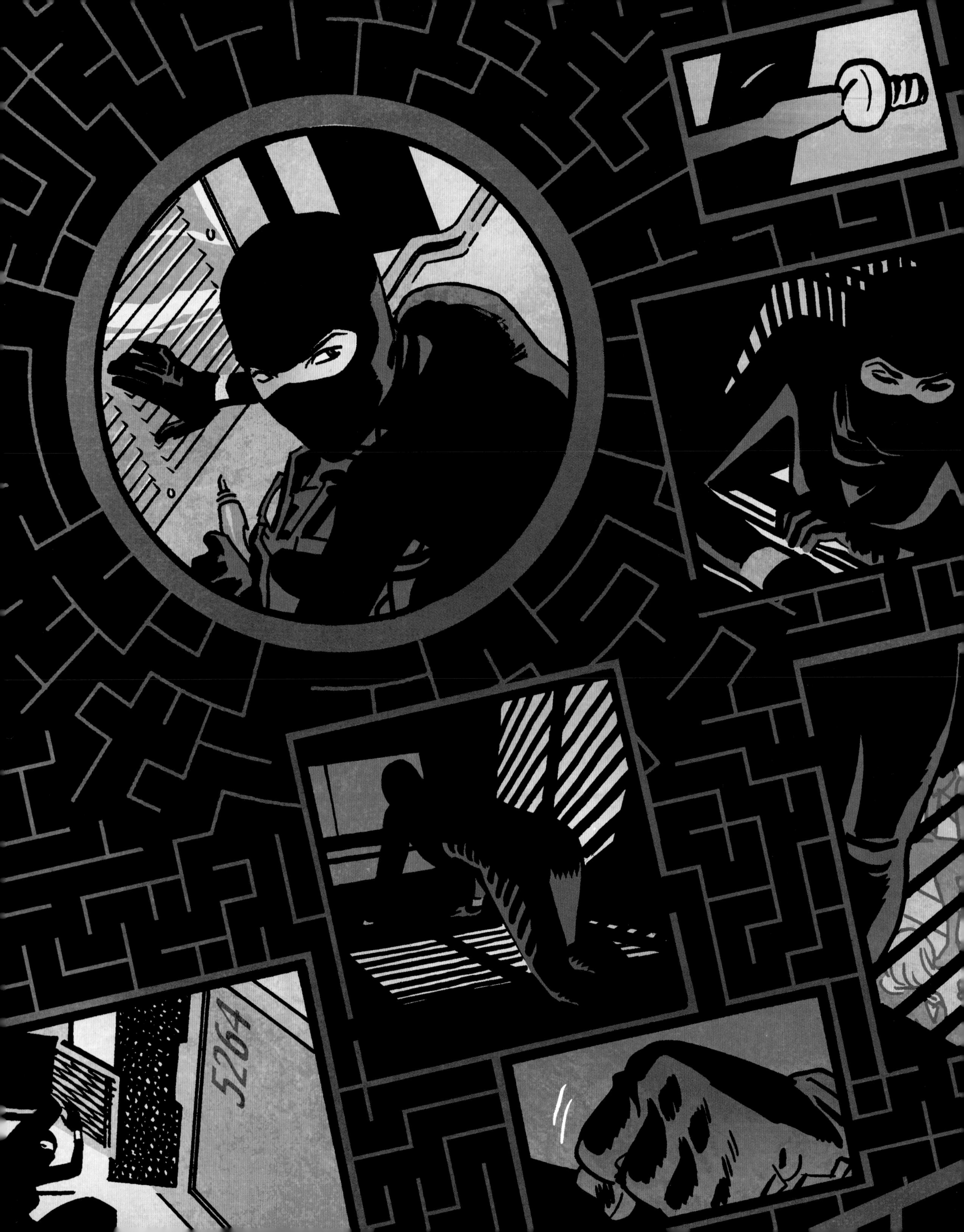
5264

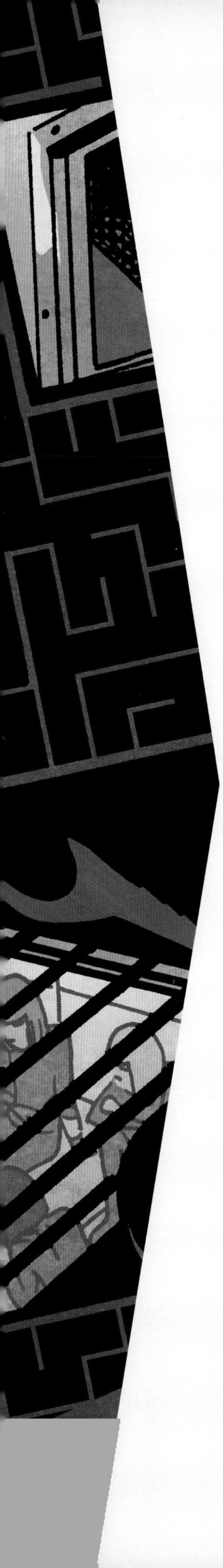

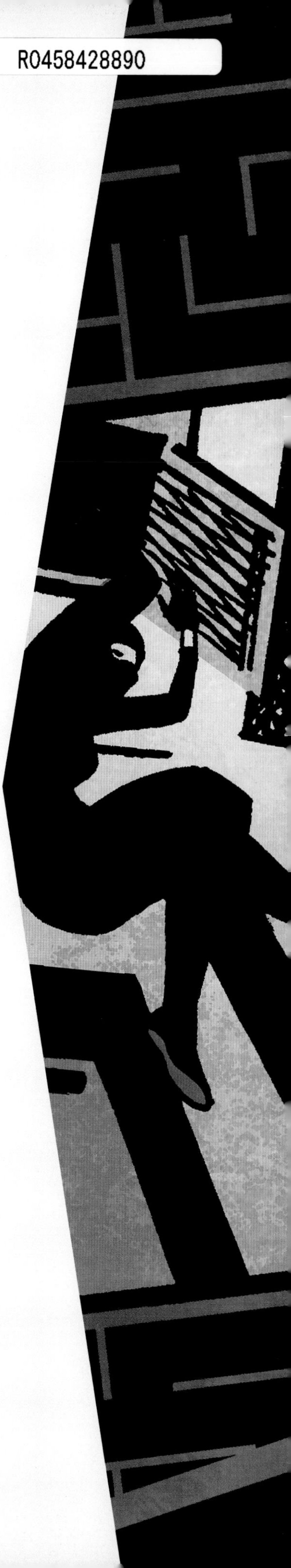

Contents

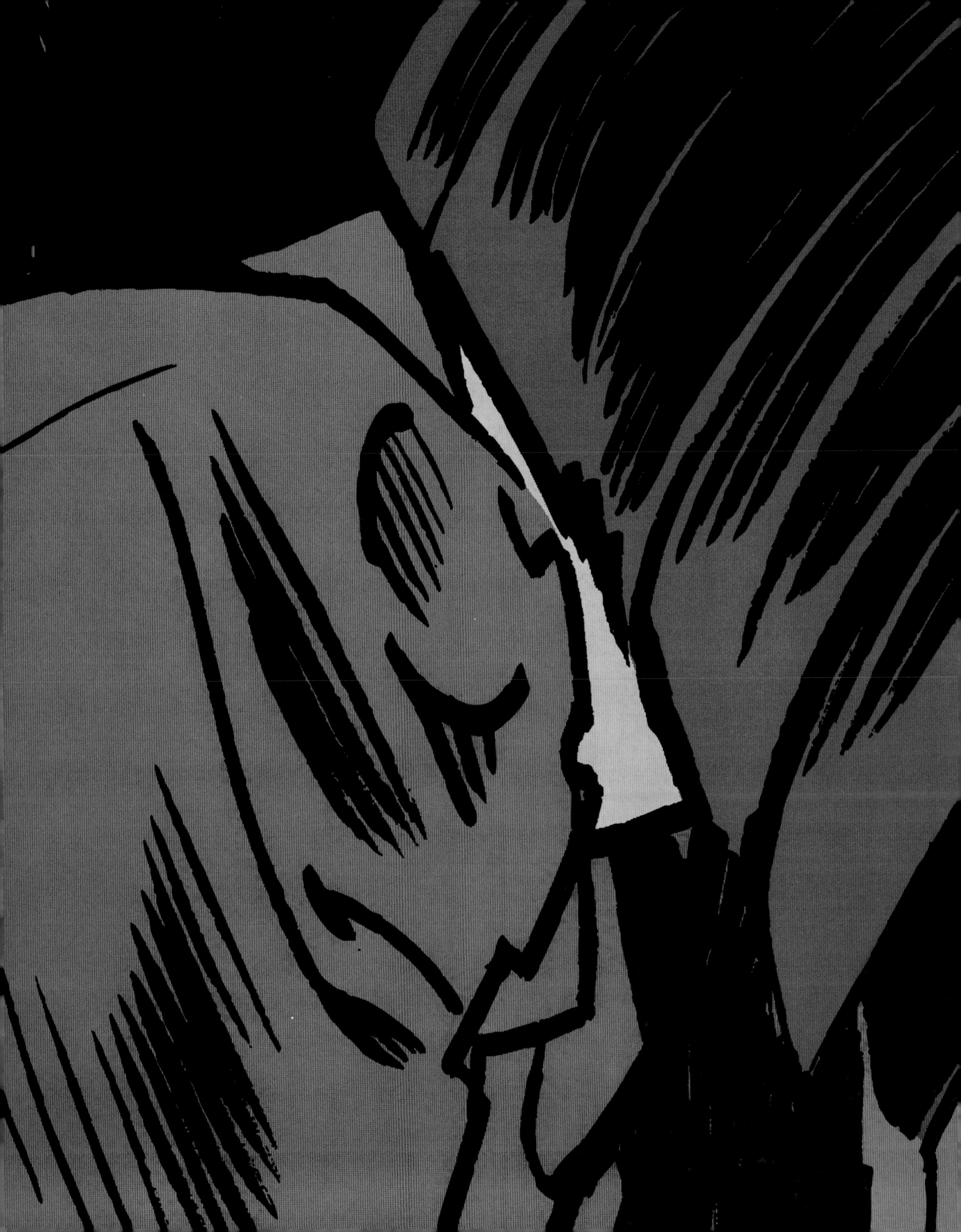

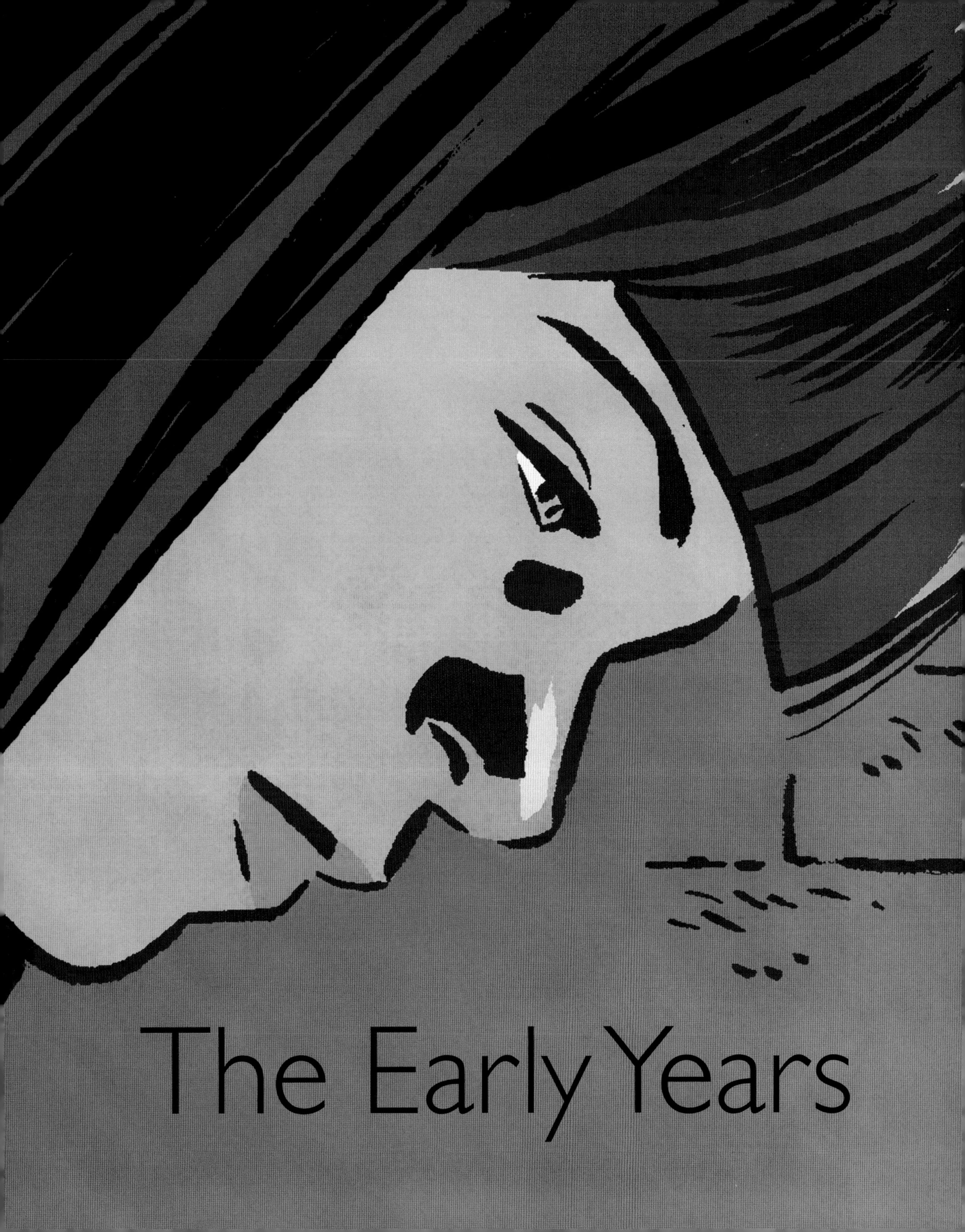

The Early Years

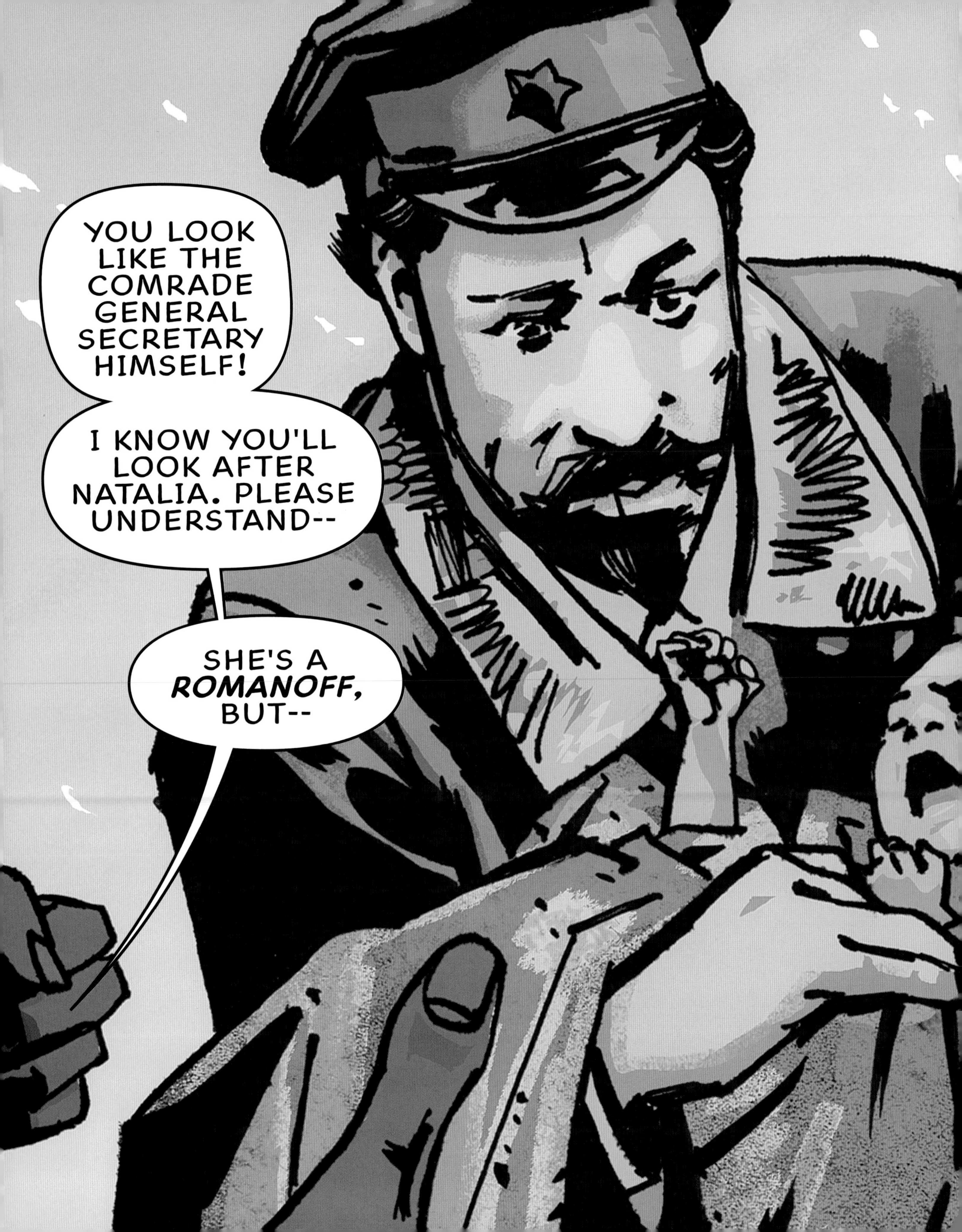
YOU LOOK LIKE THE COMRADE GENERAL SECRETARY HIMSELF!
I KNOW YOU'LL LOOK AFTER NATALIA. PLEASE UNDERSTAND--
SHE'S A *ROMANOFF,* BUT--

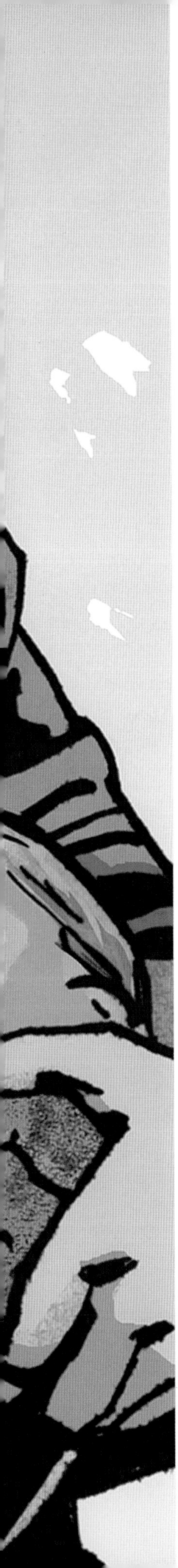

Child of Steel

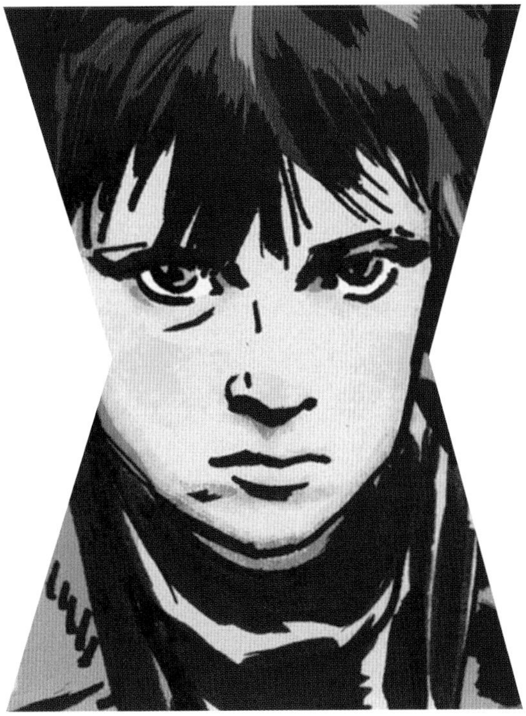

BLACK WIDOW: DEADLY ORIGIN #1 (JAN. 2010) Her rescue from the ruins of her home by soldier Ivan Petrovitch set young Natalia Romanova on a state-sanctioned path of brutality and chaos from which she would never truly escape.

The Black Widow is an inhabitant of the shadows and a keeper of secrets, habits bred through long years of espionage training and mental manipulation on the part of others. Her early history is mysterious even to herself, and it is difficult to discern the true memories from the implanted fictions. The strands of her life are tangled and uneven, just like the web of the deadly spider from which she takes her alias.

--ROMANOFF, THE FAMILY NAME OF THE CZARS. THE NAME OF THE FORMER TYRANTS, EH?

BUT THERE ARE LOTS OF US, AND WE'RE NOT **ALL** RELATED TO THEM.

INDEED, SOME OF US HAVE **PROSPERED** UNDER COMMUNISM.

BLACK WIDOW: DEADLY ORIGIN #1 (JAN. 2010) Natasha was enrolled in an intensive training program for secret agents, endorsed by the General Secretary Josef Stalin himself.

Natalia Alianovna Romanova was born in the city of Stalingrad in 1928. This place is revered as a Hero City, so it is fitting that one of the most famous members of the Avengers should be one of its children. Like Natalia, the city has a long and tortuous history, and has worn many names and identities. Called Tsaritsyn until 1925, it was rewarded for its status as a crucial battlefield of the Russian Civil War by being renamed Stalingrad, after the then Communist Party Chairman, Josef Stalin. Assigned to the area by Premier Vladimir Lenin in the aftermath of World War I, Stalin used Tsaritsyn—a strategically valuable city on the Volga River—as a testing ground for his leadership, ruthlessly purging his opponents and enforcing his will. As such, it had become a dangerous place for a child bearing the name of the despised, fallen Czars.

In the late 1920s, little Natalia Romanova—known to those close to her as Natasha—was rescued from a burning building by a soldier of the Russian Red Army, Ivan Petrovitch, as he searched for his sister. Luckily, her famous family name did not provoke Ivan's hatred, but his protective instinct: he never found his lost sibling, but took Natasha with him and decided to bring her up as if she were his own child.

Ivan Petrovitch was not the only one keeping a close eye on Natasha Romanova. While still of an age to be attending elementary school, she was selected to enter the Red Room Academy with a small number of other girls. Their ultimate destiny was mapped out for them—those who proved themselves worthy would become elite secret agents, promoting the interests of the new Union of Soviet Socialist Republics (USSR) on deadly stealth missions around the world. Like Natasha, all Red Room students were orphans, and therefore more or less the property of the state, ideal for manipulation and coercion.

"...and if the pupil is named Romanova... well, that'll show something to the world!"

JOSEF STALIN

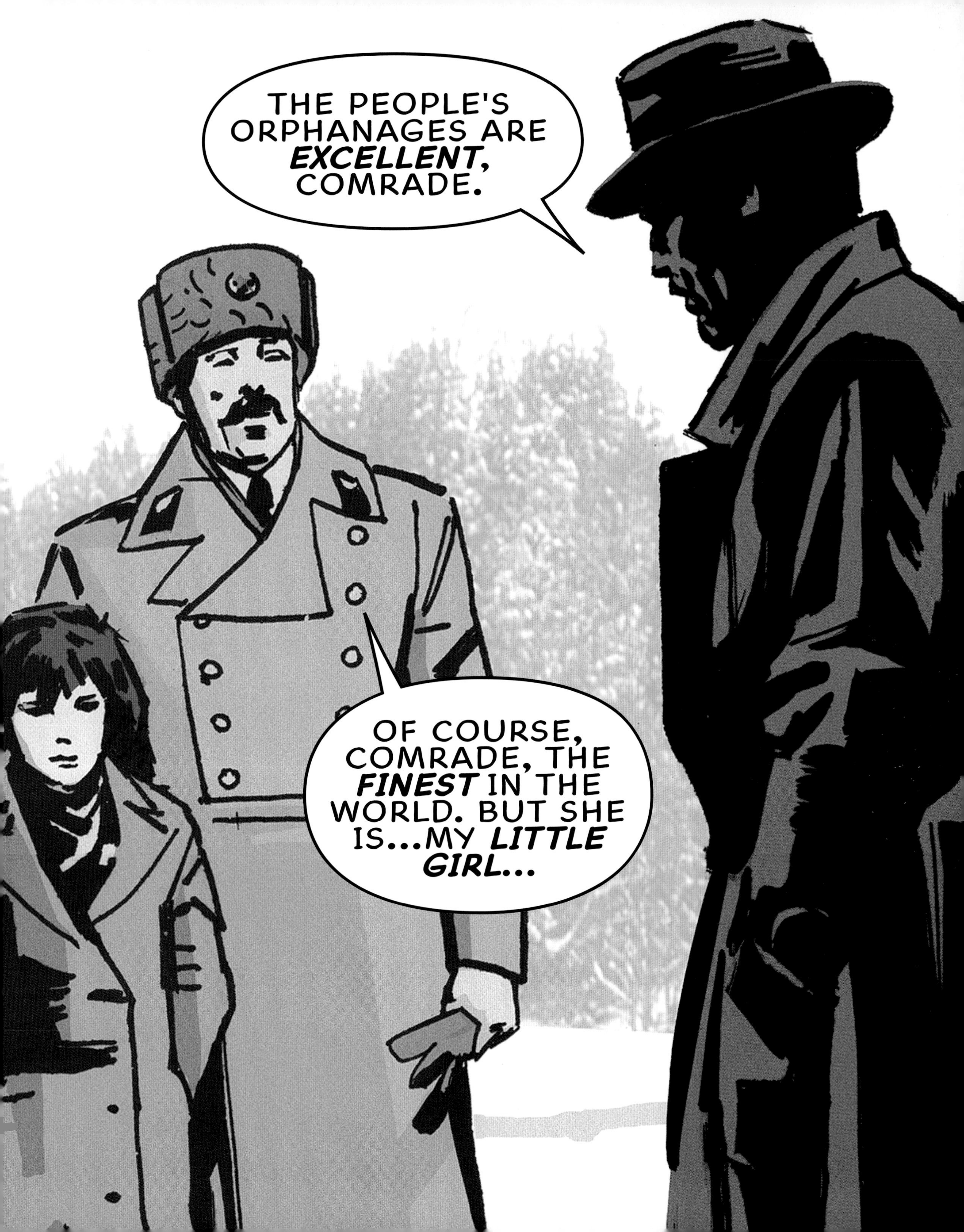
THE PEOPLE'S ORPHANAGES ARE *EXCELLENT*, COMRADE.
OF COURSE, COMRADE, THE *FINEST* IN THE WORLD. BUT SHE IS...MY *LITTLE GIRL*...

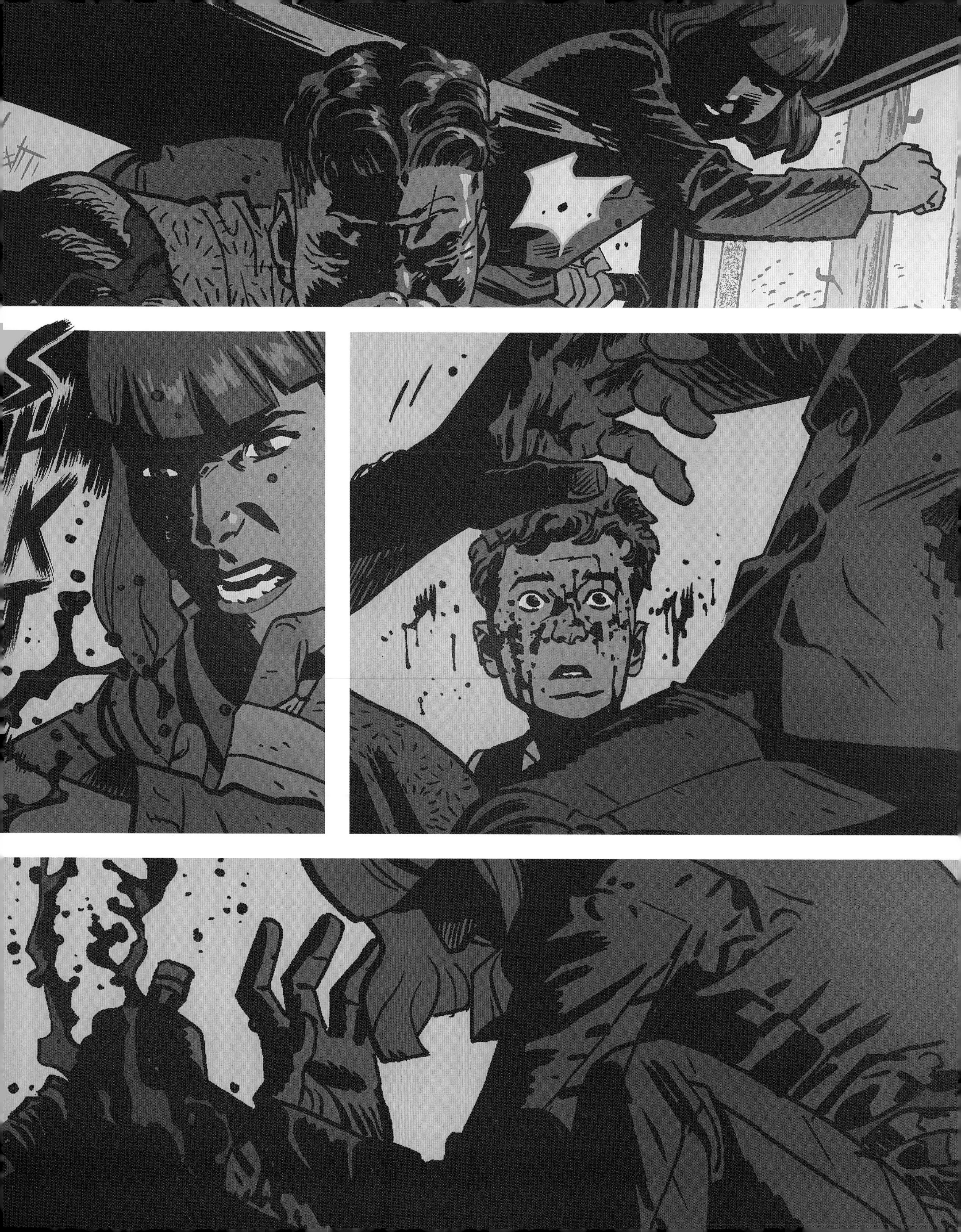

First Blood

**BLACK WIDOW #7
(DEC. 2016) Early in her
training, Natasha exhibited
a killer instinct and a
dedication to the mission
way beyond her years.**

Not long after entering the Red Room Academy,
a young Natasha made her first kill for her
nation. It said something about her character that
she chose to go out alone, without her handler,
having failed in her first attempt at the mission.
Pride and determination drove her to prove herself
to the Headmistress of the Academy by eliminating
a target known only as the Yugoslavian. She found
the man, who was considerably bigger than herself,
sitting in his car with his young son beside him.
Unhesitating, Natasha struck her target through the
vehicle's open window, fiercely stabbing him despite
the Yugoslavian wounding her with her own knife.
She also attacked the little boy in the passenger
seat, uttering the blunt declaration: "No witnesses."

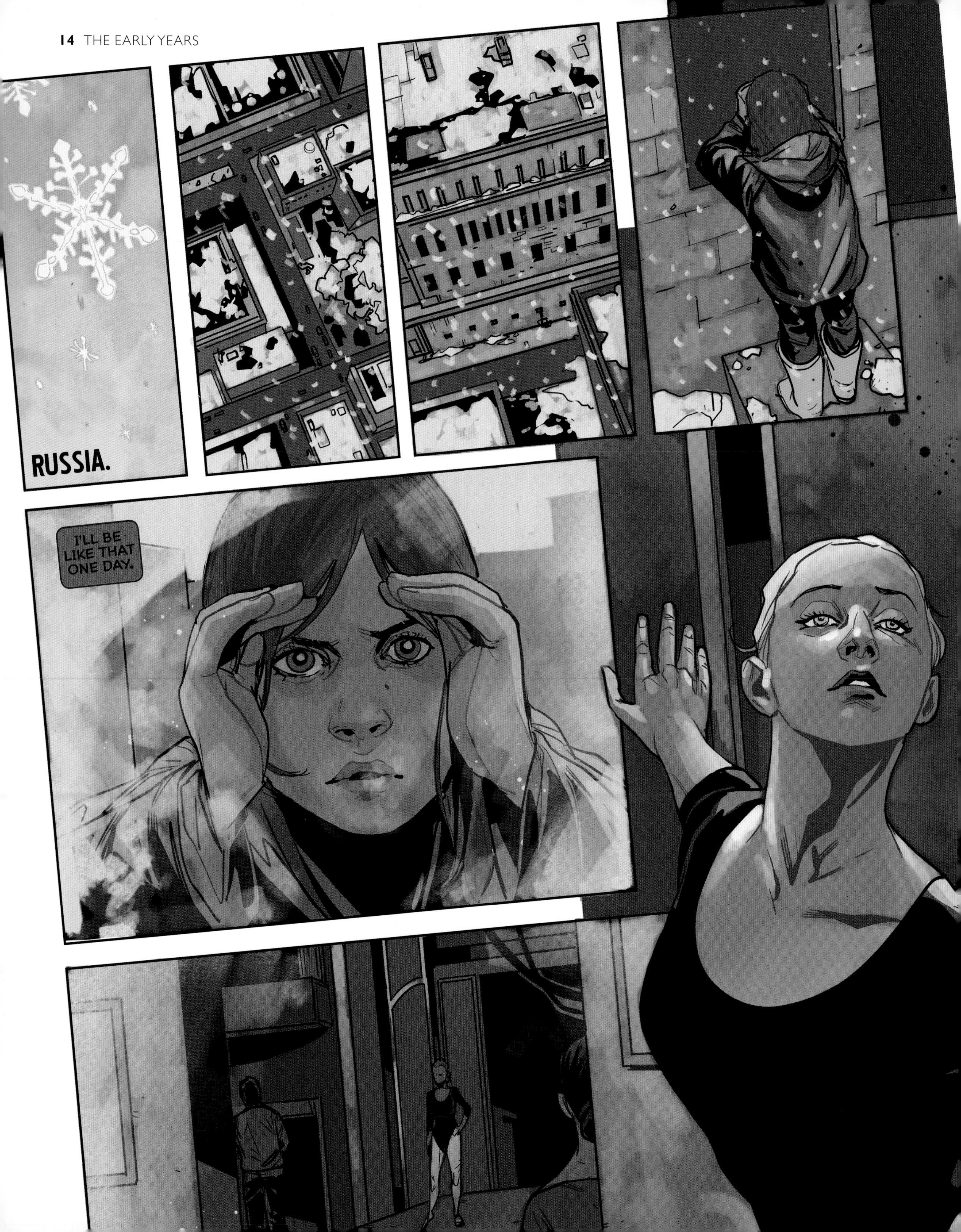
RUSSIA.
I'LL BE LIKE THAT ONE DAY.

However, allowing herself to be hurt was one of several mistakes Natasha made on this mission. Not only did she bungle killing the young eyewitness, she also failed to notice that his cousin was asleep on the back seat of the car, errors that would come back to haunt her in later life. When she returned to the Red Room, the Headmistress was most displeased that Natasha had set off on her own. She used the opportunity to teach the girl how to stitch up her own wound, advising her that the scar would serve as a useful reminder of the lessons she had learned.

The girls in the so-called "Black Widow Ops Program" spent a lot of time together, with limited contact with the outside world. Small wonder, then, that they formed close bonds with one another. These friendships, however, were forever tainted with rivalry as each strove to be the best and be granted the right to serve the USSR as a Black Widow. Natasha's closest friend at the time was called Marina. Although both girls were being trained to be deadly assassins and spies, Natasha was the more fearless, with a highly developed sense of justice that occasionally exhibited signs of tipping over into sheer retribution.

As a young girl, Natasha would spy on a talented ballerina, fantasizing that she, too, would one day dance as gracefully. Marina was usually by her side, worrying that their Red Room masters would notice that they had snuck out, but also eager to get to the local bakery in time to scoop up the day's unwanted leftovers. One day, Natasha noticed her favorite dancer on crutches, and the ballerina's gangster boyfriend parked in his car outside the ballet school. Natasha quickly surmised that the dancer had been injured by her brutal boyfriend, and became incensed. Picking up a rock, she hurled it at the thug's vehicle. When his bodyguard chased the girls, they split up: Natasha heading for an alley where she had earlier stashed a firearm. As the man advanced on her, Natasha fired the gun in desperate self-defense, shooting him down.

Later, back at the Red Room, her trainers noted how well she had dealt with the situation. The ability to react effectively in a crisis was an encouraging sign that Natasha was born to high-level espionage, although the fact that she was out without permission was also a clear sign that she possessed a less desirable rebellious streak.

Opposite: BLACK WIDOW #16 (MAY 2015) Natasha's dreams of becoming a ballerina were twisted by her harsh training in the Red Room, but her desire to see justice done stayed with her forever.

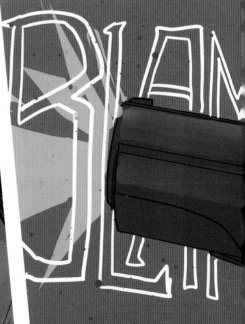

BLACK WIDOW #4 (JAN 2005) **Years of intensive psychological and chemical conditioning convinced Natasha to believe an implanted lie, that she had fulfilled her long-held ambition to train at the Bolshoi Ballet Academy.**

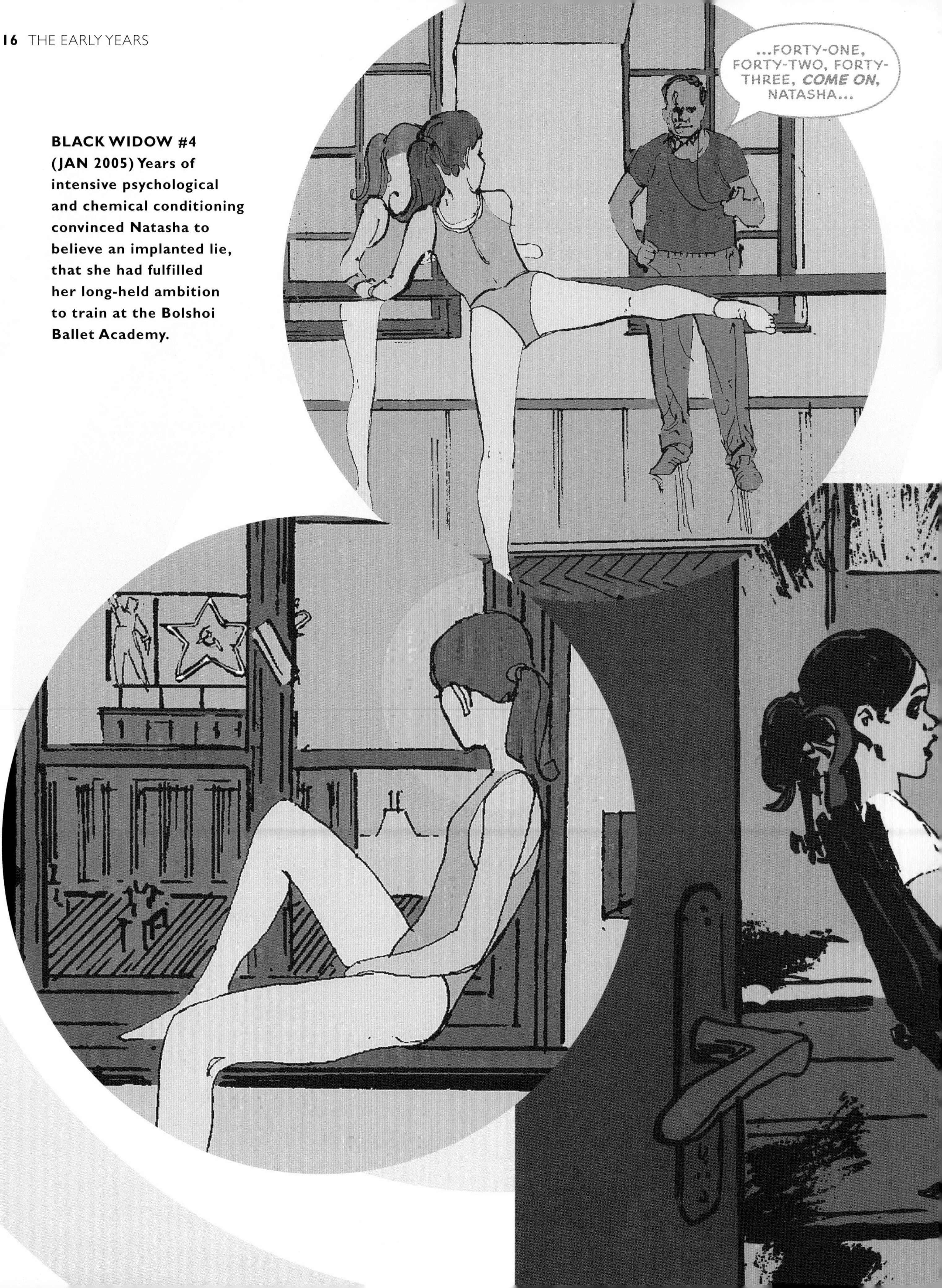
...FORTY-ONE, FORTY-TWO, FORTY-THREE, COME ON, NATASHA...

The Red Room

As well as the more traditional forms of education being used to turn young girls into loyal communist spies, the Red Room was also using an experimental psychochemical serum. This served the dual purpose of implanting false memories into subjects and causing intense pain whenever they tried to recall their true pasts. Cruelly, Natasha would be made to believe that she had in fact achieved her long-cherished dream of training as a Bolshoi ballerina.

Perhaps it was the signs of early promise that prompted the next phase in Natasha's training. She would not attend ballet lessons at the Bolshoi as she had desperately hoped, but rather a veritable school for spies. Those in charge of the Red Room had decided that Natasha should be moved from the Headmistress' Academy to learn espionage from the very best. It was arranged that she would take a place at the school of her namesake, Taras Romanoff, who was training young children to be secret agents. The move was even endorsed by no less than Josef Stalin himself. The thought of turning another with the old royal name into a weapon of the people brought the communist leader immense satisfaction.

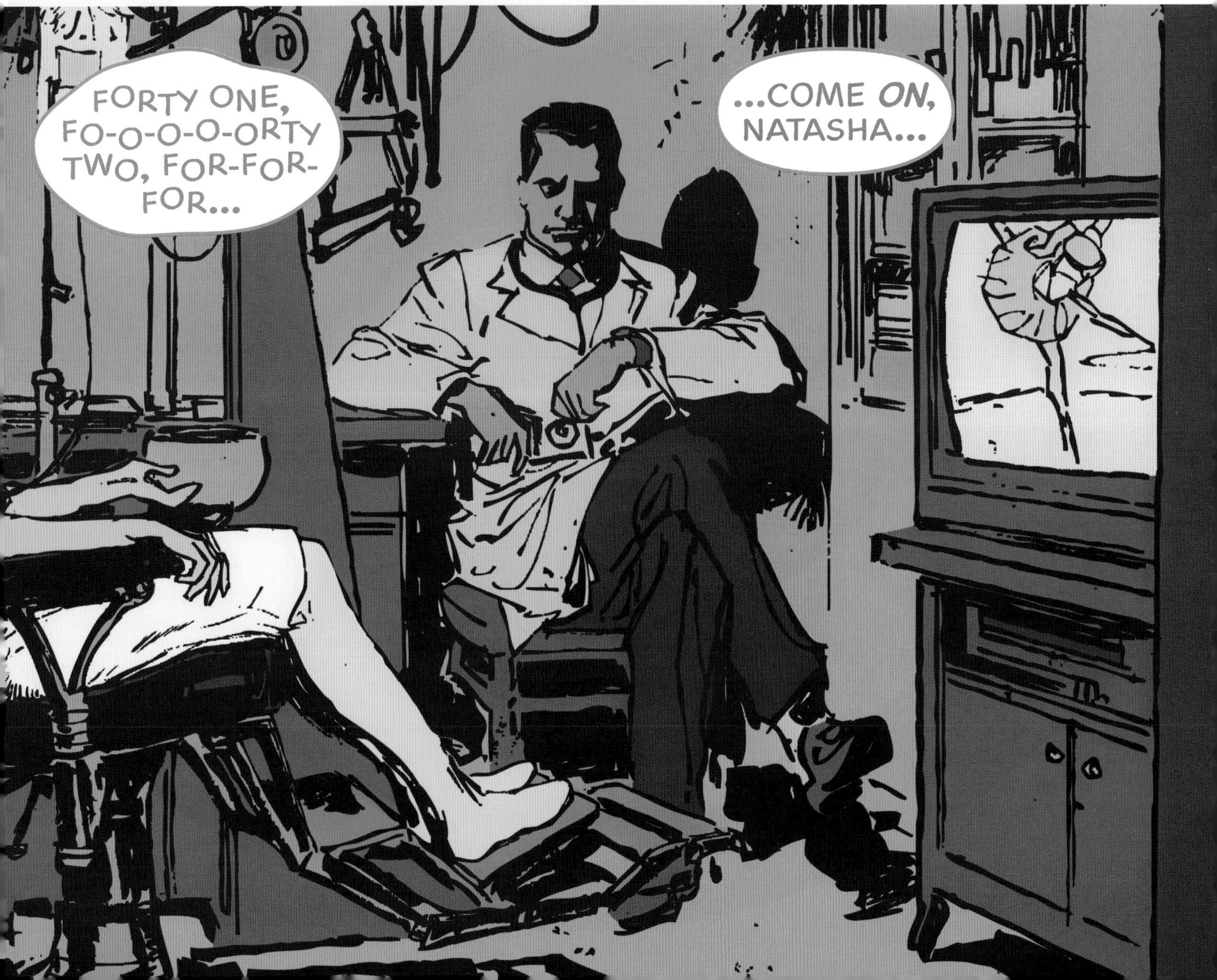
FORTY ONE, FO-O-O-O-ORTY TWO, FOR-FOR-FOR...
...COME ON, NATASHA...

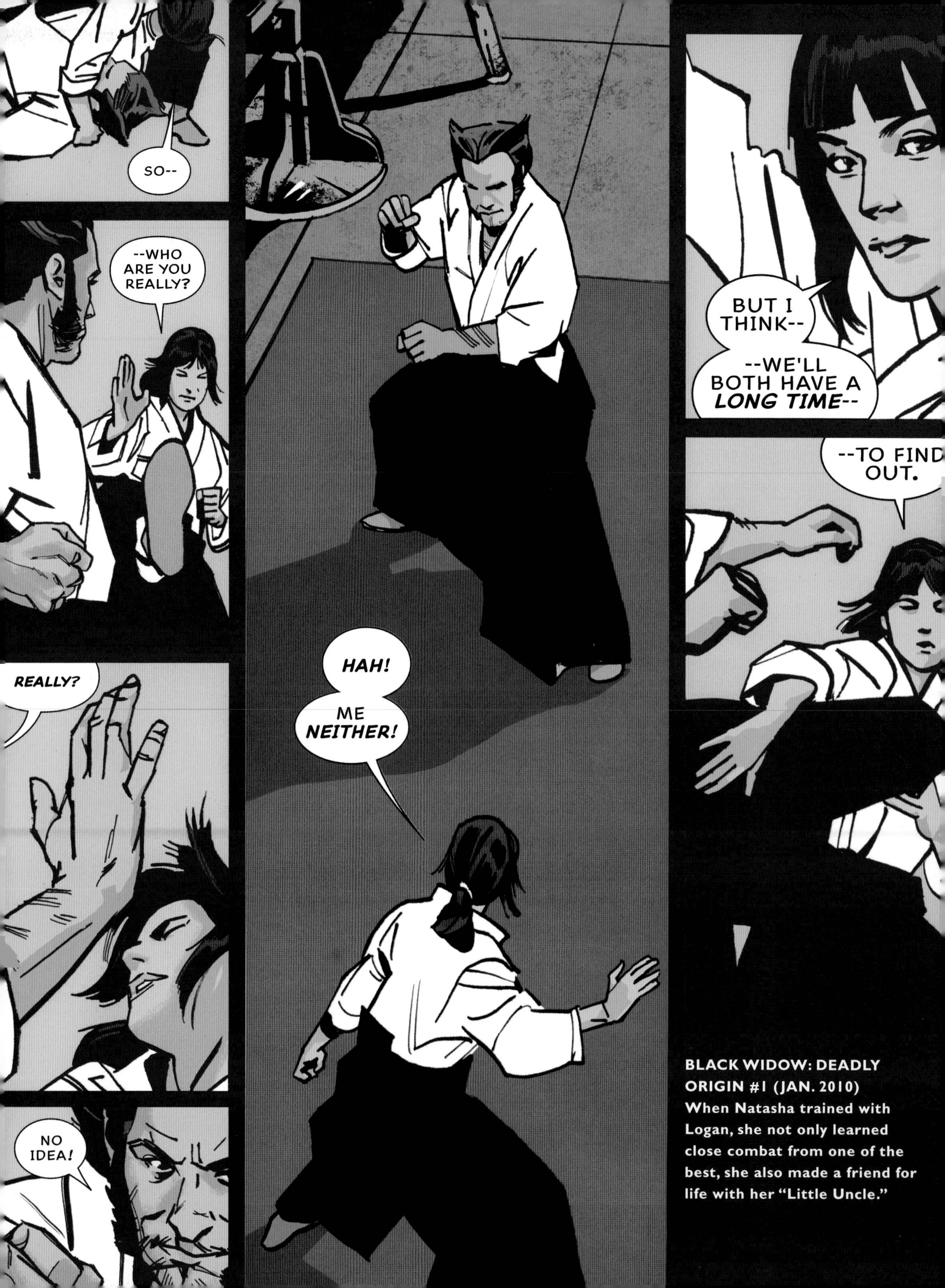
SO--
--WHO ARE YOU REALLY?
REALLY?
NO IDEA!
HAH!
ME NEITHER!
BUT I THINK--
--WE'LL BOTH HAVE A LONG TIME--
--TO FIND OUT.

BLACK WIDOW: DEADLY ORIGIN #1 (JAN. 2010)
When Natasha trained with Logan, she not only learned close combat from one of the best, she also made a friend for life with her "Little Uncle."

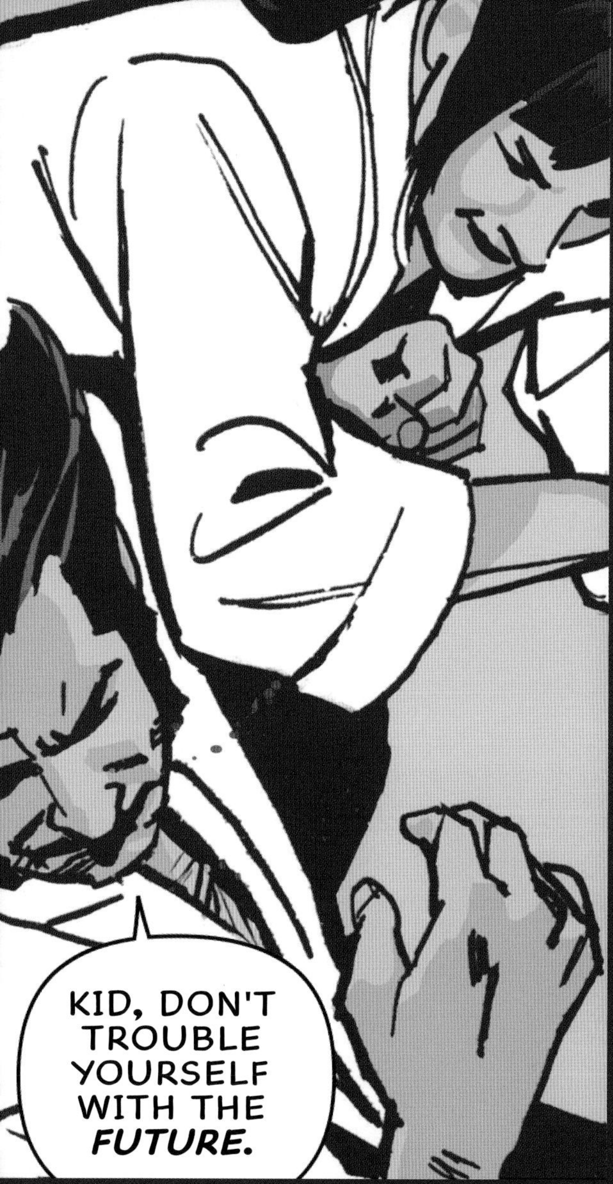
KID, DON'T TROUBLE YOURSELF WITH THE *FUTURE.*

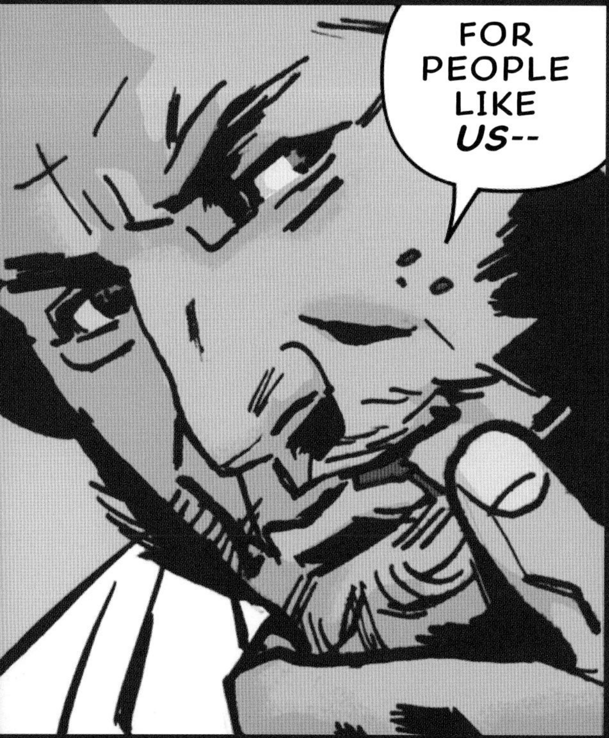
FOR PEOPLE LIKE *US*--

School for Spies

Natasha was an apt pupil for Taras Romanoff. She excelled in every area of school life, in academic subjects as well as athletic pursuits. Her hand-to-hand combat skills were enhanced by personal tuition from the notorious hired assassin Logan—the future Wolverine—while he was on a top-secret mission in Russia. Natasha bonded with Logan, and before long would give him an affectionate nickname: "Little Uncle." However, it was now the early days of World War II and the world was in tumult. Natasha soon discovered the real reason Logan was at her school was to assassinate Taras Romanoff after finding out what information he held. Rather than take Logan's life herself, which was to have been her "graduation" mission from Romanoff's school, Natasha let him escape. This was another early indication that this teenager would not grow up to be the obedient servant to communism that her handlers desired.

It was not only the Soviets who saw enormous potential in Natasha. She was kidnapped by the Hand, an ancient clan of ninja assassins, and taken to the island state of Madripoor. The Hand intended using her lethal skills to help them build an empire in a postcommunist world. But the young Natasha proved too strong-willed, and resisted the Hand's brainwashing. With the assistance of Captain America and Logan, she escaped their clutches, was reunited with her foster father Ivan Petrovitch, whose importance to her could not be wiped from her memory, and promptly returned to Russia.

> "...The future's just another bad day."
>
> **LOGAN**

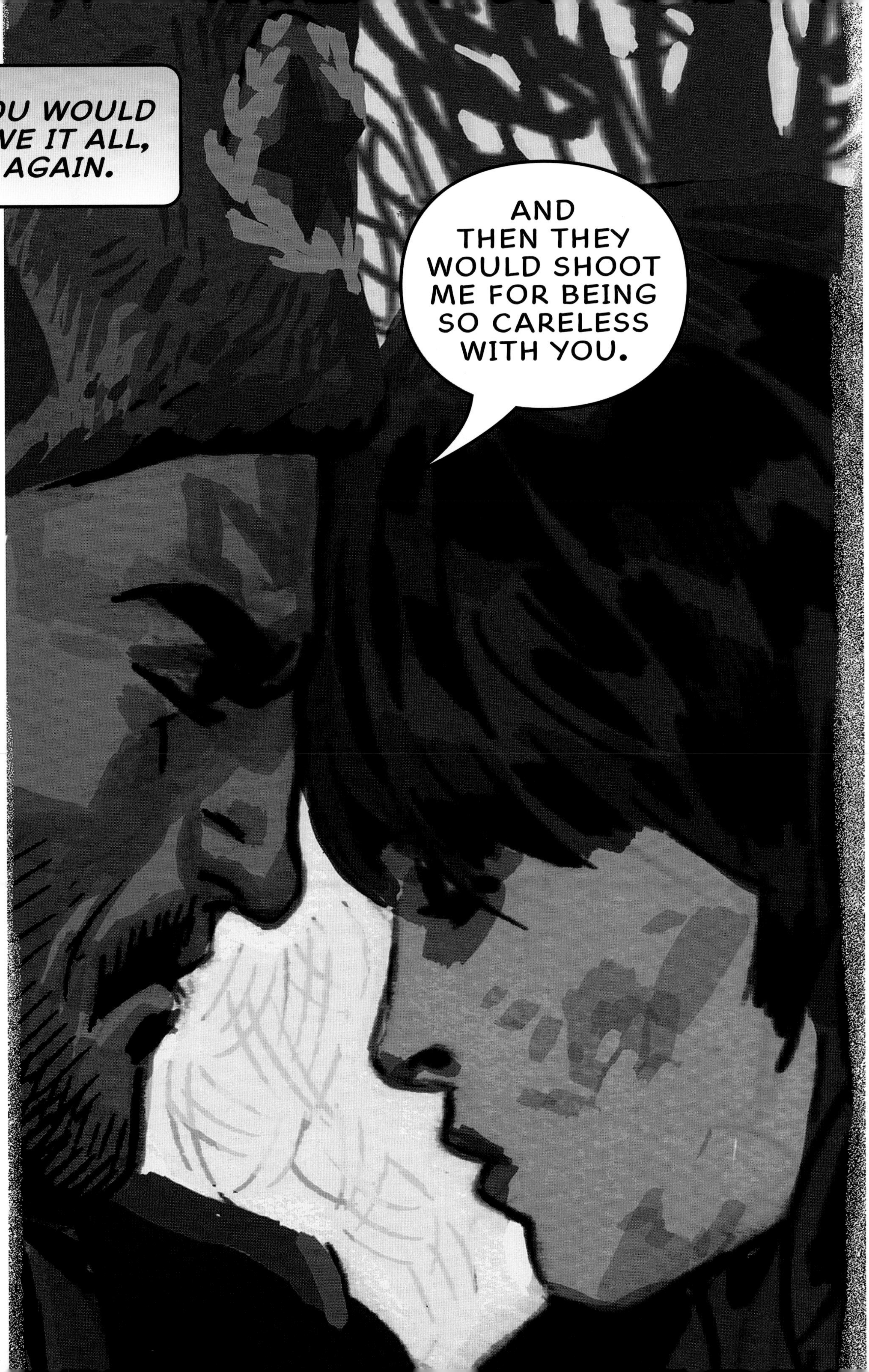
YOU WOULD LIVE IT ALL, AGAIN.
AND THEN THEY WOULD SHOOT ME FOR BEING SO CARELESS WITH YOU.

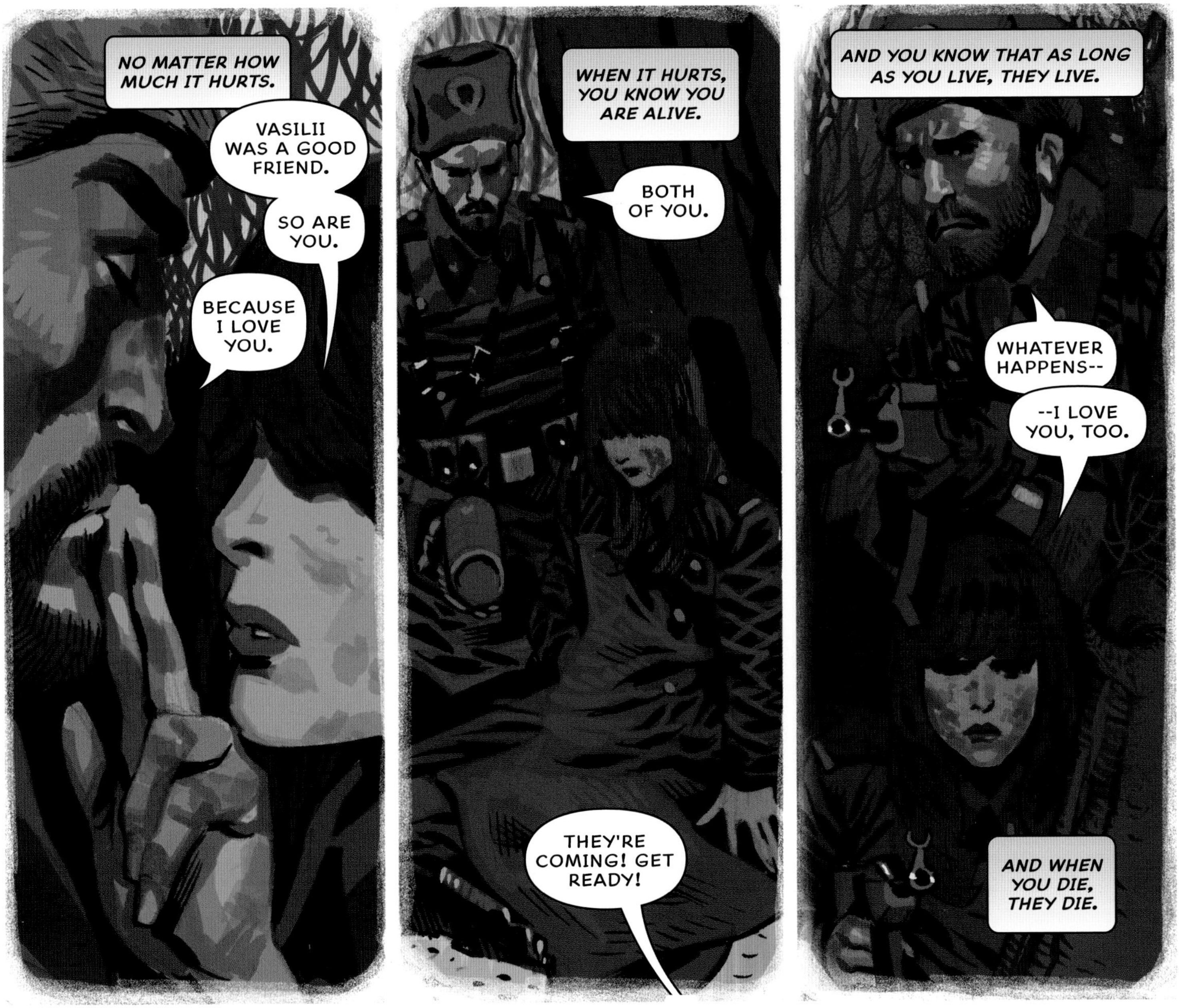
NO MATTER HOW MUCH IT HURTS.
VASILII WAS A GOOD FRIEND.
SO ARE YOU.
BECAUSE I LOVE YOU.
WHEN IT HURTS, YOU KNOW YOU ARE ALIVE.
BOTH OF YOU.
THEY'RE COMING! GET READY!
AND YOU KNOW THAT AS LONG AS YOU LIVE, THEY LIVE.
WHATEVER HAPPENS--
--I LOVE YOU, TOO.
AND WHEN YOU DIE, THEY DIE.

Back home, every Soviet citizen was being called upon to fight for their nation's survival in what the authorities called the Great Patriotic War. Even with the Nazis in retreat in the later years of World War II, young and old were still expected to stand and fight for Mother Russia, and Natasha was no exception. At just age 16, she served with a Red Army unit, falling in love with a young fellow soldier named Nikolai. Although they were never officially married, Nikolai gave Natasha a ribbon that had belonged to his mother, which she wore as a wedding band. Natasha became pregnant, but tragically the baby—a girl she named Rose—was stillborn. Her heartbreak deepened as Natasha and Nikolai were only together for a short time.

BLACK WIDOW #4 (SEP. 2010) Natasha found love in the carnage of World War II, but her happiness was cut short by tragedy. When peace finally came, she was alone once more.

Department X

WINTER SOLDIER #7 (AUG. 2012) Black Widow and the Winter Soldier were trained as part of Soviet Russia's Department X initiative. This covert agency used cutting-edge science to try to gain supremacy during the Cold War.

With one war fought—and won—at great cost, the Soviet Union embarked on a new global struggle, this time a "Cold War" against its erstwhile Western allies. In this climate of subterfuge and mistrust, the stage was set for a new breed of agent, the kind that could operate in the shadows, attempting to gain the upper hand for their nation and its ideology. Natasha, already with years of espionage training under her belt, was just the kind of person her country needed. She returned to the Red Room, which had become a part of Department X—a super-science division dedicated to advancing the Soviet cause through technological innovation.

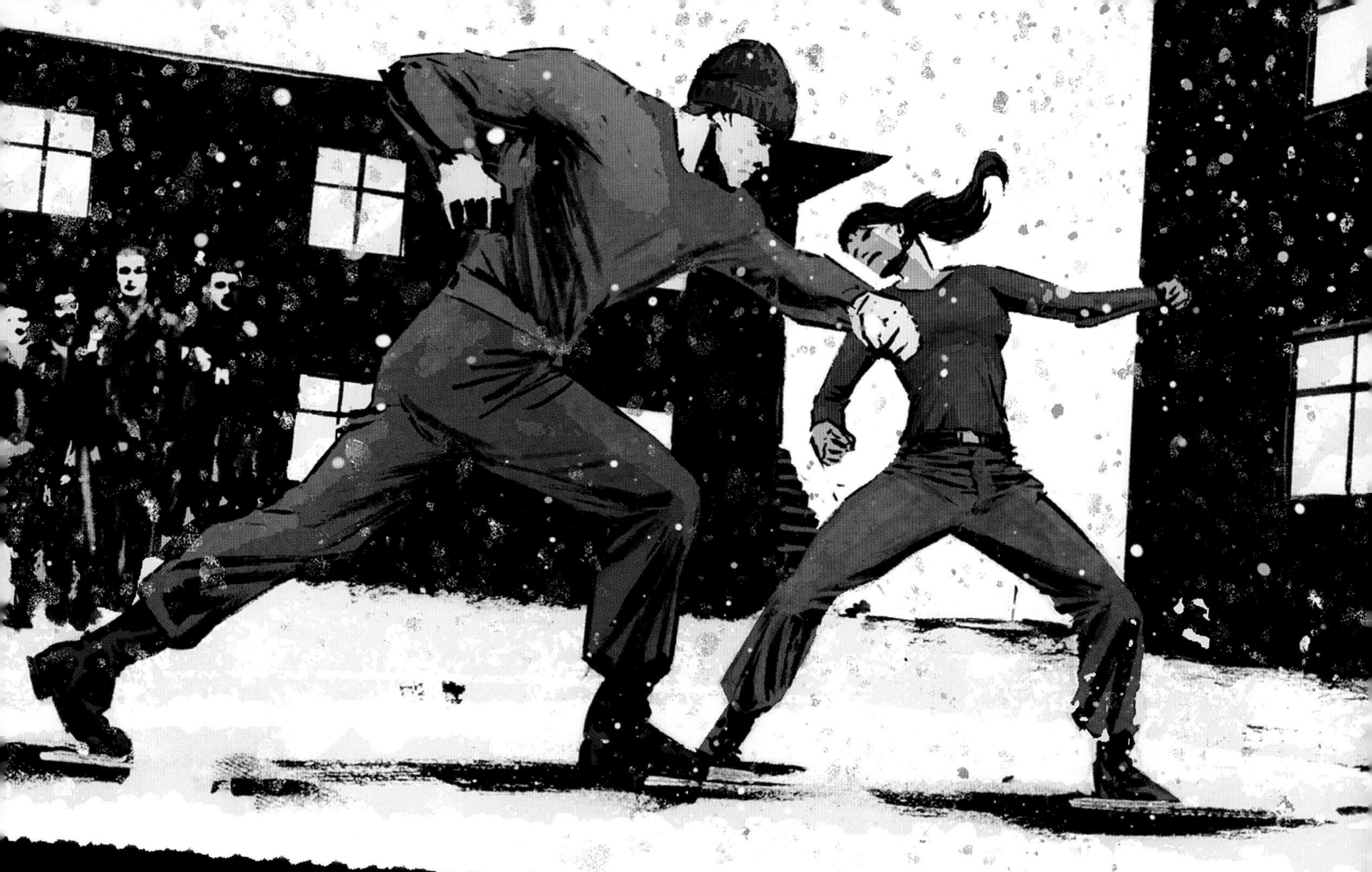
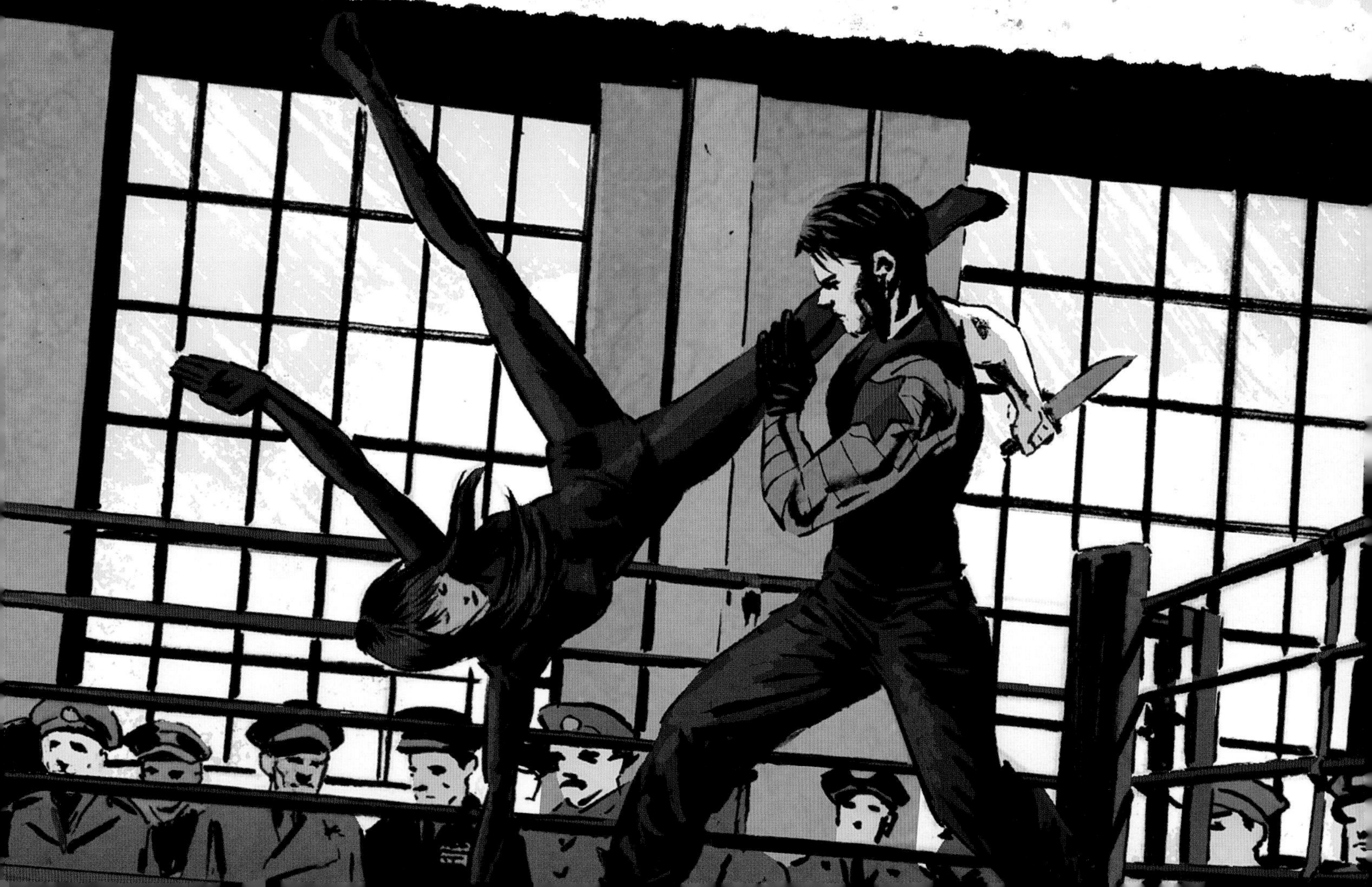

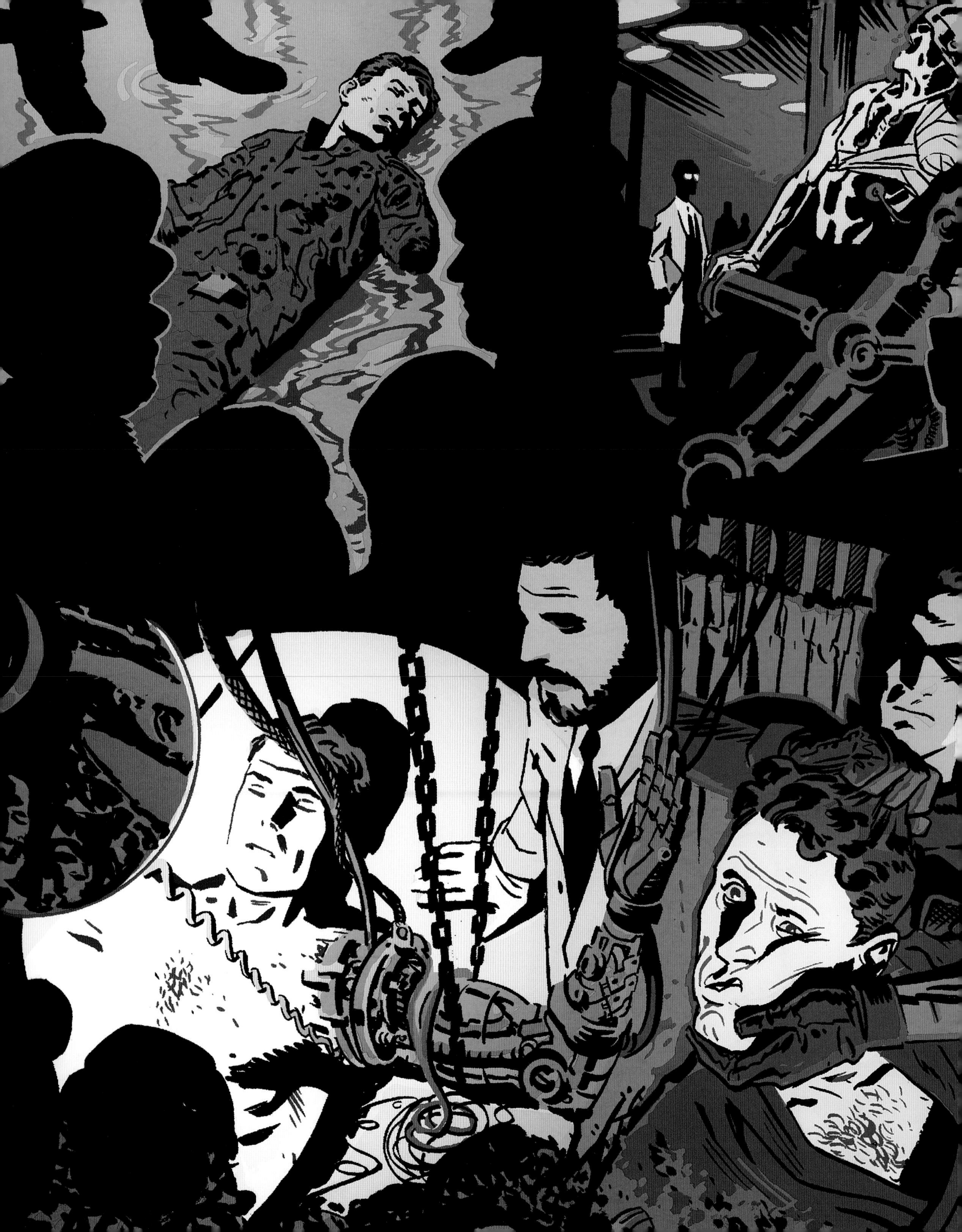

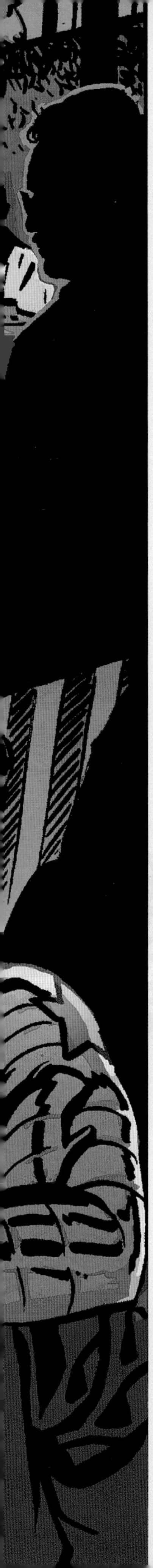

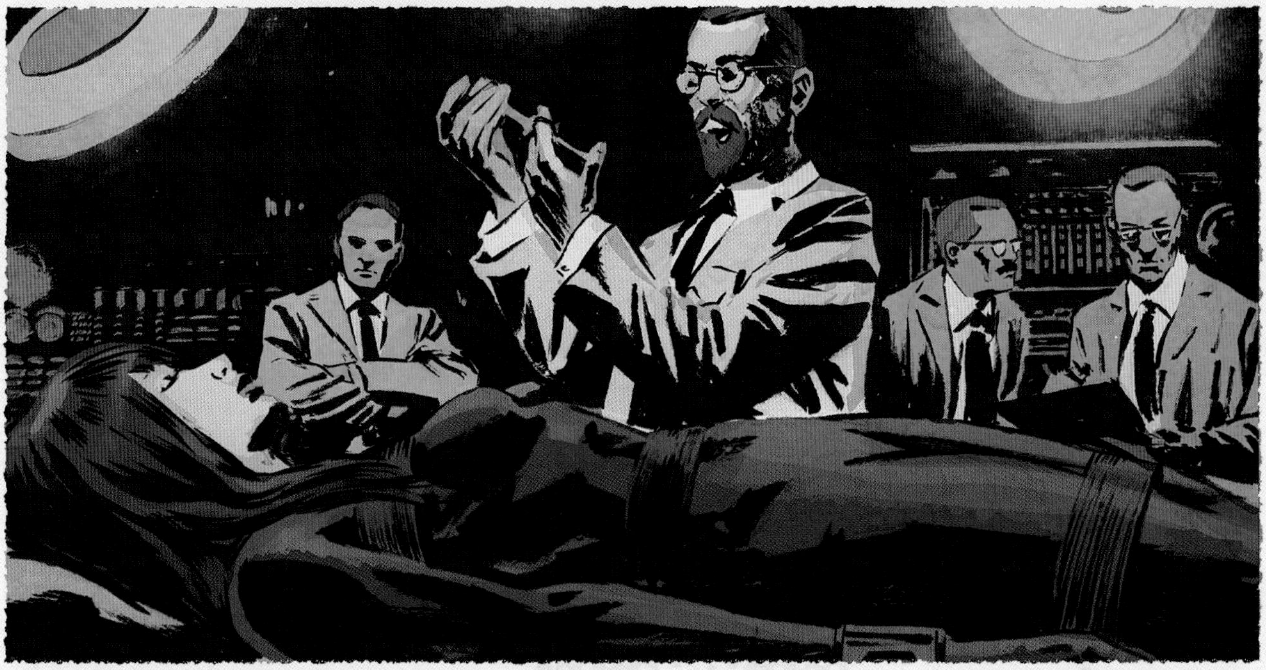

In 1954, Department X successfully created a perfect, if sometimes hard-to-manage, assassin from a captured American serviceman—one James Buchanan "Bucky" Barnes, code-named the Winter Soldier. Barnes had formerly been the youthful partner of Captain America during World War II, thought killed during the same mission that had left Cap in suspended animation in ice beneath the waves. A Russian submarine had found Bucky after the war. Like Cap, he wasn't dead, but frozen in stasis and had lost his left arm in the wartime accident that almost took his life.

The Soviets took Barnes with them, hoping that he, too, carried the Super-Soldier Serum in his blood. Although they were disappointed on that score, they devised another way he could be put to good use for the Russian cause. Barnes was given a cybernetic arm and brainwashed to obey his handlers without question. As an American he was far better suited to dangerous infiltration missions in the West than native Russians, and his extensive brainwashing made him an ideal killing machine—an assassin without qualms or conscience. In between assignments he was mind-wiped and put into stasis, which slowed his aging and prevented him from getting out of control.

Opposite: CAPTAIN AMERICA AND BUCKY #624 (JAN. 2012) Under Department X, James "Bucky" Barnes was transformed into the Winter Soldier, but the authorities found him difficult to control.

Above: WINTER SOLDIER #7 (AUG. 2012) Department X used agents like Natasha Romanova as human guinea pigs for the serums and mind-control techniques they were developing.

The success of the Soviets in creating the Winter Soldier inspired the authorities to redouble their efforts with the Black Widow Ops Program. After all, female spies could gain access to situations that would be off limits even to the Winter Soldier, like glitzy diplomatic receptions and the hotel rooms of the great and the good in the hated West. These young women were molded into living weapons, given daily training in martial arts, marksmanship, and spycraft. Yet only the best of the best would graduate from the Red Room as a Black Widow.

"If you take the gun, I drop the grenade."

NATASHA ROMANOVA

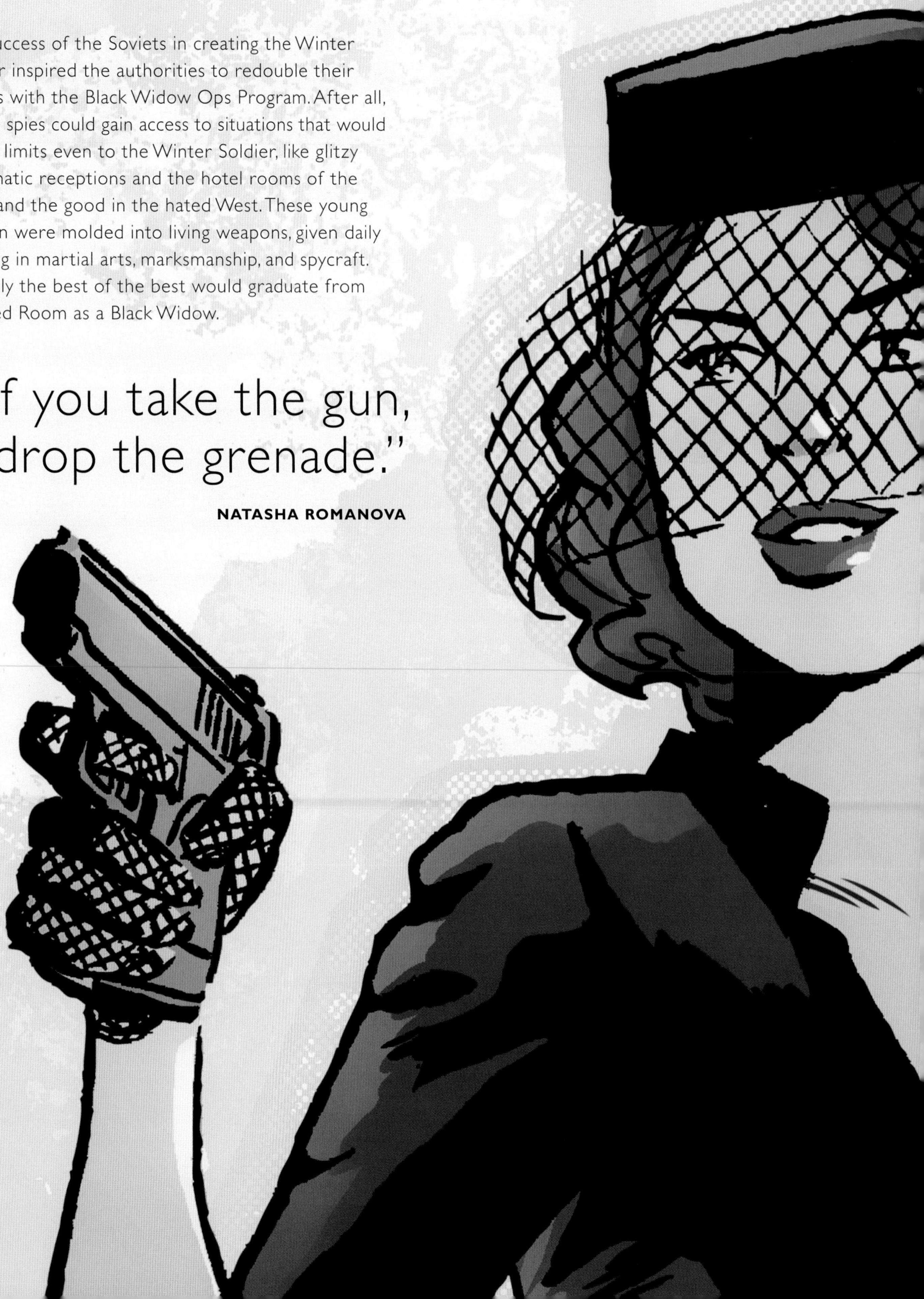

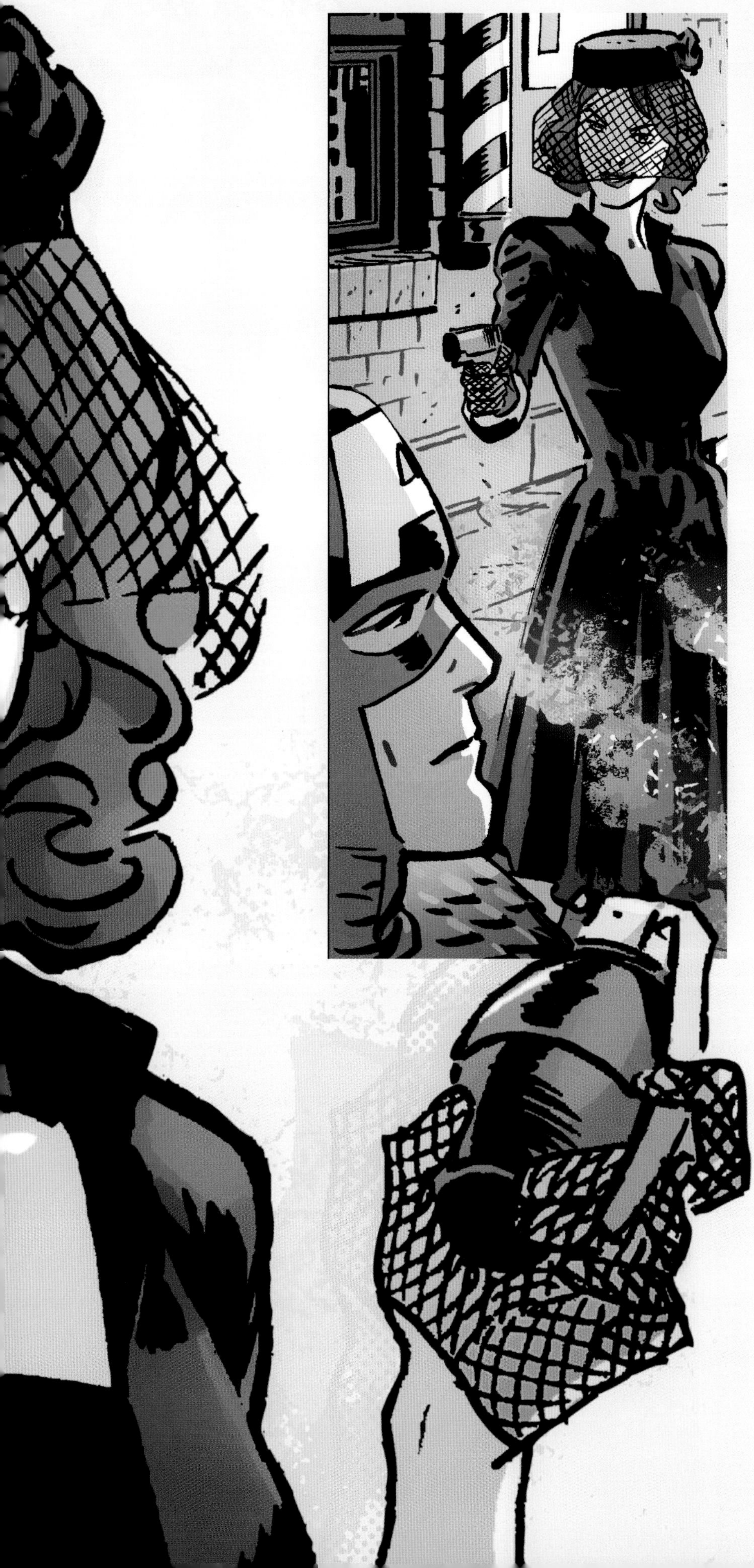

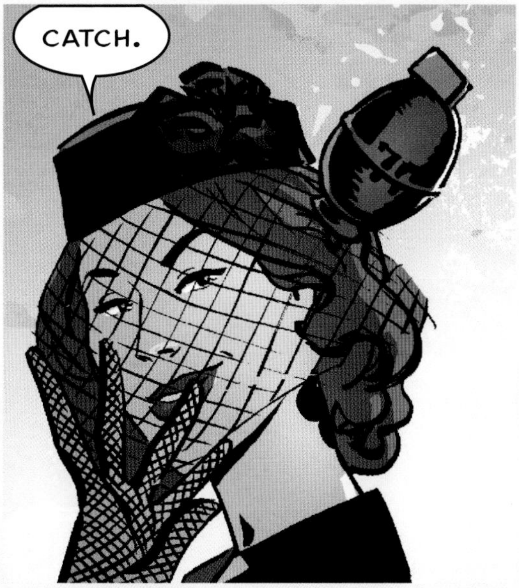
CATCH.

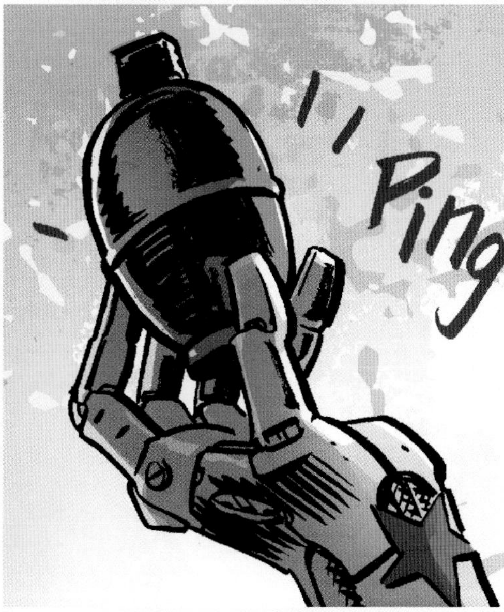
Ping

CAPTAIN AMERICA AND BUCKY #624 (JAN. 2012)
The training given by Department X was extremely realistic. In 1958, the Winter Soldier, dressed as Captain America, was impressed by Natasha's cool performance in a live exercise.

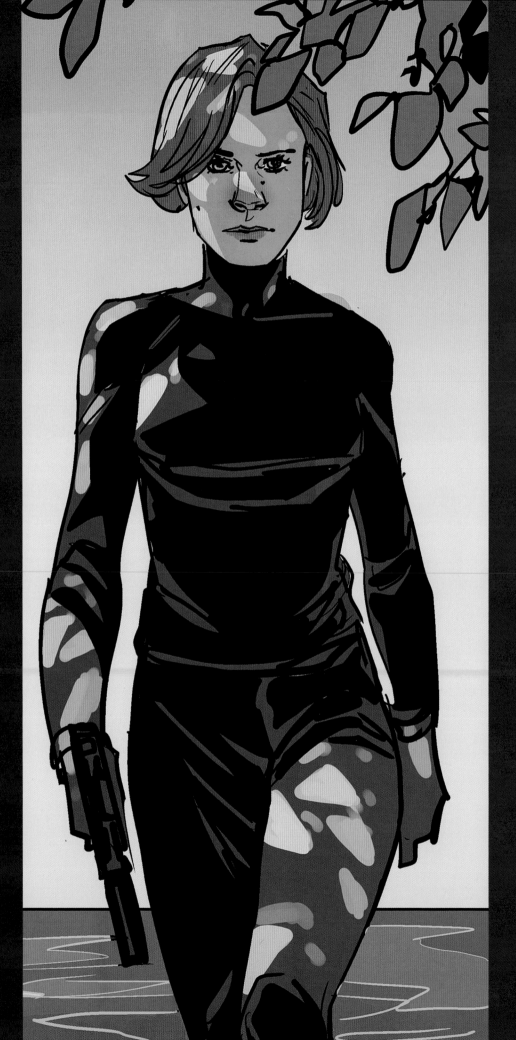

Mission to Cuba

Despite misgivings about her youth from some quarters, Natasha was trusted with an important, highly dangerous mission to Cuba. Marina, the close friend from her early Red Room days, was already working undercover on the communist island, and Natasha was sent to aid her with the extraction of a couple thought to be about to defect to the West. However, there was more to the mission than Natasha had been originally told. The Red Room doubted Marina's commitment to the Soviet Union and had decided that she needed to be "removed"—and they had earmarked her former childhood playmate for the task.

Natasha, fresh from her training and fully conditioned to support the Soviet cause, accepted the assignment with no hint of emotion. She used Marina for as long as the mission demanded, bid her farewell as if she was returning to the Soviet Union, and then broke into her friend's apartment to assassinate her, killing her Cuban boyfriend and her cat for good measure. This Natasha Romanova was a methodical, cold-hearted killer, and the deeds she committed during this time would plague her for the rest of her life. However, it was also undeniable that many of the qualities and talents of this very able assassin would prove useful to her future allies in the espionage and intelligence agency S.H.I.E.L.D., and the Earth's mightiest heroes, the Avengers.

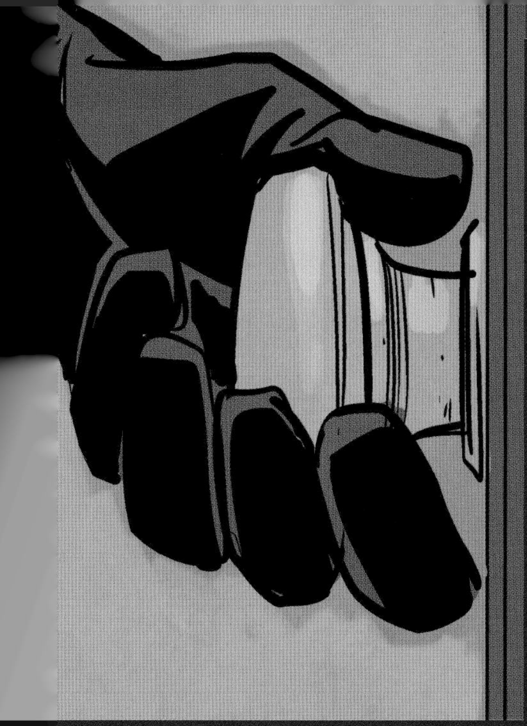

"We are agents. We have made a choice."

NATASHA ROMANOVA

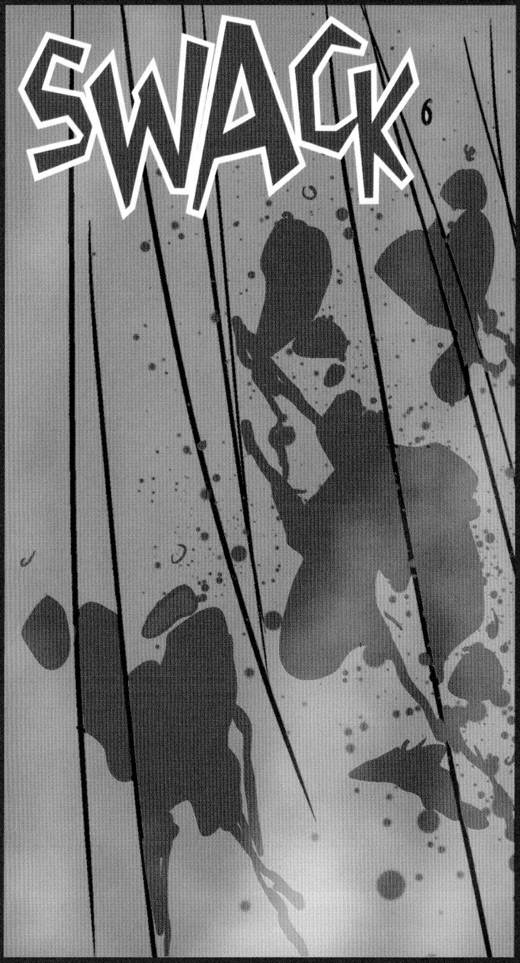
SWACK

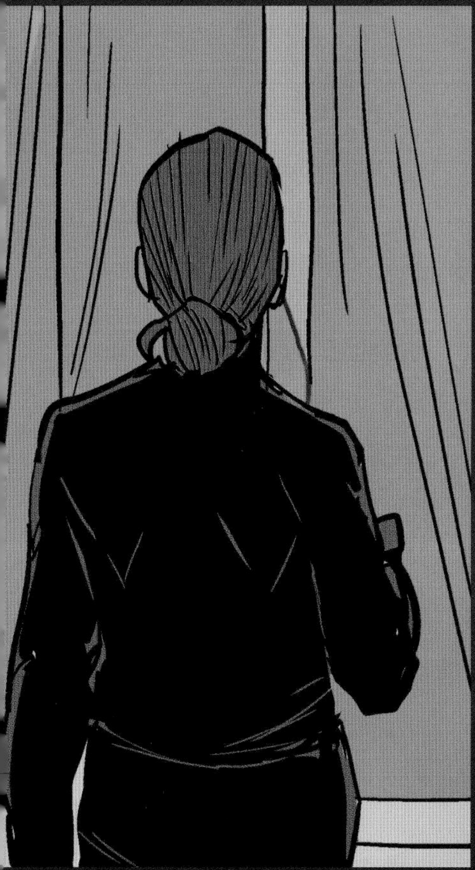

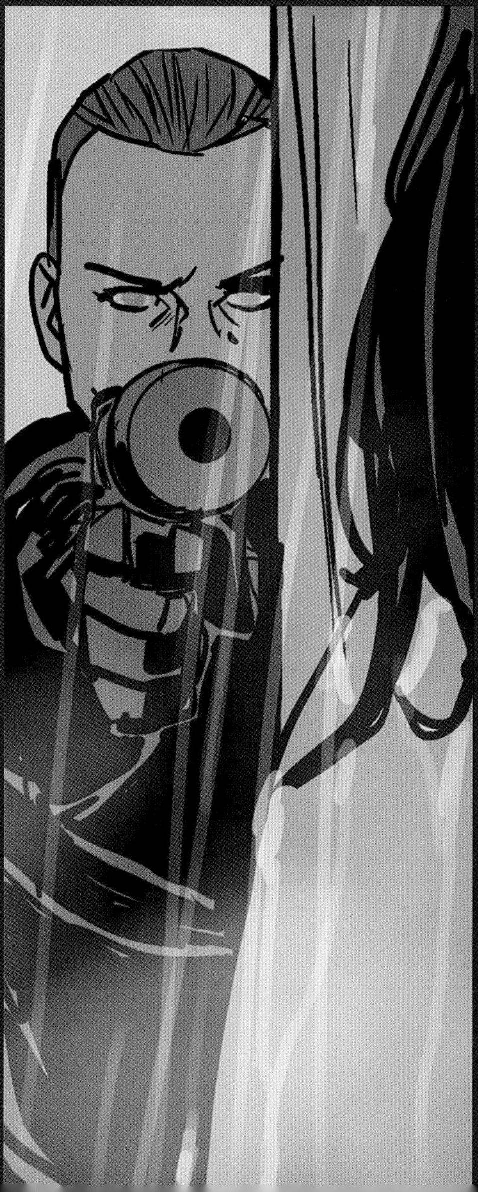

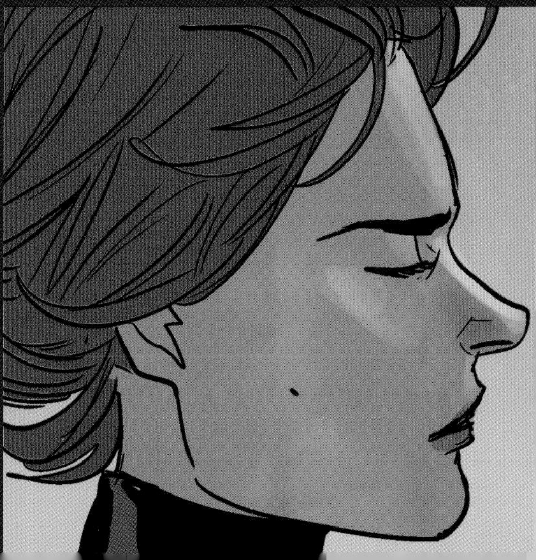

BLACK WIDOW #20 (SEP. 2015) Natasha's handlers had feared she was not ready for a mission to Cuba, but the young woman proved herself more ruthless than they could have imagined.

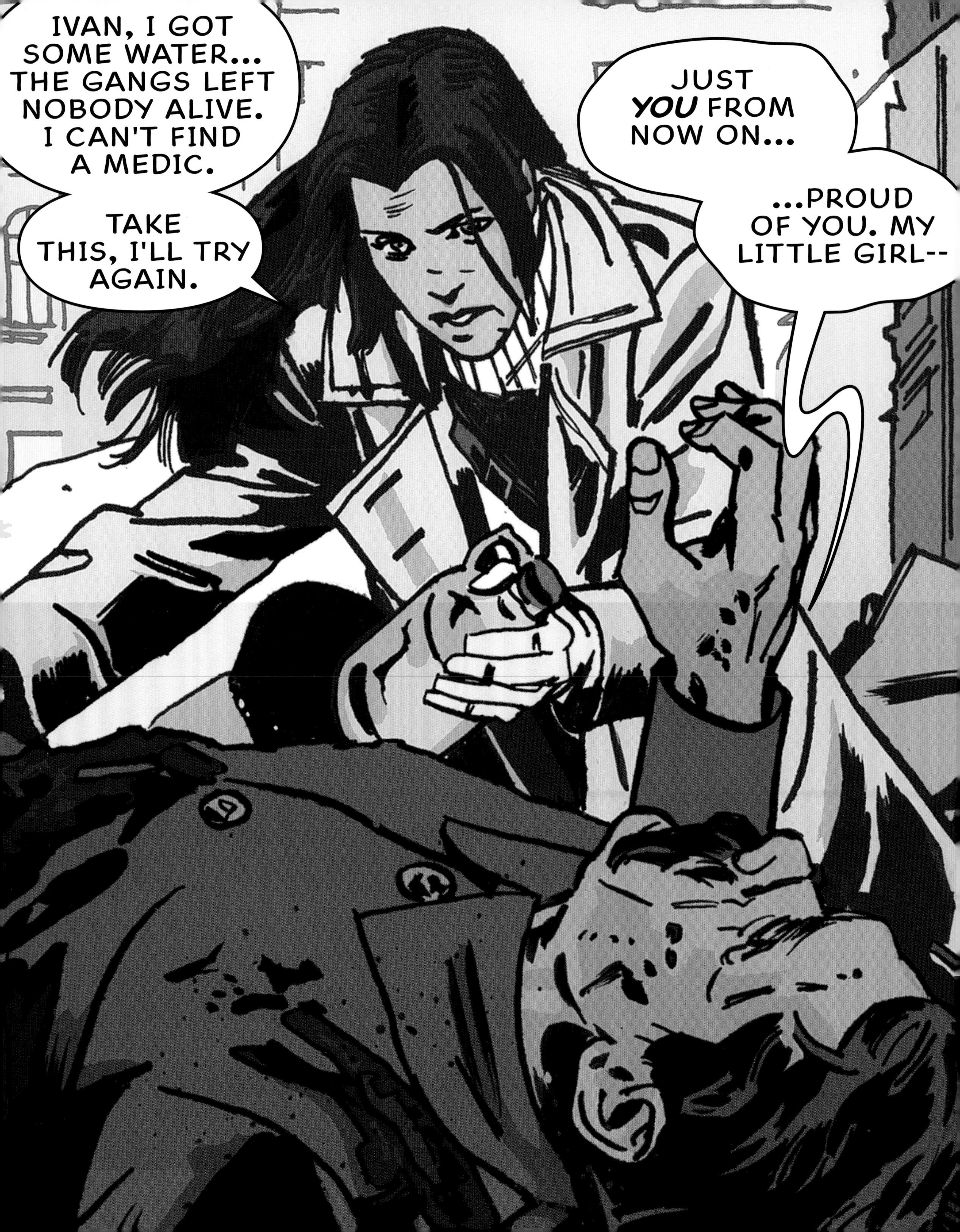
IVAN, I GOT SOME WATER... THE GANGS LEFT NOBODY ALIVE. I CAN'T FIND A MEDIC.
TAKE THIS, I'LL TRY AGAIN.
JUST *YOU* FROM NOW ON...
...PROUD OF YOU. MY LITTLE GIRL--

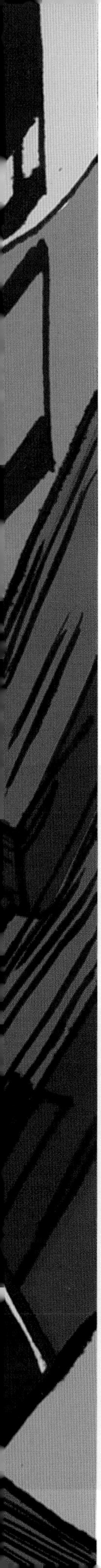

On her return to Russia, Natasha received extra combat training from the Winter Soldier and, as the two spent more time together, they developed strong feelings for each other. This sort of affection was vehemently discouraged by their superiors, as it was felt that it would make them both weak. Although the couple tried to keep their relationship secret, it was discovered and they were forced to part—the Winter Soldier being put back into stasis and Natasha manipulated into a new relationship.

Meanwhile, Natasha's earliest father figure, Ivan Petrovitch, was still very much in her life, and the two even embarked on missions together. In 1956, in the anarchic frontierland of Cold War Berlin, Germany, Ivan was mortally wounded as the duo investigated gang activity. Natasha was searching in vain for a medic to help her old friend when the Winter Soldier—thoroughly brainwashed—arrived on the scene. He had been instructed to offer Natasha and Ivan the use of a serum that would not only heal Ivan's wounds, but also grant them both greatly slowed aging. Although Ivan, who passed out from his injuries, told her to refuse, Natasha readily accepted the offer to save the life of her former mentor and guardian. This act obligated her to the Soviet authorities for years to come, as Ivan had known it would.

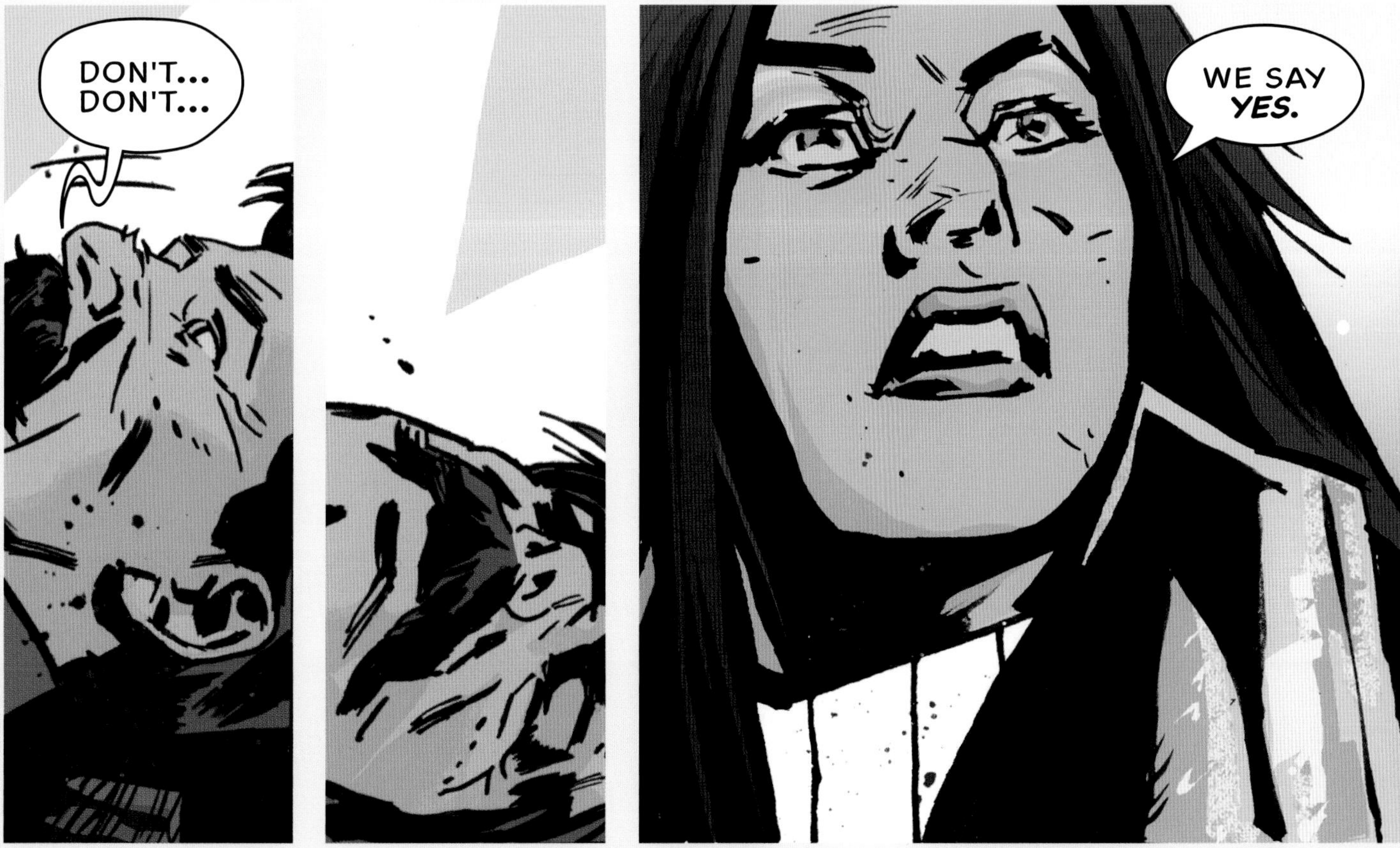
DON'T... DON'T...
WE SAY *YES.*

BLACK WIDOW: DEADLY ORIGIN #1 (JAN. 2010)
The paths of Black Widow and the Winter Soldier crossed once more in Cold War Berlin, when Barnes provided the serum that saved the life of Natasha's adoptive father, Ivan.

Love and Marriage

BLACK WIDOW: DEADLY ORIGIN #2 (FEB. 2010) The Soviet authorities created their very own power couple when they introduced handsome test pilot Alexei Shostakov to Natasha Romanova.

The authorities had long been shaping Natasha's destiny, guiding the events of her life to maximize her usefulness to the Soviet state as a lethal living weapon. After being forced to end her romance with the Winter Soldier, Natasha was informed she would be taking part in a propaganda-friendly marriage with heroic test pilot Alexei Shostakov. The seemingly happy union was even blessed behind the scenes by no less a figure than Premier Nikita Khrushchev, who had hoped to grant Natasha the gift of an early retirement and the fresh persona of a good Soviet housewife. However, the secret services had other plans.

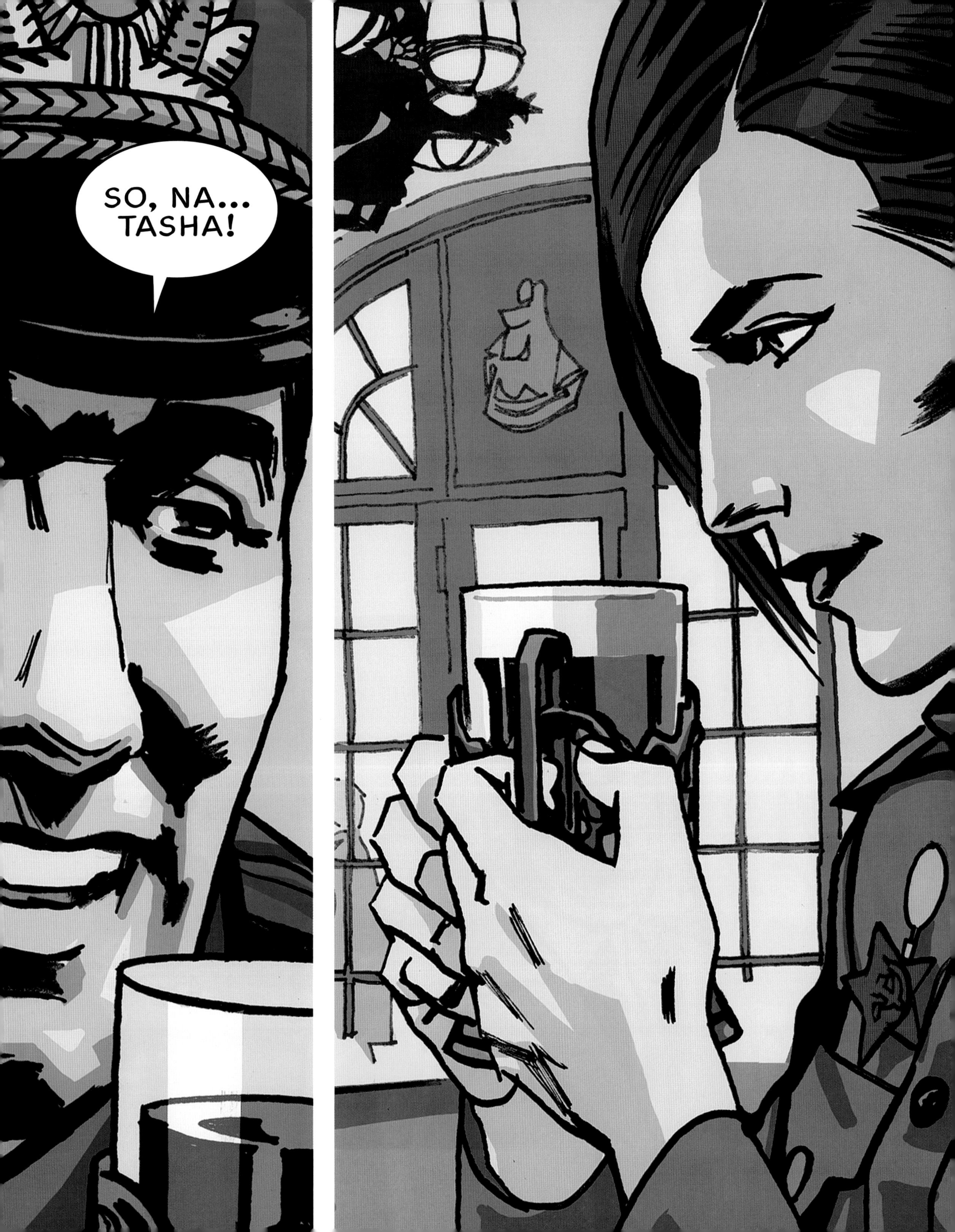
SO, NA... TASHA!

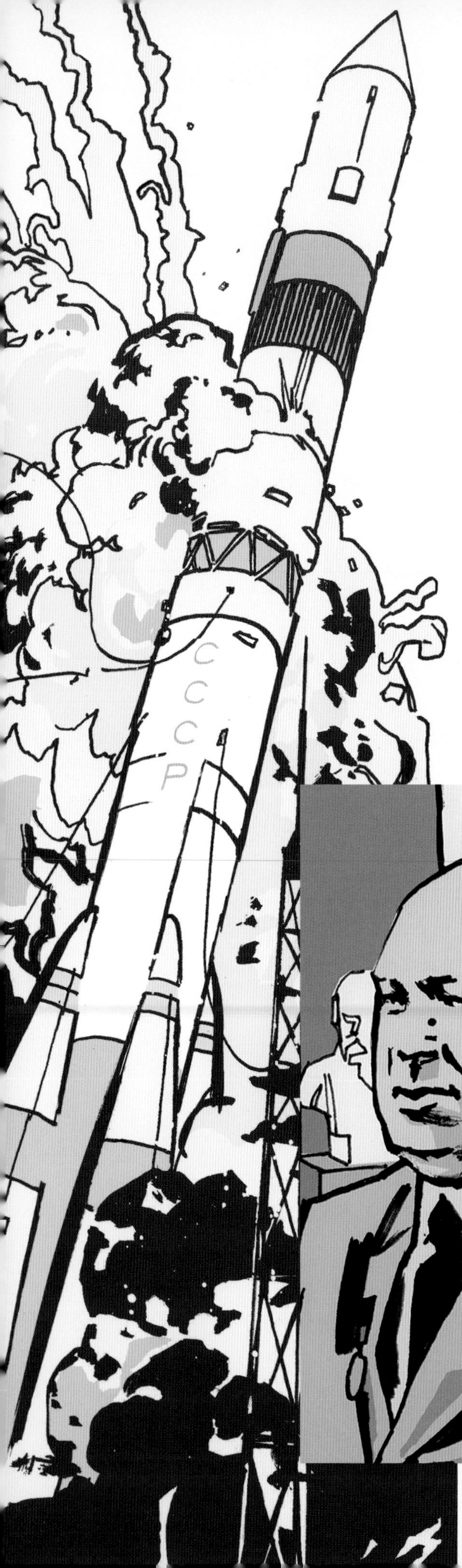
CCCP

Having accepted her new life, Natasha was soon informed that her new husband had been killed in a rocket explosion, as the USSR tried to get ahead of the West in the space race. Broken-hearted, she begged to be allowed to avenge her fallen love by working as an agent against the West. Khrushchev reluctantly agreed, privately telling Ivan to keep an eye on her, as the serum she had been given might cause mental instability.

As she became a respected and feared agent of the KGB, Soviet Russia's Committee for State Security, Natasha would come face to face with Logan again. However, the two failed to recognize each other thanks to the frequent memory wipes both had endured. Logan was on a covert mission in Russian airspace with hot-headed US Air Force test pilot Ben Grimm, prior to his transformation into the Thing. A pre-Ms. Marvel Carol Danvers was also assigned to the mission, sent by Nick Fury as a representative of the Defense Intelligence Agency.

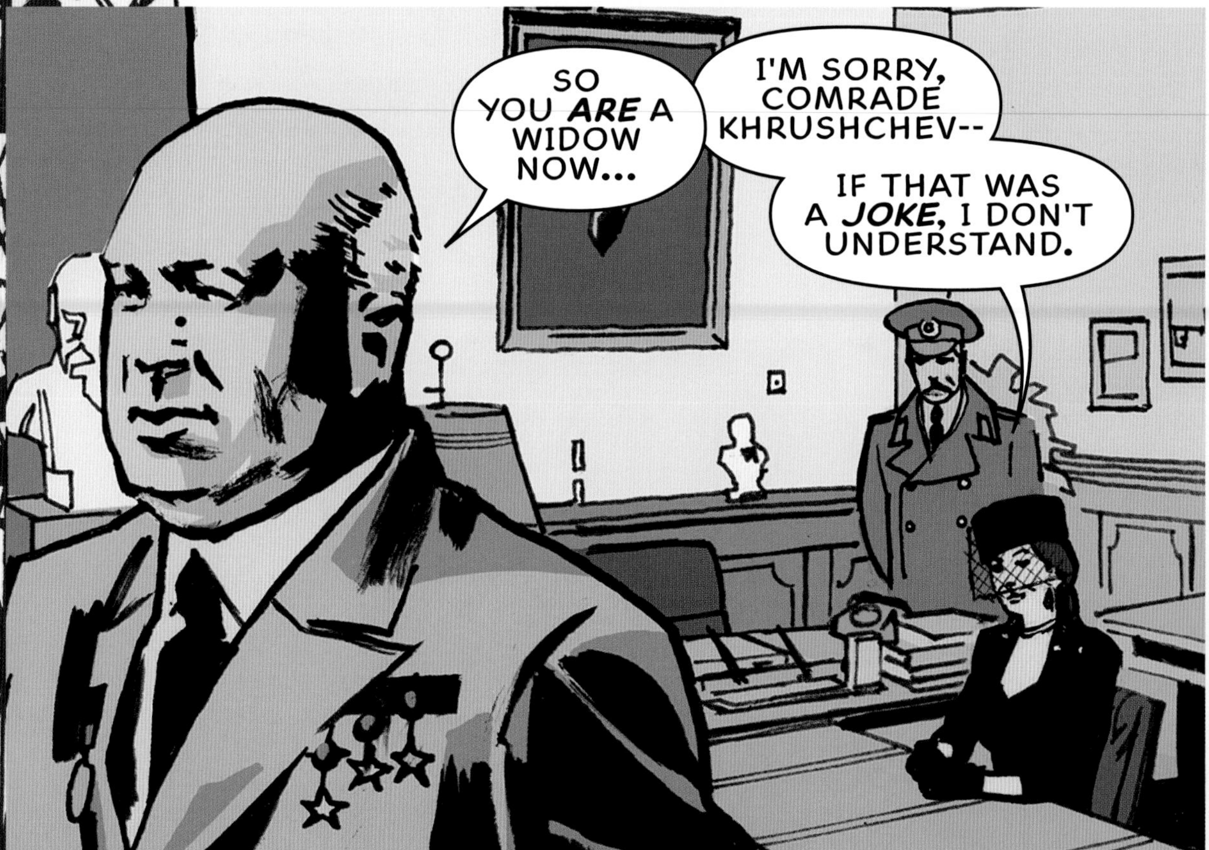
SO YOU ***ARE*** A WIDOW NOW...
I'M SORRY, COMRADE KHRUSHCHEV--
IF THAT WAS A ***JOKE***, I DON'T UNDERSTAND.

Agent Shostakova, as Natasha was then known, was piloting a jet to thwart these enemies of the Russian State. While Natasha could not help but admire the heroism of the infiltrators from the West, she was about to shoot them down when she was abruptly ordered to abort the mission and return to base. As she flew away, a confused Logan was left wondering where he had seen the beautiful Russian agent before.

The skill, strength, resourcefulness, and resolve that Natasha had demonstrated in her training and early missions had shown the authorities that she was a cut above her Red Room comrades. The loss of her husband and the life she thought she had was the final push she needed to officially take on the mantle of the Black Widow and travel to the West to fulfill her destiny. Finally, after a lifetime spent in pursuit of one purpose, Natasha Romanova could enter the Cold War battlefield and fully realize her potential as the greatest super-spy Soviet Russia had ever created.

BLACK WIDOW: DEADLY ORIGIN #2 (FEB. 2010) The news that her husband had been killed in a rocket explosion pushed Natasha to ask for a place in the front line of the Cold War: a mission to the United States.

"I request to be assigned to... infiltrate and destroy (the West's) technologies."

BLACK WIDOW

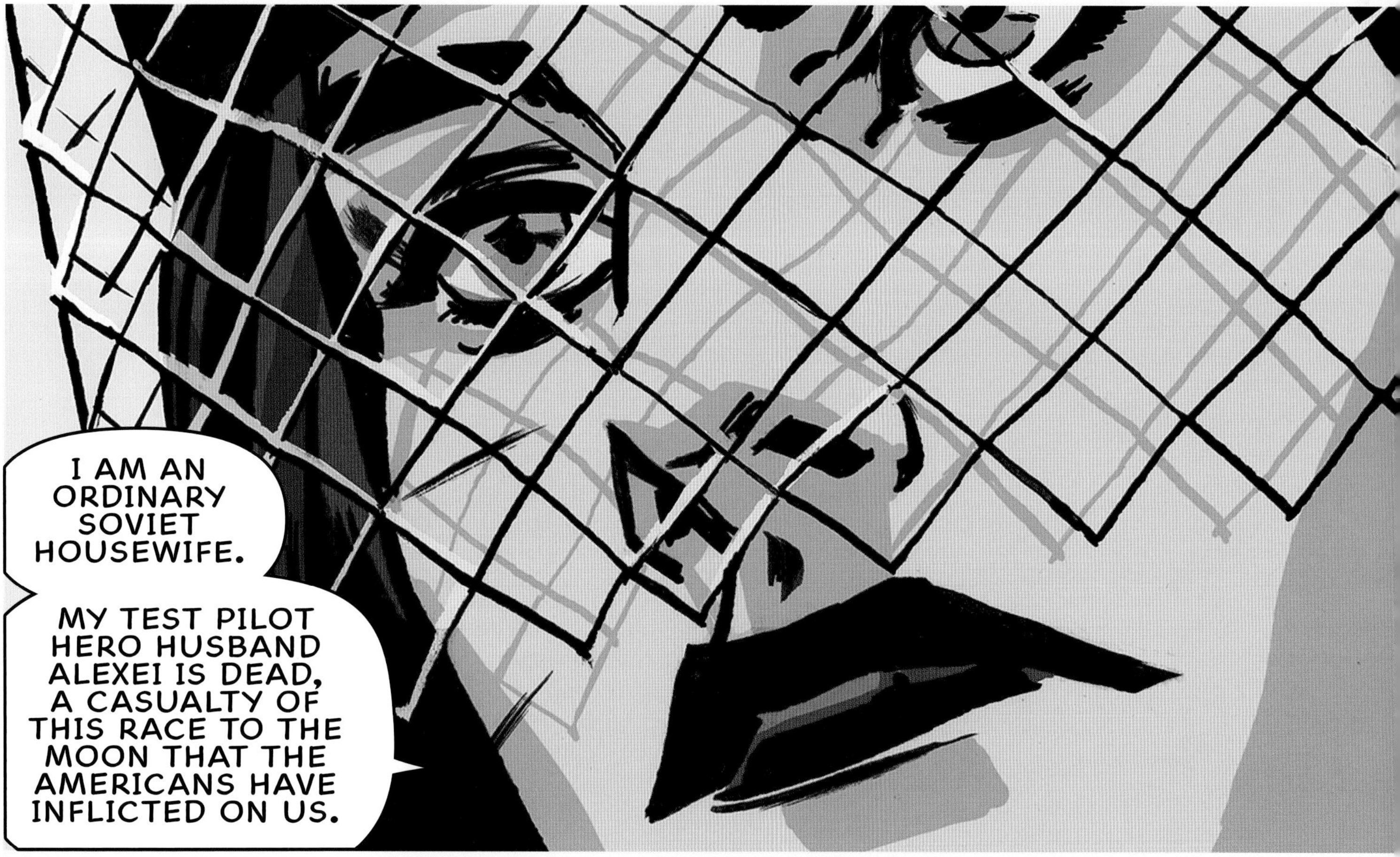
I AM AN ORDINARY SOVIET HOUSEWIFE.
MY TEST PILOT HERO HUSBAND ALEXEI IS DEAD, A CASUALTY OF THIS RACE TO THE MOON THAT THE AMERICANS HAVE INFLICTED ON US.

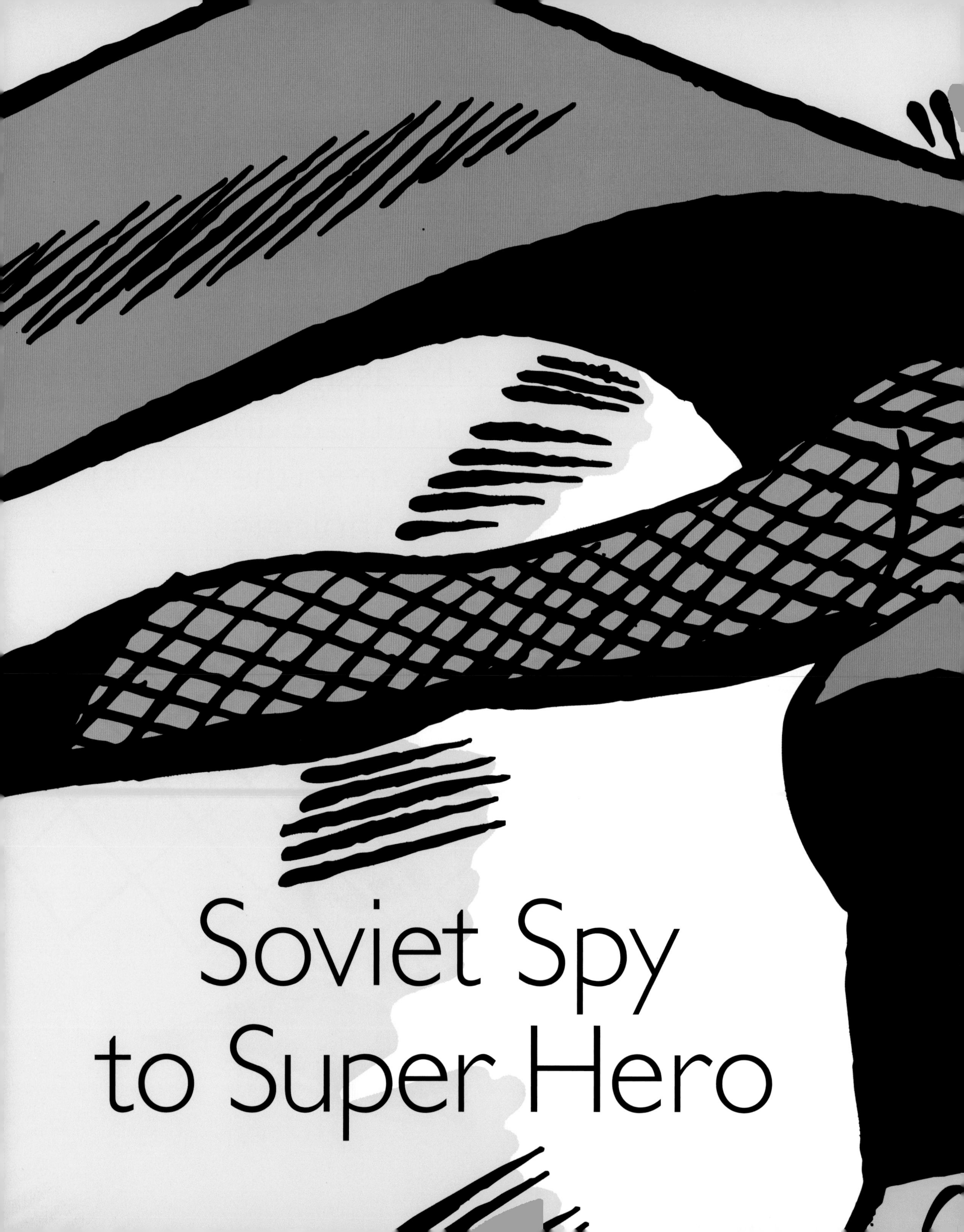

Soviet Spy to Super Hero

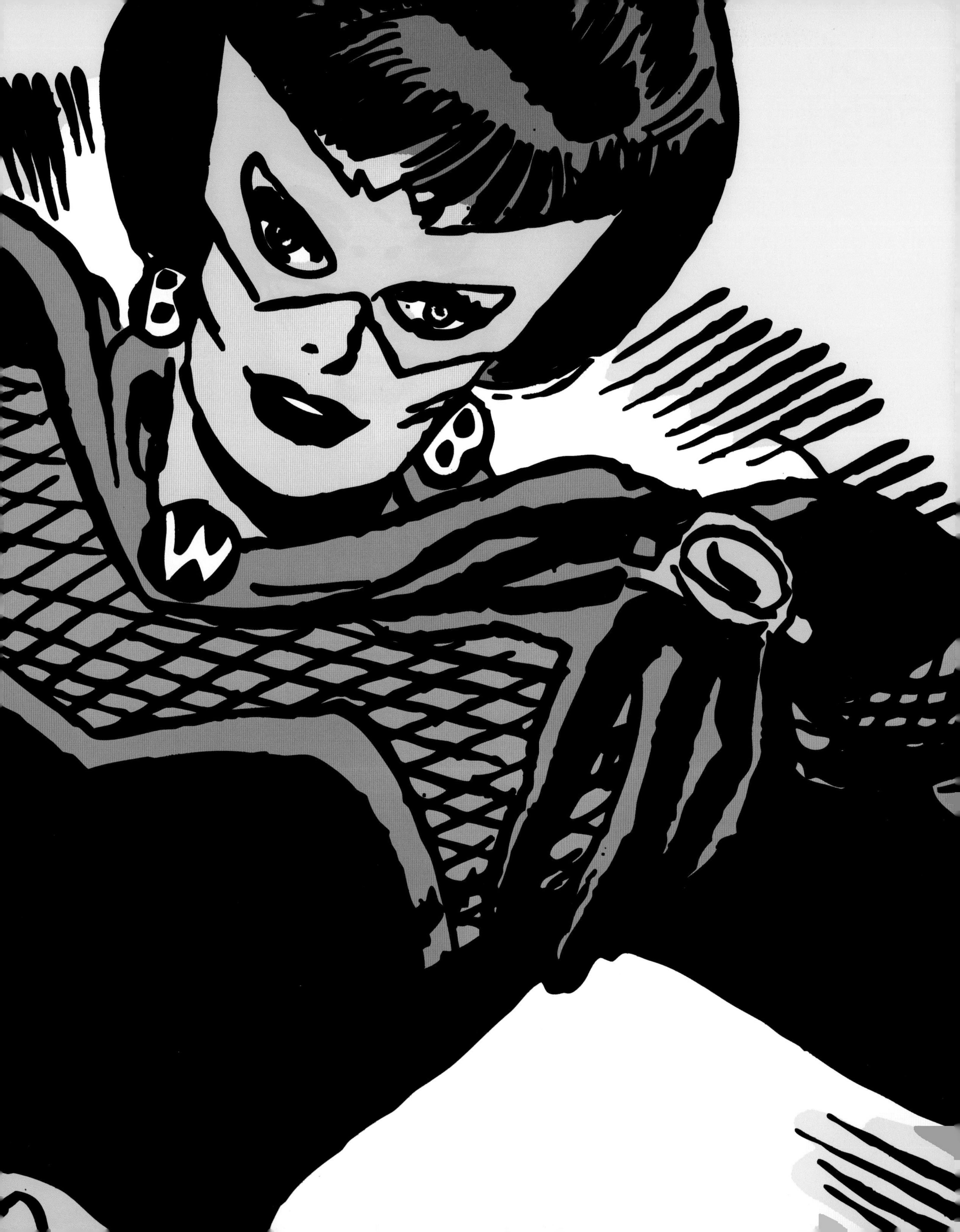

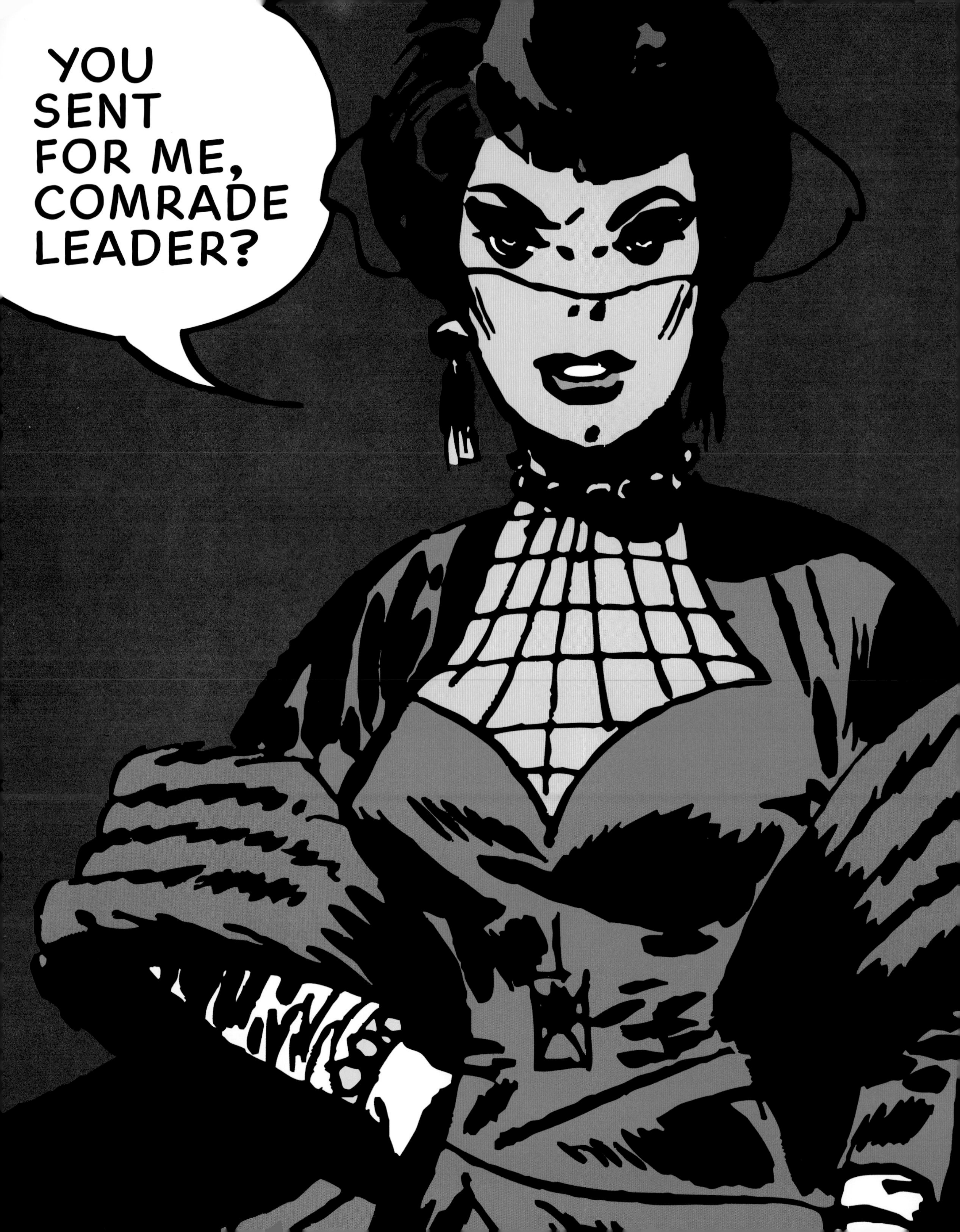
YOU SENT FOR ME, COMRADE LEADER?

In Enemy Territory

TALES OF SUSPENSE #52 (APR. 1964) After years of training, the Black Widow was deemed ready to embark on a mission to the US to take on billionaire industrialist Tony Stark and his "bodyguard," Iron Man.

Natasha Romanoff first traveled to the other side of the Iron Curtain as a highly motivated woman, determined to do her bit for her country as Black Widow. The loss of her husband, Alexei, had been the trigger she needed to push her to take on bigger challenges as an agent of the state. For her, the Cold War was anything but cold. However, although she believed that she was choosing her own path to honor Alexei's memory, in fact, from the outset, she was being led along, doing precisely what her superiors had planned for her.

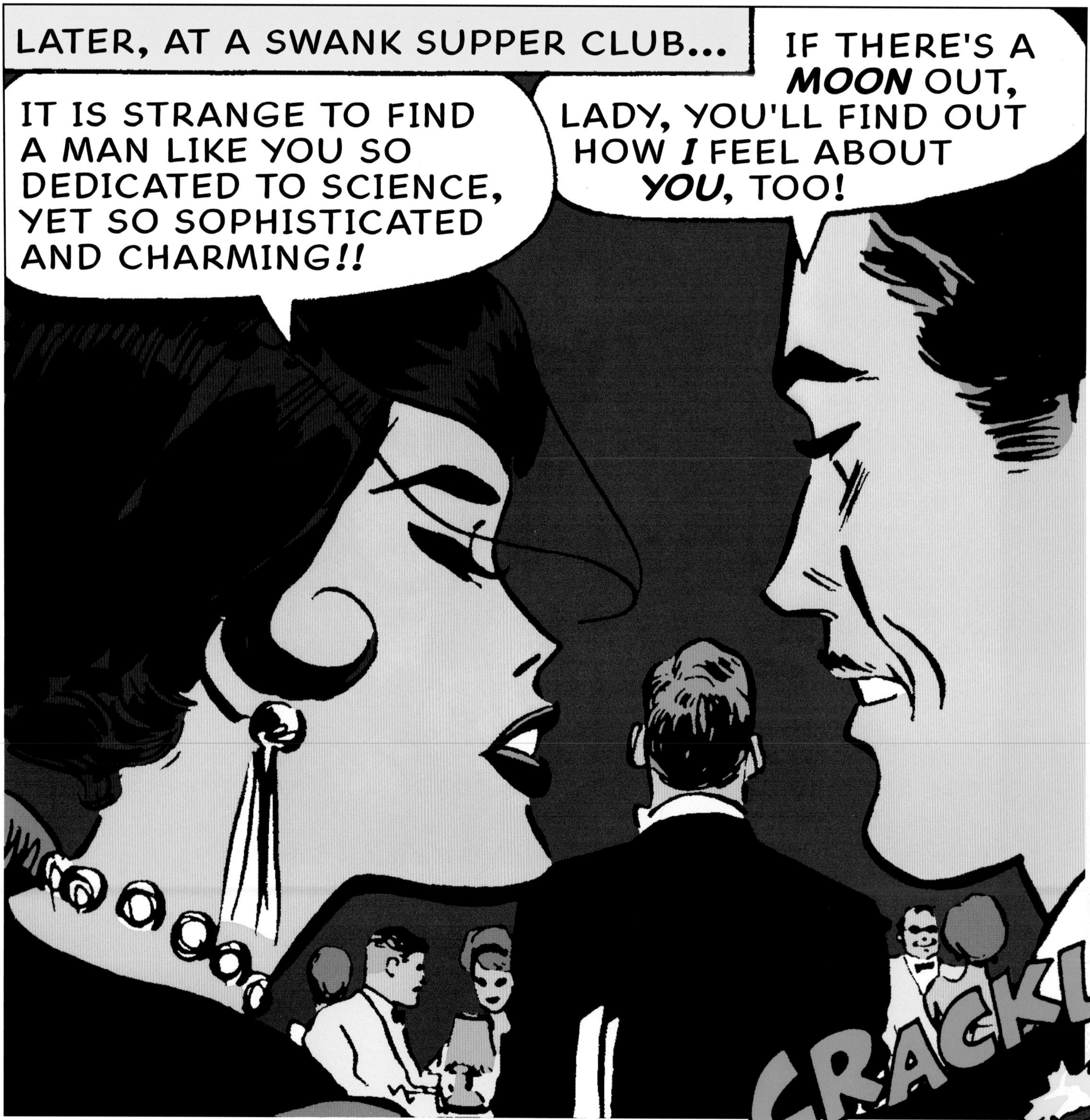
LATER, AT A SWANK SUPPER CLUB...
IT IS STRANGE TO FIND A MAN LIKE YOU SO DEDICATED TO SCIENCE, YET SO SOPHISTICATED AND CHARMING!!
IF THERE'S A MOON OUT, LADY, YOU'LL FIND OUT HOW I FEEL ABOUT YOU, TOO!

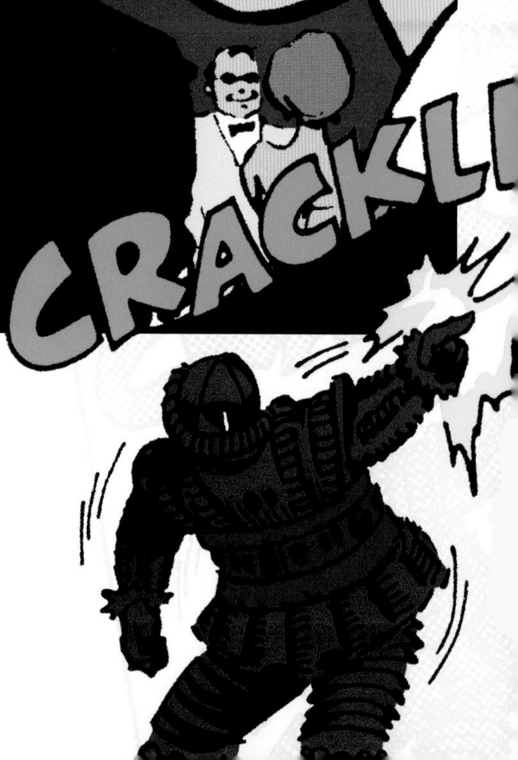

"I know too well the penalty for failure!"

BLACK WIDOW

Natasha's Soviet handlers had heard of the billionaire American genius Tony Stark and knew that his technology could be made into weapons that might be used against them. Worse still, reports had reached them that Stark was being aided by a Russian defector—Ivan Vanko, also known as the powered armor-wearing Soviet agent Crimson Dynamo. Black Widow's first US assignment would be to kill Stark, Vanko, and Stark's armored "bodyguard," Iron Man—not even the KGB's upper echelons knew that Stark and Iron Man were one and the same.

At this stage in her career, Natasha elected not to wear a costume, but rather adopt the guise of a glamorous jet-setter, clad in a fur coat and expensive jewelry. This persona—"Madame Natasha"—was calculated to be exactly what was needed to get close to Tony Stark, who, as well as being a brilliant inventor, was known for his weakness for beautiful women. Sure enough, Madame Natasha had no trouble convincing Stark to go on a dinner date with her, while her henchman Boris kidnapped Ivan Vanko, disguised himself as the Crimson Dynamo, and started trashing Stark's factory. When Iron Man arrived on the scene, he quickly discovered that his lovely companion was, in fact, a Soviet spy. During the ensuing tussle, the real Vanko saved Iron Man by shooting Boris (and tragically killing himself) with a faulty weapon, declaring: "I would dare anything for this country, which has been so good to me!" Although Black Widow would not admit it at the time, perhaps witnessing the lengths a defector would go to for his adopted country made a deep impression on her.

TALES OF SUSPENSE #52 (APR. 1964) Black Widow's first foray against Iron Man saw her use her more beguiling skills, while her comrade Boris took care of the combative side. However, Natasha would soon find reason to demonstrate her martial arts abilities in the field.

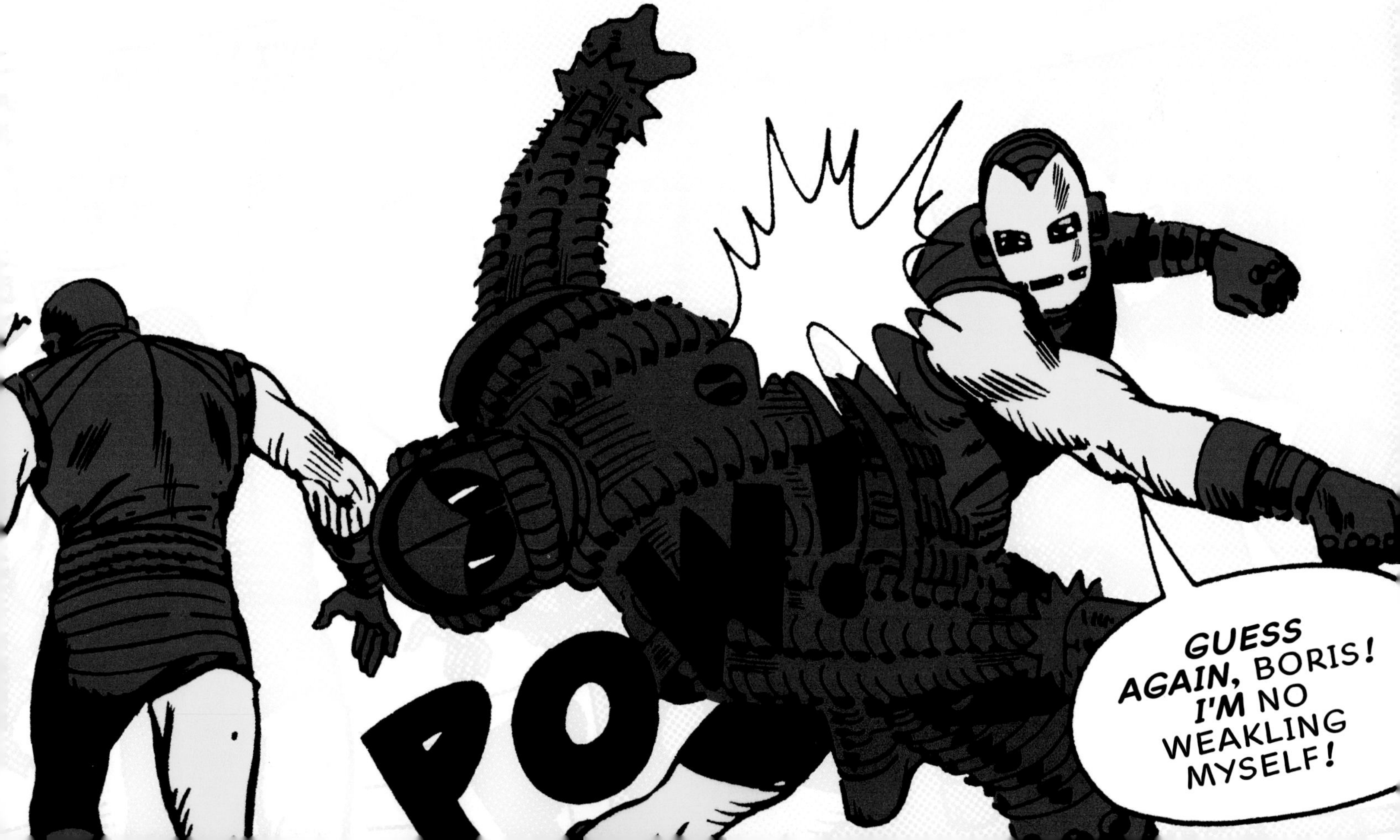
GUESS AGAIN, BORIS! I'M NO WEAKLING MYSELF!

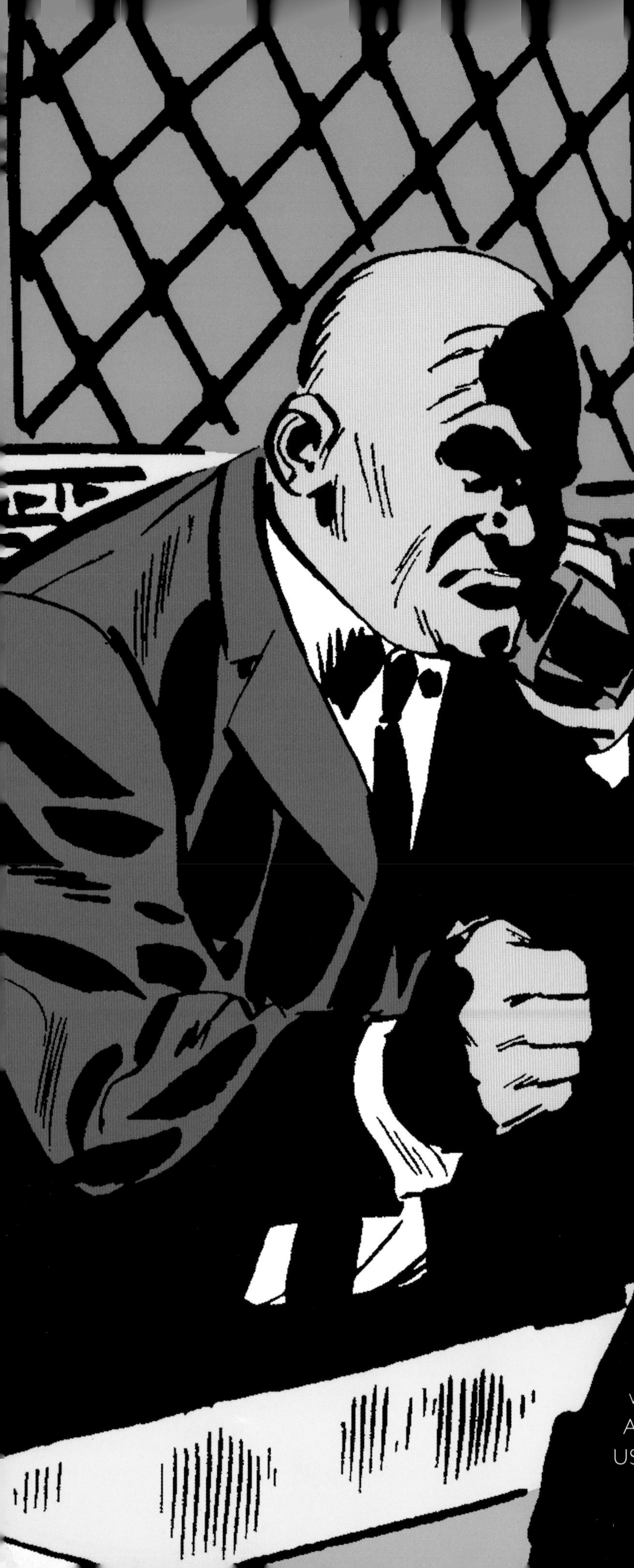

Stark Pursuit

Following her failure, Natasha retreated into hiding in the US. She did not have to wait too long before attempting to redeem herself by once more trying to defeat Tony Stark. A newspaper report on a new antigravity raygun that the billionaire inventor was developing presented Black Widow with the perfect opportunity to get back into the KGB's good books. Reasoning that Stark's instinctive American tendency to sympathize would play into her hands, she wrote him a note telling him that she wanted a chance to explain herself. Once inside his office, Natasha immediately incapacitated Stark with a paralyzing gas, stole the weapon, and made her escape. Perhaps the Western lifestyle was already influencing her, or maybe she had become too deeply engaged in her Madame Natasha persona, as she first used the ray to steal jewelry for herself before communicating her success to her KGB controllers.

Black Widow was getting into her stride. Her scheme was progressing well, and she loved the new power the antigravity weapon gave her, using it to sabotage several of Tony Stark's factories. So she did not take it well when the Soviet authorities forced her to work alongside a team of agents. Her misgivings about working with others were confirmed when one of her incompetent comrades gave away their position to Iron Man who was searching for them. Without hesitation, Black Widow went in for the kill, collapsing a building on top of the Golden Avenger. Believing him destroyed, she then moved on to her next target: the gold reserves of Fort Knox. However, Iron Man arrived—having survived her attack—to nullify the ray: accidentally triggering an enormous rockfall. To Black Widow's astonishment, the armored hero prevented her Soviet comrades from being crushed by the falling rocks. The notion that someone would risk their own life to save an enemy was inconceivable to someone raised in the Red Room. Although her bungling accomplices were captured by the US authorities, Black Widow managed to escape once again.

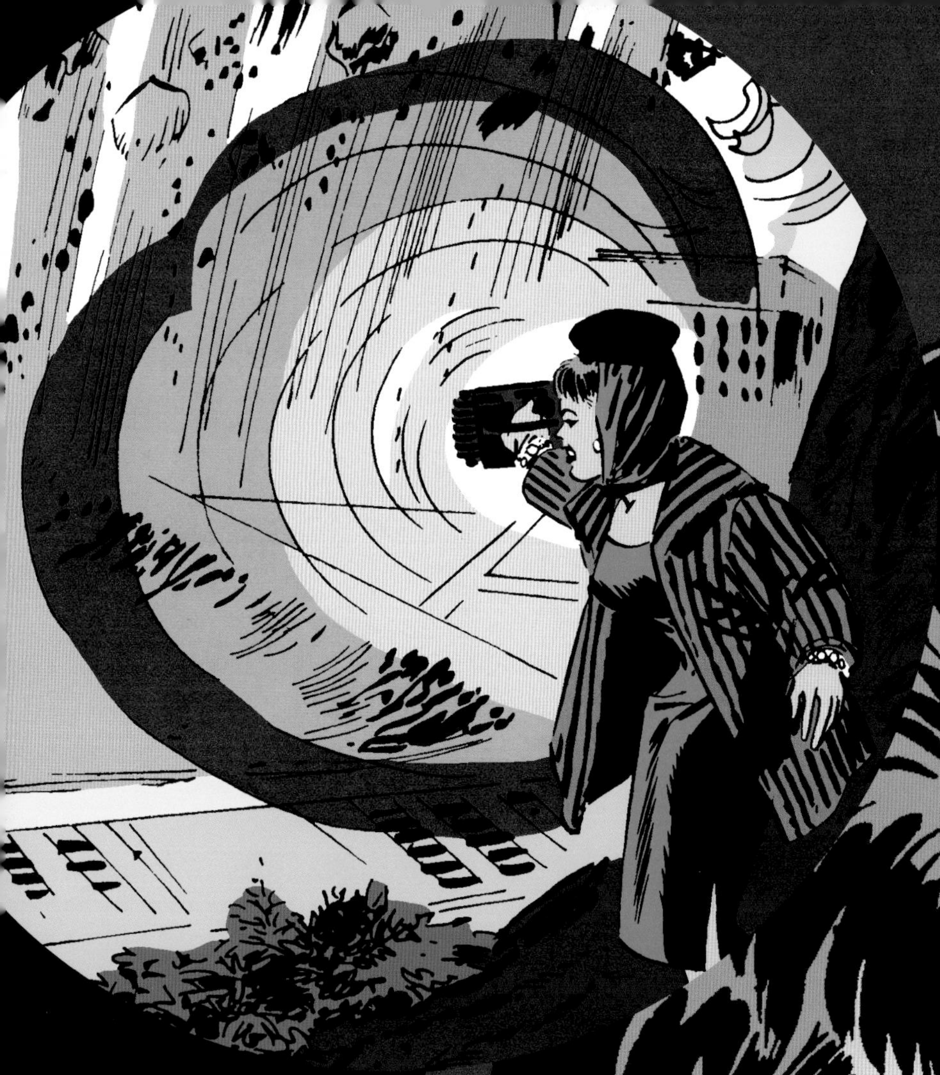

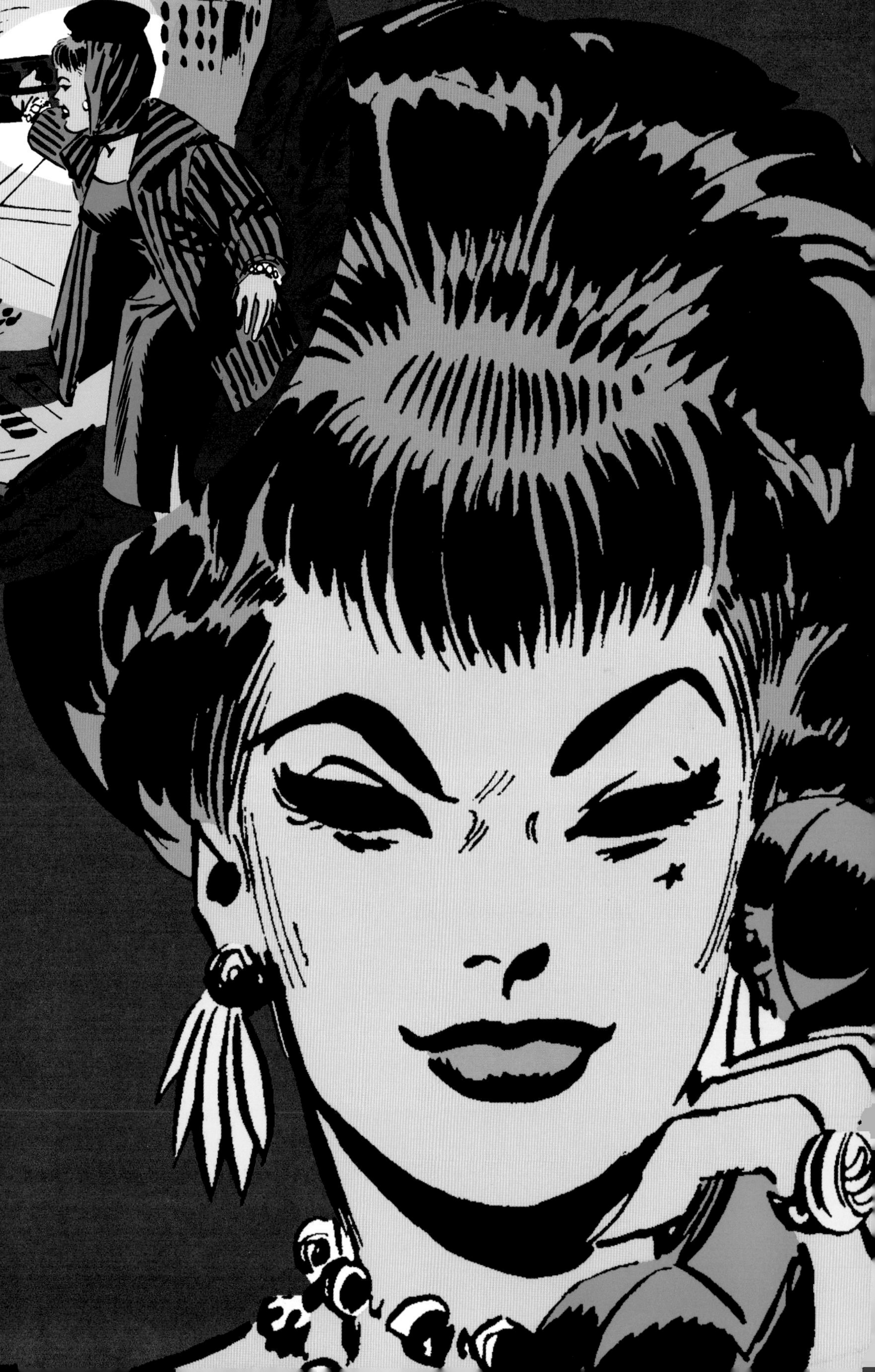

TALES OF SUSPENSE #53 (MAY 1964) Although still reporting back to her masters in the USSR, Black Widow enjoyed the freedom of operating alone in the US—giving herself her first taste of power and autonomy.

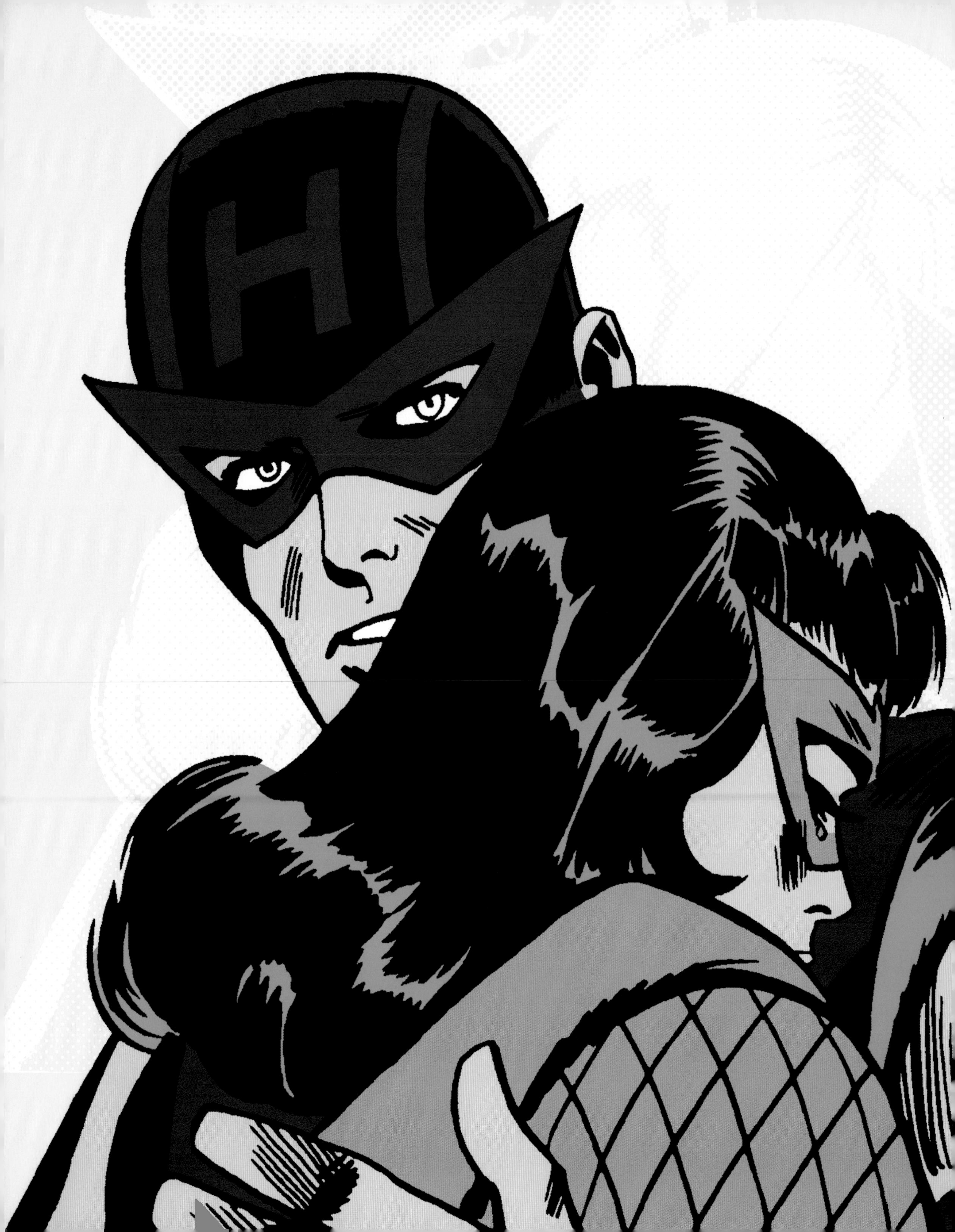

Choosing Life

TALES OF SUSPENSE #57 (SEPT. 1964) Black Widow chose Hawkeye as her partner in crime, little suspecting that the American archer would play a part in causing her to switch sides in the **Cold War.**

Black Widow was soon to find a more agreeable ally than her bumbling spy comrades, a real asset in her ongoing campaign against Tony Stark. Clint Barton, a carnival performer with a talent for marksmanship, had made himself a costume and some trick arrows. Calling himself Hawkeye, Barton was about to take the first tentative steps into a crime-fighting career when he was wrongly accused of taking part in a robbery. Fleeing the scene, Hawkeye was intercepted by a mysterious woman—Black Widow—who offered him a lift in her car. Instantly smitten, he agreed to help her take down Iron Man. Their chances of success improved after Black Widow upgraded Barton's armory with new arrows made from advanced Russian tech.

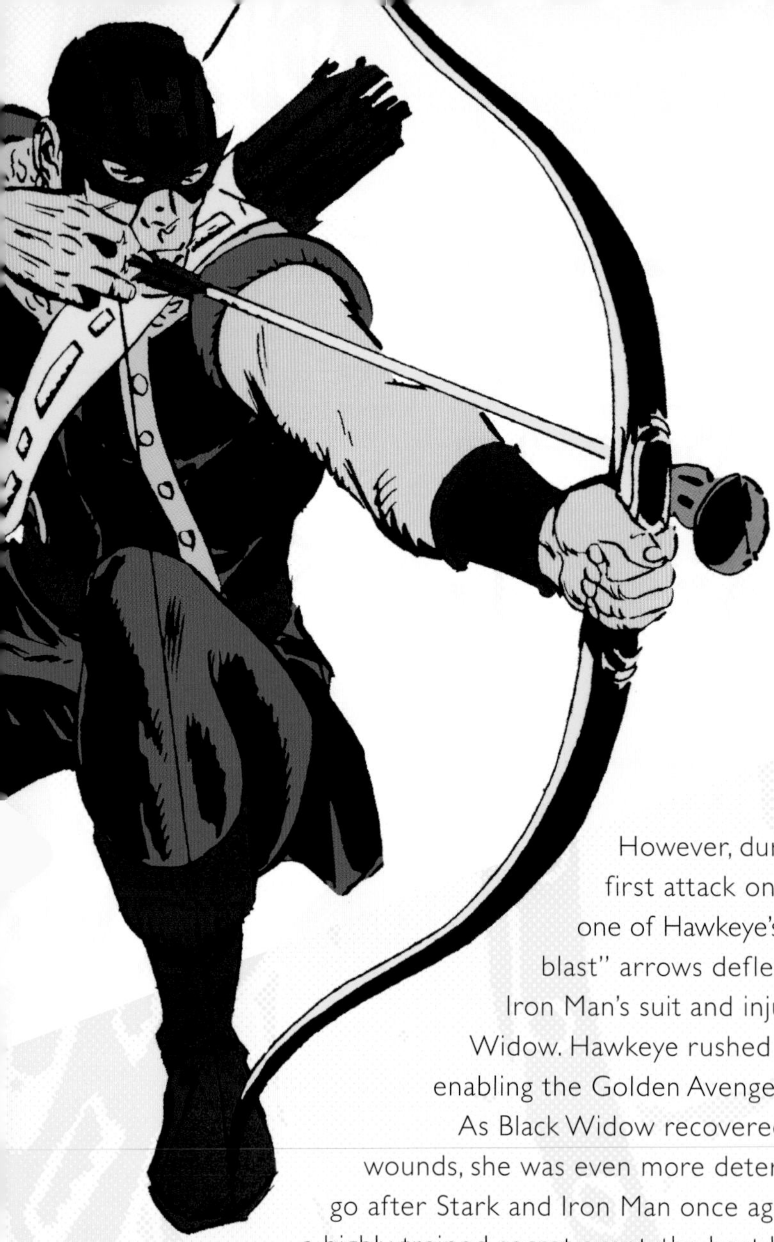

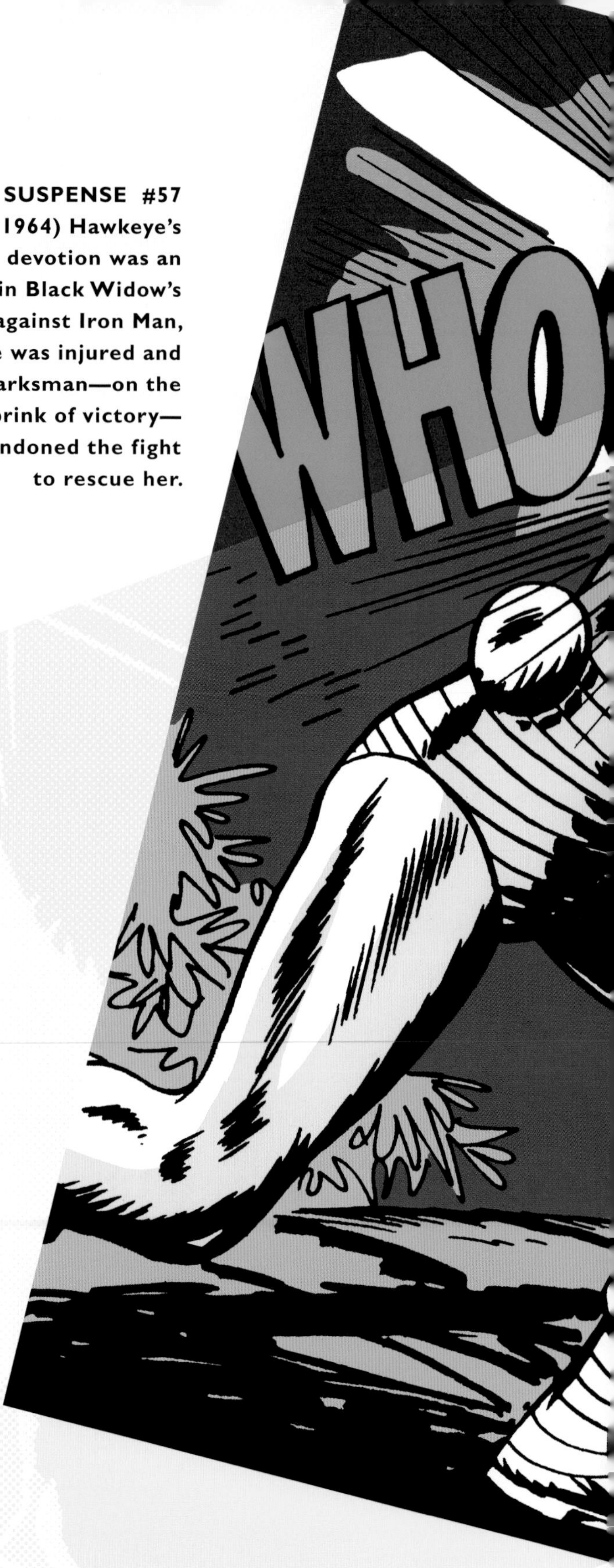

TALES OF SUSPENSE #57 (SEPT. 1964) Hawkeye's slavish devotion was an asset in Black Widow's mission against Iron Man, until she was injured and the marksman—on the brink of victory—abandoned the fight to rescue her.

However, during their first attack on Iron Man, one of Hawkeye's "demolition blast" arrows deflected off Iron Man's suit and injured Black Widow. Hawkeye rushed to her side, enabling the Golden Avenger to escape. As Black Widow recovered from her wounds, she was even more determined to go after Stark and Iron Man once again. She was a highly trained secret agent, the best her country had, but she was fast discovering that missions in the field did not always turn out like training exercises. Still unsure of her memories, being a successful agent was the only definite identity Natasha could carve for herself beyond doubt. Her failures were feeding a growing obsession with proving herself to the Soviet authorities, and her hold on Hawkeye was threatened when he started to suspect she was a Russian spy. Natasha eventually managed to persuade him that world peace was all she was striving for, and perhaps she was coming to believe it herself. But her campaign against Tony Stark was abruptly interrupted when Natasha was forcibly returned to the USSR for interrogation. Much to her surprise, she found herself wondering if she would ever see Hawkeye again—the tenderness for Barton that she had feigned to keep the archer in her thrall was turning into genuine affection.

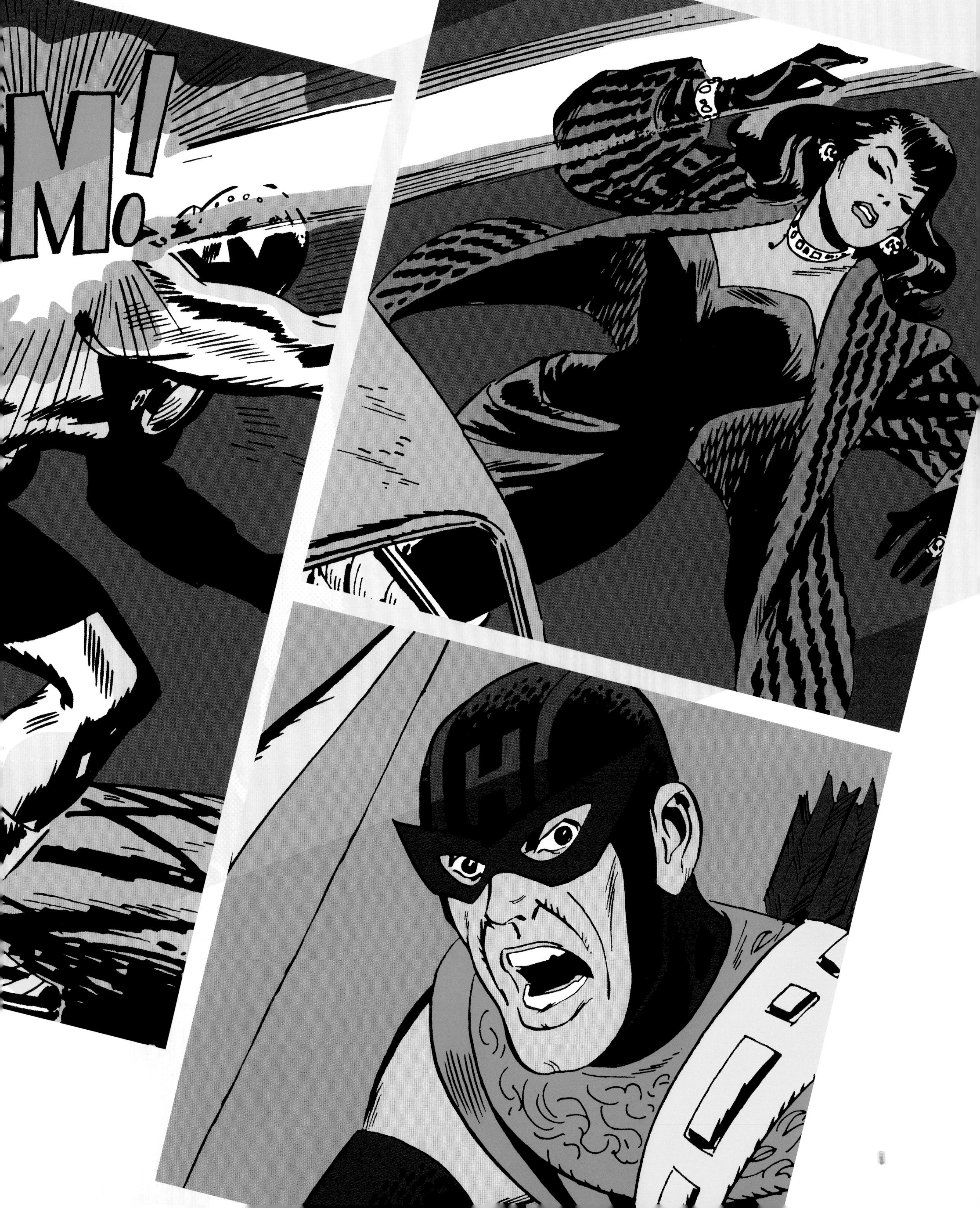

TALES OF SUSPENSE #64 (APR. 1965) Black Widow returned to the US, no longer just a femme fatale, but donning a KGB-equipped costume befitting her status as the USSR's top agent.

Back home, Natasha had to answer to Premier Khrushchev for her repeated failures. Unable to have her eliminated because—according to the comrade leader—that would prove the Soviet Black Widow plans had failed. Instead, he ordered her to return to the US and kill Iron Man once and for all.

She had seen that people on the other side of the Iron Curtain were not intrinsically evil. She had witnessed the esteem in which her compatriot Ivan Vanko held Iron Man, and how that hero had selflessly saved the lives of his enemies. And she had fallen in love with a Westerner, Clint Barton. Any or all of these factors may have led to Natasha now refusing to obey her leader's orders.

A Most Dangerous Spy

Unfortunately for Natasha, the Soviet authorities had planned for just this eventuality, introducing her to an elderly couple whom they claimed were her parents. If Black Widow were to turn traitor, these

people would suffer for it. Trapped by her own desire not to do any more harm, she was forced to comply. She was handed into the care of a scientist named Brushnev, who designed her a new costume befitting the most dangerous of all Russian spies. The soles of her feet would now be equipped with suction devices that enabled her to climb walls and even hang upside down, like her spider namesake. She was also fitted with a "bracelet" that could fire out suction-tipped nylon to enable her to swing between buildings. All that remained was to adopt a mask, and Natasha chose one resembling Hawkeye's, in the hope that they could be partners once again.

When Black Widow returned to the US, Hawkeye was overjoyed when he learned that she hadn't left him of her own free will, but was removed from American soil by her own countrymen. He even agreed to help her in her renewed effort to bring down Iron Man. However, after engaging the armored Avenger in battle, their wily foe quickly recognized that Hawkeye's affection for Black Widow was the duo's weak spot. Seizing the chance, he took Natasha down with an electric blast. Sure enough, although he was on the brink of victory, Hawkeye abandoned the fight and rushed Black Widow to safety, ruining yet another of her plans. Natasha was furious with Barton, and bluntly told him so: "Because of your love… I've failed again!"

"I have waited so long... so very long... for this moment!"

BLACK WIDOW

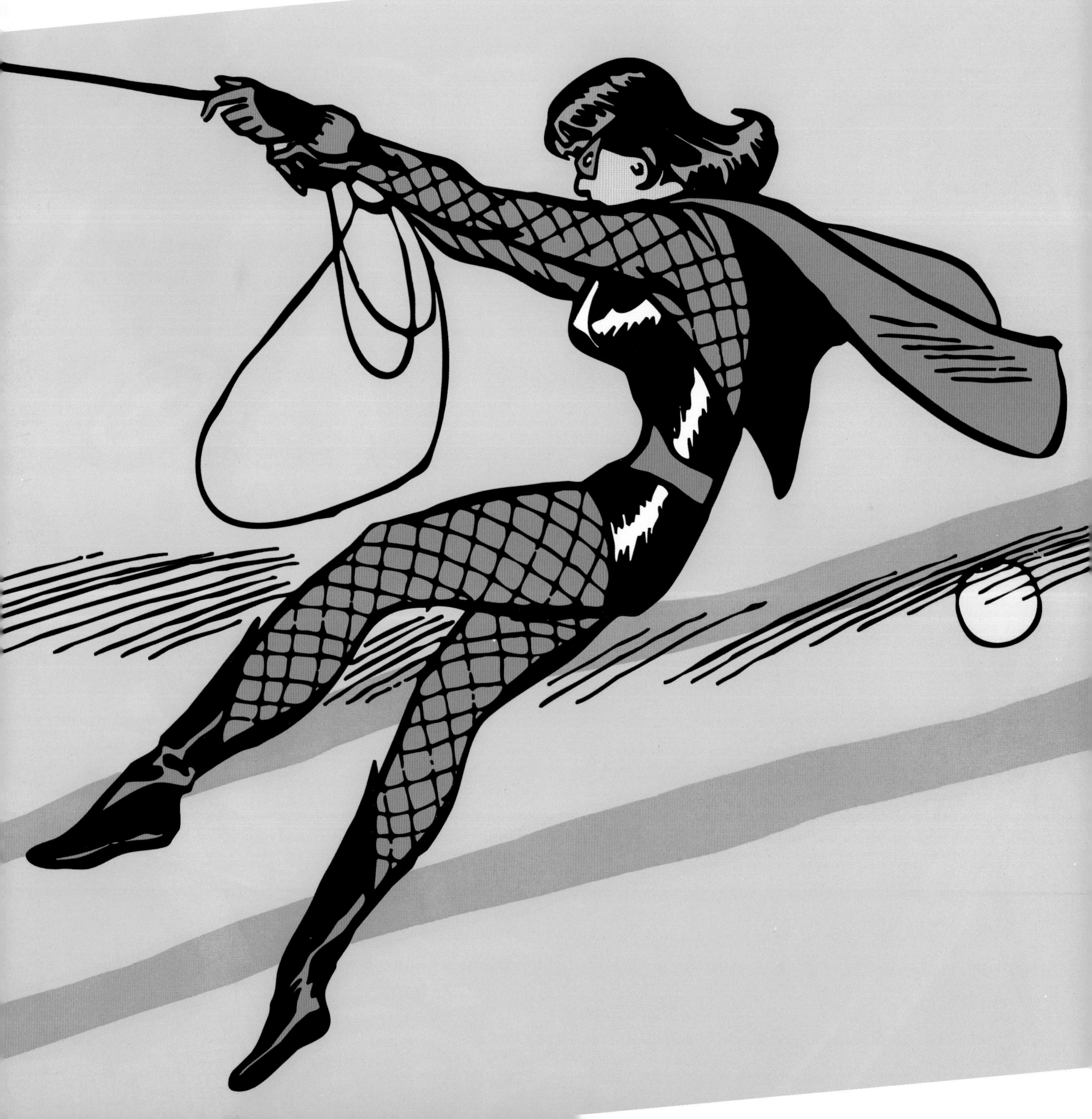

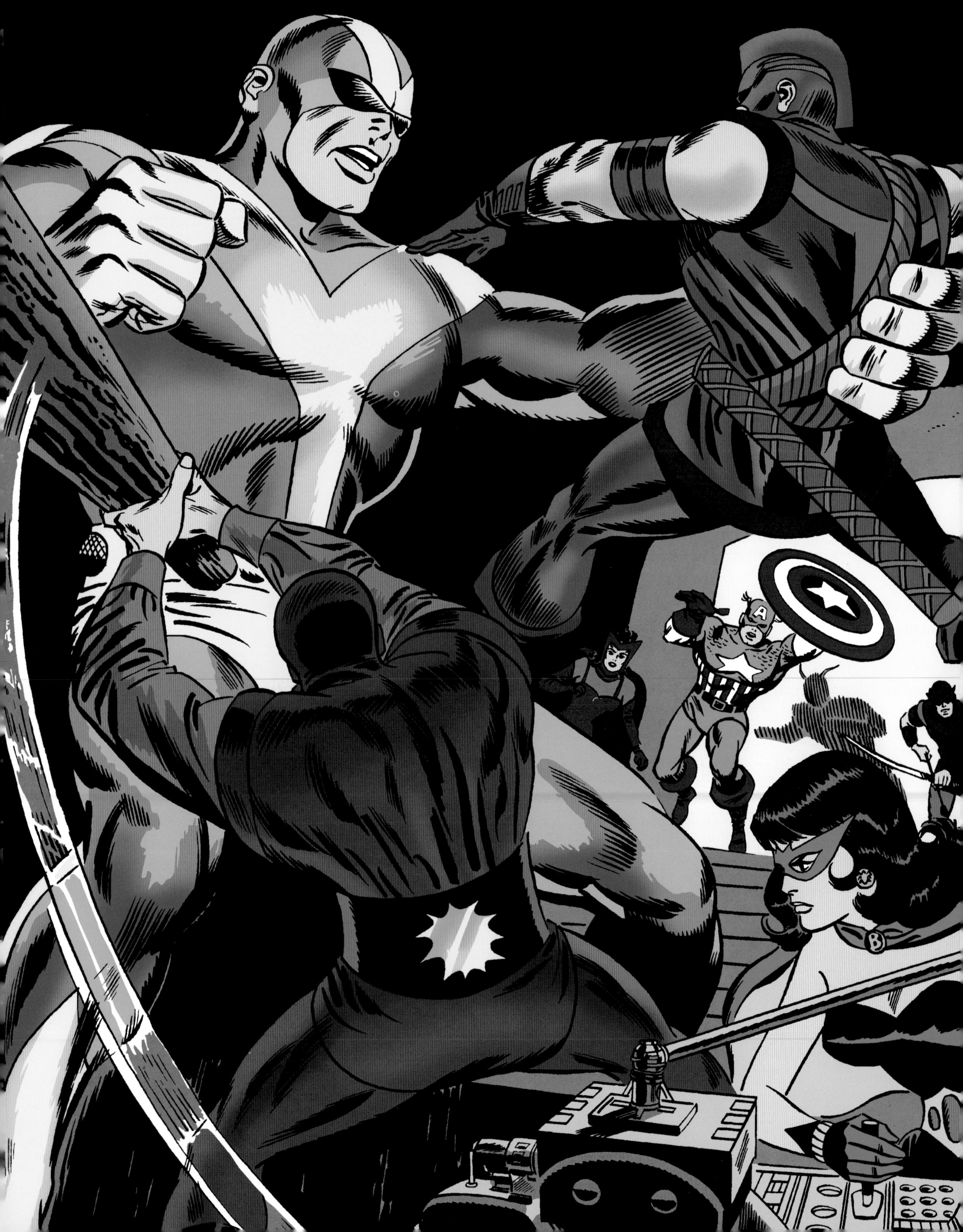

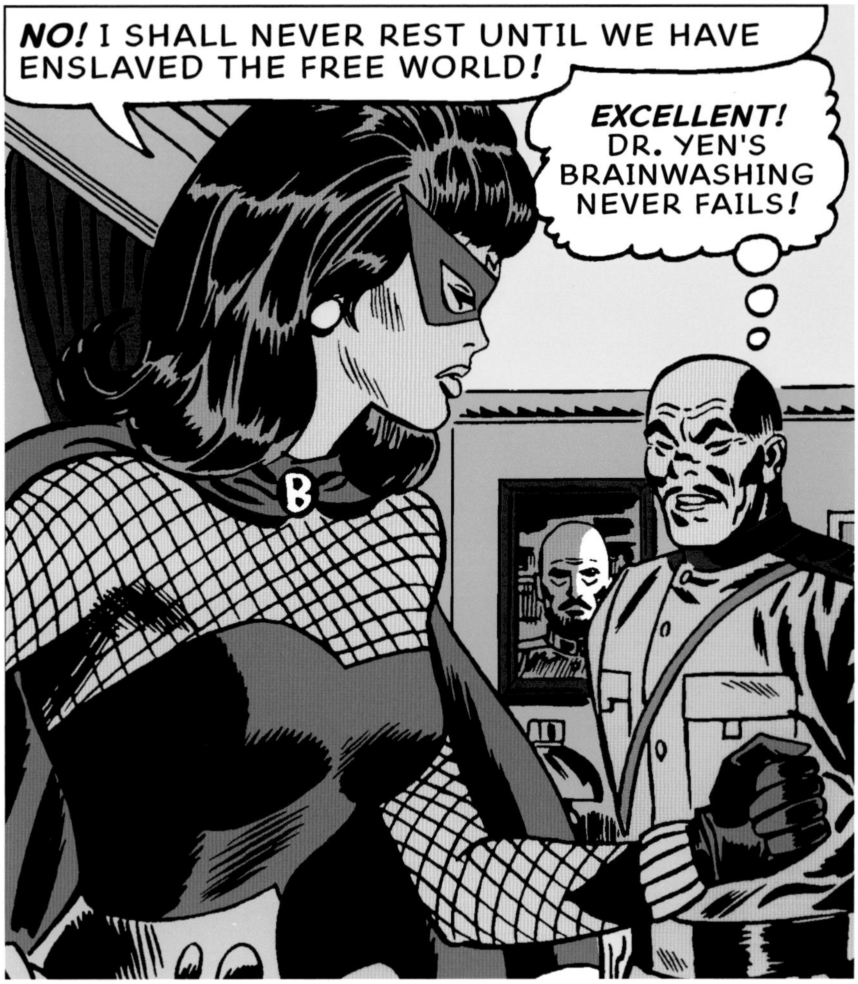
NO! I SHALL NEVER REST UNTIL WE HAVE ENSLAVED THE FREE WORLD!
EXCELLENT! DR. YEN'S BRAINWASHING NEVER FAILS!

THE AVENGERS #29 (JUN. 1966) Fighting the Avengers put Black Widow on the opposing side to her paramour, Hawkeye, but the archer could not bring himself to shoot down his brainwashed beloved.

This lack of success caught up with Natasha in the most brutal of ways, as she always knew it would, and she was hospitalized after being targeted by the Soviets. Extracted and taken back behind the Iron Curtain to be imprisoned, Black Widow was released when a brainwashing expert was found who could turn her back into an obedient agent. After all, many years of effort and cutting-edge science had gone into creating Black Widow, and the authorities were determined to find a way she could still be used. Her new target was the US Super Hero team known as the Avengers, which her old adversary Iron Man helped found and in which Hawkeye was now a member. However, Natasha acknowledged that she might need assistance against the Earth's Mightiest Heroes, and recruited two powerful villains for her cause: the Swordsman (Jacques Duquesne) and the original Power Man (Erik Josten).

When news of her return reached the Avengers, Captain America (Steve Rogers) warned Hawkeye that Natasha was likely to be brainwashed. Barton didn't care, however; he rushed to find her in the hopes that he could help her break free. He was painfully disavowed of that idea when she told him in a cold, emotionless tone, that she had come to defeat the Avengers. However, Black Widow and her allies were thwarted in their attempt, and she only escaped thanks to Hawkeye, who could not bring himself to shoot down his former love.

As her communist handlers feared it might, Black Widow's brainwashing began to wear off. She found herself unable to explain why she hated the Avengers so much, and why she couldn't stop thinking about Hawkeye. The marksman himself, overcome with shame about his part in her recent escape, was driven to prove himself to the Avengers by capturing Black Widow and her allies single-handedly. As he battled the trio, Hawkeye dropped his arrows. Natasha retrieved them and, for a brief moment, Hawkeye thought she was going to hand them to him. Instead, he received an electric shock from her new weapon: the Widow's Bite. Unable to bring himself to fight her, Barton returned to the fray. But just as Power Man was about to deliver Hawkeye a final blow, Black Widow used her gauntlets again—this time to save him. Natasha had finally shaken off her brainwashing, although Barton was still quite skeptical about her true motives.

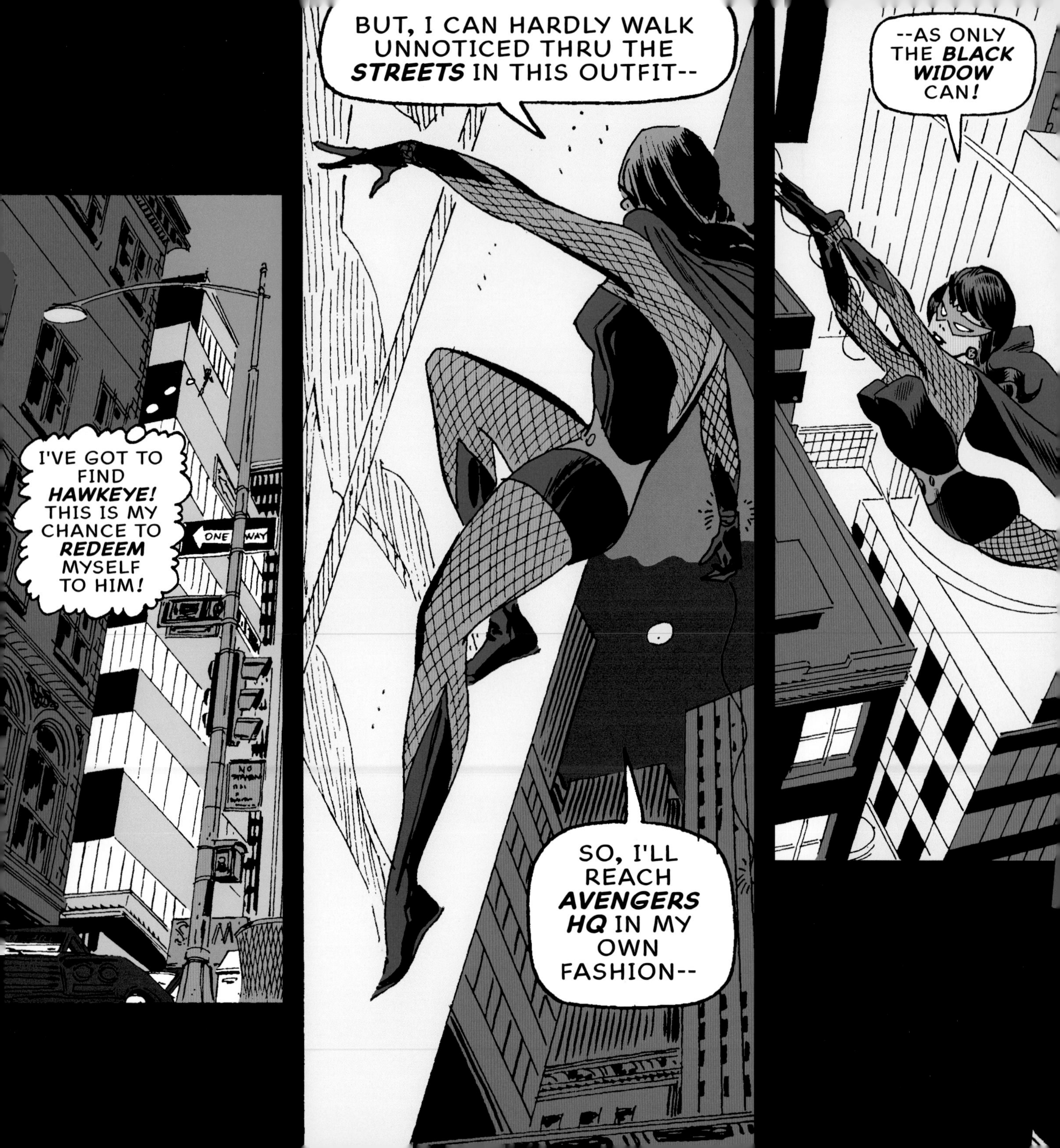
I'VE GOT TO FIND **HAWKEYE!** THIS IS MY CHANCE TO **REDEEM** MYSELF TO HIM!
ONE WAY
BUT, I CAN HARDLY WALK UNNOTICED THRU THE **STREETS** IN THIS OUTFIT--
SO, I'LL REACH **AVENGERS HQ** IN MY OWN FASHION--
--AS ONLY THE **BLACK WIDOW** CAN!

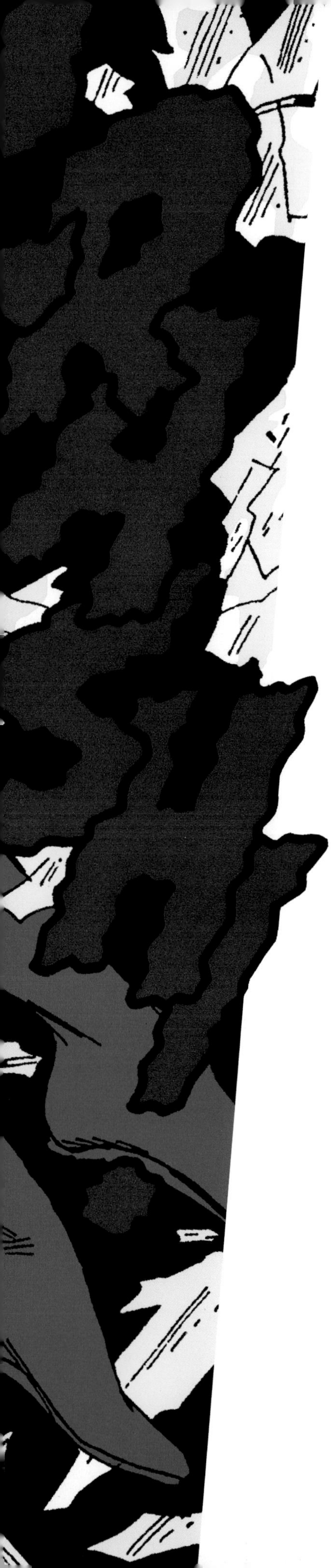

Avengers Ally

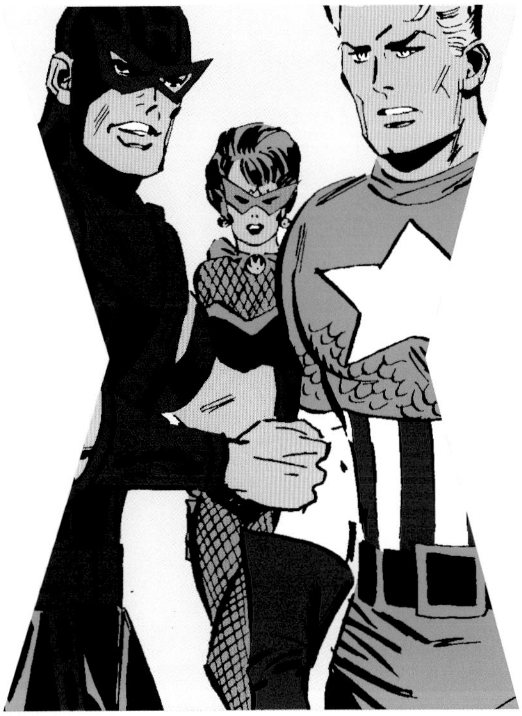

THE AVENGERS #32 (SEPT. 1966) Black Widow had decided to leave her life as a spy, and swung through the streets of the Big Apple to find Hawkeye and convince him that she was now a worthy ally of the Avengers.

Now free of her Soviet brainwashing, Natasha realized she wanted to use her impressive skills to do good, rather than serve the bidding of tyrants. Actively seeking a mission for herself, she infiltrated a meeting of the evil group Sons of the Serpent. Disliking their talk of driving foreigners out of the US, Black Widow sought out Hawkeye so she could prove that her redemption was genuine. The pair teamed up again, but this time for a heroic cause. Hawkeye now trusted Natasha, and tried to convince the other Avengers that she should join the team.

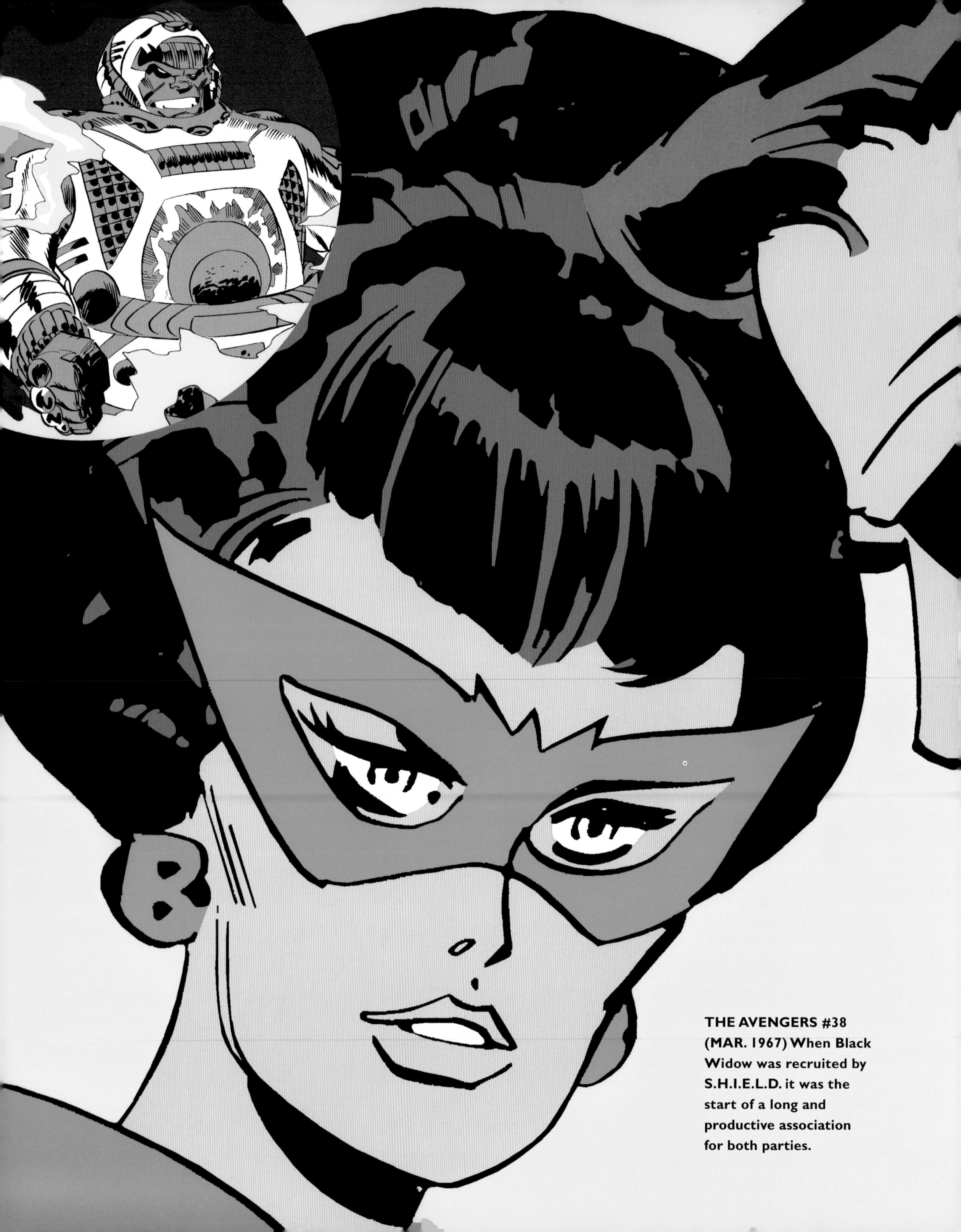

THE AVENGERS #38 (MAR. 1967) When Black Widow was recruited by S.H.I.E.L.D. it was the start of a long and productive association for both parties.

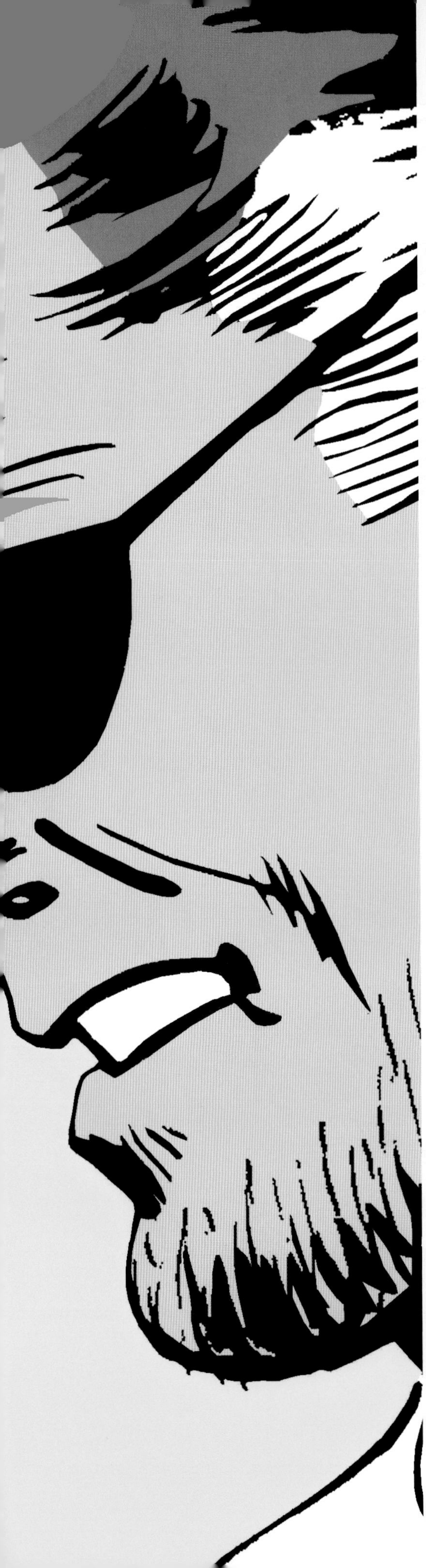

Black Widow fought alongside the Avengers for the first time on an assignment to stop alien warlord Ixar. Her contribution was crucial to the victory, although she and Hawkeye chose not to divulge that she had forced the villain's surrender by threatening to kill him. Such lethal action went against the Avengers' code of conduct. Natasha was taking steps to become a hero, but her instincts were still influenced by the Red Room.

Hawkeye continued to press his Avengers colleagues to vote Black Widow onto the team. However, another organization was more eager to recruit someone of Natasha's unique skill set—S.H.I.E.L.D. They were so determined to get her to work for them that they kidnapped her en route to Avengers Mansion. S.H.I.E.L.D. commander Nick Fury told Natasha that he had the perfect opportunity for her to prove her loyalty to her adopted country, but that she had to keep it a secret from the Avengers—even Hawkeye. Black Widow was unhappy at having to deceive her new friends, but she wanted to prove herself. Putting her own feelings aside for the sake of the mission—as she was so experienced at doing—she advised Hawkeye to forget their romance.

Before long, reports reached the newspapers of Black Widow breaking into a top-secret defense installation and stealing plans for a nuclear submarine. The Avengers read the reports in dismay, but what neither they—nor almost anyone else—knew, was that Natasha was now a double agent working for S.H.I.E.L.D., and news of her apparent treachery was intended to reach the ears of her former communist masters.

Inset opposite: THE AVENGERS #37 (FEB. 1967) Black Widow was crucial in the Avengers' defeat of alien warlord Ixar, but her methods were outside the team's code of conduct.

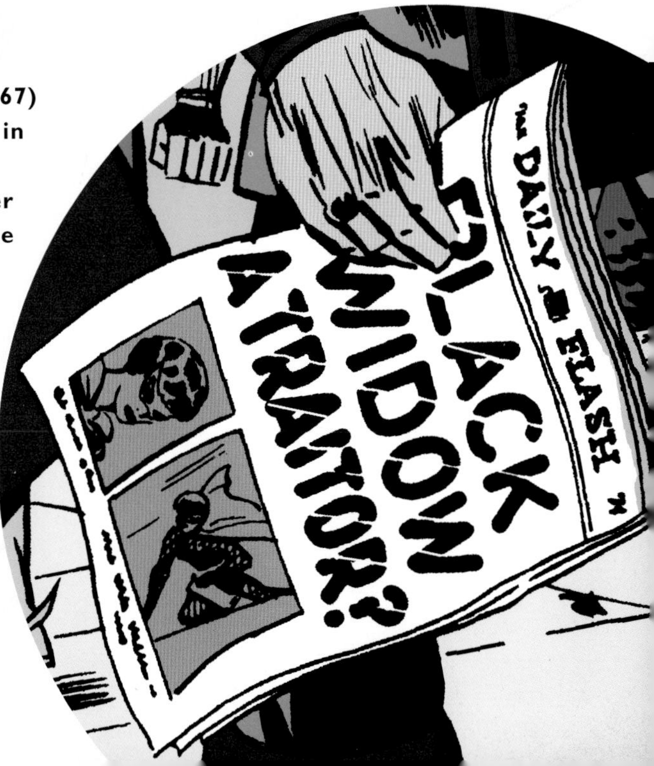
DAILY FLASH
BLACK WIDOW A TRAITOR?

Right: THE AVENGERS #39 (APR. 1967) Natasha's work for S.H.I.E.L.D. called for her to fool people into thinking she had returned to her old life as a Soviet spy.

Beyond the Bamboo Curtain

For the next phase of her assignment, Natasha traveled beyond the so-called Bamboo Curtain, the communist Far East, where she handed over the stolen submarine plans to Colonel Wai Ling. In return, Ling offered to show her his new weapon, the Psychotron. It had the power to drive people mad with fear, which would enable communist nations to take over the West. However, it was a trap—Ling had somehow found out that Natasha was working for S.H.I.E.L.D. and had resolved to make her the first human victim of the Psychotron. When the diabolical machine was switched on, Black Widow found herself in a literal living nightmare.

Much to the chagrin of Colonel Ling and his cronies, however, the Psychotron was no match for Black Widow's strength of will. Although she pretended to be broken by the device and ready to tell them everything she knew about S.H.I.E.L.D. operations, in reality she was just waiting for her moment to escape. She broke out of her cell, ruthlessly dispatching more than half a dozen guards with her martial arts skills and her Widow's Bite. As a furious Ling screamed that she was a traitor to the communist cause, Natasha returned the insult, saying that he was a traitor to humanity itself. Her loyalties now lay with the greater good, not some ideology. Despite her valiant heroics, though, she was eventually brought low by a poisonous gas and imprisoned again, her captors bent on discovering how she had been able to resist the Psychotron.

"Enough lies! Activate the machine!"

COLONEL WAI LING

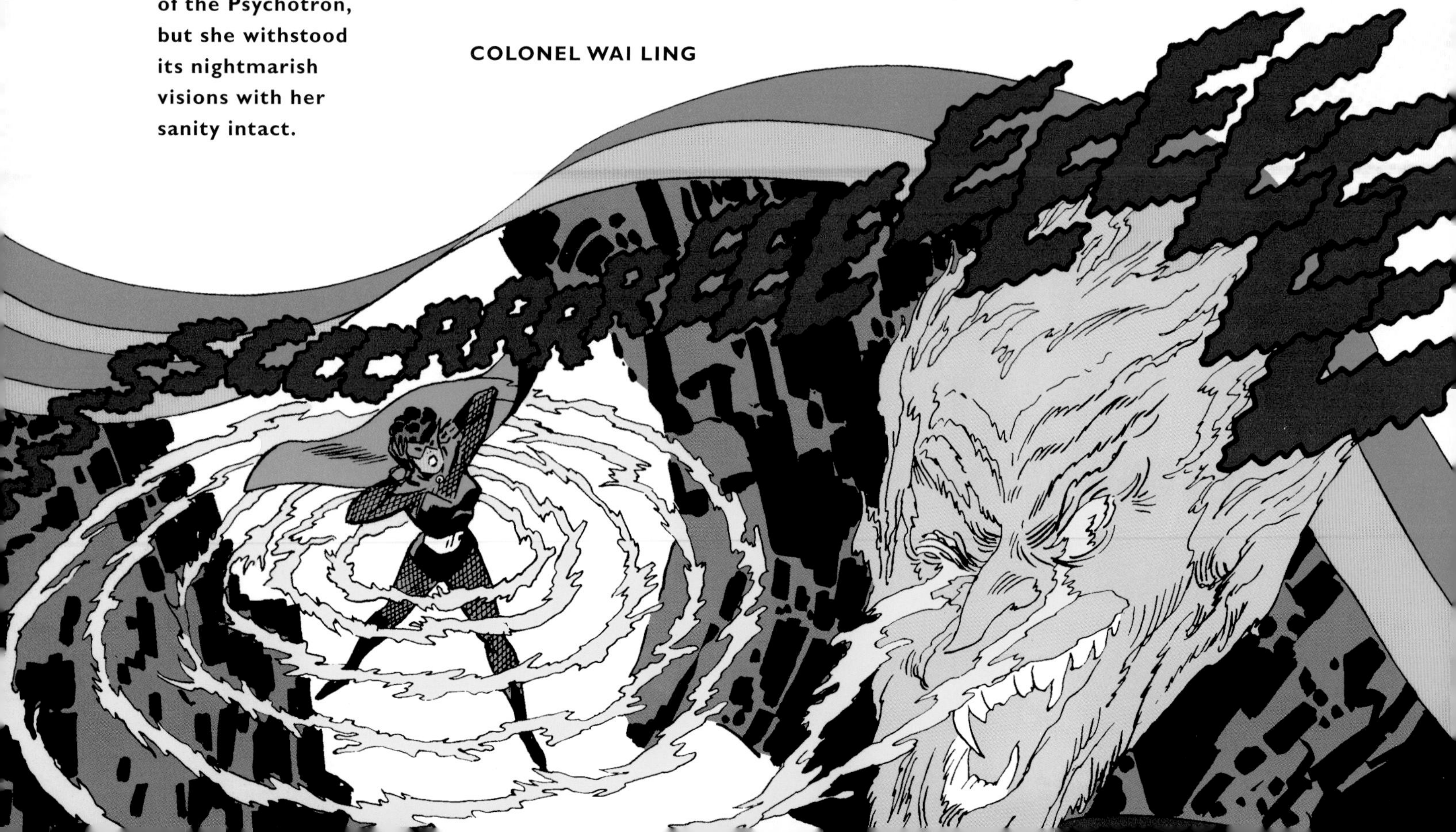

THE AVENGERS #41 (JUN. 1967) Black Widow was the first human victim of the Psychotron, but she withstood its nightmarish visions with her sanity intact.

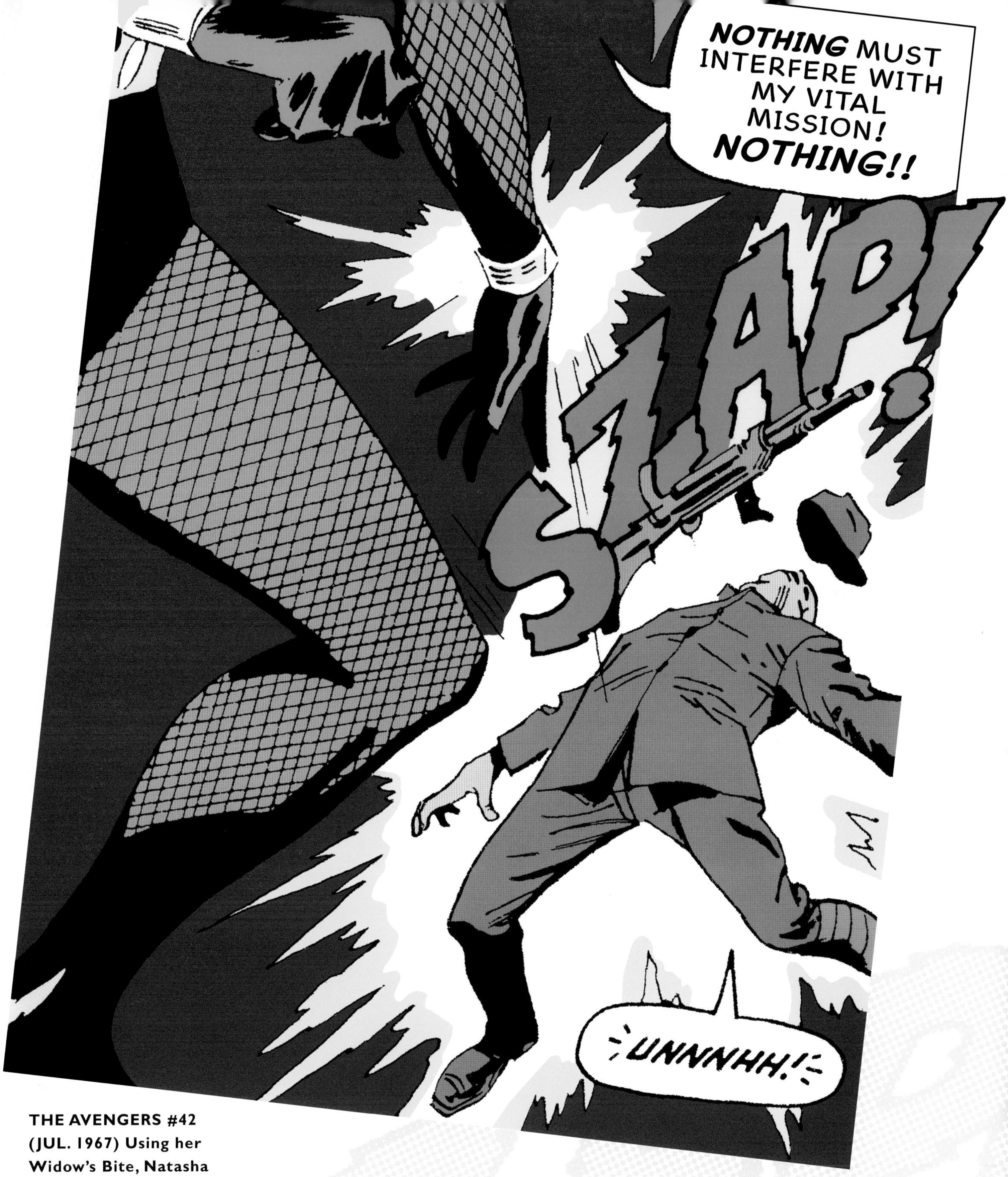
NOTHING MUST INTERFERE WITH MY VITAL MISSION! NOTHING!!
ZZAP!!
UNNNHH!

THE AVENGERS #42 (JUL. 1967) Using her Widow's Bite, Natasha took on her communist captors so that their terrible plans for the world would be stopped.

The Red Guardian

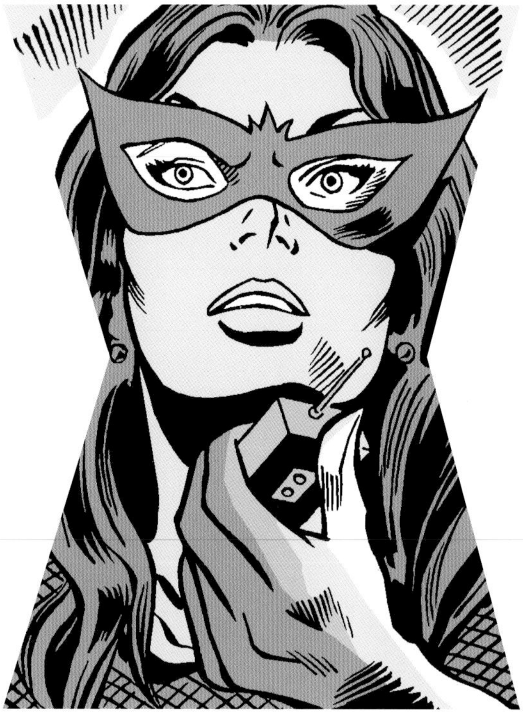

THE AVENGERS #43 (AUG. 1967) The Red Guardian, like Black Widow, was a Russian whose patriotism had been twisted to serve someone else's agenda.

Back in New York, the Avengers learned that Natasha had been working for S.H.I.E.L.D. and was now a prisoner in Asia. After taking down a bunch of lowlifes and criminals, a determined Hawkeye caught up with his reluctant informant, from whom he coerced the exact location where Natasha was being held. He also learned that she had been betrayed by an unknown asset within S.H.I.E.L.D. He and Hercules—the powerful demigod who was on the Avengers roster at the time—set out to bring her back.

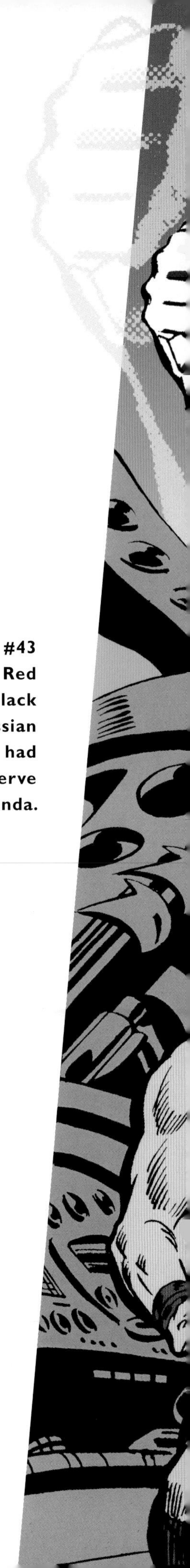

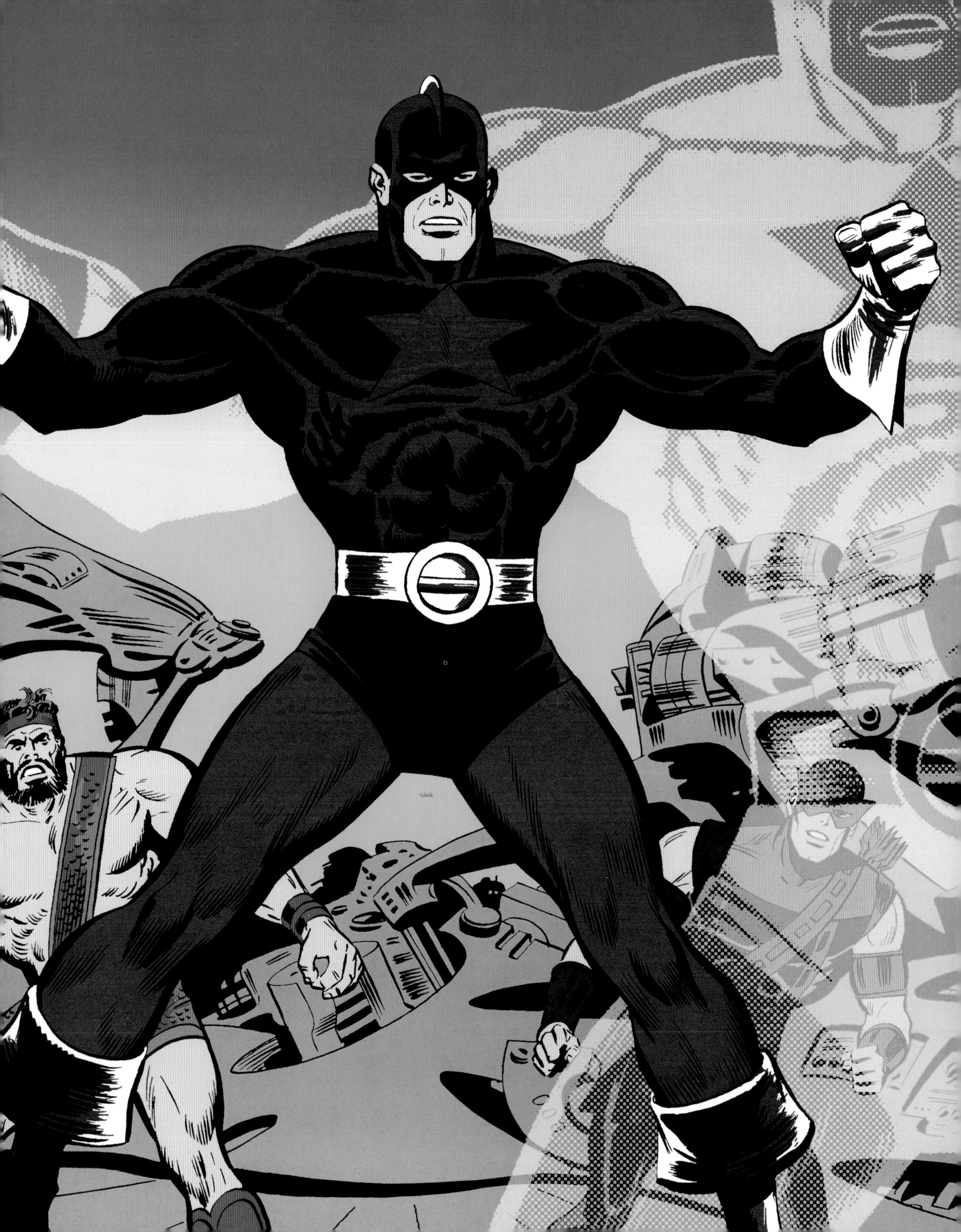

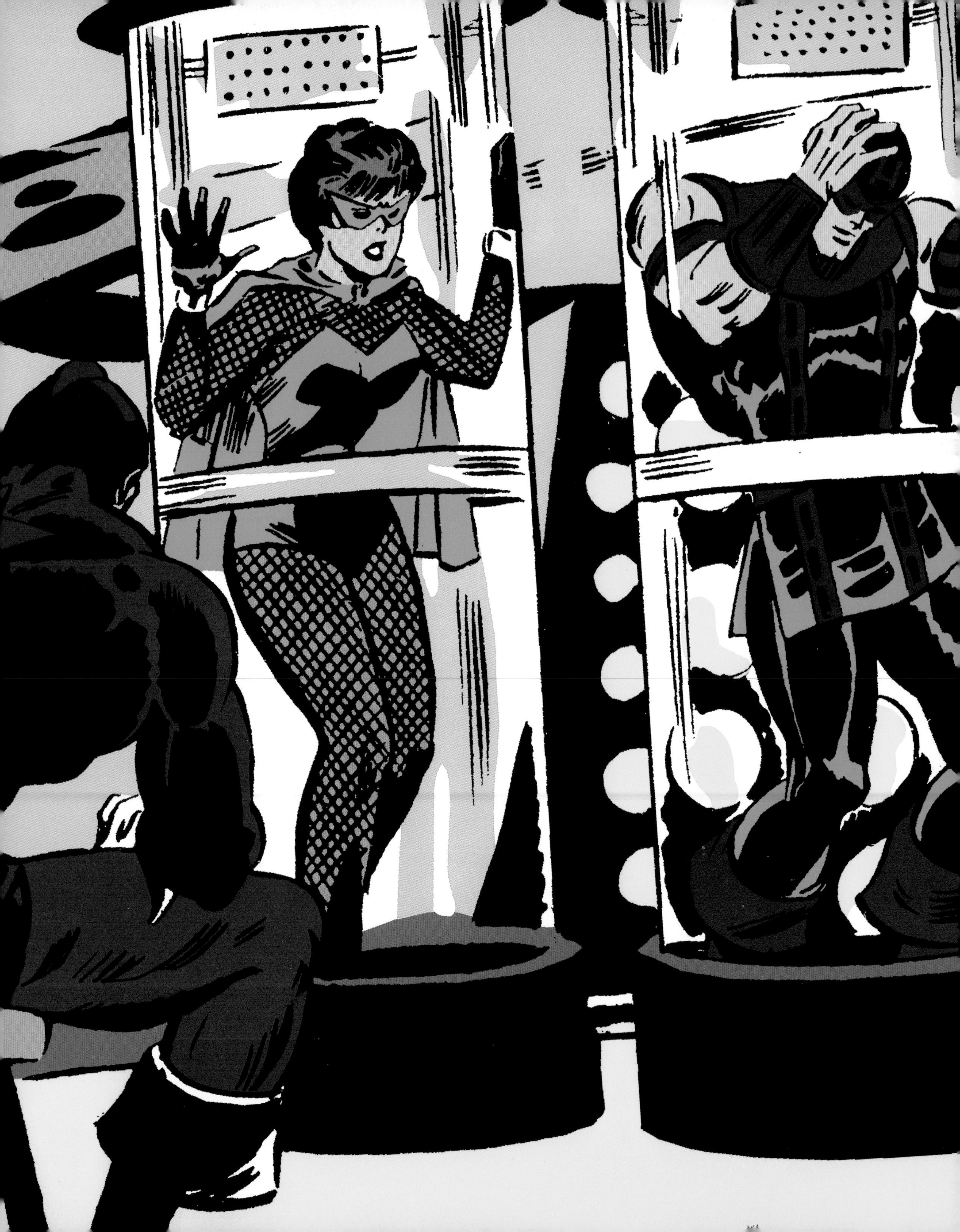

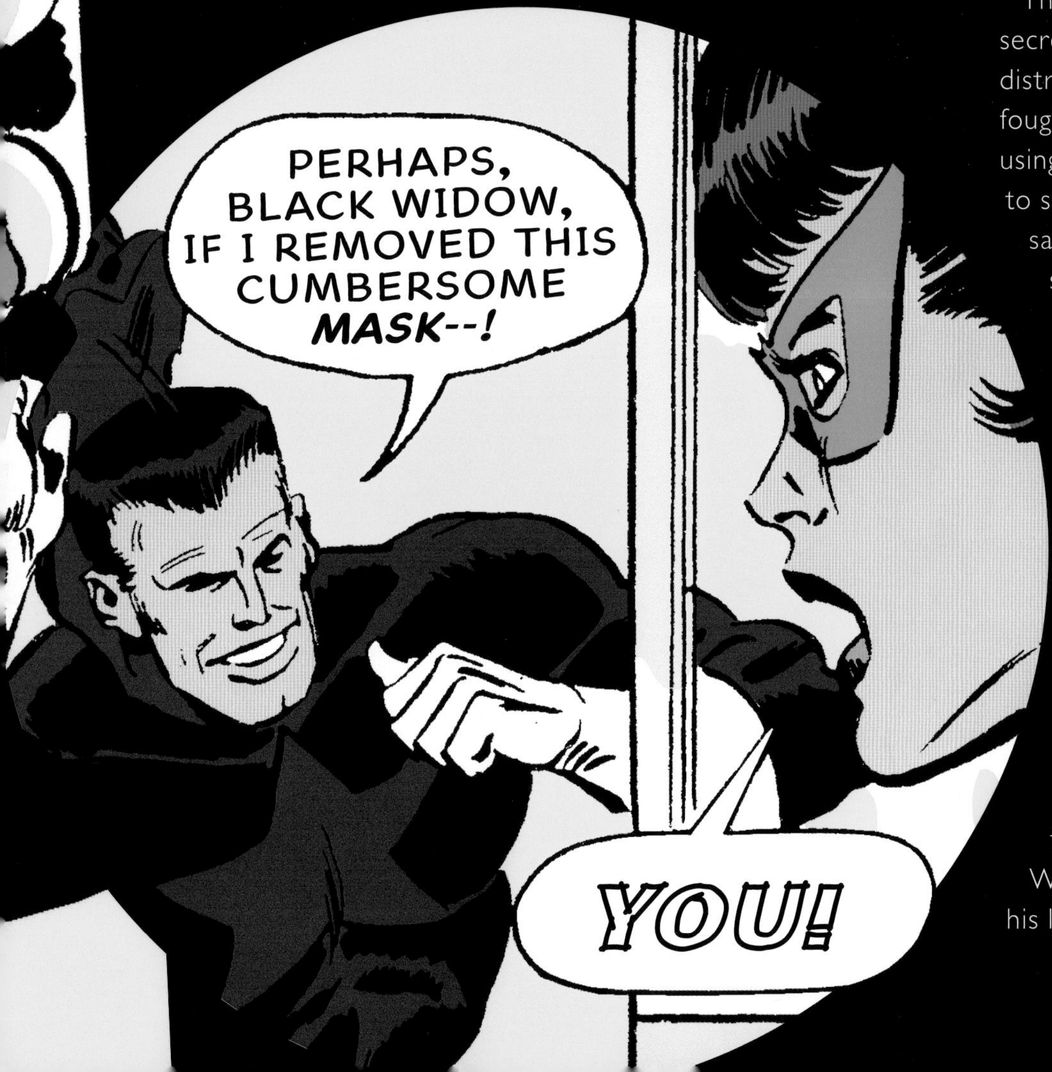
PERHAPS, BLACK WIDOW, IF I REMOVED THIS CUMBERSOME *MASK--!*
YOU!

THE AVENGERS #43 (AUG. 1967) Natasha was shocked to discover that her husband Alexei was not dead—as she thought—but had become the Soviet answer to Captain America: Red Guardian.

Meanwhile, Natasha's captors had invited a Soviet representative, General Brushov, to come and witness the unveiling of the communist answer to Captain America—the Red Guardian.

Although created and trained in Asia, Ling revealed that the Red Guardian was Russian by birth. His aim was to defeat Cap in combat, but first he had to face Hawkeye and Hercules as they arrived on their rescue mission. While he succeeded in taking down Hawkeye, Red Guardian realized he was no match for Hercules, so instead lured him into the Psychotron chamber. With the machine switched on, Hercules believed he was battling a mythical beast, and was out of the fight.

Hawkeye succeeded in finding Black Widow; however, they were both trapped and apparently at the mercy of the Red Guardian and his masters. Natasha realized in horror that the man behind the red mask was none other than her former husband, Alexei Shostakov. His "death" had been a lie, a way for the Soviet authorities to manipulate her and turn her into a lethal weapon with no thought for her—or Alexei's—humanity.

Natasha did not have long to reflect on this turn of events, as she was forced to submit to a lie detector to prove whether or not she had betrayed her native country. She passed with flying colors (thanks to a post-hypnotic suggestion implanted by S.H.I.E.L.D.) and was freed. So convincing was her professed allegiance that even the Red Guardian declared that he was still proud to call Natasha his wife.

The arrival of the Avengers, summoned secretly by Black Widow, provided a useful distraction. As her estranged husband fought Captain America, Natasha set about using the last charge of her Widow's Bite to sabotage the Psychotron. Colonel Ling saw what she was doing and went to shoot her, but the Red Guardian hurled himself into the path of the bullet, saving his former wife. Ling fired again, wounding Natasha, but not before she destroyed the Psychotron, saving untold lives in the process. She had come to see that her own life was of little importance compared to preserving the lives of others. This selfless attitude was shared by Alexei, who, while mortally wounded after protecting Black Widow, had also prevented Ling from shooting Captain America.

While the Red Guardian had sacrificed his life, he had not sacrificed his honor.

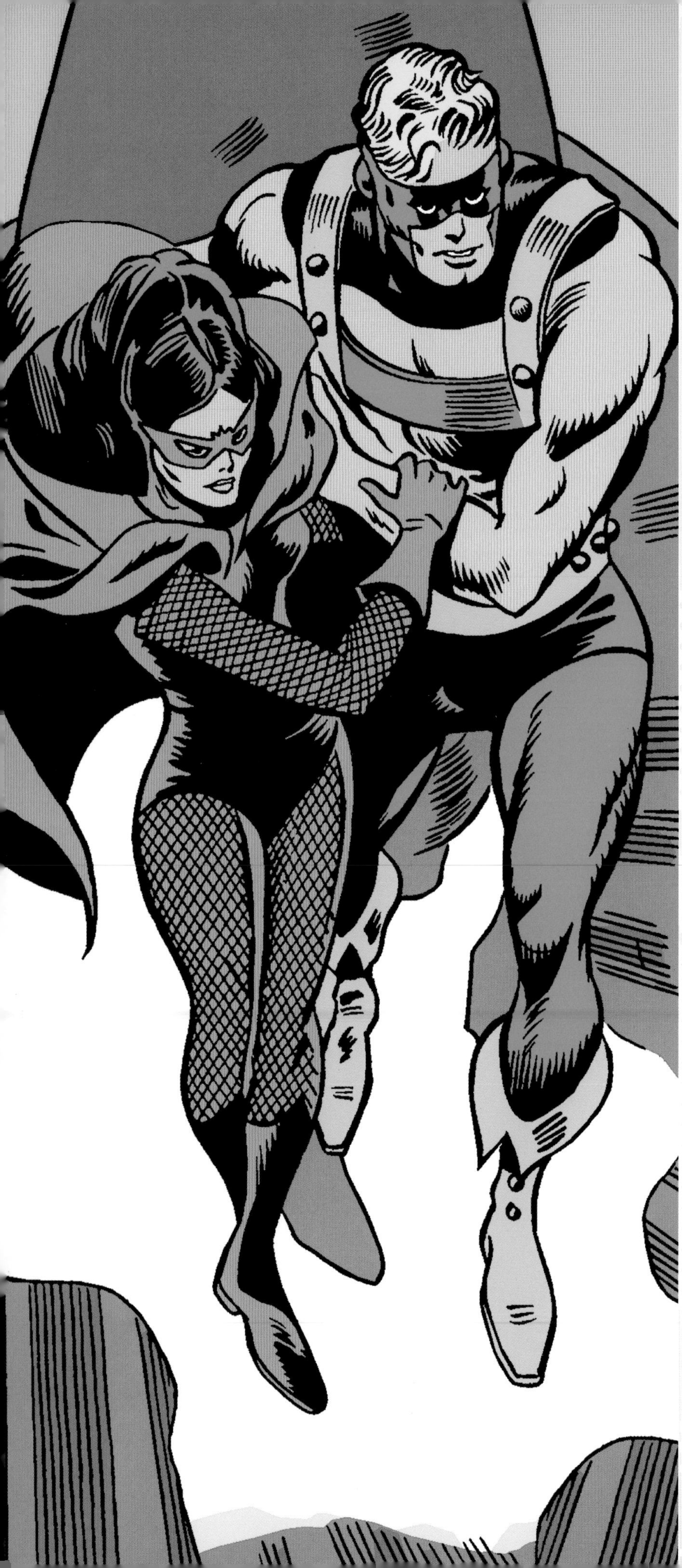

Call to Action

As she recovered back in the US, Natasha decided to give up her Black Widow identity and try to make a new life with Hawkeye. She was now simply Natasha, a woman with a dark past, but a present that she had chosen for herself, and, hopefully, a bright future. But being Natasha the ordinary woman seemed just like assuming another persona. It didn't seem real to her, and it certainly didn't feel right. Now excluded from the heroic world and unable to share in Hawkeye's adventures, Natasha grew bored and restless. When Nick Fury asked her to take on another assignment for S.H.I.E.L.D. as Black Widow, she jumped at the chance. Better danger than dullness.

After training with S.H.I.E.L.D., Black Widow traveled to the Caribbean to investigate a strange laboratory thought to hold a terrible threat to mankind. She discovered that the Mad Thinker—a genius obsessed with computers and probabilities—had created a giant android programmed to destroy the moon rocket being developed in the US. Although captured by the evil genius' plastic android minions, Black Widow was able to fire off a micro-bomb from beneath her thumbnail, shattering the giant android's energy transmitter and stopping its rampage. However, she was then gassed and taken away to be imprisoned by the Mad Thinker.

THE AVENGERS #63 (APR. 1969) After taking Pym particles, Hawkeye, as Goliath, was able to defeat the Mad Thinker's giant construct and rescue Black Widow.

After deducing that Natasha was being held in Coney Island, Hawkeye used the Avenger Hank Pym's old suit and serum to become the new size-changing Goliath and rescue his beloved. However, their reunion was short-lived: Black Widow's work for S.H.I.E.L.D. was now the most important thing in her life, and she told Barton that they could never be together. Consequently, the stage was set for a new phase in Natasha's life as she sought to carve out an identity for herself in the US.

THE AVENGERS #76 (MAY 1970) Wanting a clean break, Natasha told Hawkeye—now Goliath—that she could no longer be with him.

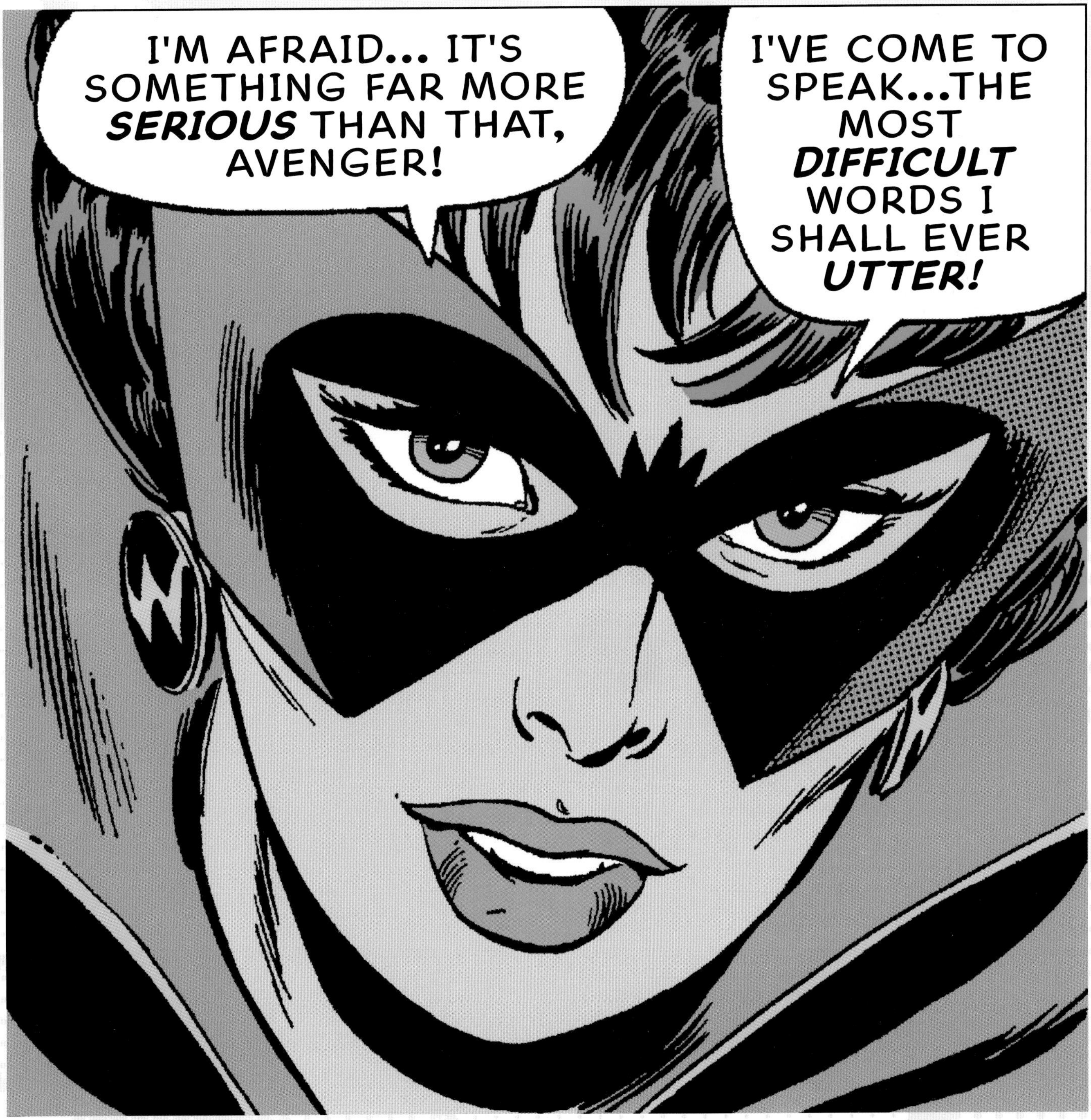
I'M AFRAID... IT'S SOMETHING FAR MORE *SERIOUS* THAN THAT, AVENGER!
I'VE COME TO SPEAK...THE MOST *DIFFICULT* WORDS I SHALL EVER *UTTER!*

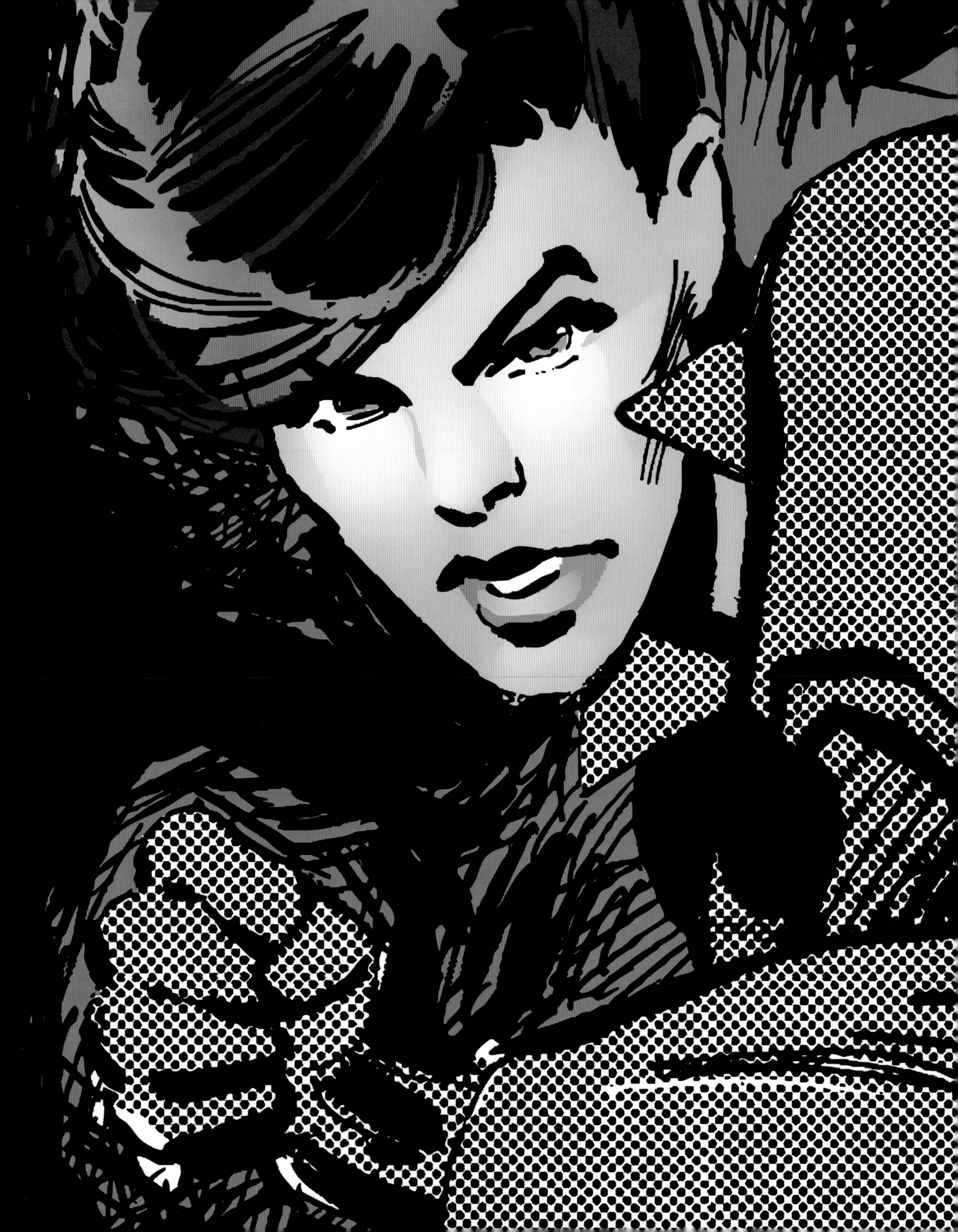

A New Life

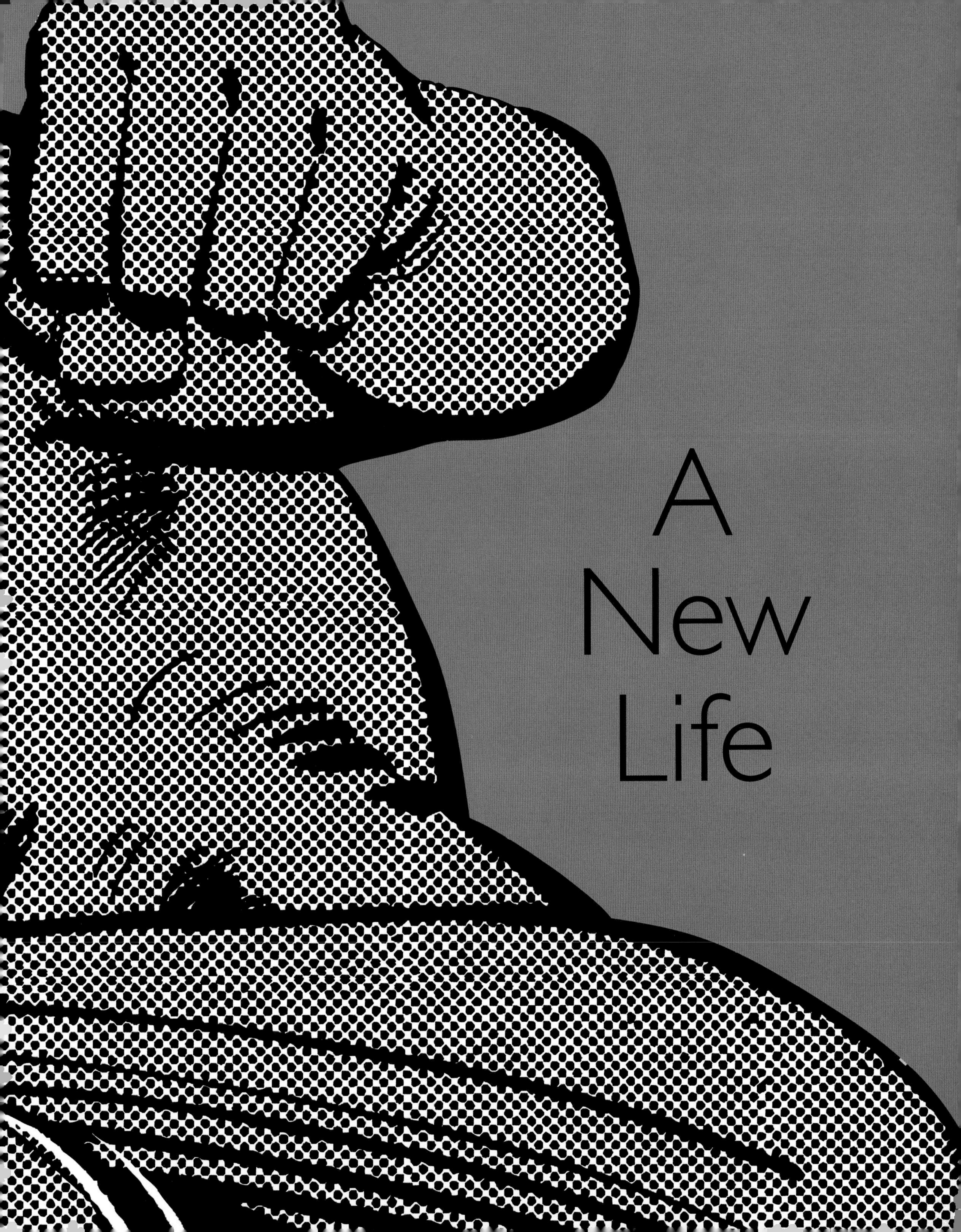

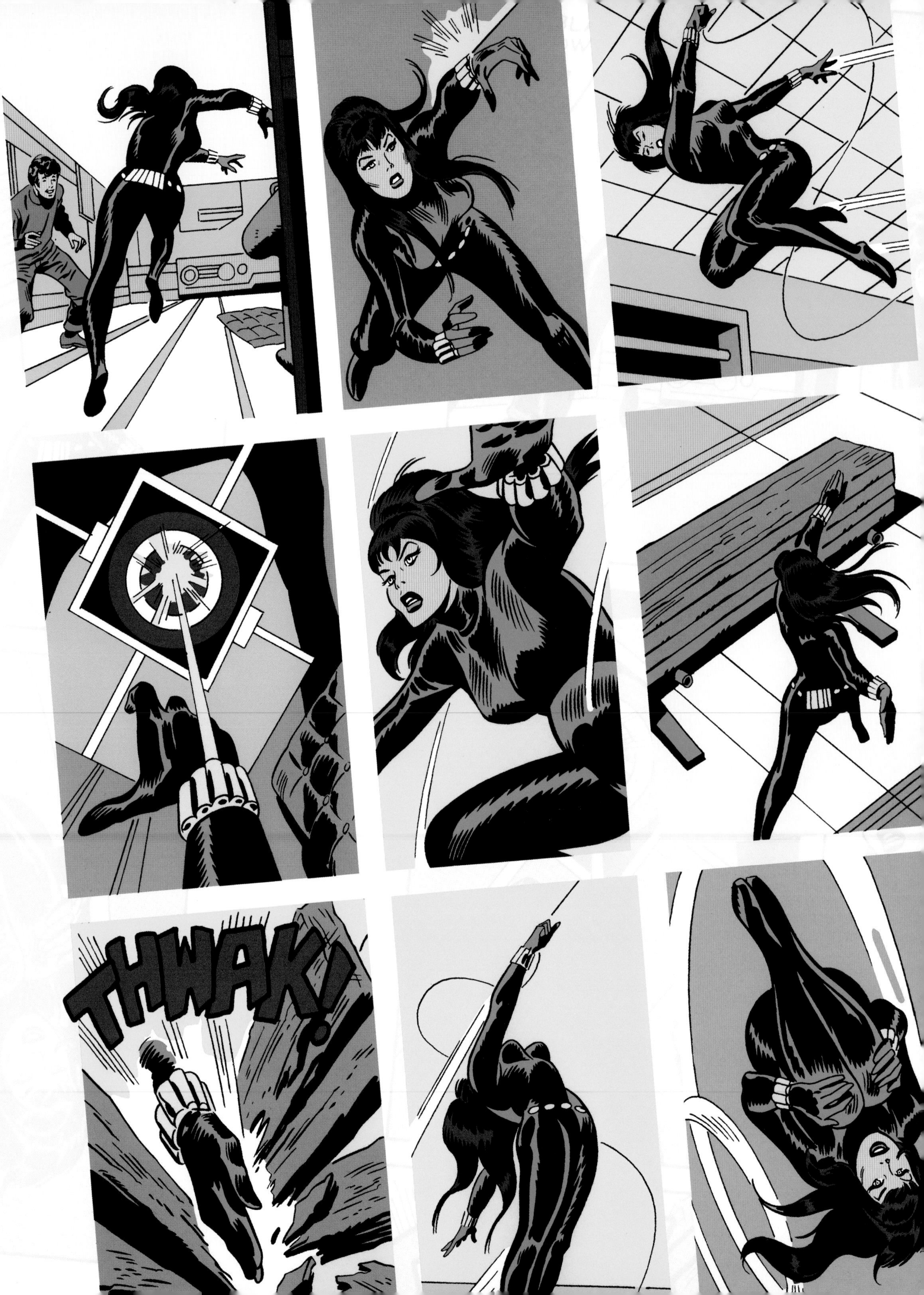
THWAK!

The Widow Alone

AMAZING SPIDER-MAN #86 (JUL. 1970)
Black Widow was ready to walk her own heroic path, protecting the vulnerable and bringing justice to the streets.

Following the apparent death of her husband Alexei Shostakov—aka the Red Guardian—and her decision to walk away from Hawkeye, the Avengers, and S.H.I.E.L.D., Natasha found herself at a crossroads. When she looked at her past, she saw heartbreak, tragedy, and guilt. She had tried to escape these ghosts by throwing herself into the life of an international jetsetter, but she was forced to admit that luxury and frivolity bored her and left her unfulfilled. She needed to get back to doing what she did best—being Black Widow.

"I've got to become the Black Widow once again!"

BLACK WIDOW

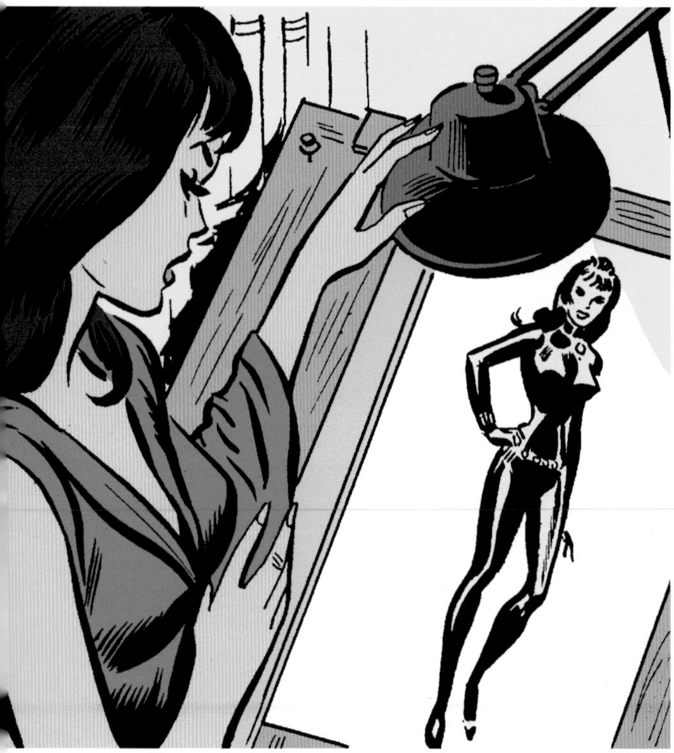

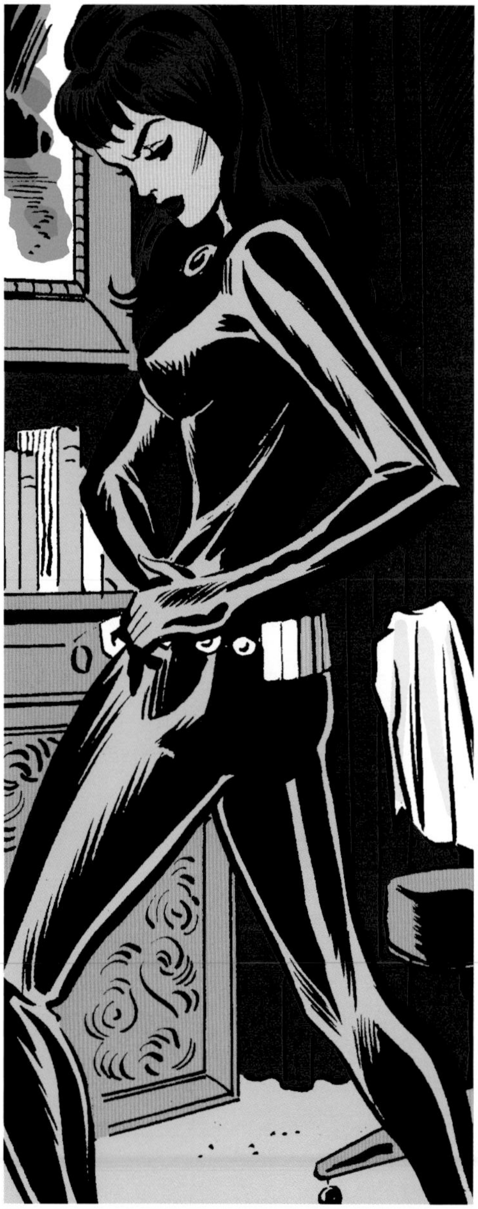

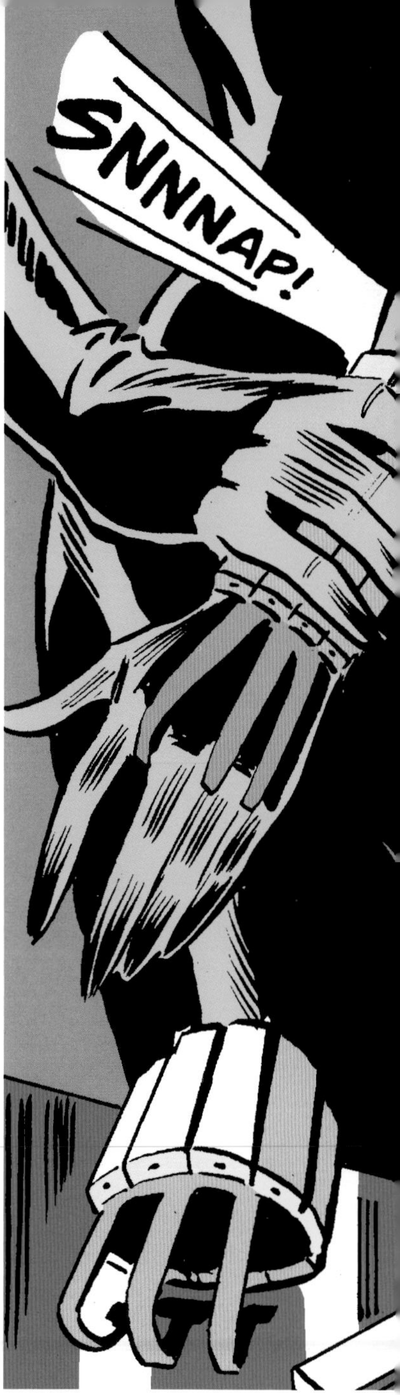
SNNNAP!

Having set up home in a New York City penthouse, Natasha decided that for her new career as a lone vigilante—accompanied by her loyal foster father Ivan Petrovitch, now her chauffeur and occasional sidekick—she needed a new outfit. The costume she designed would become her iconic look for many years—a simple, black, belted catsuit. It was equipped with a Widow's Line, enabling Natasha to swing between buildings, and antigravity boots for climbing walls, technology that she had acquired from S.H.I.E.L.D. Unlike her old costume, the new one did not have a mask; perhaps Black Widow wanted her identity to be known to prove to people in her adopted nation that Natasha Romanoff would be fighting the good fight from now on.

The arachnid overtones of her Black Widow identity gave Natasha the idea of following Spider-Man to see if she might be able to better understand his powers and maybe even take some for herself. However, failing to best him in a fight, Black Widow came to the conclusion that she should not be imitating someone else, but rather carving her own identity as a hero using her unique skill set. Whatever dangers lay ahead, she resolved to face them her way.

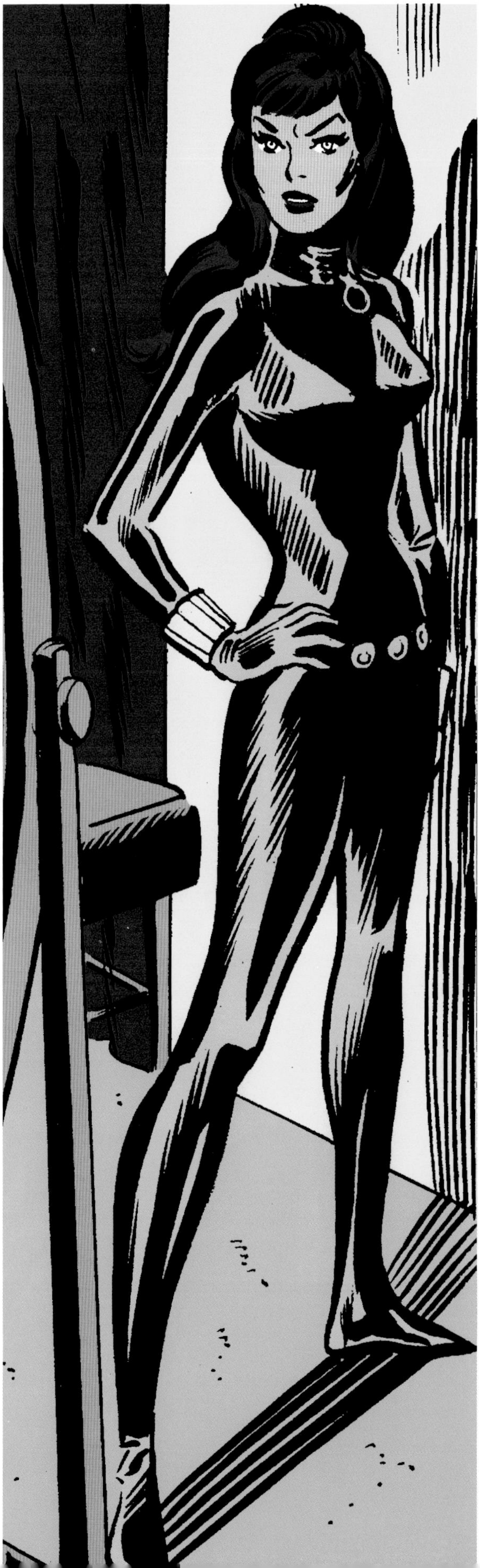

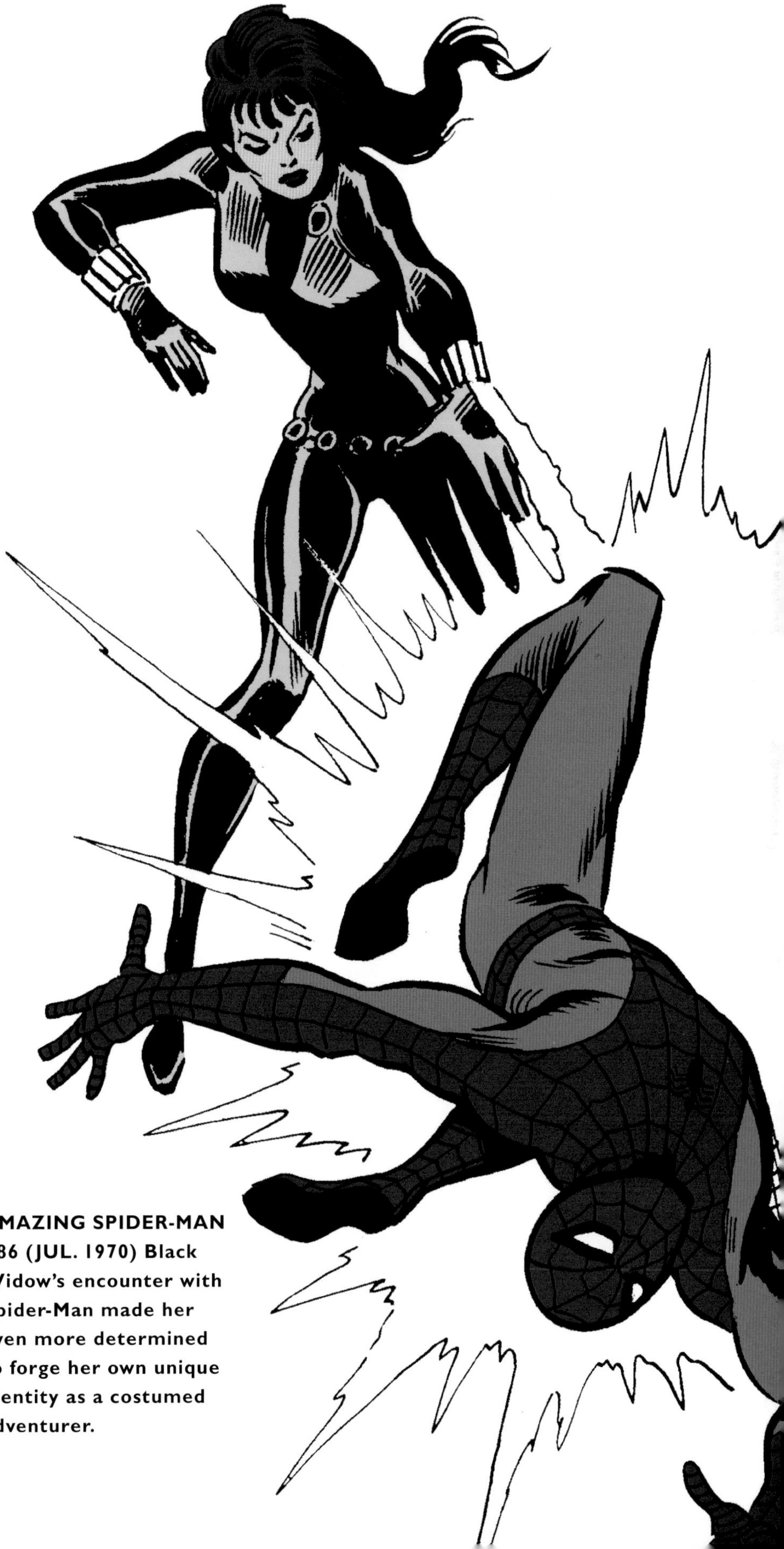

AMAZING SPIDER-MAN #86 (JUL. 1970) Black Widow's encounter with Spider-Man made her even more determined to forge her own unique identity as a costumed adventurer.

Black Widow's first solo mission saw her taking on the gang of a corrupt politician who was threatening to kill her housekeeper's son, Carlos. While Natasha approved of Carlos' plan to start a center for underprivileged children with his friends, the Young Warriors, she was concerned about their militant tactics after they forcibly occupied a building to use as their center, and were prepared to fight the police to keep hold of the premises. The press quickly jumped on the story, casting Black Widow in the role of Russian radical interfering in internal US politics by trying to convert young people to communism. However, Natasha showed off her lesser-known diplomatic skills when she succeeded where the police—and even the mayor—had failed by talking the Young Warriors out of a building they had seized illegally and defusing a tense situation.

Despite her diplomatic success, Natasha's sense of guilt was becoming ever-present. The accidental deaths of a gangster she was fighting and later a teenage boy who had tried to save her simply added fuel to the fire. Her feelings of remorse took on a whole new dimension, and she began to believe that she was cursed: that people who encountered her were inevitably put in harm's way.

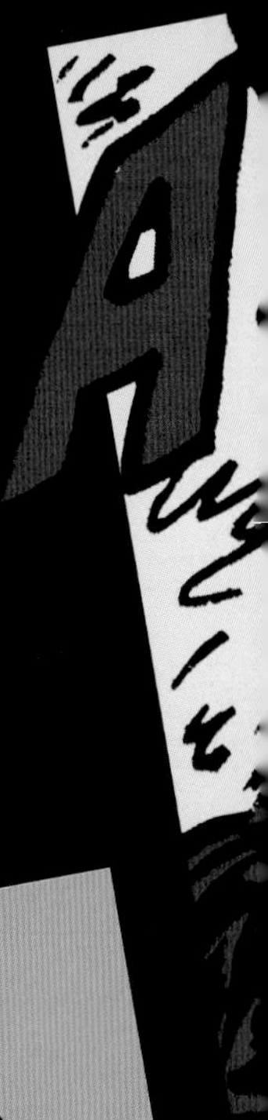

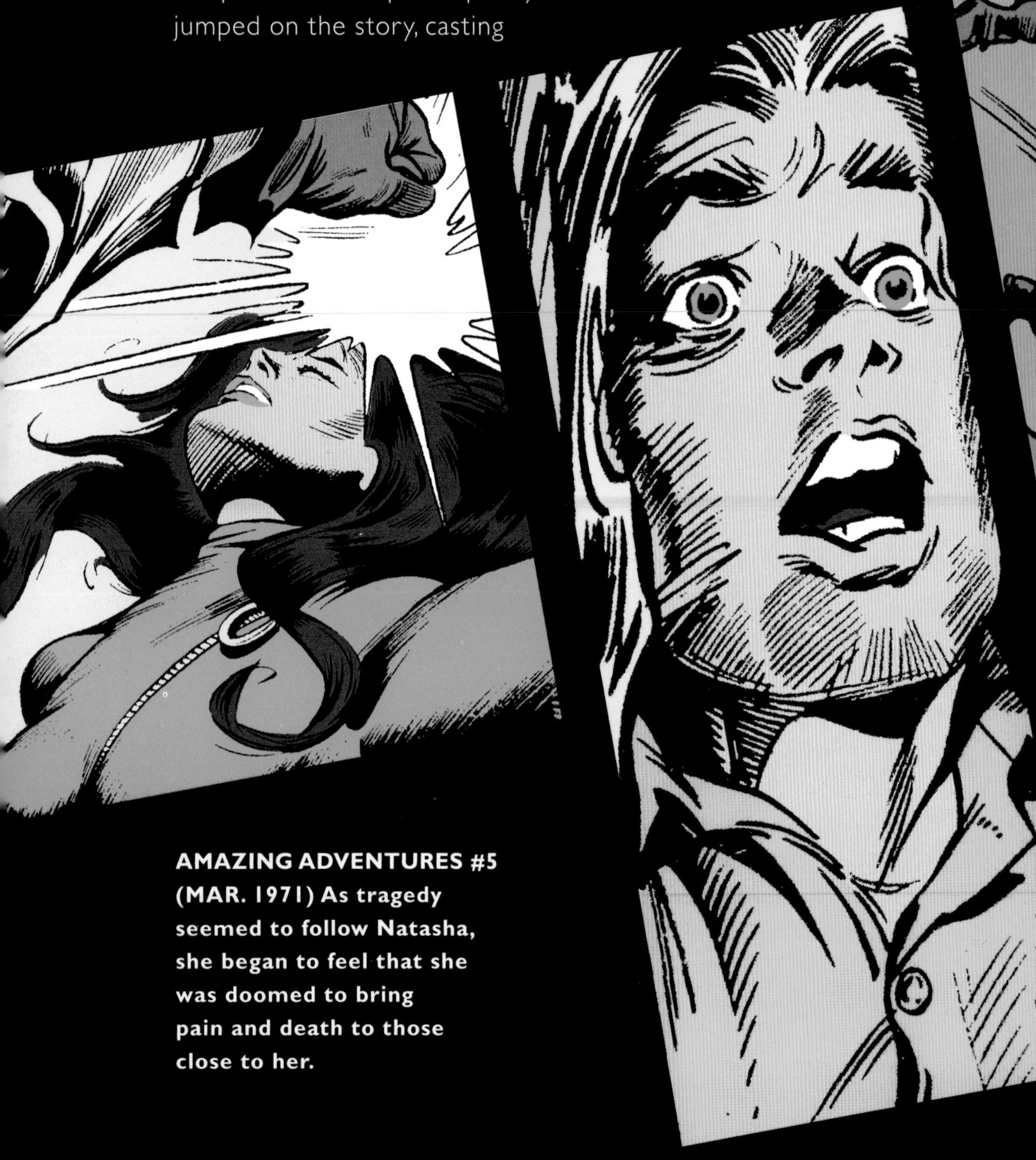

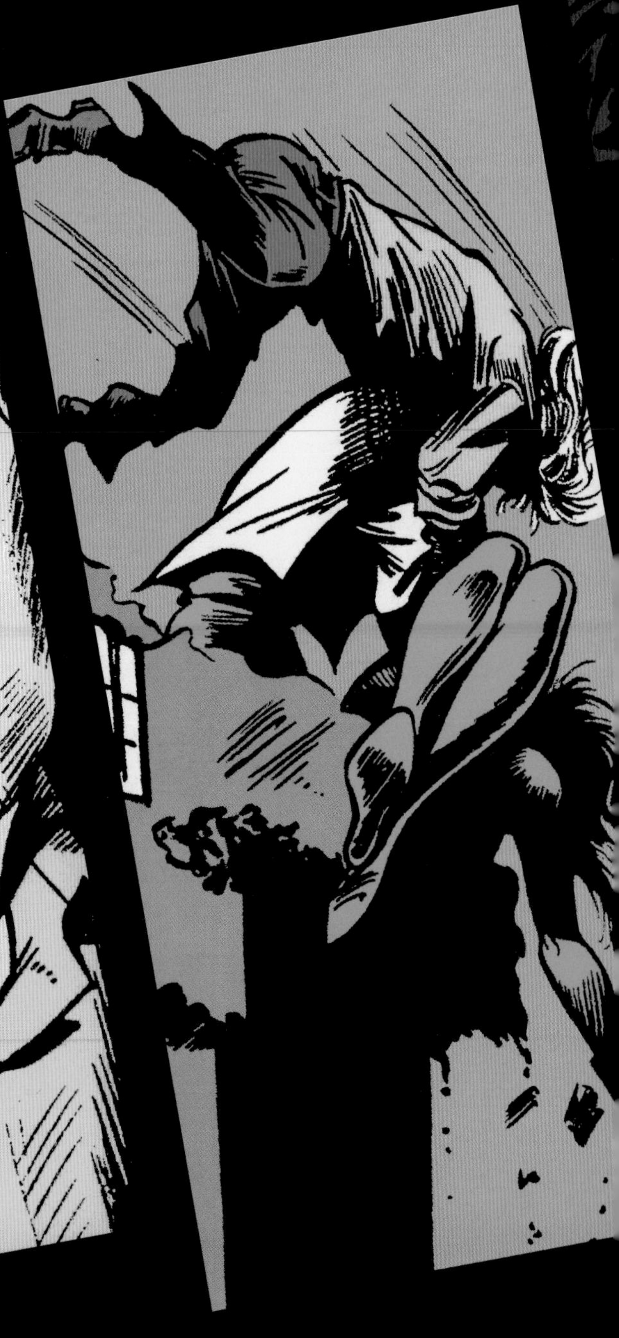

AMAZING ADVENTURES #5 (MAR. 1971) As tragedy seemed to follow Natasha, she began to feel that she was doomed to bring pain and death to those close to her.

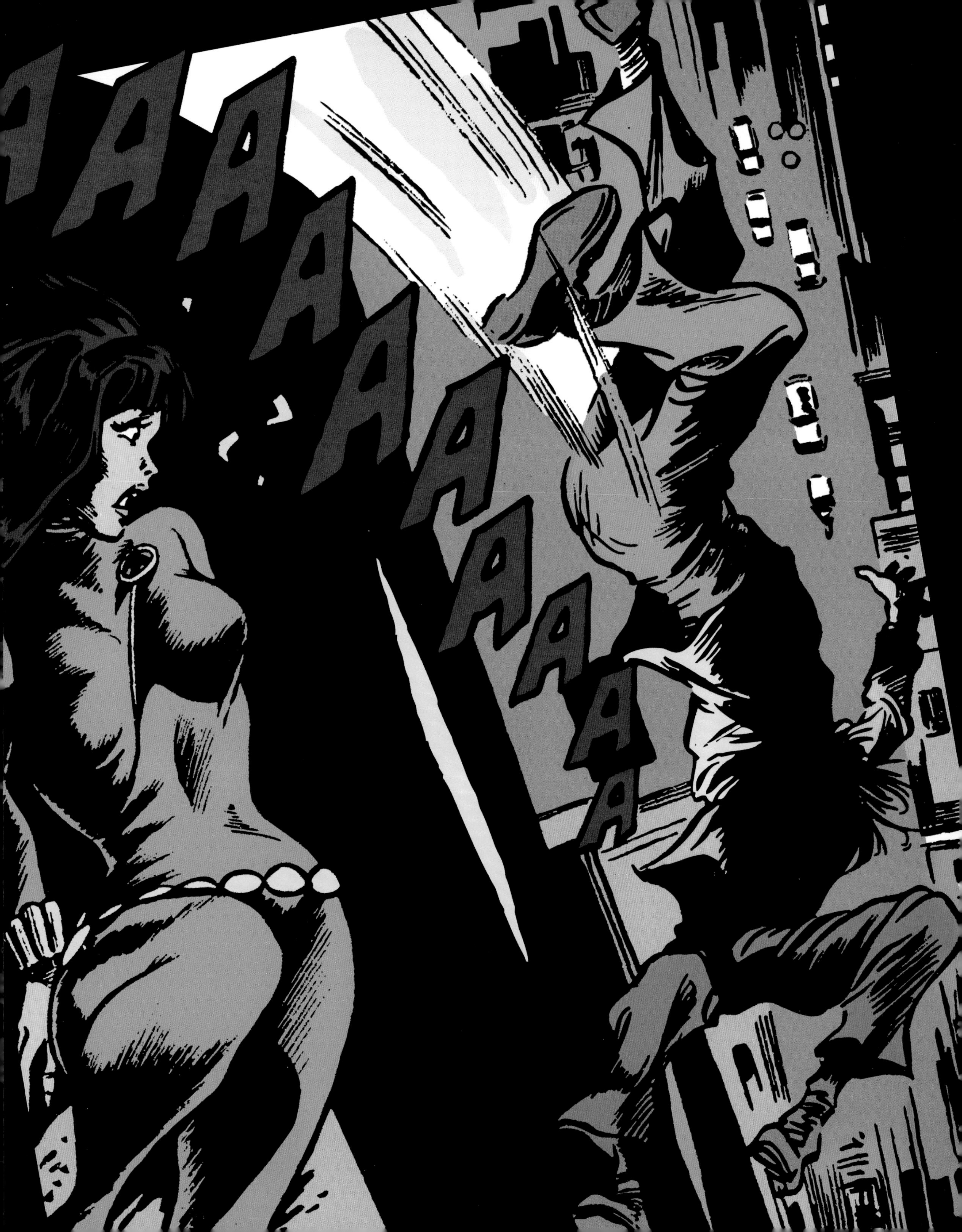
AAAAAAAAAAAAA

Daring to Dream

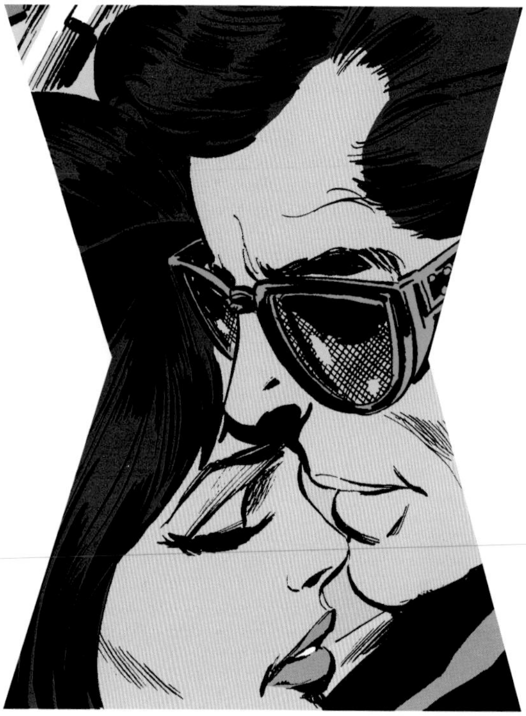

DAREDEVIL #81 (NOV. 1971) When Black Widow plunged into the harbor to save Daredevil, it marked the start of a long and sometimes tempestuous relationship in the lives of both heroes.

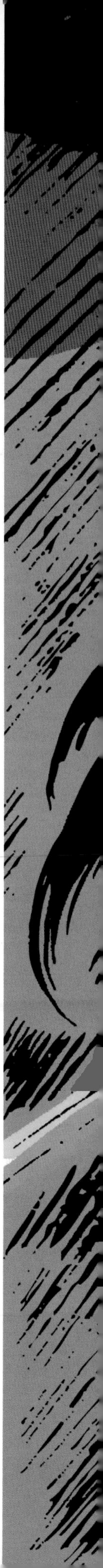

The machinations of a villain called the Assassin brought Natasha together with someone who would become one of her most significant partners, both in crime-fighting and on a personal level.

After rescuing the sight-impaired Super Hero Daredevil from drowning in New York City's harbor, the two heroes later fought the Super Villain the Scorpion, who seemingly died during the fierce encounter. This provided further proof for Natasha of the existence of her "curse."

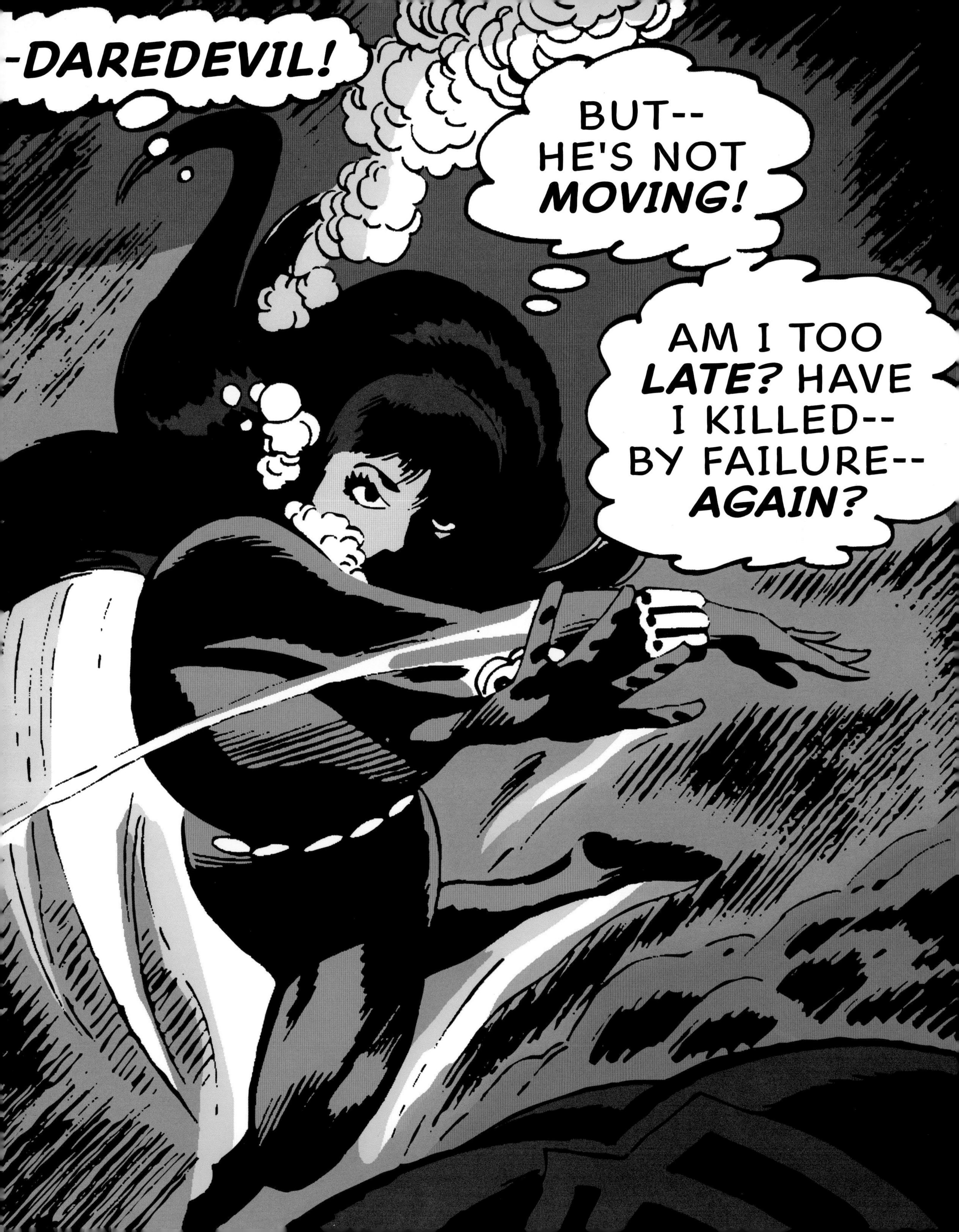
-DAREDEVIL!
BUT-- HE'S NOT MOVING!
AM I TOO LATE? HAVE I KILLED-- BY FAILURE-- AGAIN?

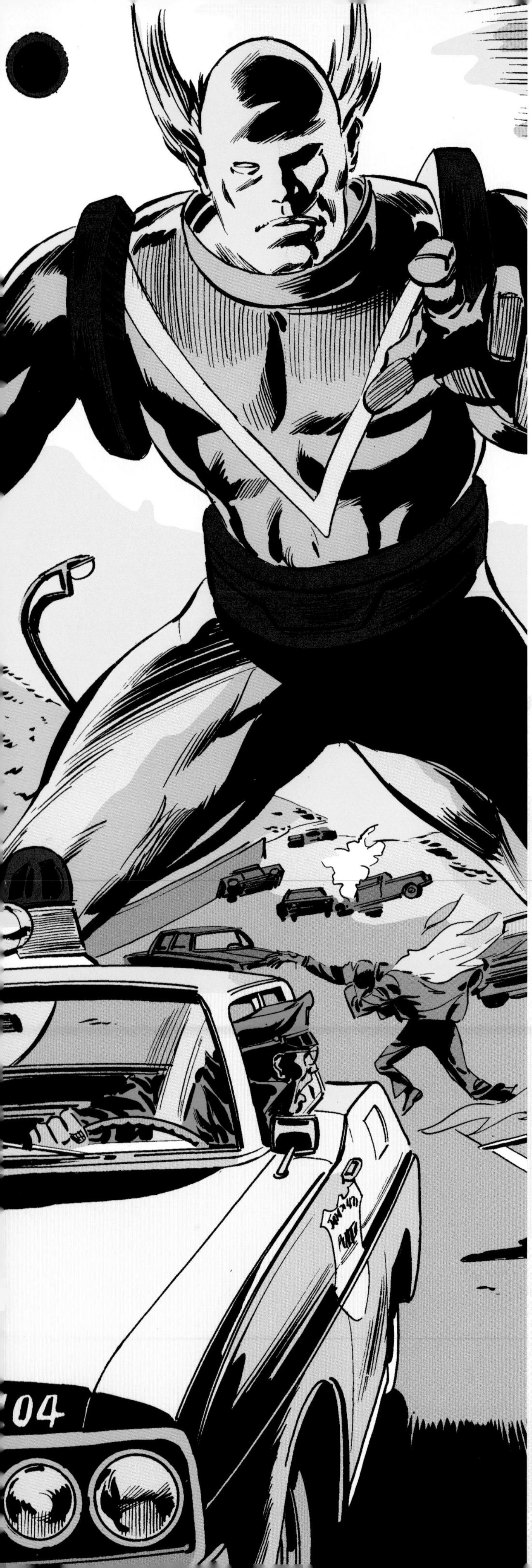
04

When she was put on trial for the Scorpion's murder, Daredevil's alter ego, Matt Murdock, was her defense lawyer. At this time, Natasha did not realize that they were the same person. Although the case against her was dropped, Natasha felt persecuted, and asked herself if she could continue to live in the US. However, now she had a reason to stay: her blossoming relationship with Daredevil. Soon enough, the two decided to move to San Francisco to begin a new life together.

Life on the West Coast started promisingly for Black Widow as she rented a large house with the intention of using one room as a studio for fashion design. Relying on Matt Murdock's lawyer salary was not an option for her; she was determined to earn her own money. However, it wasn't long before her past once more caught up with her in the form of Danny French, an old colleague from one of her first spy missions in the US. The assignment had not gone as planned, leading to the accidental deaths of all the scientists involved in the project the pair had been investigating. French then disappeared with a mystical sphere that was at the heart of the investigation.

Not long after, the villainous weapons manufacturer Damon Dran stole the sphere, using it to turn himself into the gigantic Indestructible Man. Despite the size and strength of the opponent, Black Widow took the lead in

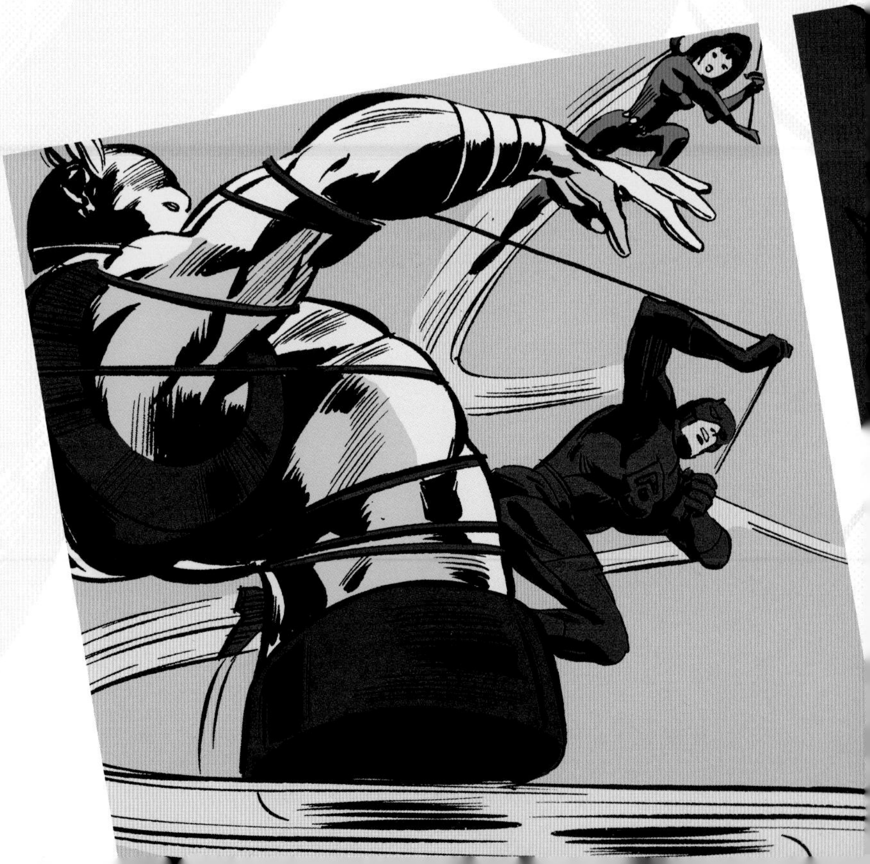

urging Daredevil, Ivan, and French to take the fight to Dran. Although naturally courageous, Widow's training gave her added confidence to battle much stronger, more powerful enemies, knowing that she was wily and agile and could use their size and strength against them. Although the heroes won, Danny French was killed in the fight. Natasha was devastated that one of her comrades had again been lost to her "curse."

As well as dealing with the specters of her earlier life, Natasha was also having trouble adjusting to being in a team, and a relationship. She resented the way Daredevil called her "kid," and accused him of not seeing her as an individual and an equal partner with her own motivations. Something that did give her satisfaction, however, was her newfound status as an icon for women after she overheard a group of female office workers comparing her to the high-profile feminist, Gloria Steinem.

DAREDEVIL #94 (DEC. 1972) When the villain Damon Dran turned himself into Indestructible Man, Black Widow and Daredevil swung into action with the courage and capability that typified both of them.

"Don't fight me, sister... I've got you!"

DAREDEVIL

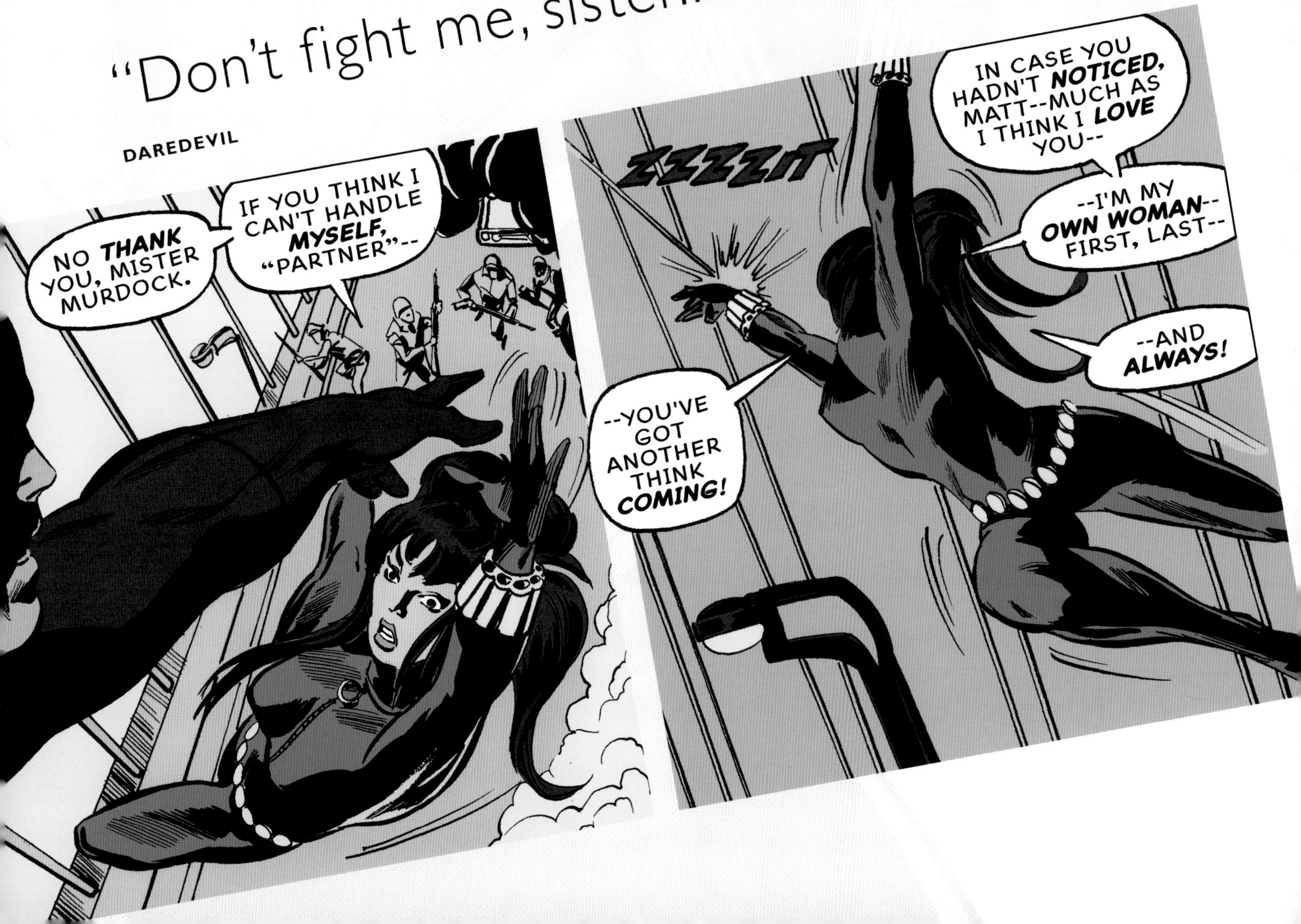
NO THANK YOU, MISTER MURDOCK.
IF YOU THINK I CAN'T HANDLE MYSELF, "PARTNER"--
--YOU'VE GOT ANOTHER THINK COMING!
ZZZZIT
IN CASE YOU HADN'T NOTICED, MATT--MUCH AS I THINK I LOVE YOU--
--I'M MY OWN WOMAN--FIRST, LAST--
--AND ALWAYS!

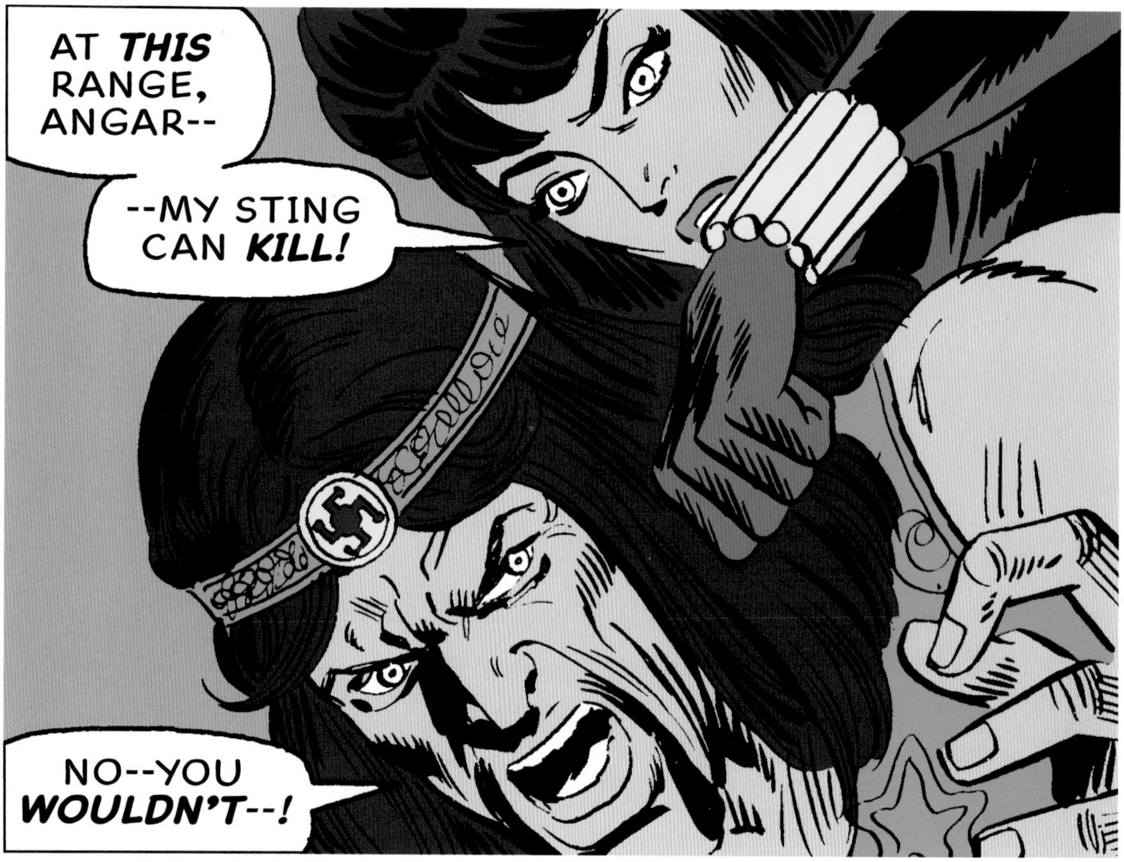
AT *THIS* RANGE, ANGAR--
--MY STING CAN *KILL!*
NO--YOU *WOULDN'T*--!

End of the Affair

After some time, Natasha's ex-lover Hawkeye showed up in San Francisco and bickered with Daredevil over her. She was furious that neither man gave a thought to what Natasha might want for herself, thinking she could be won like a prize. When the Avengers asked Black Widow and Daredevil to join their ranks to fight Magneto, Matt declined for both of them—the audacity of this was the last straw for Natasha and she informed her shocked partner that actually, she *would* join the Avengers, and get some space to think.

Her first mission with her new team went well, and Black Widow was instrumental in vanquishing the celestial Lion God. However, she decided to return to Daredevil and give their partnership another chance. She wasn't yet ready to be part of a large team, and explained to the Avengers that she was more of a "do-it-yourself type."

Although Natasha and Daredevil cared deeply for one another, their partnership continued to be beset with problems. Daredevil was uncomfortable with how far Black Widow was willing to go to defeat her enemies. In a battle against the hallucination-inducing Angar, Black Widow threatened to kill the villain, and Daredevil realized she meant it. Later, when stopping the violent mugging of an elderly woman, Daredevil had to physically restrain Black Widow to stop her from beating to death one of the criminals. Also coming between them were Daredevil's relationships with other people: his old friend Foggy Nelson—whom Black Widow had not forgiven for being the prosecutor in her murder trial—and the mystical hero Moondragon, to whom Matt was obviously attracted. When Daredevil returned to New York City with Moondragon to visit Foggy, who was in the hospital, a jealous Black Widow told Murdock it was over between them.

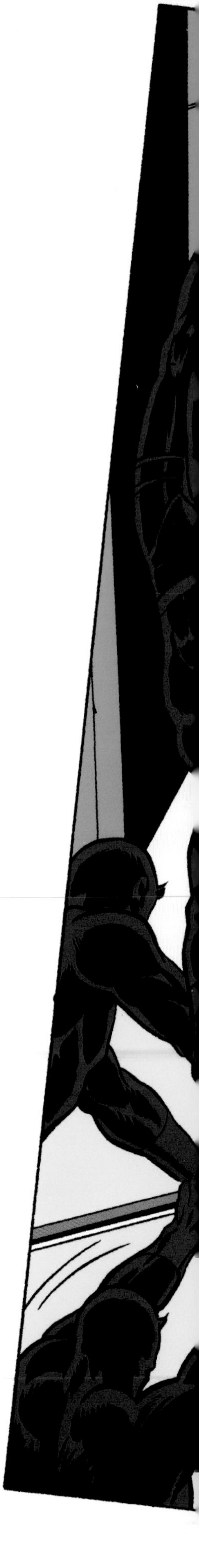

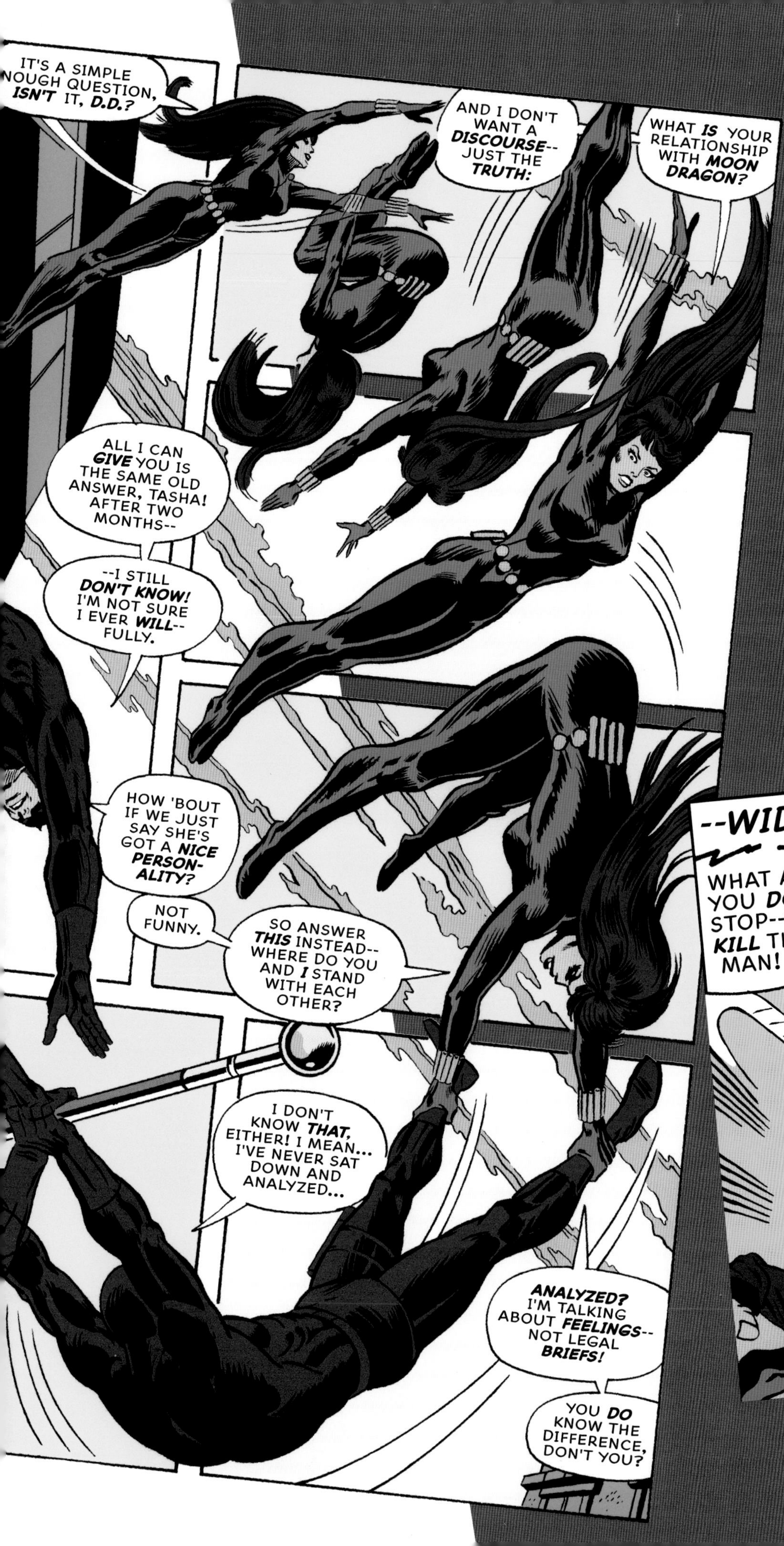
IT'S A SIMPLE ENOUGH QUESTION, ISN'T IT, D.D.?
AND I DON'T WANT A DISCOURSE-- JUST THE TRUTH:
WHAT IS YOUR RELATIONSHIP WITH MOON DRAGON?
ALL I CAN GIVE YOU IS THE SAME OLD ANSWER, TASHA! AFTER TWO MONTHS--
--I STILL DON'T KNOW! I'M NOT SURE I EVER WILL-- FULLY.
HOW 'BOUT IF WE JUST SAY SHE'S GOT A NICE PERSON-ALITY?
NOT FUNNY.
SO ANSWER THIS INSTEAD-- WHERE DO YOU AND I STAND WITH EACH OTHER?
I DON'T KNOW THAT, EITHER! I MEAN... I'VE NEVER SAT DOWN AND ANALYZED...
ANALYZED? I'M TALKING ABOUT FEELINGS-- NOT LEGAL BRIEFS!
YOU DO KNOW THE DIFFERENCE, DON'T YOU?

Opposite page: DAREDEVIL #101 (JUL. 1973) Natasha's ruthlessness in defeating her opponents caused friction between herself and more straitlaced allies like Daredevil and the Avengers.

Left and below: DAREDEVIL #108 (MAR. 1974) Cracks started to appear in Black Widow's relationship with Daredevil that would ultimately signal its end, although the couple would continue to care for each other.

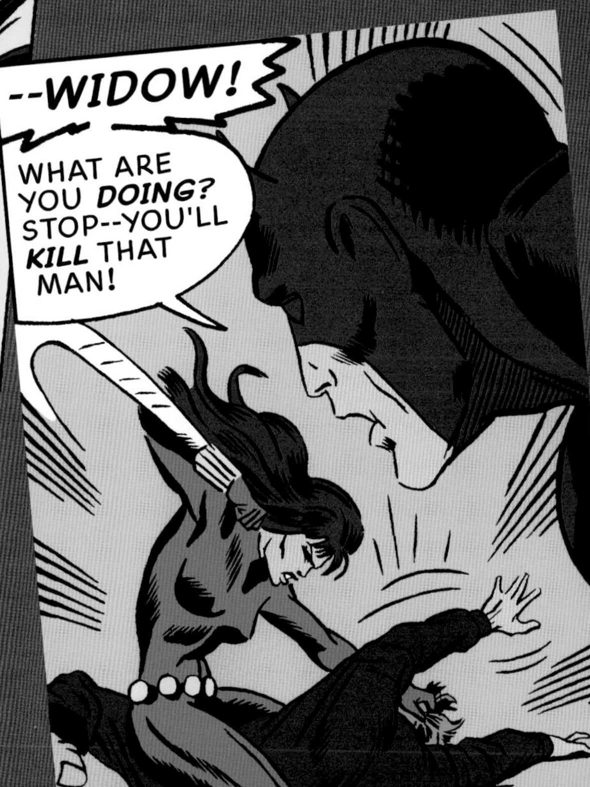
--WIDOW!
WHAT ARE YOU DOING? STOP--YOU'LL KILL THAT MAN!

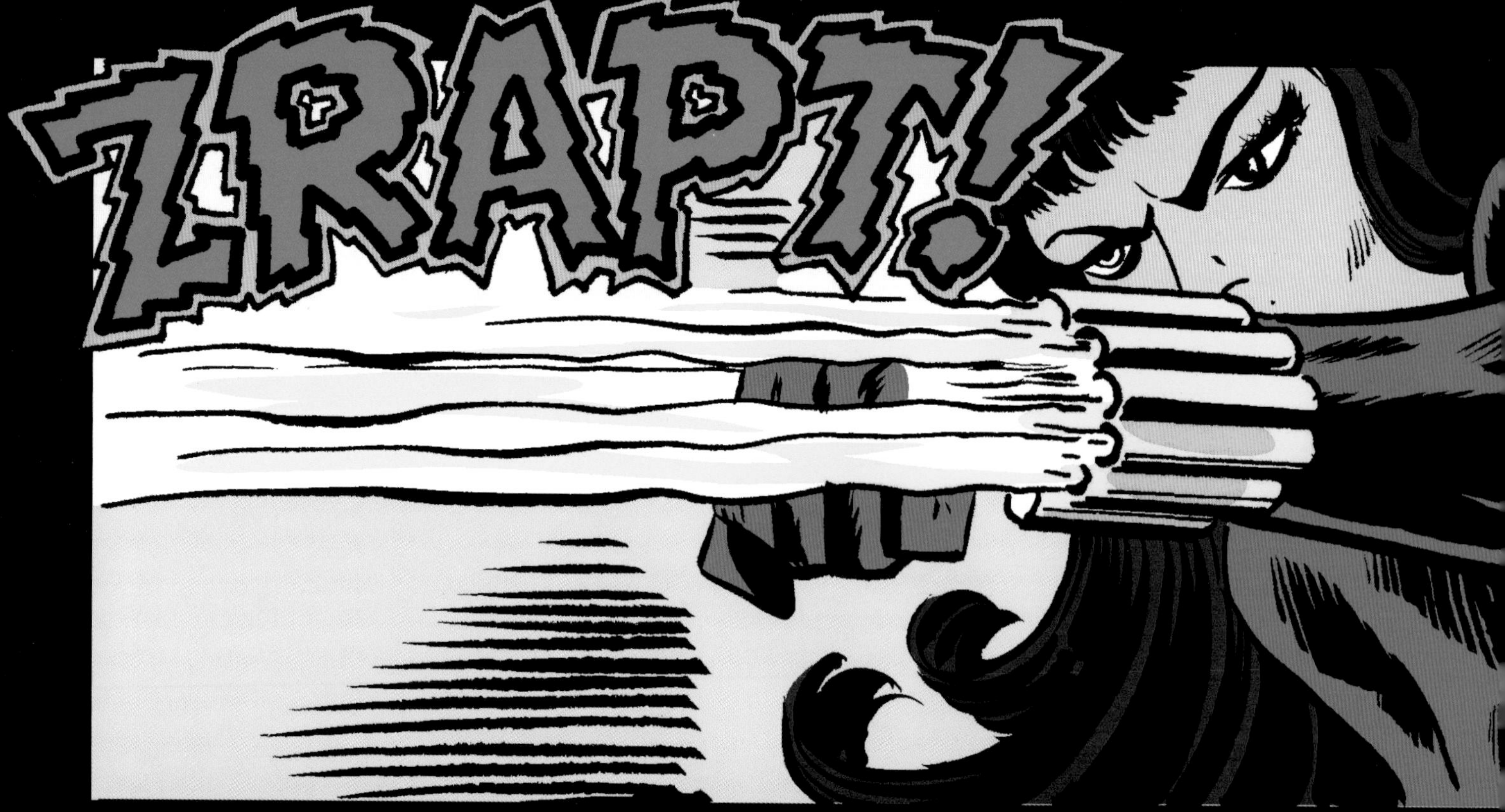
ZRAPT!

With Daredevil now absent, Natasha and Ivan were forced to live in their Rolls Royce for a time, having run out of money to pay the lease on their San Francisco home. Although she had been scanning the "Wanted" ads for jobs, Natasha was starting to conclude that the Black Widow might be unemployable. When Daredevil returned to the city to check that Natasha was okay, the pair were kidnapped by the villainous Owl. Black Widow used all her skills to escape her bonds, thwart the Owl's plot to steal information from Daredevil's brain, and beat all his henchmen singlehandedly, while also finding time to berate one of the goons for calling her "chick." The thugs were no match for Black Widow's athletic prowess and combat abilities.

After the battle was won, Daredevil offered to take Natasha back to New York with him, but she decided to stay and settle her debts herself so that she could come to him as an equal. A few months later she arrived in the Big Apple, but she and Daredevil were not sure how to move forward. Natasha told him that she used to be the most dangerous spy in the world, although she hadn't liked herself then. Her noble deeds with the Avengers and S.H.I.E.L.D. made her feel better about herself, but her time with Daredevil had diminished her identity, making her feel like her strength and resolve were slipping away. However, her affection for Daredevil remained—as it would do forever—and Natasha threw herself wholeheartedly into the rescue mission when Matt's friend Foggy Nelson was abducted by the terrorist organization Hydra. This episode again tempted her to stick with Daredevil, so much so that she once more turned down Avengers membership to stay with him.

Ultimately, it was a mission with the Fantastic Four's the Thing that pushed Black Widow to make the break from Daredevil. The unlikely duo stumbled on a plot by a former comrade of Natasha's to cause a tsunami that would engulf the entire eastern seaboard of the United States. On an installation in the middle of the Atlantic Ocean, Black Widow used her stealth and experience to take a hundred henchmen out of the game so that the Thing could stop the disaster. Having proved her credentials as the best spy in the world, Natasha returned to Daredevil to say goodbye. The role of sidekick was not for her: she needed to strike out on her own and discover who she was before Natasha Romanoff was lost forever.

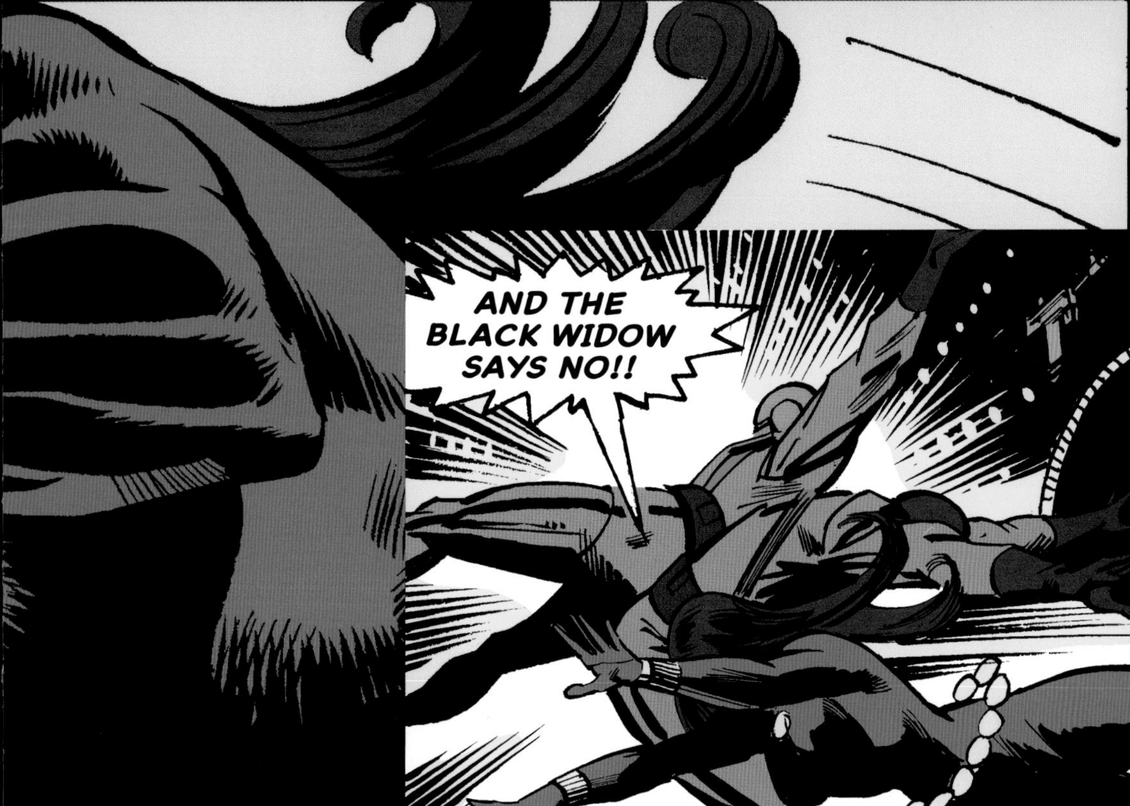

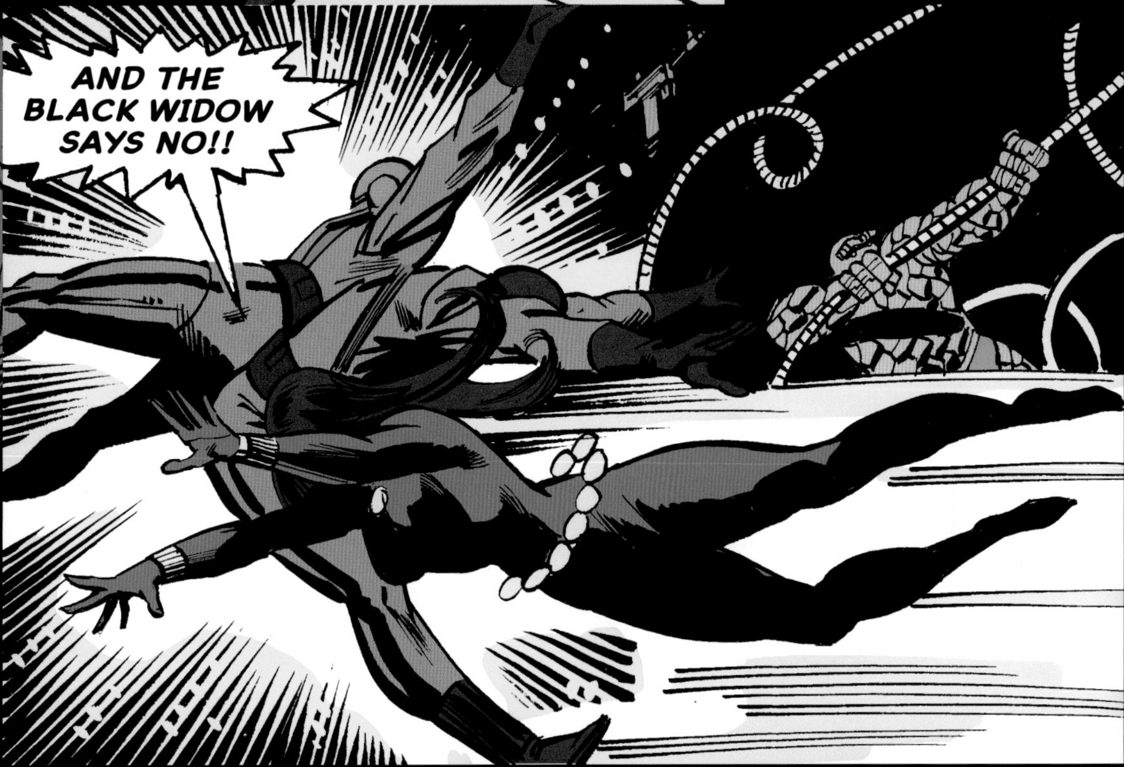

AND THE BLACK WIDOW SAYS NO!!

Above: DAREDEVIL #117 (JAN. 1975) Black Widow used her Widow's Bite to stop the villainous Owl from downloading the information in Daredevil's brain.

Above right: MARVEL TWO-IN-ONE #10 (JUL. 1975) A mission with the Fantastic Four's Thing gave Black Widow the confidence to break away from Daredevil and fight her own battles.

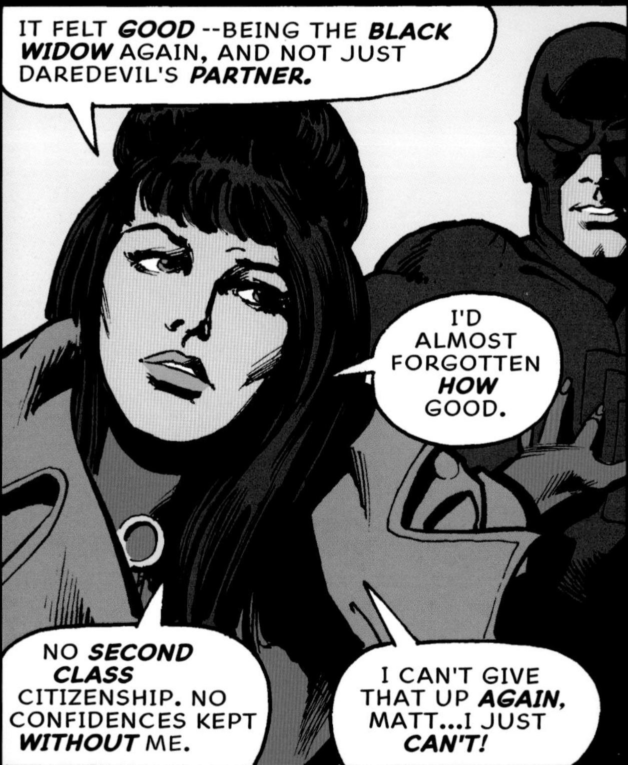

IT FELT GOOD --BEING THE BLACK WIDOW AGAIN, AND NOT JUST DAREDEVIL'S PARTNER.
I'D ALMOST FORGOTTEN HOW GOOD.
NO SECOND CLASS CITIZENSHIP. NO CONFIDENCES KEPT WITHOUT ME.
I CAN'T GIVE THAT UP AGAIN, MATT...I JUST CAN'T!

Right: DAREDEVIL #124 (AUG. 1975) Black Widow broke the news to Daredevil that they could never go back to how they were—maintaining her own identity was more important to her.

"I do not like the term... 'chick'. Nor do I like men with guns. Remember that!"

BLACK WIDOW

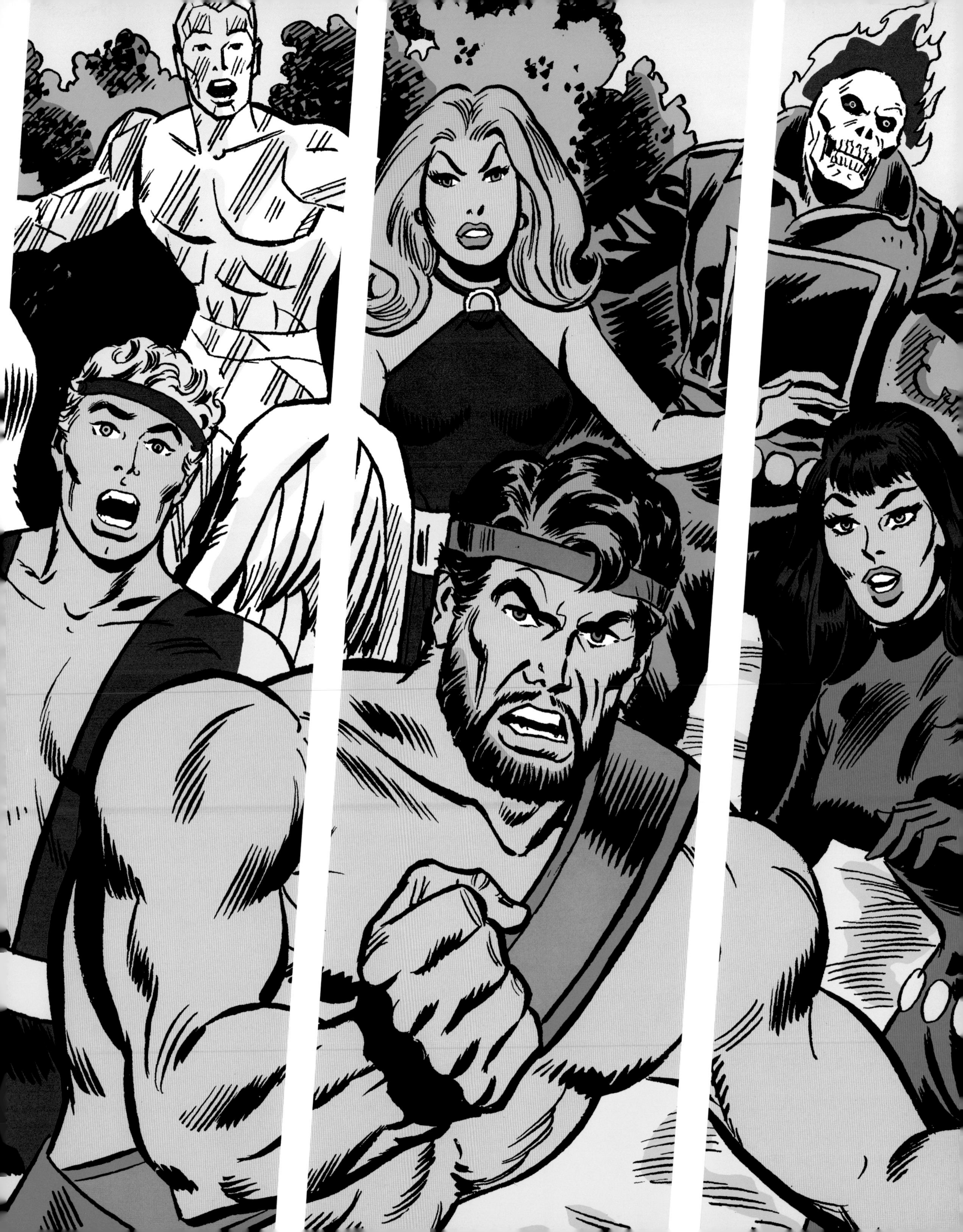

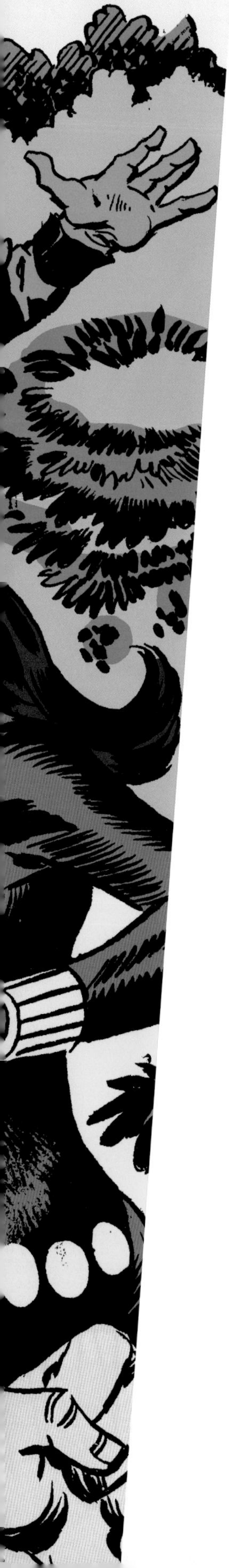

Champion of Champions

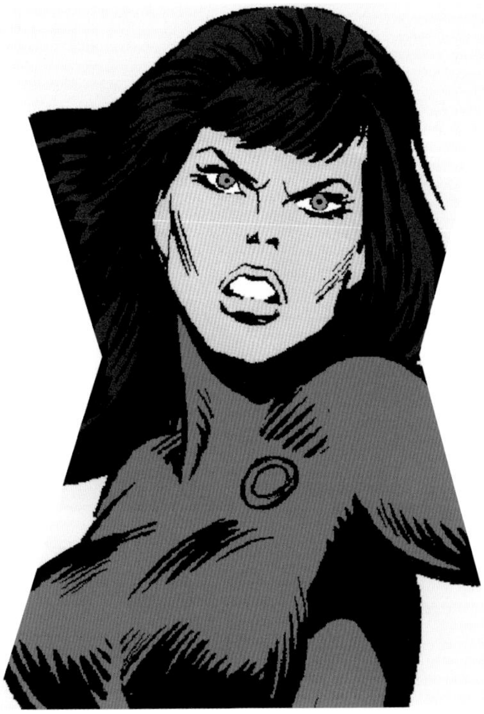

THE CHAMPIONS #2 (JAN. 1976)
Natasha led her new team, the Champions, in a mission to help demigods Hercules and Venus escape the machinations of Pluto, God of the Underworld.

Natasha returned to the West Coast, applying for a position teaching Russian at the University of California, Los Angeles. As usual, trouble was not far away, and she became embroiled in a battle against the all-powerful Olympian god of death, Pluto, alongside a group of unlikely allies: the demigod Hercules, Ghost Rider (Johnny Blaze), and two former X-Men, Iceman (Bobby Drake) and Angel (Warren Worthington III). Her participation in the conflict could not have been better timed.

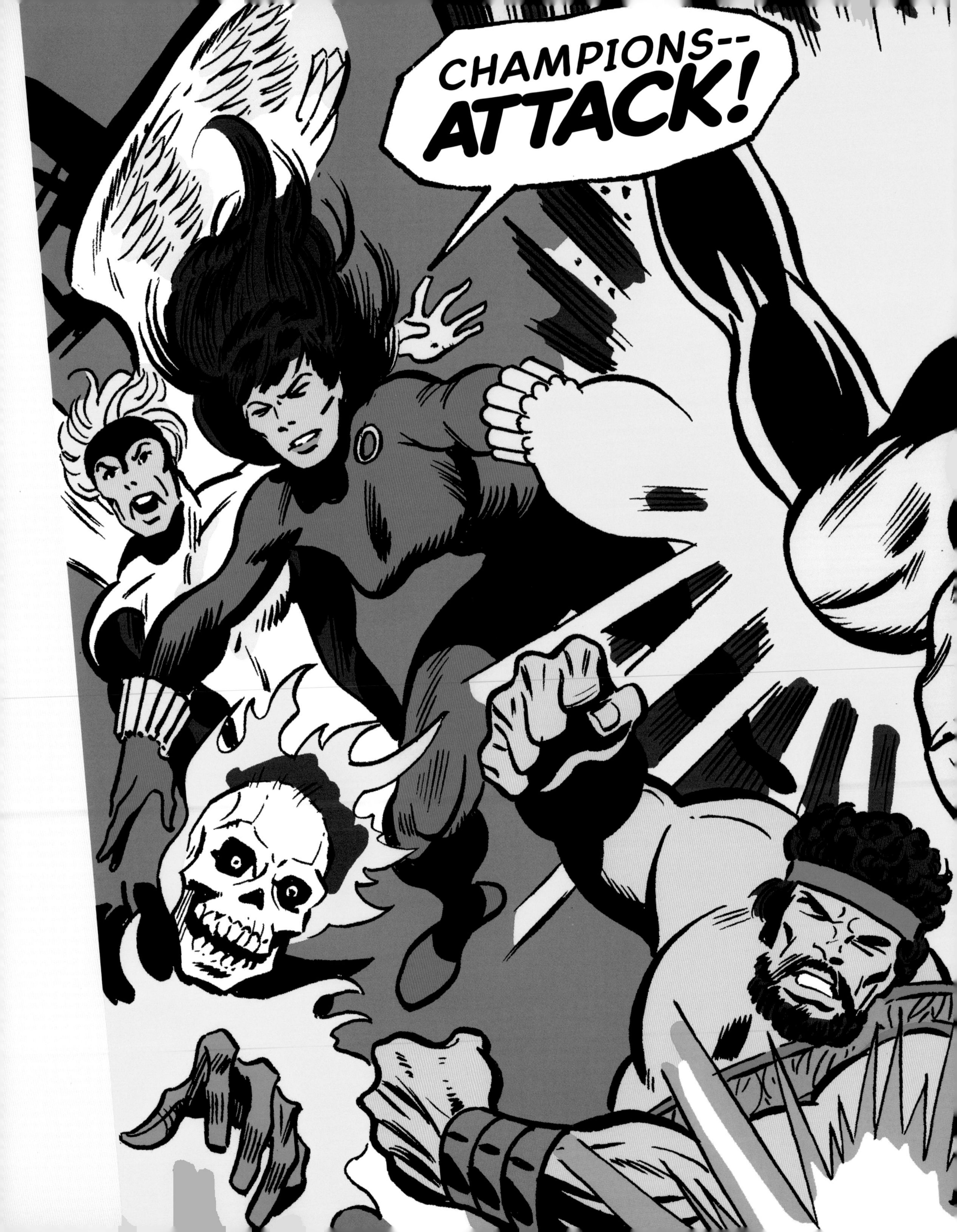
CHAMPIONS-- ATTACK!

THIS *FOREST* HATH BEEN BLESSED BY THE *GODS,* MILADY!

THERE WERE PLACES LIKE THIS IN *RUSSIA* --WHEN I WAS A *GIRL!*

MY FATHER WOULD *LIFT* ME TO HIS *SHOULDERS--*

--*THUS,* MY FAIR COMPANION?

IRON MAN ANNUAL #4 (AUG. 1977) During a mission with Iron Man, Natasha grew closer to her Champions teammate Hercules, sharing her innermost feelings with the Olympian.

The ad hoc, disparate team was in dire need of leadership, and Natasha stepped up, her tactical and strategic experience proving just the right ingredient to guide her teammates to victory. Black Widow knew when to fight, and when to step back and make a plan.

Following their triumph over Pluto, Black Widow and her team gathered together to determine their next move. They decided that the West Coast lacked a team of Super Heroes to help ordinary people in extraordinary situations, and so they would take on that role for themselves. Calling their team the Champions, they officially elected Black Widow as their leader. Her main responsibilities revolved around strategy and planning, as her powerful teammates did not need much

instruction when it came to battling the bad guys. Ivan Petrovitch, still her loyal companion, was concerned about Natasha teaming up with others again as it had so often led to heartbreak in the past, but she was optimistic. After all, her fellow Champions were like her—loners who did not really fit in anywhere else.

Natasha had found herself a new niche, and, drawn to his immense strength and brash charm, even began a fledgling relationship with her Olympian teammate Hercules. Settled in Los Angeles, both she and Hercules turned down an opportunity to return to the Avengers in New York, although Natasha was fully aware of the debt of gratitude she owed Earth's Mightiest Heroes for giving her a chance to prove herself in the early days after her defection.

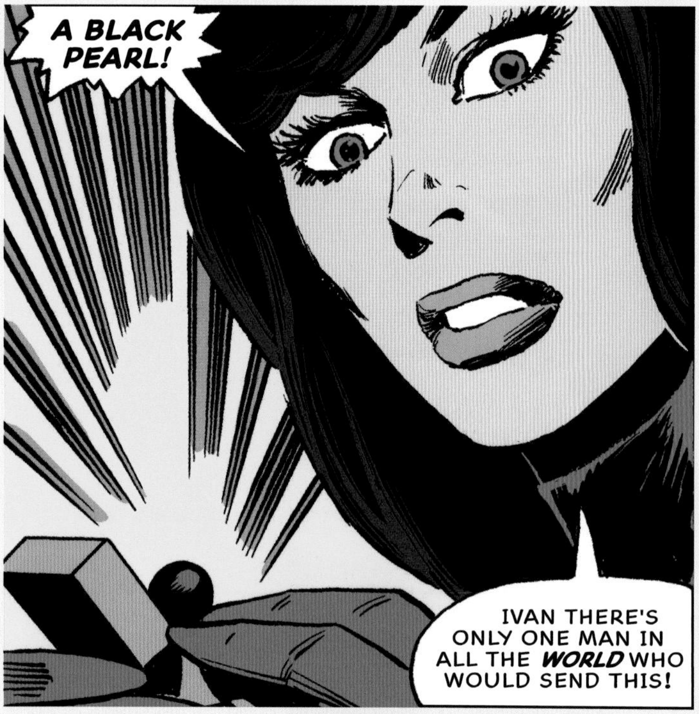
A BLACK PEARL!
IVAN THERE'S ONLY ONE MAN IN ALL THE *WORLD* WHO WOULD SEND THIS!

Several months after the team was established, a bomb was thrown through the window of the Champions' HQ. Ivan discovered it contained a black pearl. He instantly recognized it as a reference to a nickname given to Natasha by an old teacher from her Soviet days, Commissar Bruskin. Black Widow went to meet Bruskin, but she was ambushed and captured by the Titanium Man. He was part of a group sent by the Soviets to retrieve three Soviet defectors: Natasha, Ivan, and Bruskin. When Natasha heard that she was wanted "home," the word struck despair into her heart.

Further shocks were in store when the leader of the group was revealed to be the Crimson Dynamo. Puzzled, Natasha remarked that she had witnessed his death back in Tony Stark's factory during an early assignment to the US. However, this was a new version: it was Ivan's son, Yuri, thought to have been killed as a child. Yuri's demise had been faked by the Soviet authorities, who

Above: THE CHAMPIONS #7 (AUG. 1976) A black pearl sent to Natasha was a shocking reminder of a life she thought she had left behind: her days training as a KGB agent in the USSR.

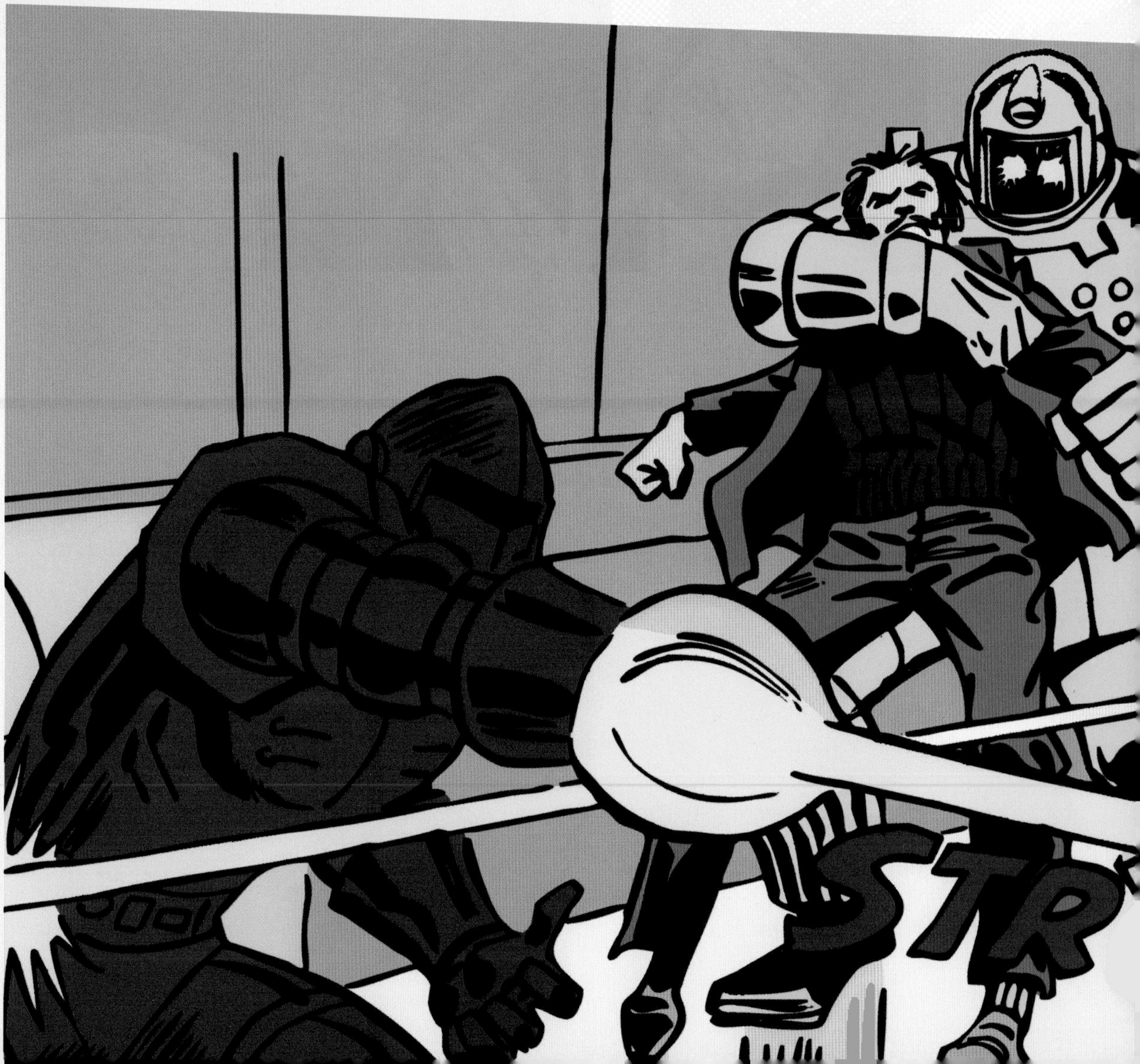
STR

Right: THE CHAMPIONS #10 (JAN. 1977) After being freed by Darkstar, Black Widow takes the fight to her Soviet captors, Crimson Dynamo and the Titanium Man.

had abducted him and brought him up as an agent who hated the West with a zealot's passion. When Yuri learned that his father had defected, he was furious, and determined to bring Ivan back to face punishment. Natasha and Ivan were horrified to hear that Bruskin himself had been involved in the deception around Yuri's "death" and had even sanctioned the murder of his mother, Ivan's wife. Like Black Widow, Ivan's life had been controlled and manipulated by the authorities.

The clash between the Champions and the Soviet group led to two further outcomes: the defection to the West of a young Russian agent known as Darkstar, who unofficially joined the team, and the discovery that there were secrets about the Crimson Dynamo that Black Widow was not sharing with her teammates. She grew concerned about Darkstar: the young woman reminded Black Widow of herself in her earlier years, and she knew how hard defecting could be. Perhaps Natasha also felt a hint of jealousy as Darkstar possessed powers such as control of dark energy and flight.

Natasha's old insecurities were bubbling to the surface again—after a dangerous mission in space she worried that her leadership was putting her teammates in too much peril. She was unsettled further by the departure of Ivan, who told her he was returning to Russia to try and reach out to his son, who had returned there. However, in reality he was acting on a call from S.H.I.E.L.D.

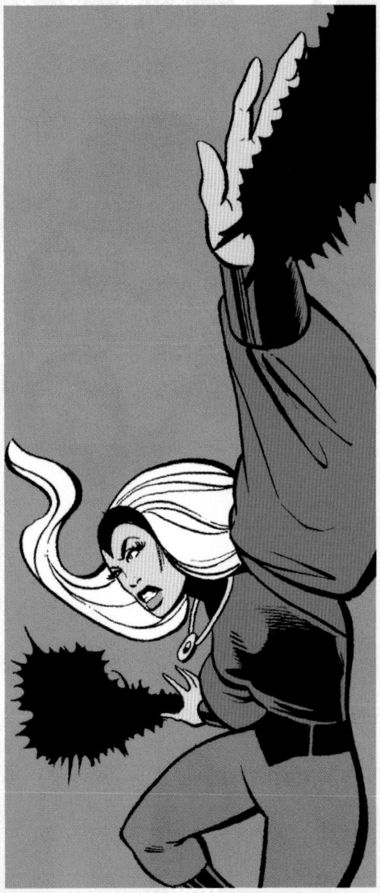

Above: THE CHAMPIONS #13 (MAY. 1977) Fellow Soviet defector Darkstar (Laynia Petrovna) reminded Natasha of a younger version of herself, albeit one with greater super-powers.

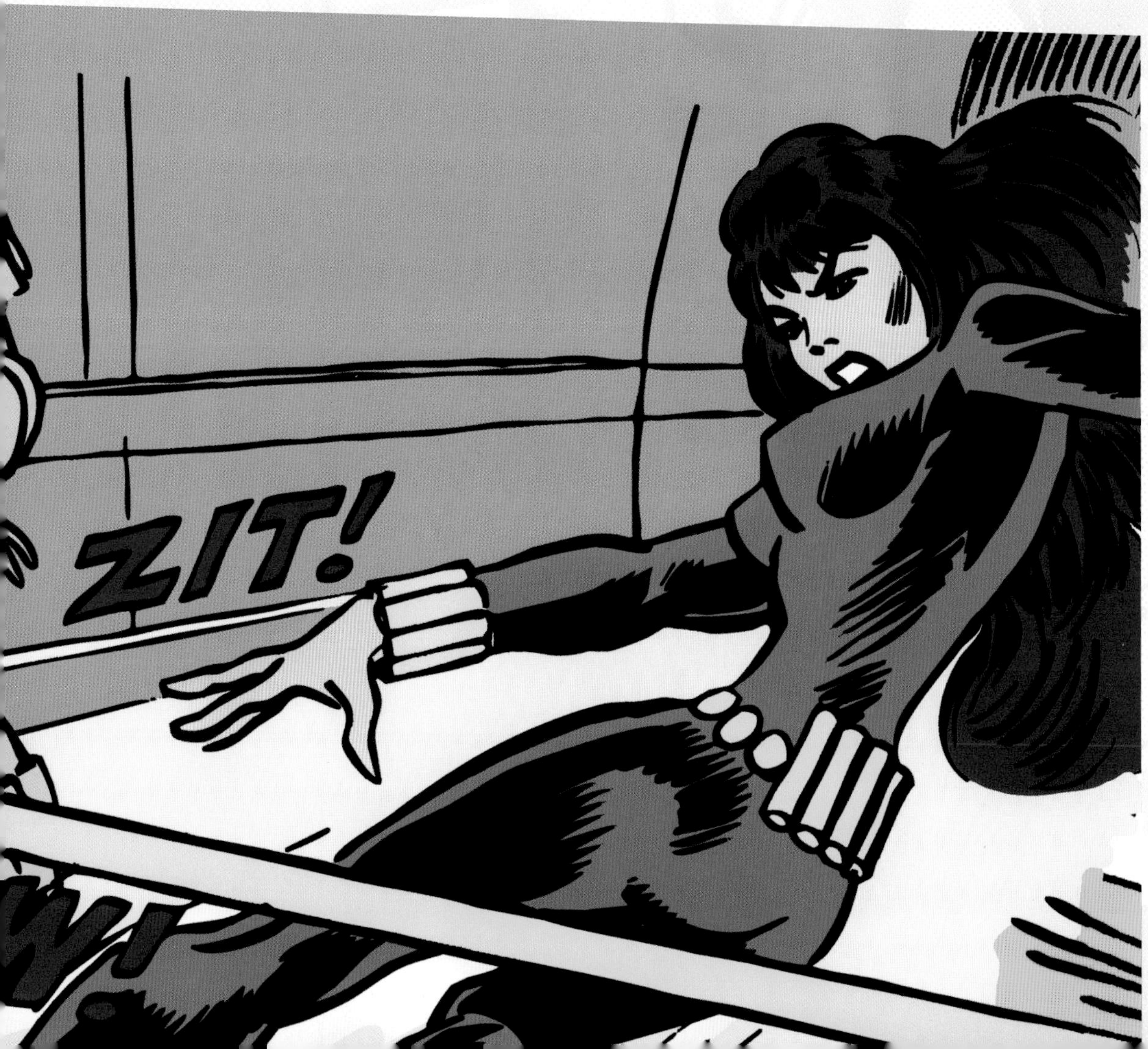
ZIT!

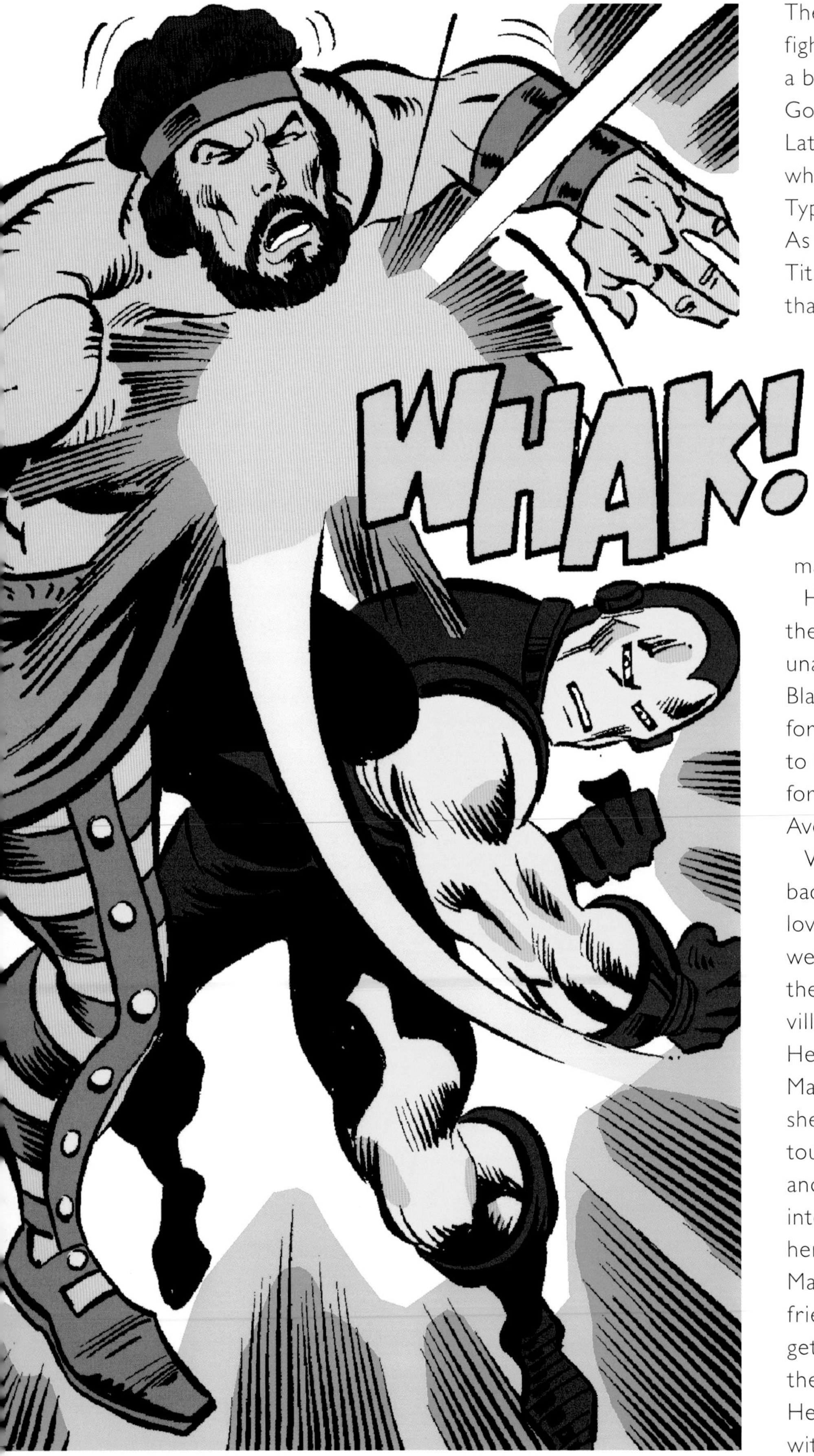
WHAK!

The Champions' lack of experience fighting as a team was highlighted during a battle against the mighty monster Godzilla as he attacked San Francisco. Later, the team was attacked by Iron Man, who was being forced by the immortal Typhon to try to take down Hercules. As the Champions rallied to fight the Titan, Typhon was surprised to find that Black Widow—a mere mortal—could hurt him. She told him in no uncertain terms that every enemy had a weak point. She then demonstrated how strength could be used against an opponent by flooring the giant, making her only the second being to ever manage this after Hercules.

However, despite their many victories, the Champions ended up disbanding, unable to work together anymore. Black Widow blamed herself as leader for the breakup of the team, and decided to travel to New York with Hercules for another new start—staying at Avengers Mansion for a time.

When Daredevil heard that she was back in town, he had to talk to his former love. However, the reunion did not go well. At the time, Daredevil was under the influence of the interdimensional villain known as Death-Stalker. He attacked everyone at Avengers Mansion and angrily told Natasha that she destroyed everything she ever touched. Although he was possessed and clearly not himself, Black Widow's internalized guilt immediately caused her to agree with her ex-lover. When Matt recovered, Natasha was able to be friends with him again, but chose not to get romantically involved. It also spelled the end of Black Widow's dalliance with Hercules, whose ego had not coped well with seeing her so close to Daredevil.

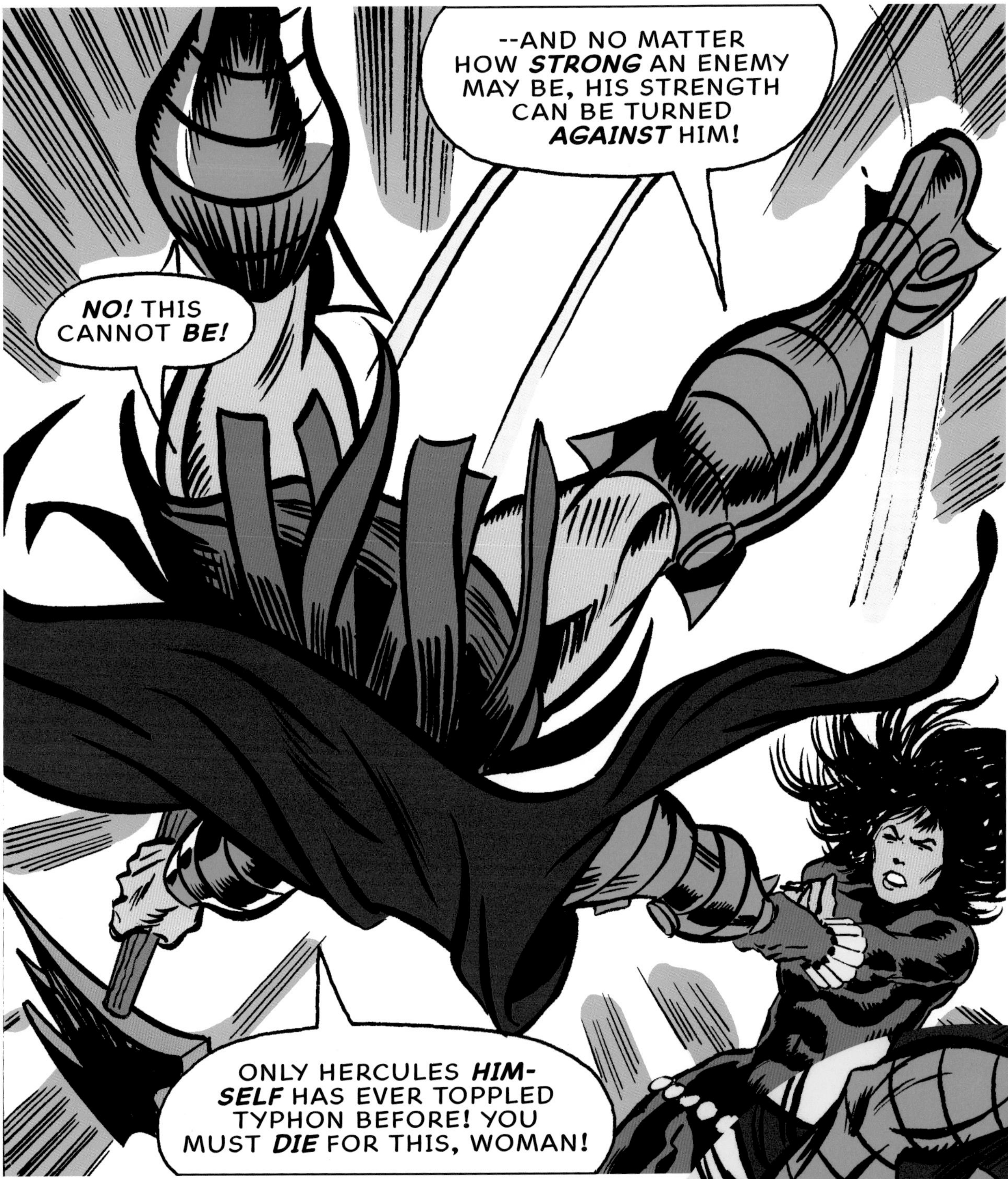
--AND NO MATTER HOW STRONG AN ENEMY MAY BE, HIS STRENGTH CAN BE TURNED AGAINST HIM!
NO! THIS CANNOT BE!
ONLY HERCULES HIM-SELF HAS EVER TOPPLED TYPHON BEFORE! YOU MUST DIE FOR THIS, WOMAN!

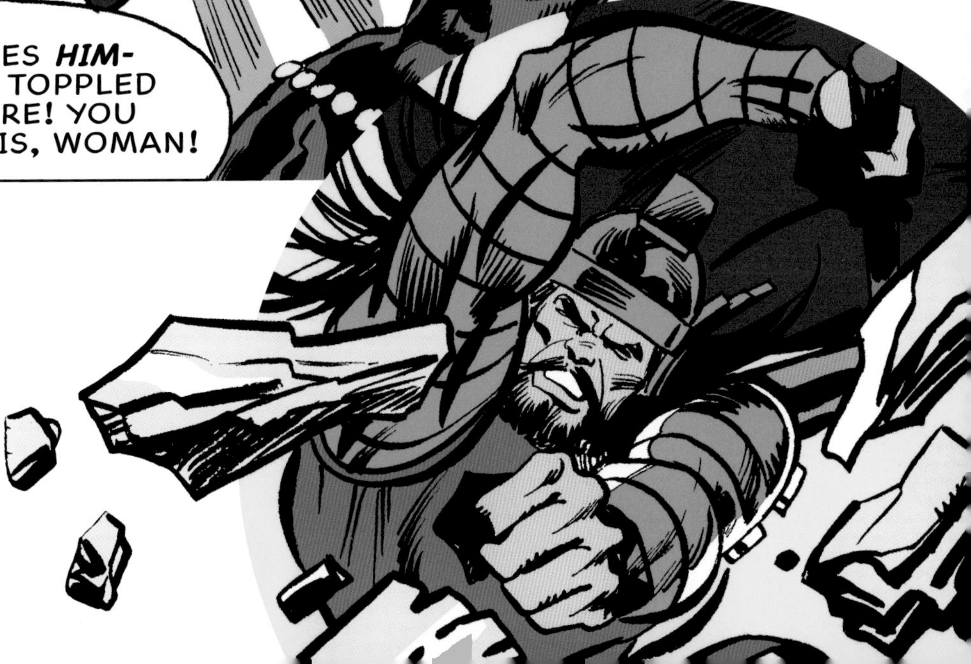

THE AVENGERS #163 (SEP. 1977) When the villain Typhon forced Iron Man to attack Black Widow's Champions team, she scored a memorable victory against the powerful immortal.

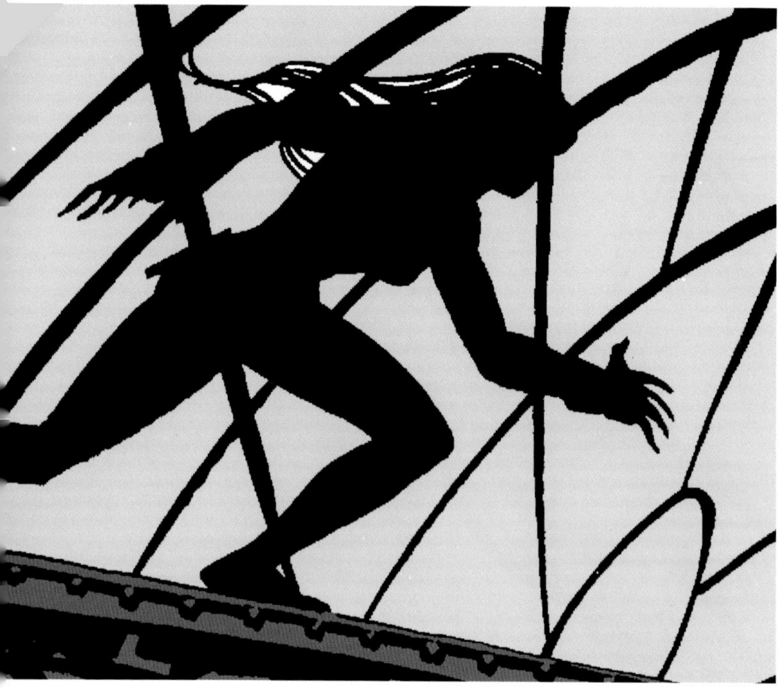

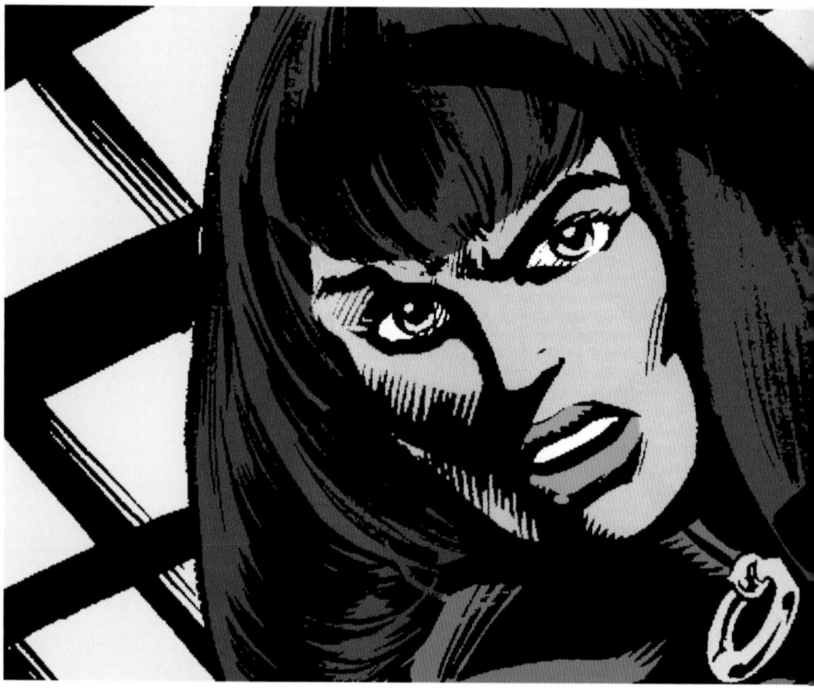

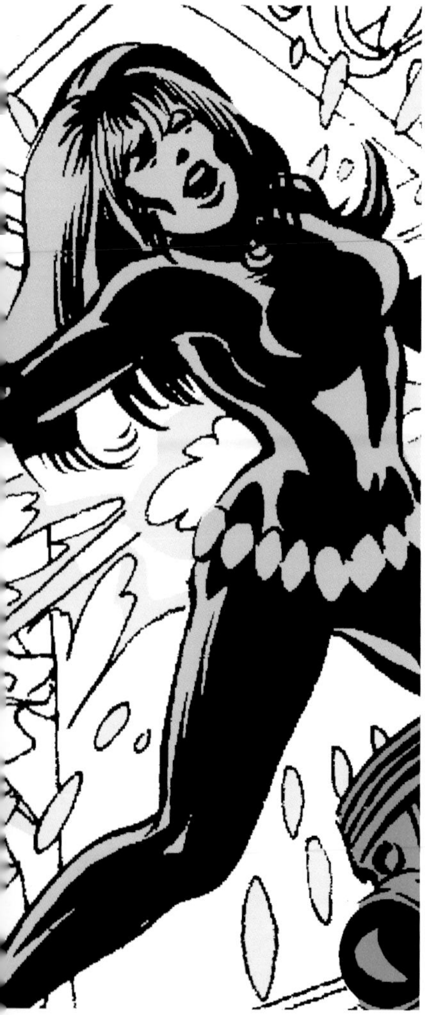

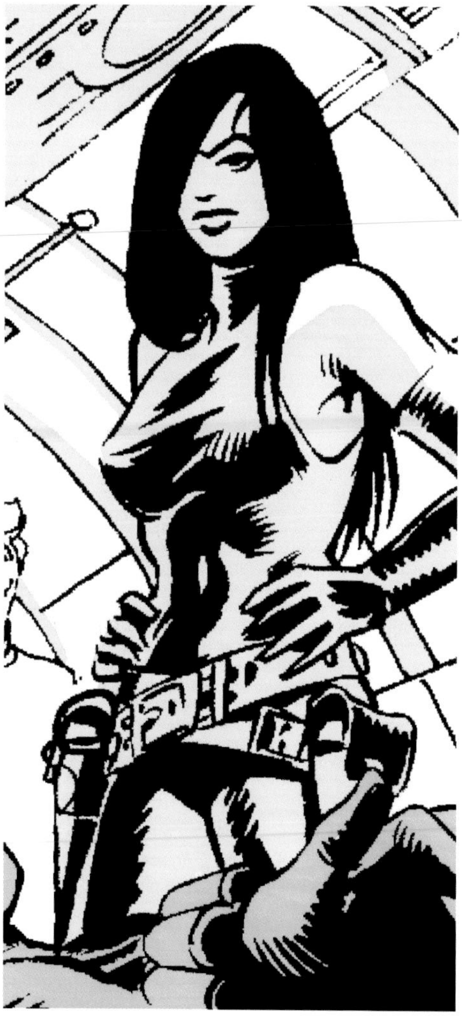

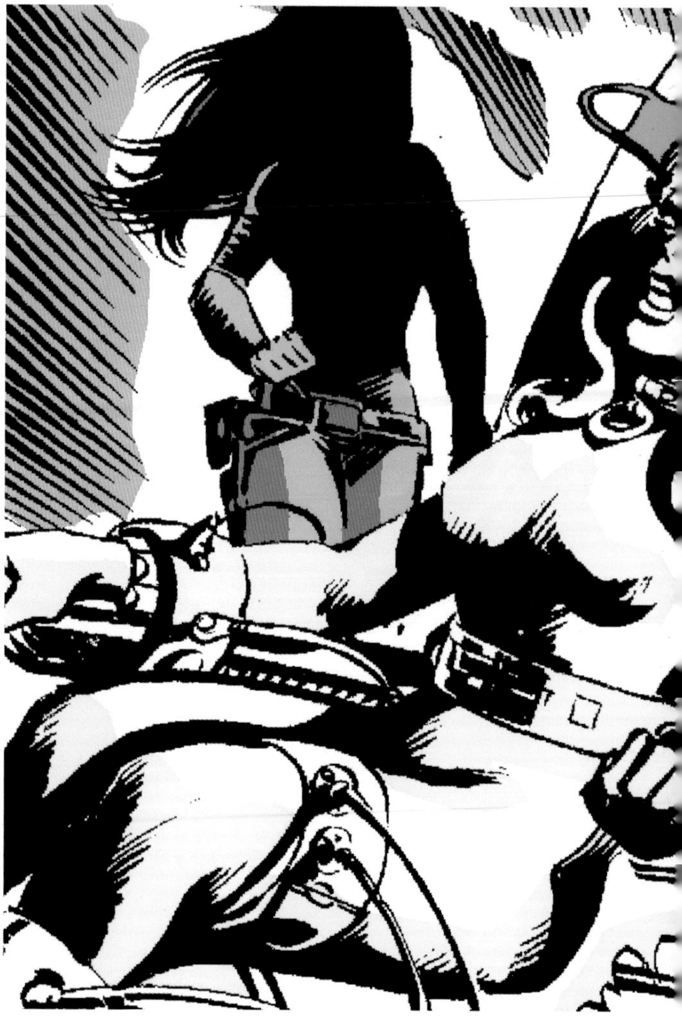

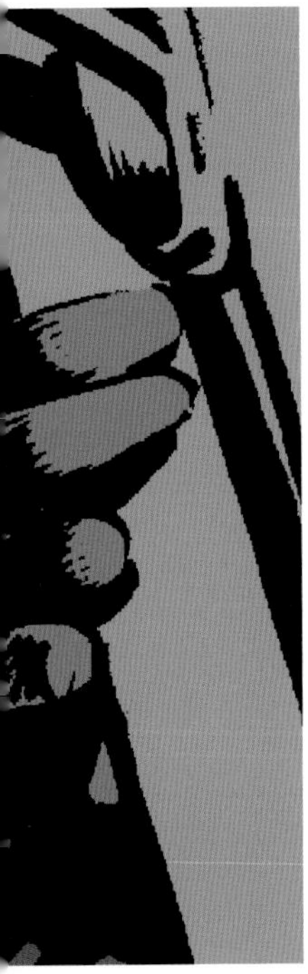

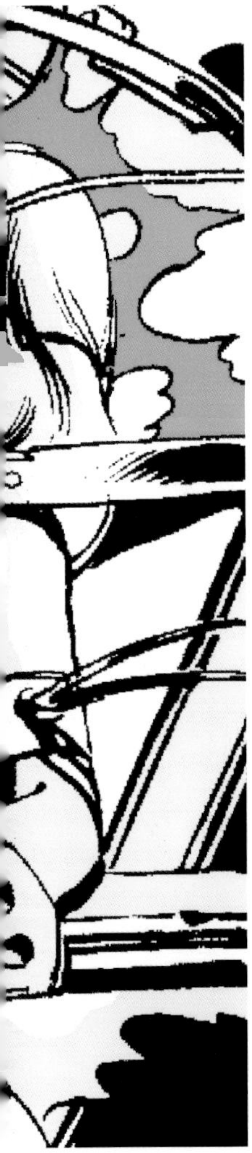

Agent for Hire

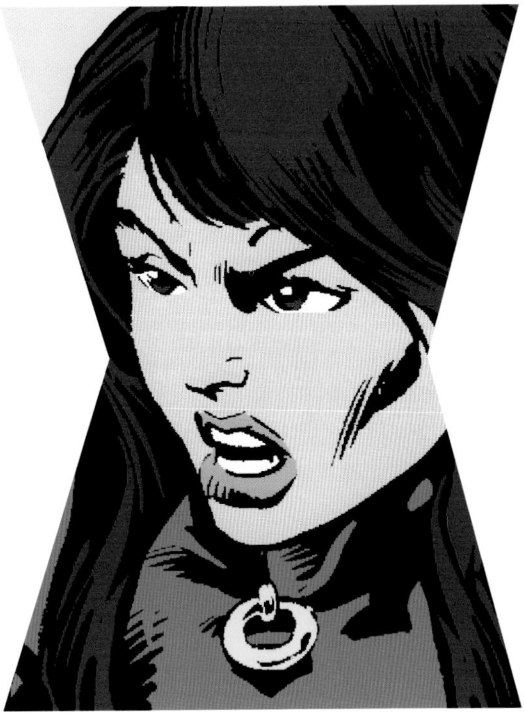

MARVEL TEAM-UP #85 (SEP. 1979) When she was tortured by Viper on a mission to the Far East, Black Widow reverted to the persona of meek schoolteacher Nancy Rushman.

When the Avengers were ordered by the National Security Council to cut their numbers to a core team of seven, Black Widow was not in the final lineup. Striking out solo as a freelance agent, she was on a mission to the Far East when she was betrayed by a mind-controlled S.H.I.E.L.D. agent and captured by Viper, formerly Madame Hydra. For days Black Widow was brutally tortured for information about S.H.I.E.L.D. and Nick Fury, but she did not talk. As a result of Viper's torture, and finding herself back home in New York City, Natasha's traumatized mind reverted to one of her old cover identities from her Soviet spy days—Nancy Rushman, elementary teacher from upstate New York.

Opposite: MARVEL TEAM-UP #85 (SEP. 1979) When Spider-Man took "Nancy Rushman" under his wing on a dangerous mission, Black Widow's true personality returned and she joined in the fight.

When "Nancy" found herself walking New York City's streets late at night, she was set upon by thugs. Luckily Spider-Man was nearby, and swung in to help, but the web-slinger was soon on his back after slipping on a patch of ice. With one of the muggers about to stab Spider-Man, the meek schoolteacher floored the bad guy with a powerful display of martial arts that surprised everyone. Looking more closely at the "victim," Spider-Man immediately recognized Black Widow, but the frightened woman was adamant that she was not her, even when the famous costume was discovered in her bag. Spider-Man took Nancy Rushman under his wing, hoping to coax the truth out of her in time, but his plan was derailed by rogue S.H.I.E.L.D. agents, pursuing the confused woman with the intent to kill her. Her instincts again kicking in, "Nancy" fought the agents—they were no match for her deadly grace. However, she was defeated by an anesthetic bullet fired by Nick Fury, who wanted to bring her in and try to work out what was going on. Was Black Widow's whole defection a sham—was she actually working undercover for the Russians?

However, Fury soon realized that the problems instead lay inside S.H.I.E.L.D., and many of its operatives had been compromised by mind control from an unknown source. The risks posed to the world at large by a renegade S.H.I.E.L.D. were clear, and Nancy/Natasha realized that, whoever she was, she had to try and help. She and Spider-Man boarded a S.H.I.E.L.D. helicarrier controlled by corrupted agents only to discover that the mastermind behind the whole plot was Viper. Black Widow recalled what she had suffered at Viper's hands and confronted her, disgusted by her casual attitude to the deaths she would cause by her actions. As they fought atop a propeller casing on the helicarrier, Black Widow told Viper that she had grown up with death, enough to know how precious life was. Despite being physically and mentally exhausted, Natasha dug deep to draw on her indomitable will, and thus was returned fully to herself again. The Viper did not have a prayer against the best secret agent in the world. After the battle, Black Widow bid farewell to Spider-Man. The web-slinger and Nancy Rushman had a special connection, but Natasha Romanoff was different. She had fought to be free all her life, to choose her own path. She knew that if she was to fly free like an eagle, she had to fly alone.

MARVEL TEAM-UP #82 (JUN. 1979) Natasha had retreated so far into her Nancy Rushman persona that Spider-Man had to play along with it to avoid causing her further mental distress.

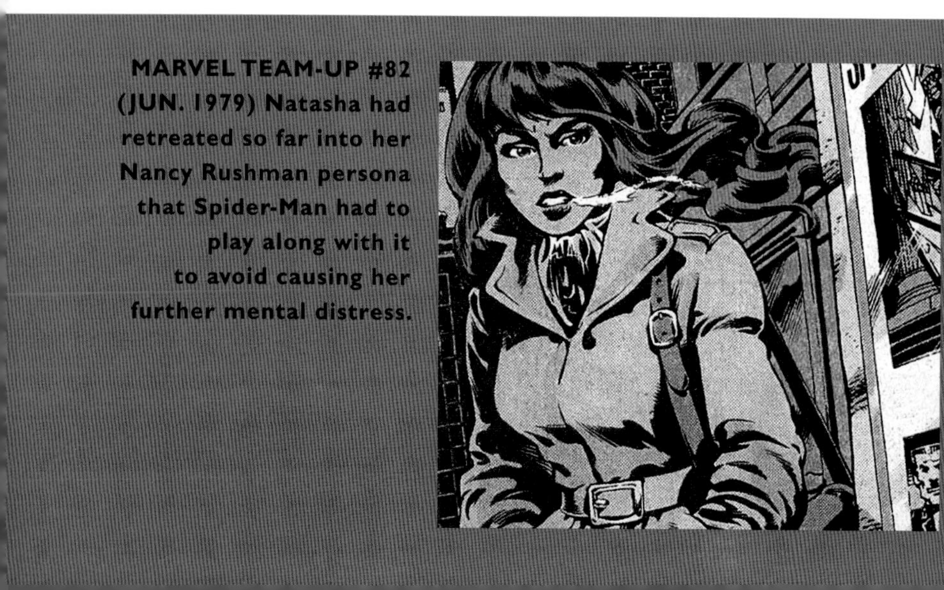

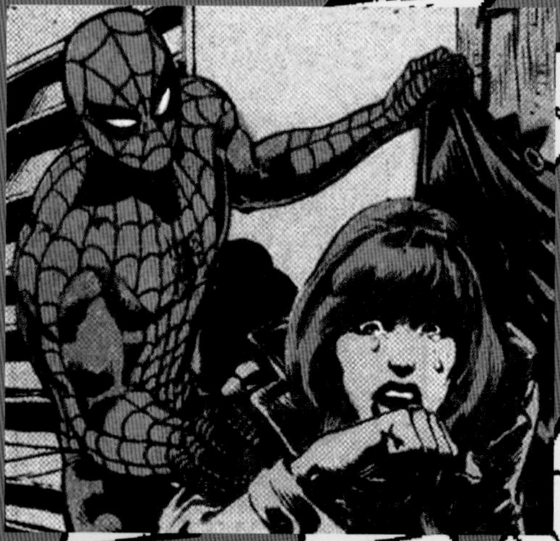

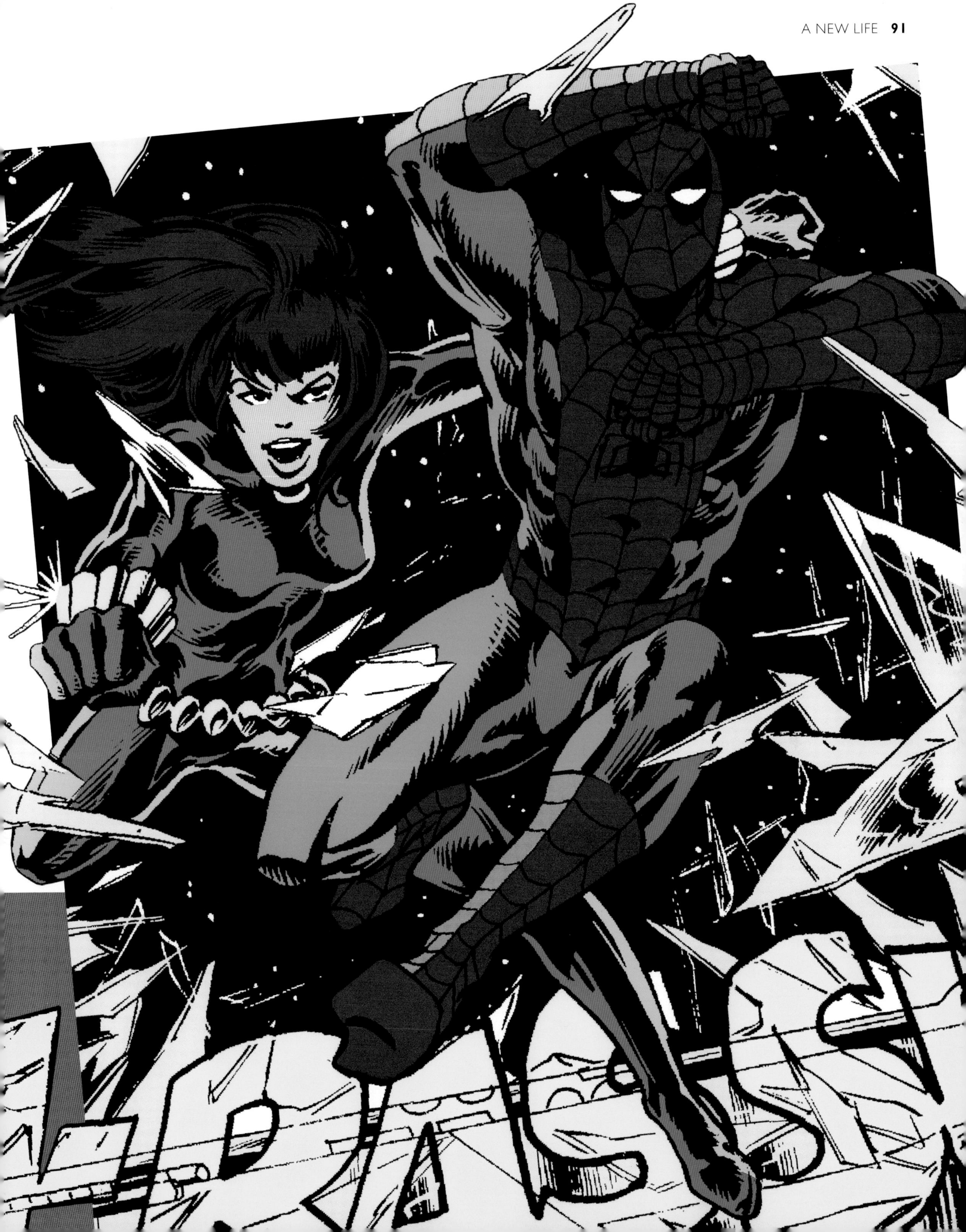

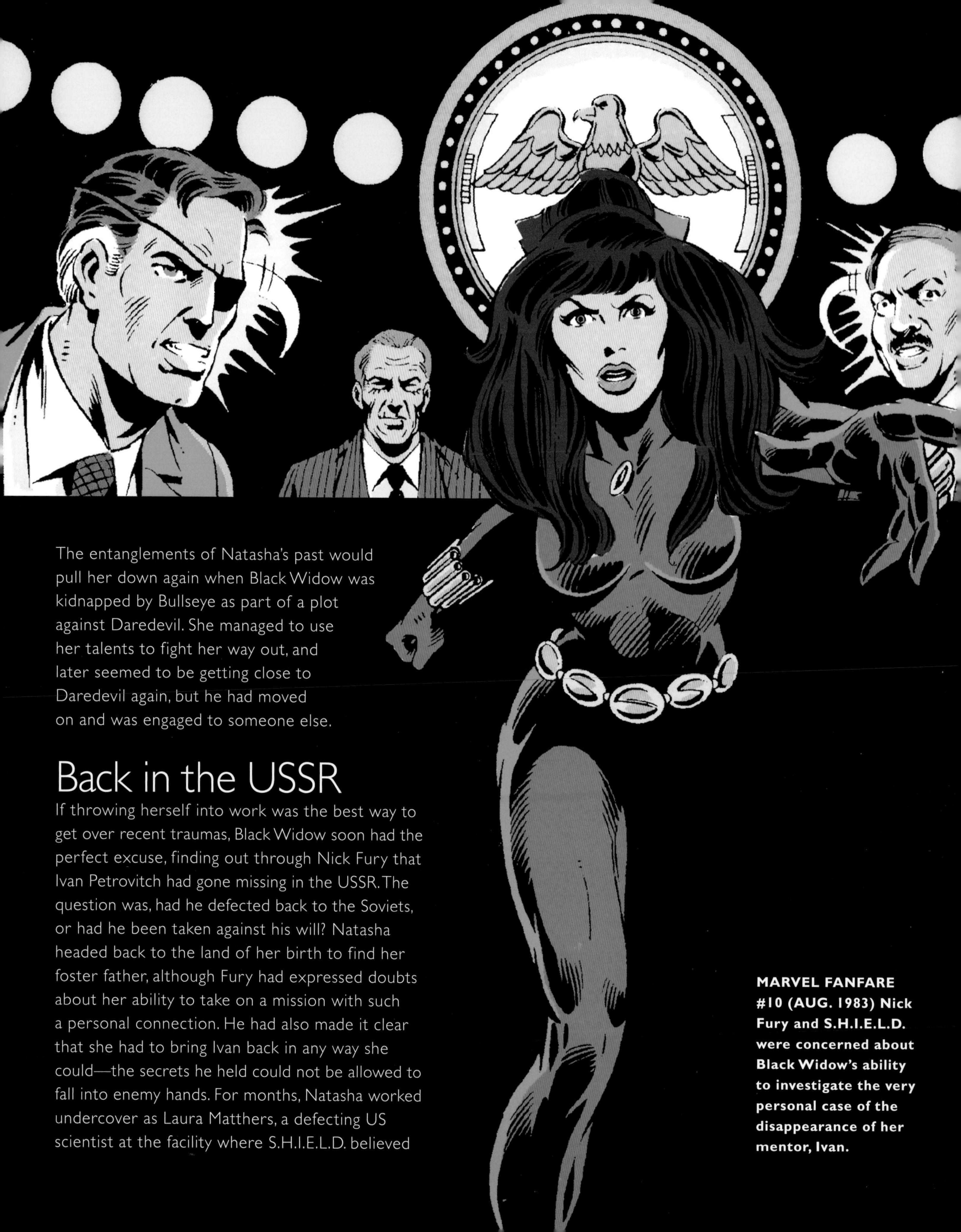

The entanglements of Natasha's past would pull her down again when Black Widow was kidnapped by Bullseye as part of a plot against Daredevil. She managed to use her talents to fight her way out, and later seemed to be getting close to Daredevil again, but he had moved on and was engaged to someone else.

Back in the USSR

If throwing herself into work was the best way to get over recent traumas, Black Widow soon had the perfect excuse, finding out through Nick Fury that Ivan Petrovitch had gone missing in the USSR. The question was, had he defected back to the Soviets, or had he been taken against his will? Natasha headed back to the land of her birth to find her foster father, although Fury had expressed doubts about her ability to take on a mission with such a personal connection. He had also made it clear that she had to bring Ivan back in any way she could—the secrets he held could not be allowed to fall into enemy hands. For months, Natasha worked undercover as Laura Matthers, a defecting US scientist at the facility where S.H.I.E.L.D. believed

MARVEL FANFARE #10 (AUG. 1983) Nick Fury and S.H.I.E.L.D. were concerned about Black Widow's ability to investigate the very personal case of the disappearance of her mentor, Ivan.

"But I'll come back for you, Ivan. I swear it."

BLACK WIDOW

Ivan to be, all the while keeping watch for any clues as to his whereabouts. Even the American Embassy knew nothing of her mission. "Laura" was told her research was vital, but never given any details about what her work would achieve for the USSR. She even grew close to a man she believed to be a fellow American defector, Michael Corcoran. However, like so much of Natasha's Russian experience, it was all a web of deception. The Soviet authorities knew who she was, knew she was working for S.H.I.E.L.D., and had used Michael to feed her false intel on Ivan. Michael, having outlived his usefulness, was killed in cold blood by agents at the facility, but Natasha escaped and went on the run. It was made public that she had killed Michael, and she was now wanted for murder.

Luckily S.H.I.E.L.D. was able to extract Black Widow before she could be arrested by the Soviets. She followed a lead to Hong Kong, but that turned out to be a trap. Accosted by six of the world's deadliest assassins, she managed to best them all before finally being captured and led to a secret island hideout. Here she found out the mastermind of the plot was Damon Dran, seeking revenge for his earlier defeat by Widow and Daredevil. Ivan had been kidnapped and brainwashed as part of the scheme, but when the time came for the burly Russian to hurt his "little Czarina," he couldn't do it.

Widow's next problem was to save Nick Fury from a duplicate version of herself, created by Dran to board the helicarrier without suspicion and kill the S.H.I.E.L.D. commander. Managing to communicate with Fury, Black Widow and Ivan escaped the island just before it was destroyed.

MARVEL FANFARE #11 (NOV. 1983) Assuming the identity of defecting scientist Laura Matthers gave Black Widow the chance to get closer to Ivan Petrovitch's captors.

MARVEL FANFARE #12 (JAN. 1984) The mission to find Ivan brought Black Widow into the clutches of a squad of the world's deadliest assassins.

MARVEL FANFARE #13 (MAR. 1984) Natasha rescued her old friend Ivan from Damon Dran, and helped him break free from his brainwashing.

KLIK

Back in the US, Black Widow continued working for S.H.I.E.L.D. and adopted a new look. Cutting her hair fashionably short, she donned a new gray costume with spider emblems. Her luck seemed to have run out when—while pursuing members of the shadowy ninja organization, the Hand—she was poisoned after treading on toxic foot spikes thrown by the ninjas. S.H.I.E.L.D. doctors gave her just one week to live. They wanted to keep her at their HQ to run tests, but Black Widow was not one to lie around and wait for death. She fought her way out, running first to Ivan—who had returned to the US with her following their dramatic escape from Dran's island—to break the news, and then to Daredevil. It was a life-saving decision. Natasha died shortly after tracking down her old flame who was with his mentor, the ninja Stick, and Stick's favorite pupil, Stone. Stone used his *chi* power to resurrect Black Widow, restoring her to full health. Following this pivotal moment, Black Widow helped out Daredevil whenever she could, often training with him so that they could both keep their strength and reflexes operating at their full potential.

Later, Natasha was visited by Russian agents who told her that her former husband Alexei Shostakov was not dead. She believed he had died in Asia years before when, as the Red Guardian, he had saved her life, but the Russians showed her recent photos and even video footage of him appearing to be alive and well. They explained that he had been found still breathing—just—and taken back to Russia for extensive treatment. He seemed to have forgotten all of his previous life… except his wife. The Russians informed her that his medical treatment might be stopped unless she performed a "small service" for them. Natasha angrily told them to get out. She then turned to her former partners, Hawkeye and Daredevil, but when she found

BLACK WIDOW: THE COLDEST WAR #1 (NOV. 1983) When she heard reports that her former husband Red Guardian (Alexei Shostakov) was still alive, Black Widow had to return to Russia to see him for herself.

that they had moved on with their lives, she decided to make contact with the Russians after all. Maybe she could help her former husband. Her mission for the Russians involved first stealing something from the UN headquarters, and then from S.H.I.E.L.D.: near-impossible tasks for most people, which Black Widow achieved in short order. She stole a computer control chip for S.H.I.E.L.D.'s new generation of LMDs (Life Model Decoys, incredibly lifelike androids), on the condition that she would take it to Russia, see Alexei for herself, and bring him back with her to the US.

Arriving in Russia with Ivan, every street held a memory for Natasha, some warm, others painful. And falling into both categories were

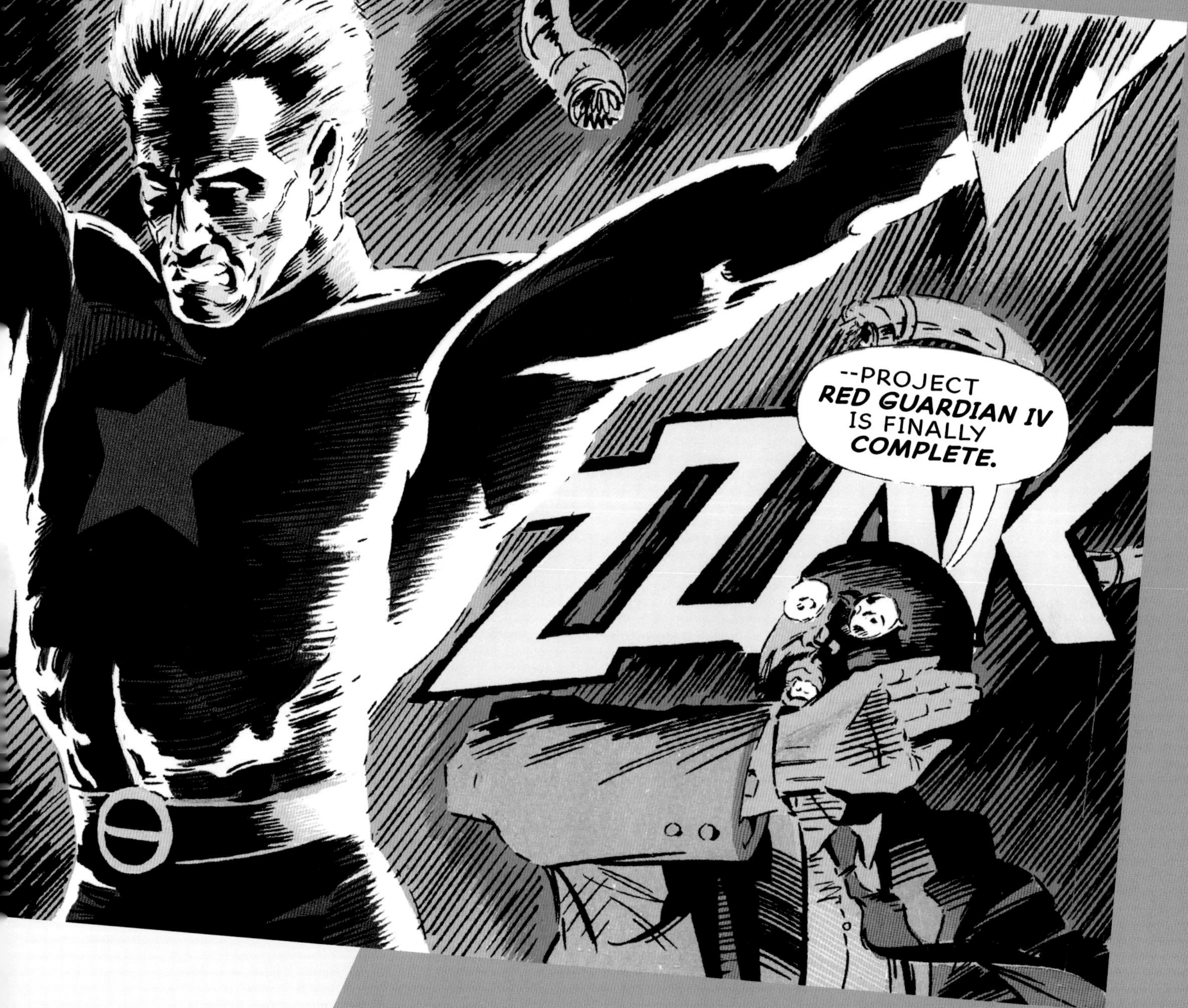
--PROJECT
RED GUARDIAN IV
IS FINALLY
COMPLETE.
ZAK

the memories of Alexei, her husband, whom she had already twice lost to death. At Moscow University, the two were ushered into a lab, where Natasha was overjoyed to see Alexei coming to greet her. But when he reached her, he fell forward, attached by wires to the wall behind. Alexei was an LMD, or the Russian equivalent of one. The Soviets had needed the S.H.I.E.L.D component to make him the most powerful of his kind in the world. Now they had it, they ordered "Alexei" to kill them both. But Black Widow knew how the LMDs were operated, and removed the control chip to disable the Alexei android. She had also been ready for the Soviet deception, knowing they were using her attachment to Alexei for their own ends, and had alerted S.H.I.E.L.D. to their activities. But despite knowing it was likely to be a lie, she still needed to see Alexei for herself… just in case.

When the Cold War ended, Natasha felt a great sense of personal freedom that aligned with the newfound liberty of the people of Eastern Europe. The landscape for secret agents was changing forever, but of course, new enemies would quickly rise to take the place of the old.

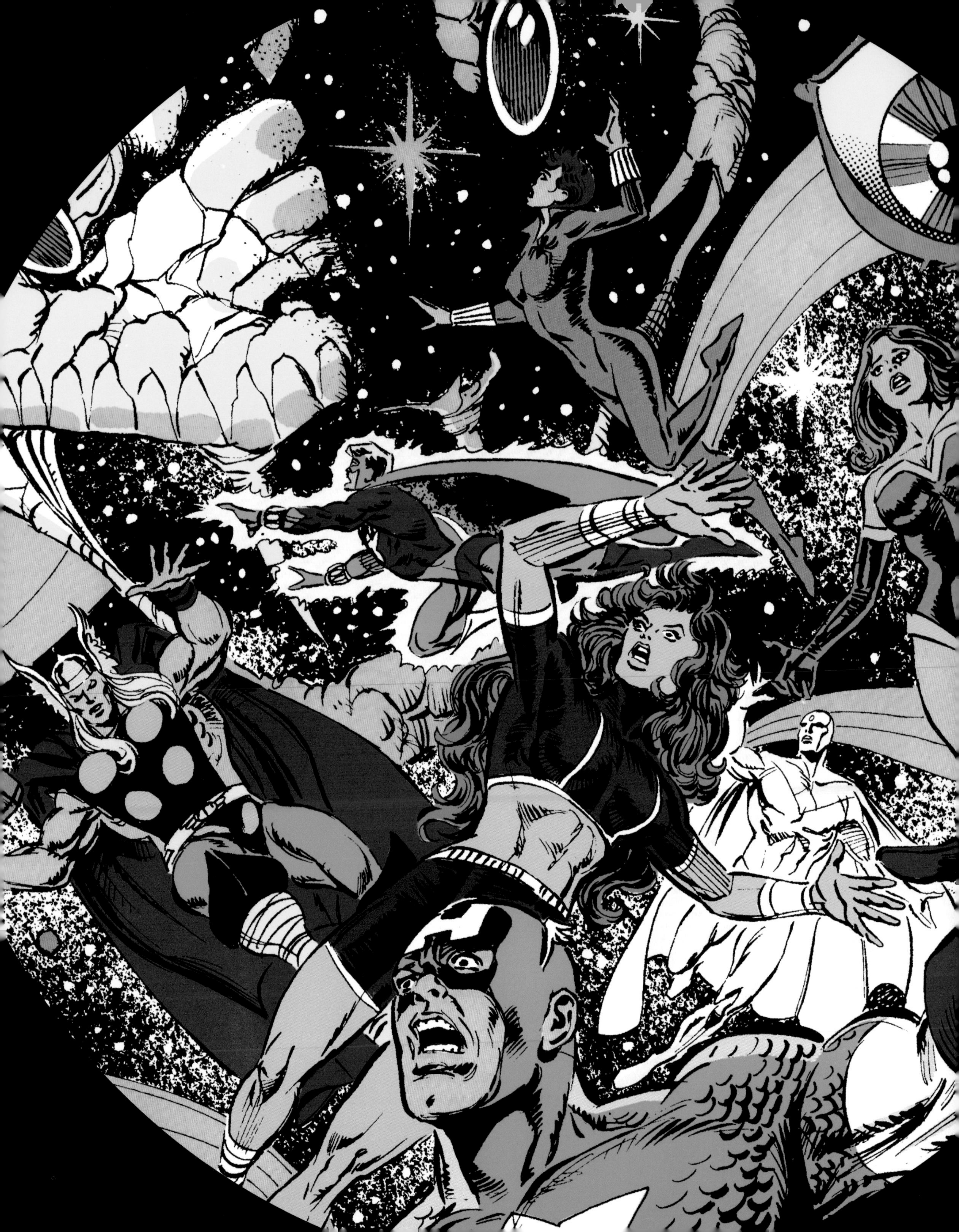

Avenger at Last

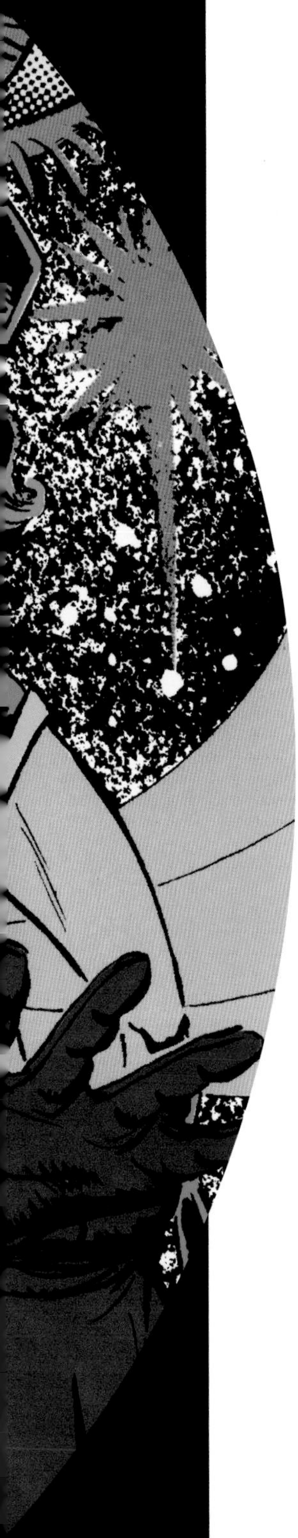

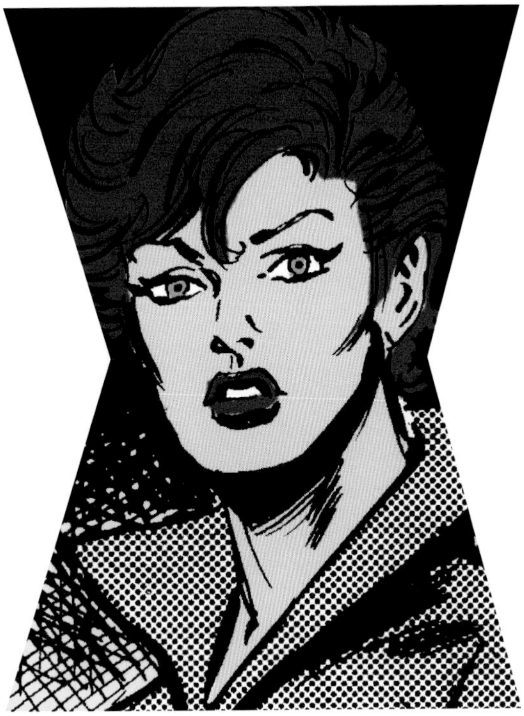

AVENGERS #330 (MAR. 1991) Black Widow's first mission as an official Avenger showed her just how different her new life would be from the shadowy world of espionage.

With the new era came a milestone moment—after years as a reserve Avenger, Black Widow was finally named as one of the team's core members. Any celebrations were short-lived, however. At the ceremony to introduce the lineup to the press and the public, the entire team was sent to the Dimension of Exile by a group of cosmic beings called the Tetrarchs of Entropy. This adventure into the cosmos, followed by a battle with demons on Brooklyn's streets, was a perfect example of the kind of mission Natasha would find herself facing as an Avenger. But even in this world of super-powered aliens and alternate dimensions, she would still find her place as someone with good old-fashioned espionage skills and a head for strategy.

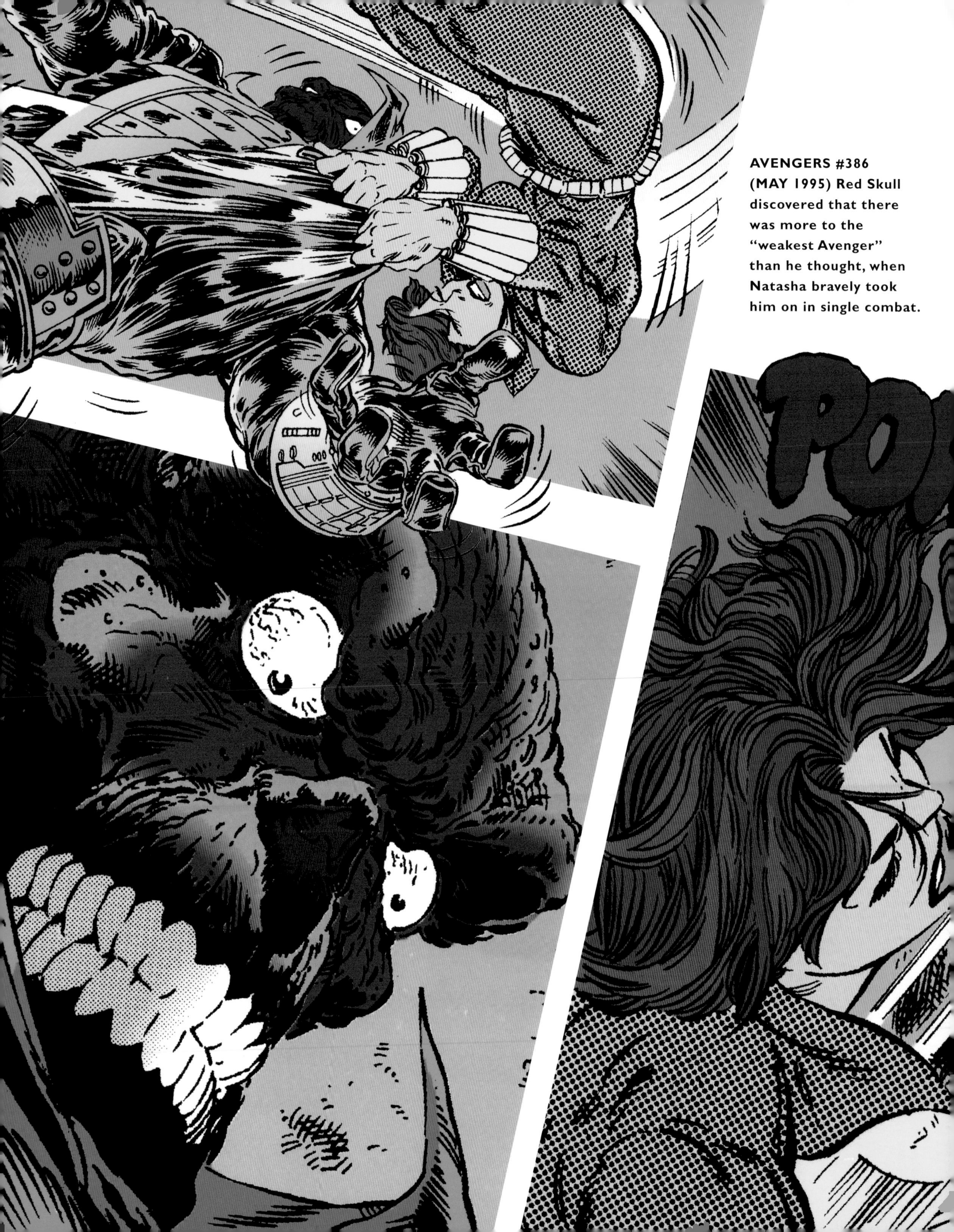

AVENGERS #386 (MAY 1995) Red Skull discovered that there was more to the "weakest Avenger" than he thought, when Natasha bravely took him on in single combat.

Hunt for Red Oktober

Some areas of Natasha Romanoff's undiscovered past had deadly ramifications that went way beyond just her and the people she knew. When she heard that an agent codenamed "Oktober" was planning to set off US nuclear missiles to trigger World War III, she enlisted the help of Iron Man as the most suitable hero for the job. Evading several layers of lethal security, the pair got into the NORAD (North American Aerospace Defense) Command installation and into the locked room containing the nuclear buttons. At first, Iron Man thought that Agent Oktober was not there, but he was disavowed of that a moment later when Black Widow revealed that she was Oktober! She was, in fact, brainwashed and under Soviet control.

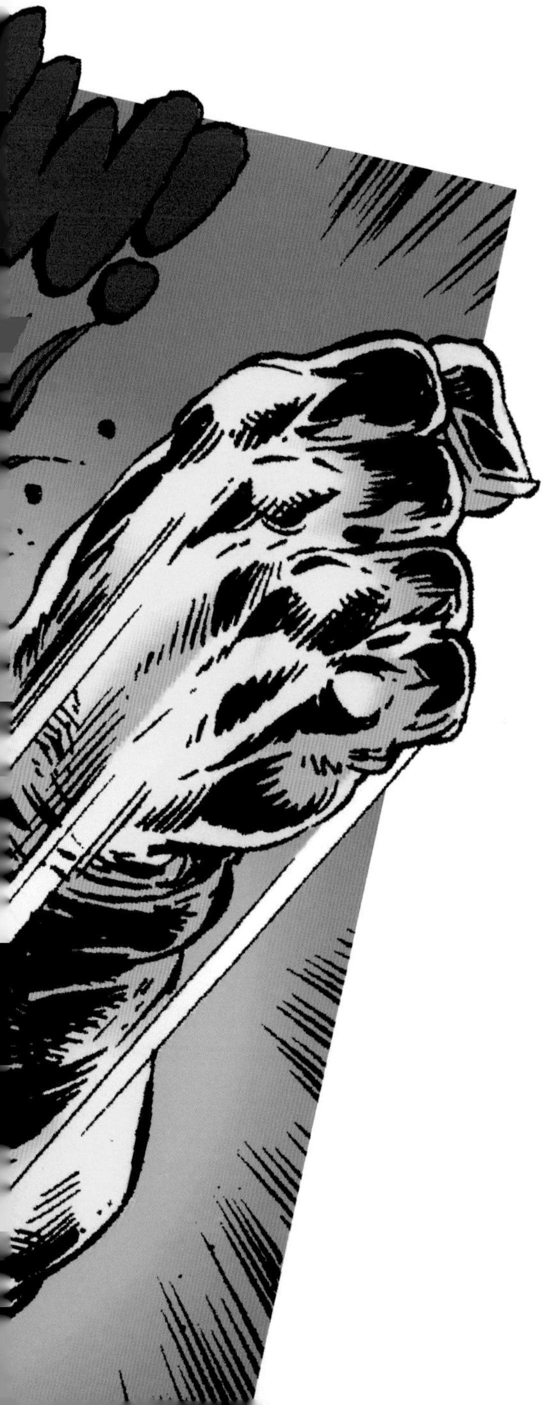

Natasha then immobilized Iron Man and fired the missiles before leaving, apparently having caused inevitable nuclear war between the US and Russia. Shocked, Iron Man got to his feet, and took to the skies to stop the missiles reaching Russian airspace. When he returned, he found Black Widow had commandeered a jet. Now no longer under an external influence, Natasha was going after the person she believed to be responsible for turning her into an unwilling sleeper agent. She had deduced that it was the Russian attaché to the UN—and a former teacher of hers from the KGB—who had pledged to cause Armageddon if communism failed. He had been responsible for implanting the necessary commands in Natasha's brain many years before. When they caught up with him, Black Widow and Iron Man broke the news of the failed plot to the attaché, and stopped him from taking his own life. As a result, he was able to corroborate Natasha's innocence in the whole Oktober affair.

By this point, Black Widow was such an established figure in the Avengers that Steve Rogers named her chairperson while he took a leave of absence. Busy with her team, Natasha Romanoff was nevertheless delighted to see Ivan Petrovitch again after a long separation. He, too, had been busy on missions for S.H.I.E.L.D., and had discovered a strange energy pulse in Canada's North-West Territories, intel he passed to his little Czarina so she and the Avengers could investigate.

Natasha led a reconnaissance team who found a huge crater at the site of the energy source. At the bottom lurked the Red Skull with Ivan, whom he had taken prisoner. Seeing Ivan hurt, Natasha angrily confronted the villain, who scornfully derided her as the weakest Avenger. She fought him valiantly, and was just about to deliver a crucial blow with her Widow's Bite when he teleported away. She was furious with herself for not acting more quickly, although Ivan, returning to consciousness, reminded her that few people went one-on-one with the Red Skull and lived to tell the tale.

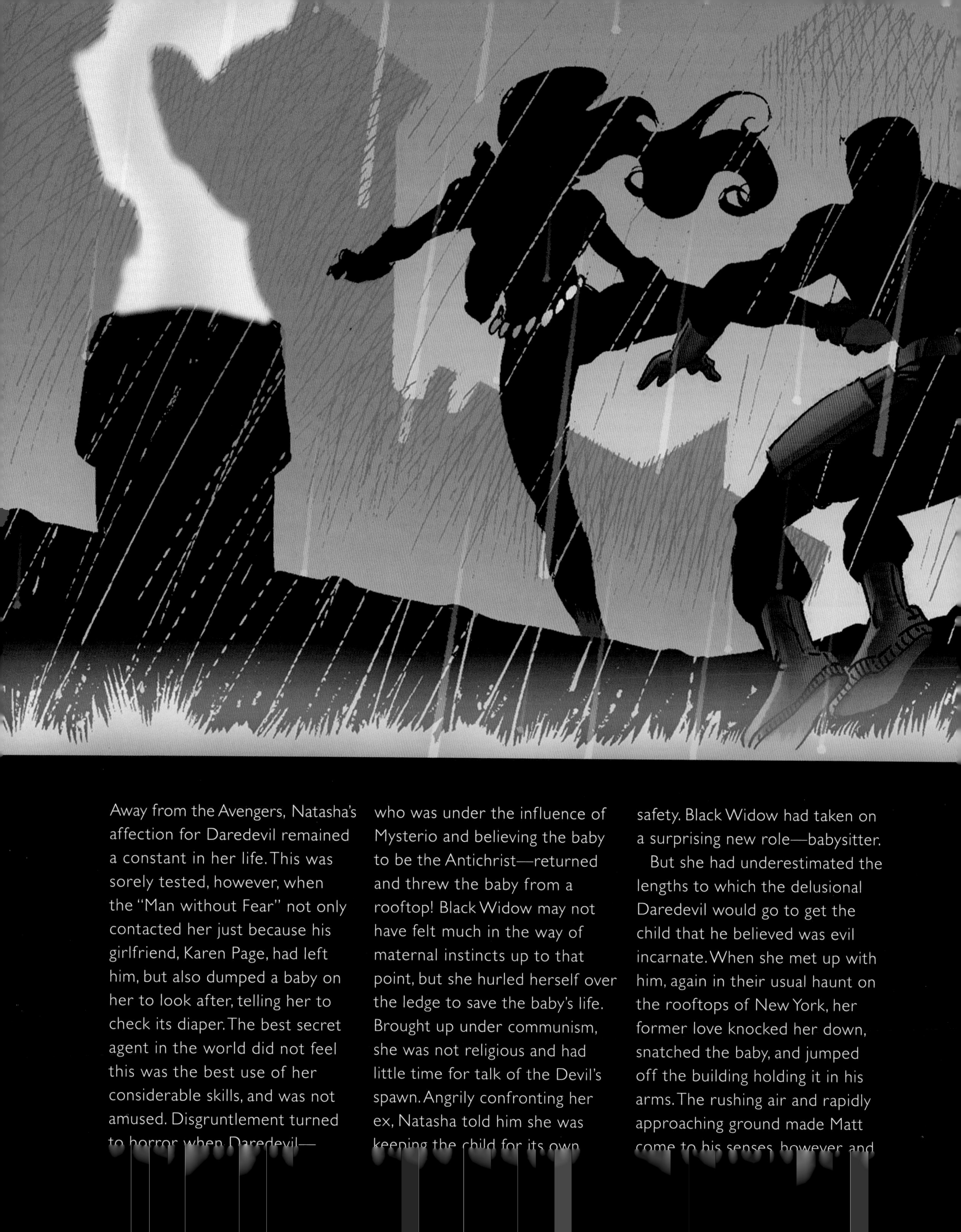

Away from the Avengers, Natasha's affection for Daredevil remained a constant in her life. This was sorely tested, however, when the "Man without Fear" not only contacted her just because his girlfriend, Karen Page, had left him, but also dumped a baby on her to look after, telling her to check its diaper. The best secret agent in the world did not feel this was the best use of her considerable skills, and was not amused. Disgruntlement turned to horror when Daredevil—who was under the influence of Mysterio and believing the baby to be the Antichrist—returned and threw the baby from a rooftop! Black Widow may not have felt much in the way of maternal instincts up to that point, but she hurled herself over the ledge to save the baby's life. Brought up under communism, she was not religious and had little time for talk of the Devil's spawn. Angrily confronting her ex, Natasha told him she was keeping the child for its own safety. Black Widow had taken on a surprising new role—babysitter.

But she had underestimated the lengths to which the delusional Daredevil would go to get the child that he believed was evil incarnate. When she met up with him, again in their usual haunt on the rooftops of New York, her former love knocked her down, snatched the baby, and jumped off the building holding it in his arms. The rushing air and rapidly approaching ground made Matt come to his senses, however, and

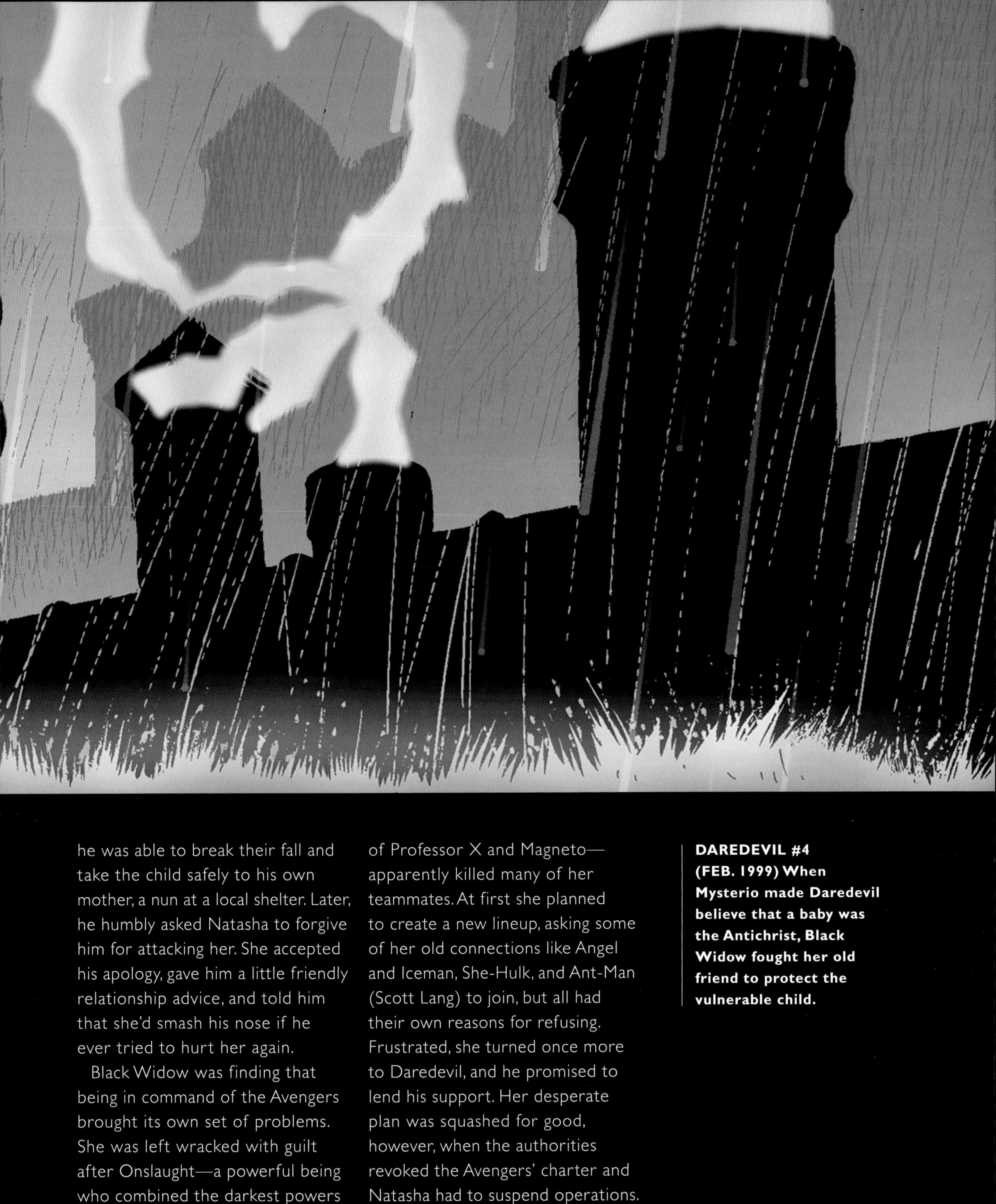

he was able to break their fall and take the child safely to his own mother, a nun at a local shelter. Later, he humbly asked Natasha to forgive him for attacking her. She accepted his apology, gave him a little friendly relationship advice, and told him that she'd smash his nose if he ever tried to hurt her again.

Black Widow was finding that being in command of the Avengers brought its own set of problems. She was left wracked with guilt after Onslaught—a powerful being who combined the darkest powers of Professor X and Magneto—apparently killed many of her teammates. At first she planned to create a new lineup, asking some of her old connections like Angel and Iceman, She-Hulk, and Ant-Man (Scott Lang) to join, but all had their own reasons for refusing. Frustrated, she turned once more to Daredevil, and he promised to lend his support. Her desperate plan was squashed for good, however, when the authorities revoked the Avengers' charter and Natasha had to suspend operations.

DAREDEVIL #4 (FEB. 1999) When Mysterio made Daredevil believe that a baby was the Antichrist, Black Widow fought her old friend to protect the vulnerable child.

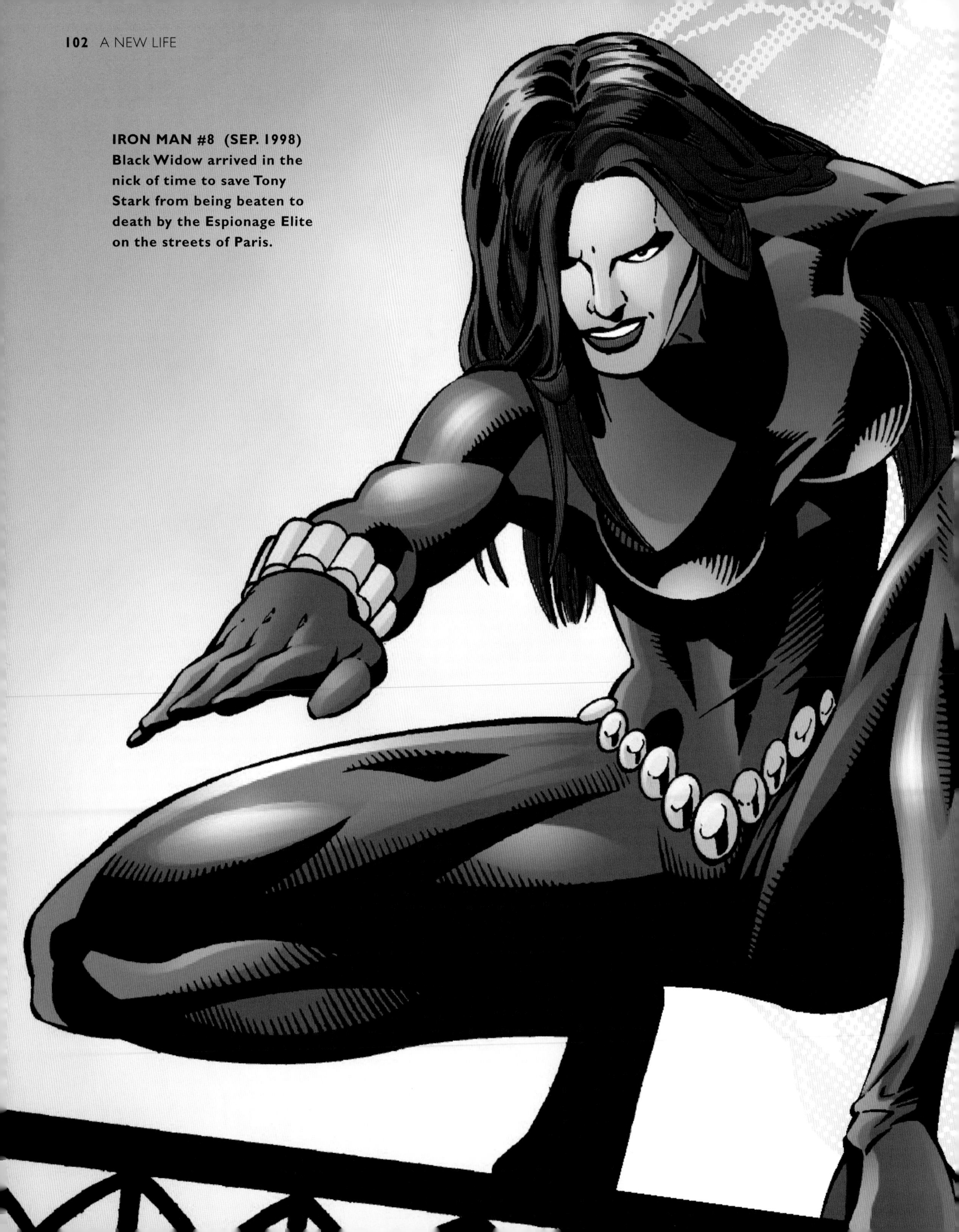

IRON MAN #8 (SEP. 1998)
Black Widow arrived in the nick of time to save Tony Stark from being beaten to death by the Espionage Elite on the streets of Paris.

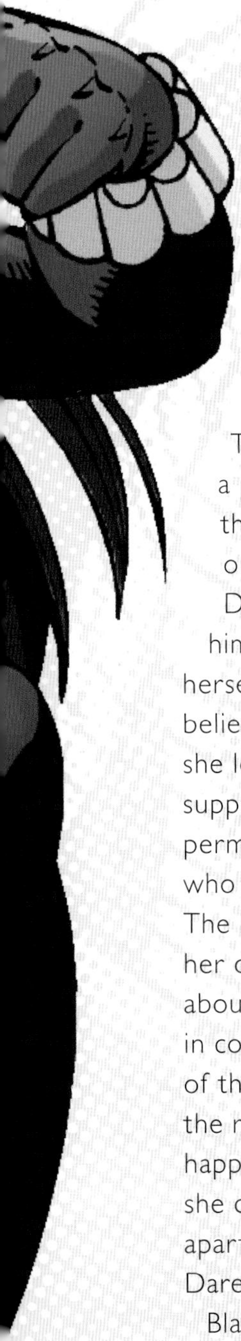

Rough Justice

Tormented by survivor's guilt, Natasha made a pledge to personally destroy all the villains that the Avengers had ever fought. Number one on her list was the Grey Gargoyle, but when Daredevil swung in to help she angrily pushed him aside—she wanted to take on the Gargoyle herself, as her penance for the curse that she believed had struck again to take away those whom she loved. Black Widow had long struggled to suppress a darker side, a side that favored more permanent solutions to the problem of villains who returned again and again to plague humanity. The loss of her teammates seemed to have pushed her over the edge, and Daredevil later found her about to shoot the villainous mutant Omega Red in cold blood. When Natasha told him to get out of the way, Matt refused, only to find himself on the receiving end of a bullet. The unthinkable had happened—his old partner had shot him. However, she did patch him up and carry him back to his apartment before disappearing. Her actions gave Daredevil hope that perhaps he could still reach her.

Black Widow resurfaced in a Russian expatriate community in Brighton Beach, where certain interested parties had heard what had happened with Daredevil and her deadly quest, and were eager to discover whether she could be brought back into the fold to work for the land of her birth. When Daredevil followed her, he was captured by the Russians. The fact that he had survived aroused their suspicions, and Natasha was put in a cell with him. As they talked, Black Widow stuck with the story that she had shot him when he stopped her killing Omega Red, but Matt soon realized that she was tapping her fingers ever so slightly, sending him Morse code messages that only he, with his heightened senses, could hear. Her "Avenging Avenger" stance had been a ruse: a S.H.I.E.L.D. mission to enable her to get close to certain underworld figures. They were ex-KGB and thought to have access to powerful agents and weapons that she had been sent to stop. However, Natasha's countrymen were not buying her act, and as they took her away to be interrogated she slipped Daredevil one last kiss—and a lock-pick for his handcuffs. By the time he had freed himself and reached her, she had already managed to escape herself, cornering her interrogator, General Tskarov, in the tunnels beneath the building. At first she seemed to be toying with the idea of using some of her most painful KGB tricks on the general, but she declared that she was not that person any more. After she and Daredevil shared a lingering kiss, they departed, friends once more.

Later, Natasha's guilt was assuaged in the best possible way, when all the lost heroes of the Avengers were found to be still alive, having been kept safe in a pocket universe. However, Natasha still felt that she had failed as a Super Hero, and wanted to return to being an agent again. She stepped back from the Avengers and began taking missions from S.H.I.E.L.D. One such assignment involved tracking down a gang who had been abducting brilliant scientists and engineers, and Black Widow knew the perfect person to use as bait—Tony Stark. Having successfully rescued the missing scientists, Black Widow's path would cross Iron Man's once again in Paris. He had been set upon by a shady group known as the Espionage Elite while out of his armor. Luckily, Black Widow was in the area. She dispatched the Espionage Elite with her close combat skills, but not before they had left Stark without a pulse. Unable to revive him any other way, Natasha used her Widow's Bite to shock his heart back to life.

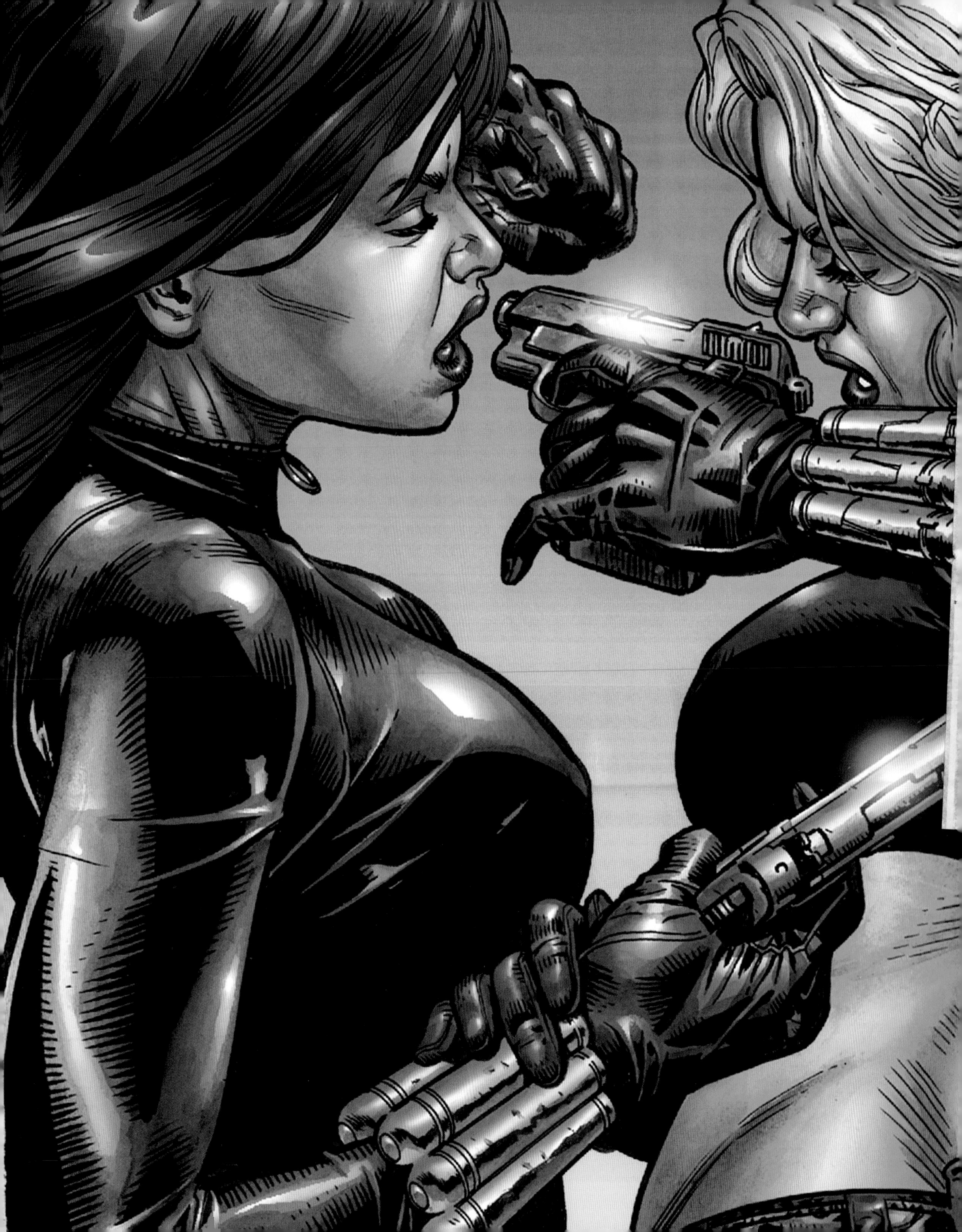

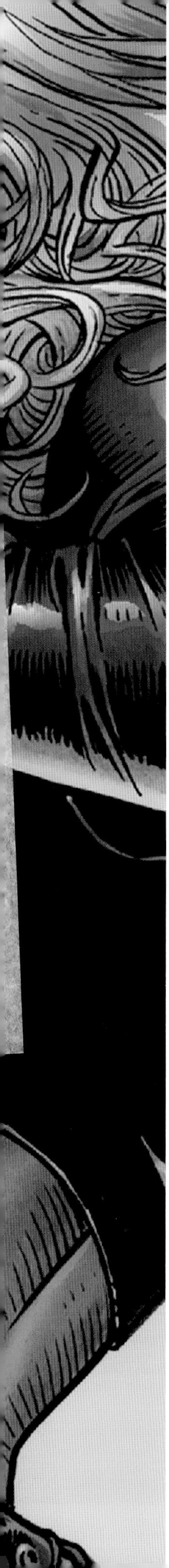

Widow vs. Widow

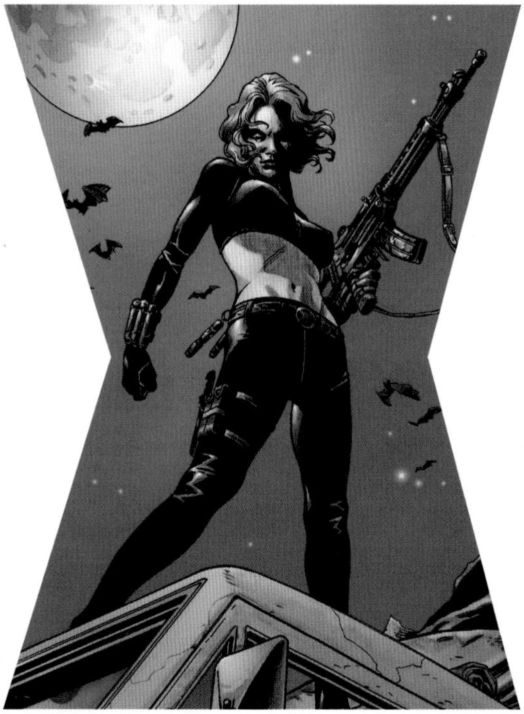

BLACK WIDOW #3 (AUG. 1999) Natasha discovered that she was not the only Black Widow when she ran into Yelena Belova on a mission, but experience gave the original the edge.

Past and present collided when Black Widow was on a mission in Rhapastan. Sent to retrieve a sample of a terrifying new bio-weapon and bring it back to the US, she encountered a foreign agent on an identical mission for her own country… named Black Widow. It seemed that the end of the Cold War had not signaled the end of the Red Room, and Russia was still training agents who were taught to admire the exploits of the great Natasha Romanoff, even if they were not encouraged to follow her defector's path.

BLACK WIDOW #3 (MAR. 2001) When Natasha had her appearance changed to resemble Yelena Belova, and vice versa, many felt she had crossed a line, no matter how good her intentions.

Yelena Belova had also been granted the title of Black Widow, and boasted to Natasha that she was the first student ever to achieve better marks than the original. However, it was Natasha, not Yelena, who walked away with the bio-weapon. Experience counted for a lot more than test scores, it seemed.

The new Black Widow, though, did not give up so easily, and tracked Natasha to Zurich, where she had taken the scientist who had created the bio-weapon and ordered him to create an antidote. This had not been a part of her assignment, but Natasha saw the bigger picture: looking beyond the petty motivations of national governments and trying to act in humanity's best interests. When Yelena showed up again to attack her, Natasha gave her the benefit of some of the wisdom she had learned in her years as a spy. She urged the young woman to think again about the path she had chosen, which would lead her to surrender her identity and her personal life to do the Russian state's bidding. Better to be Yelena than be Black Widow. But before the younger woman could reply, Natasha was shot in the back, falling into Yelena's arms.

Yelena continued with her mission, traveling back to Rhapastan to stop the army commander of that nation infecting anybody with the bio-weapon. However, she was captured, and all looked lost until Natasha arrived. She had faked her death to shake off Yelena, telling her she did not like working with a shadow. Natasha had managed to vaccinate all the soldiers in the area, so when the weapon was deployed, only the commander was infected. When the US Army arrived, Natasha debriefed them. As for Yelena, she had learned enough from following Natasha to be able to slip away from the authorities.

Later, when Natasha heard about a rogue Russian trying to steal nuclear weapons from the US, she saw an opportunity to teach her counterpart Yelena Belova a little more about espionage, while also saving her life in the process. Natasha was concerned that Yelena's youth and naiveté would get her killed, so she came up with a drastic and shocking plan. She had S.H.I.E.L.D. kidnap Belova and then subject both Black Widows to plastic surgery, in effect swapping their faces. Now Romanoff could take on Belova's mission and use her years of experience and wisdom to stop the younger woman getting killed by her unscrupulous employers. In the meantime, Yelena had woken up in Natasha's apartment, struggling to make sense of it all. When the mission was over, and their faces later swapped back, Yelena was furious that Natasha had taken such a drastic step without her knowledge. But Natasha emphasized that Yelena should not see herself as a hero—she was a spy, and she had to learn that espionage was a nasty business, and that she would be controlled and manipulated by others.

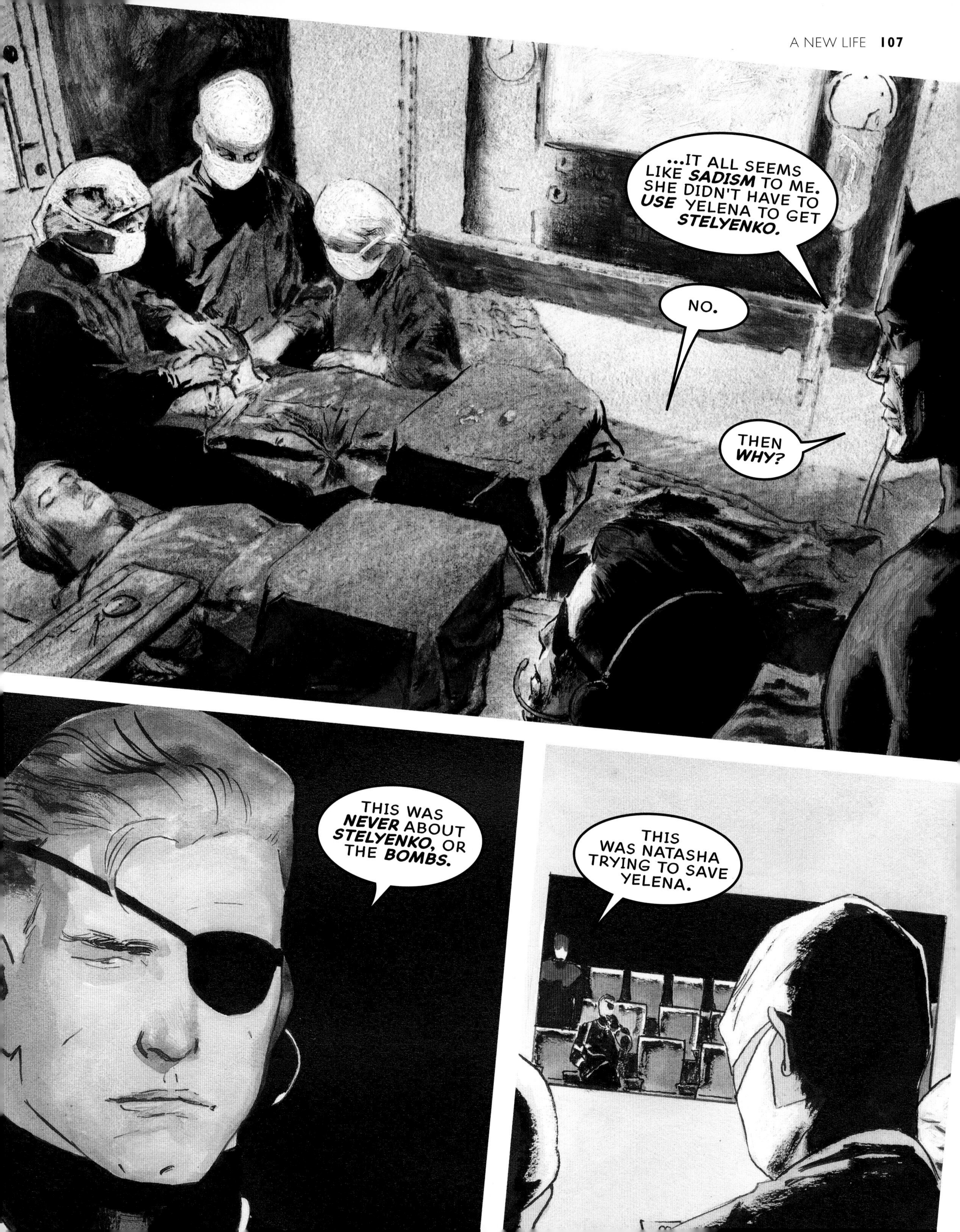
...IT ALL SEEMS LIKE SADISM TO ME. SHE DIDN'T HAVE TO USE YELENA TO GET STELYENKO.
NO.
THEN WHY?
THIS WAS NEVER ABOUT STELYENKO, OR THE BOMBS.
THIS WAS NATASHA TRYING TO SAVE YELENA.

Secrets and Lies

SECRET WAR #2 (JUL. 2004) In a mission that demanded the utmost secrecy, Black Widow was the obvious choice to be Nick Fury's right hand in Latveria.

Natasha played a pivotal role in the most secret of covert ops when she discovered that the villainous engineer known as the Tinkerer was in Latveria meeting with its head of state, Lucia von Bardas. Relaying the information to Nick Fury, the two concluded that Latveria was helping the Tinkerer arm all the villains in the US who used technology to commit crime. When Fury told the US authorities, they were unwilling to act due to the risk it would pose to international relations. Fury knew he had to deal with it himself, even without the oversight of S.H.I.E.L.D. He also knew he could trust Black Widow to do what needed to be done, and enlisted her as part of a team to assassinate Lucia before she could facilitate an act of mass terror.

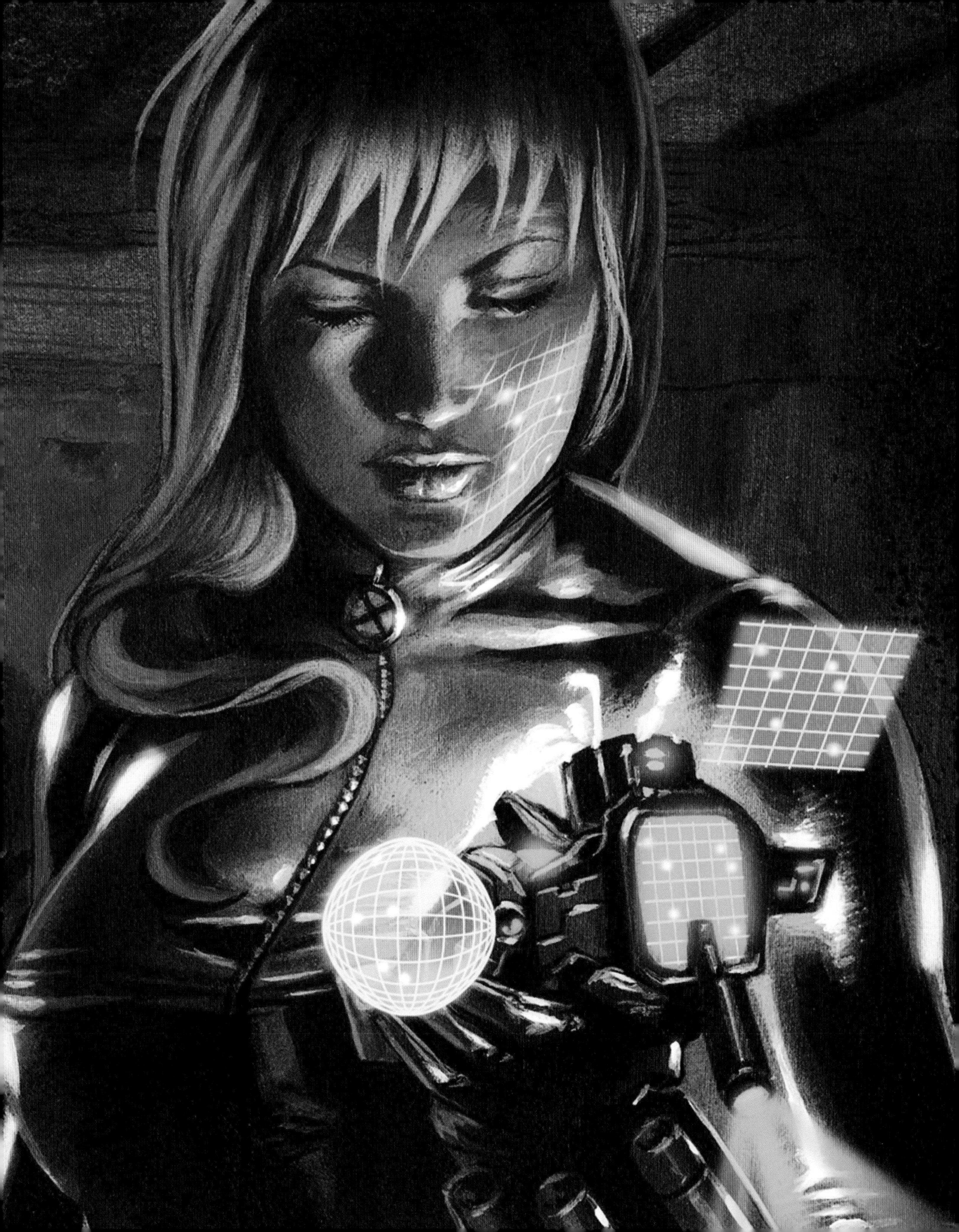

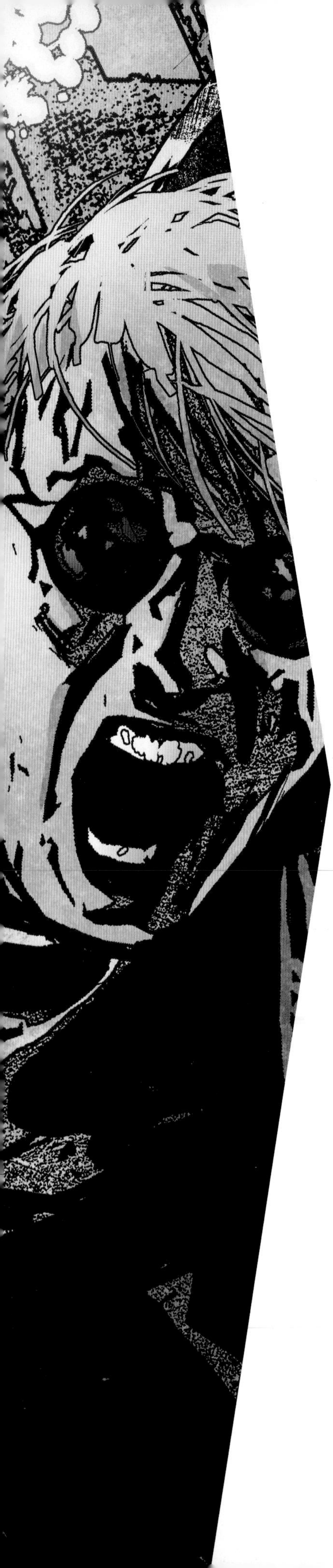

Black Widow and Nick Fury by this point had known each other long enough to have a mutual trust and respect greater than they had for almost anyone else. After her involvement in Fury's "Secret War," their loyalty to each other was proven once again when Fury risked his job to tip off Natasha that the government had agreed to swap her for Madame Hydra in an exchange deal with Bulgaria, so that Black Widow could answer there for her alleged crimes. Natasha went to Daredevil, hoping to hide in plain sight. She suspected that there was more to it than even Fury or the government knew, and that someone in her past had orchestrated this opportunity to get her into their clutches. She soon found out that whoever the mystery person was, they were happy to get her dead or alive, after she and Daredevil were shot at as they sat outside a busy New York café.

She told Matt defiantly that, while she accepted some day she might be killed in this way, and that she may even have it coming after the many shady deeds of her long life, she would not go quietly, and she would go on her terms. When her would-be assassin was caught, Fury made him talk about who had paid him to go after Black Widow. The answer was shocking—it had been Natasha's husband, Alexei Shostakov, alive after all and living in Bulgaria. The years had not been kind to him, leaving him so embittered and resentful of his wife that all he could think of was to use the money and power he had amassed to bring her down. But Natasha demonstrated that she had plenty of friends who were willing to stand by her, traveling to Bulgaria and arresting Alexei with the backup of S.H.I.E.L.D. agents and the Avengers.

Natasha's brush with death at the behest of Alexei was followed by the devastating loss of her former boyfriend, Hawkeye, who was killed in the chaos caused by the Avenger Scarlet Witch going insane (Hawkeye was later returned to life when the Scarlet Witch restored reality). The events made Natasha ever more determined to get away from New York, away from the places that held so many dark memories. She made a big decision—retiring from her activities as Black Widow and going to live in Arizona. Here she sought to lose herself in rock-climbing and the wonders of nature. But that was never destined to be the life for Natasha Romanoff, and trouble would soon draw her back into the great game…

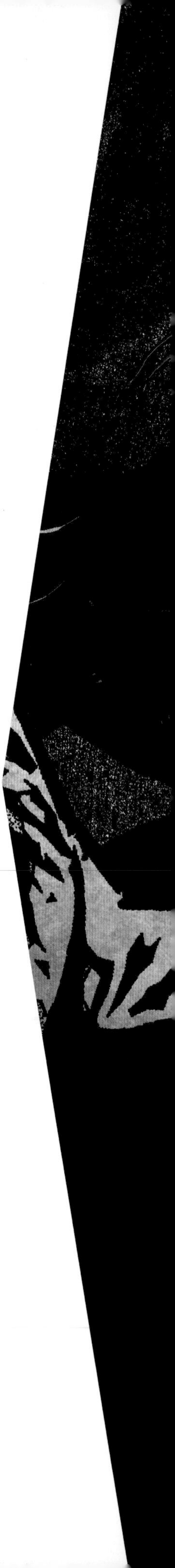

DAREDEVIL #62 (SEP. 2004)
Hunted by her ex-husband Alexei, Natasha's friends were again endangered as she and Daredevil narrowly avoided a sniper's bullets.

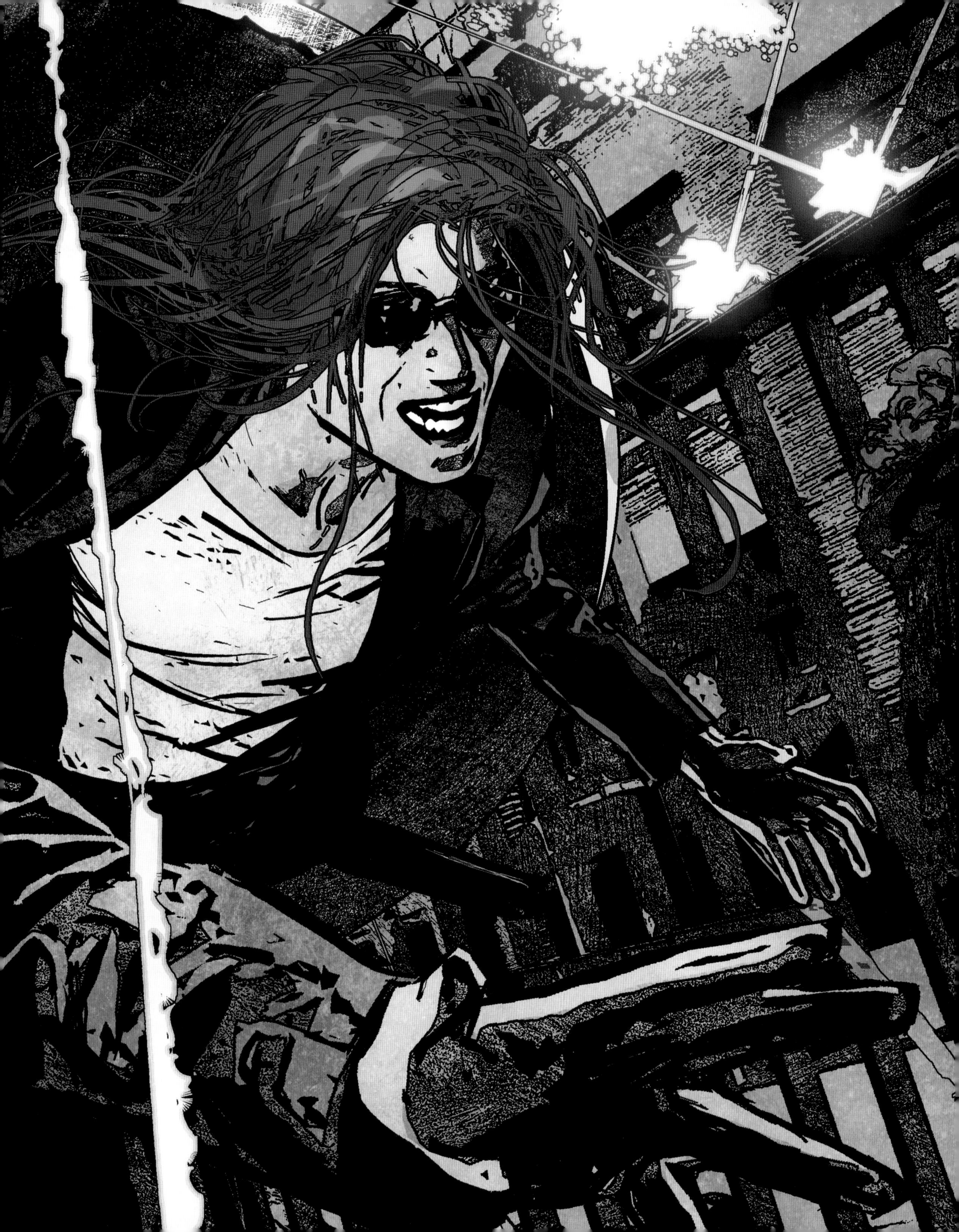

The Battle Within

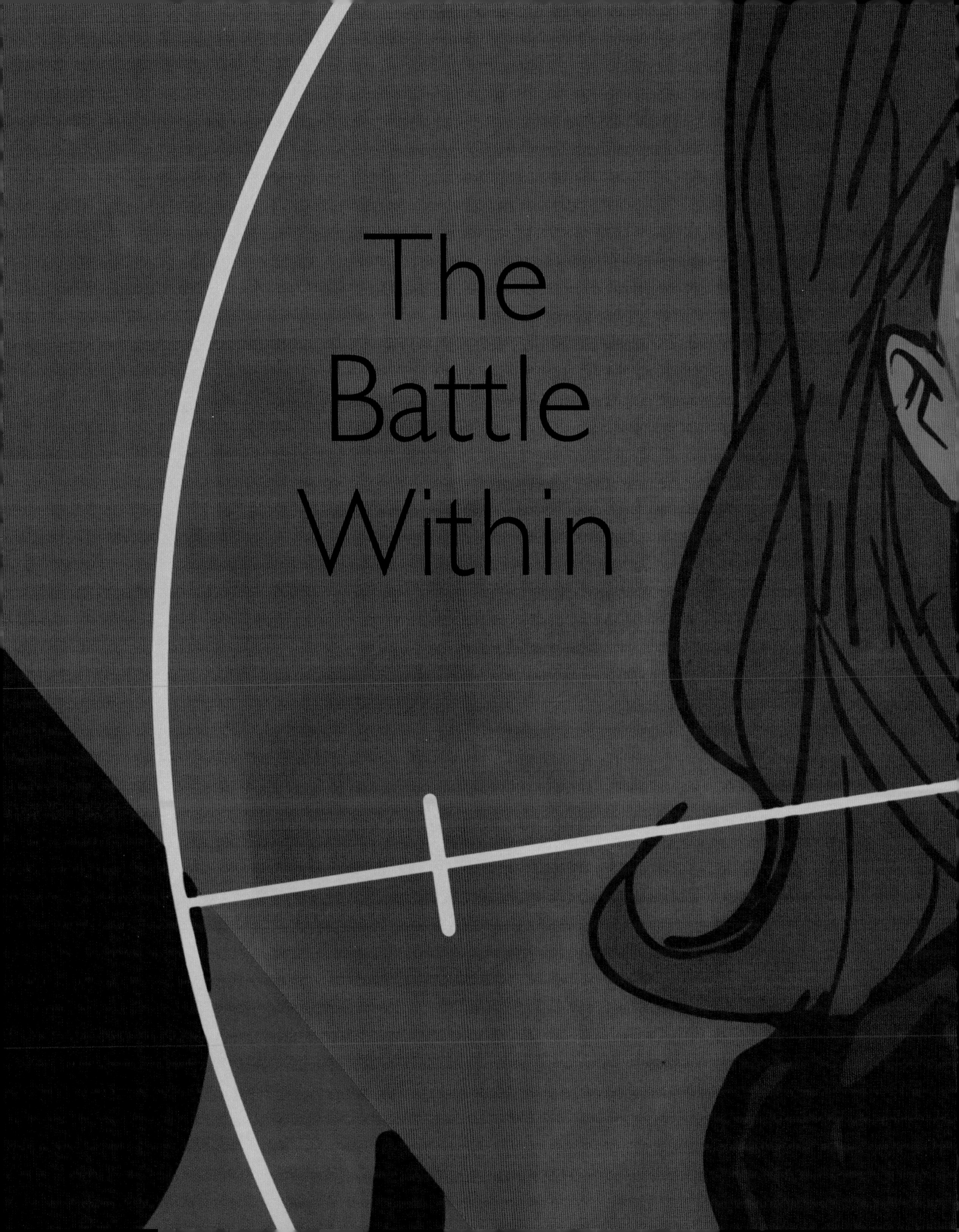

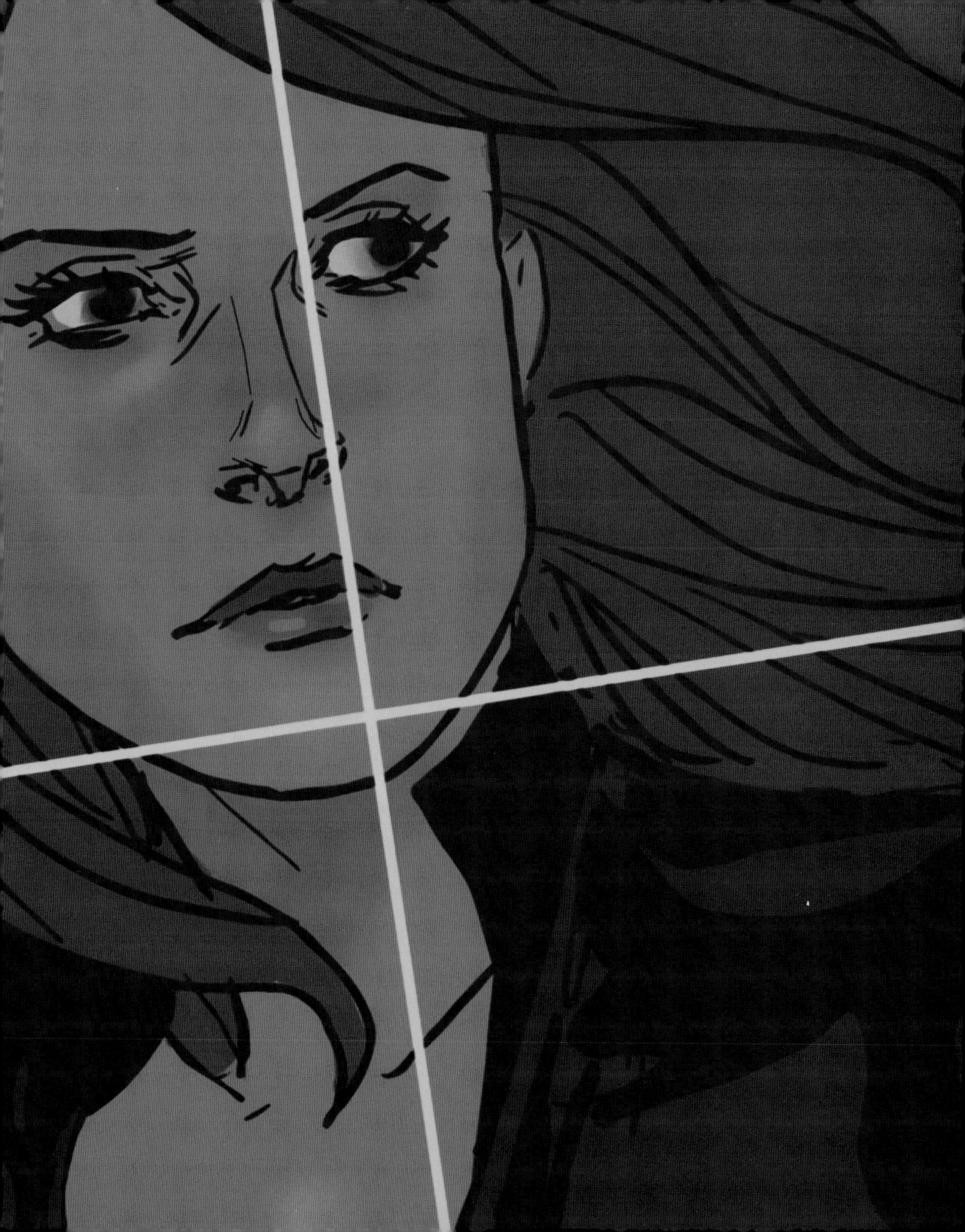

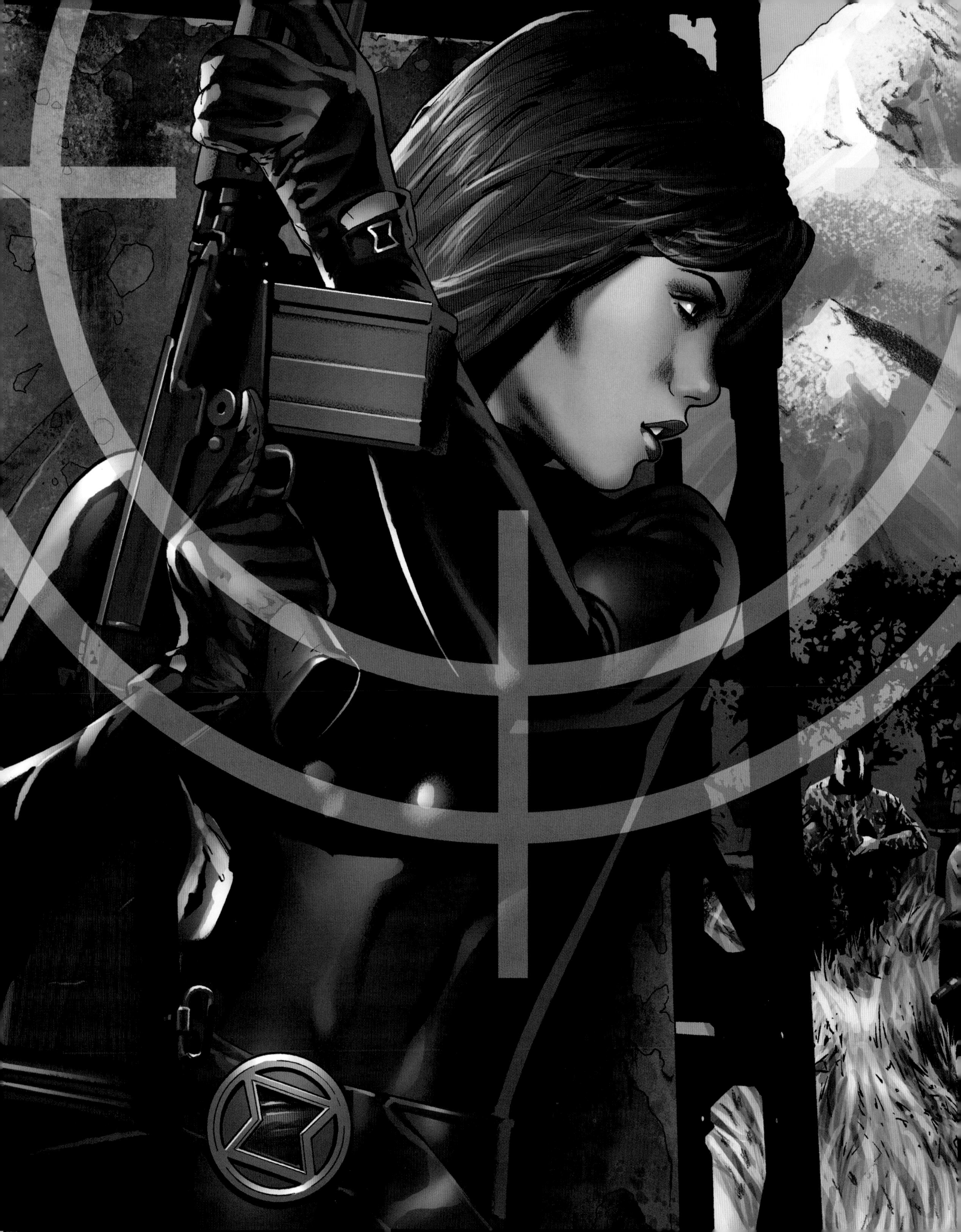

America's Most Wanted

BLACK WIDOW #5 (MAR. 2005) Investigating the deaths of former Red Room agents led Natasha deep into her past, and onto the wrong side of the law.

Black Widow had retired, moving away from the life of a super-spy to a tranquil haven in the wilds of Arizona. After one too many losses and injuries to those she held dear, perhaps total solitude would provide a shield against her "curse." It was not long, however, before the ex-hunter became the hunted. When a stranger flagged her down on a lonely desert road pleading car trouble, Natasha Romanoff's natural instincts kicked in, and she knew that, however reluctantly, she was going to have to get back into the game.

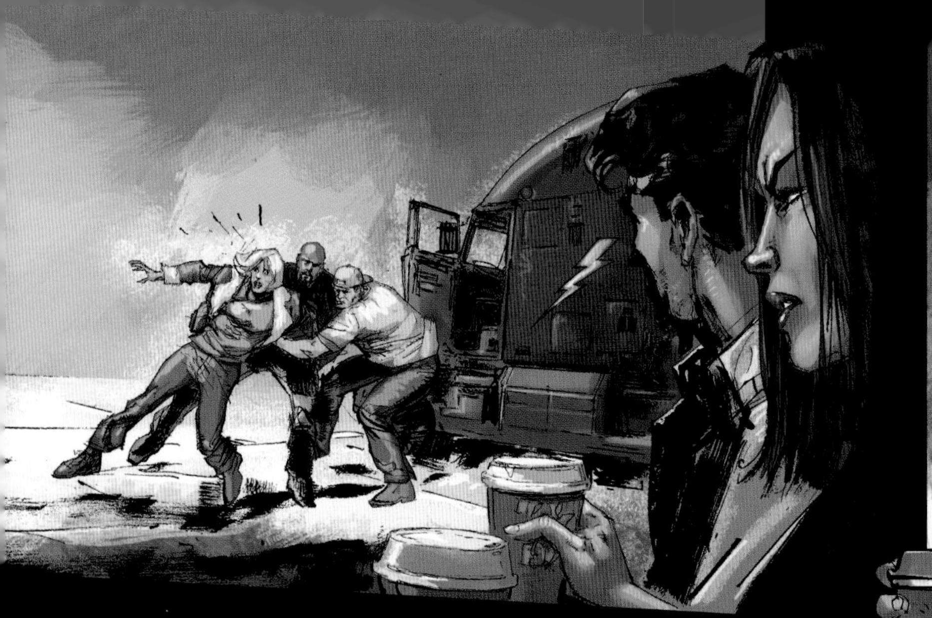

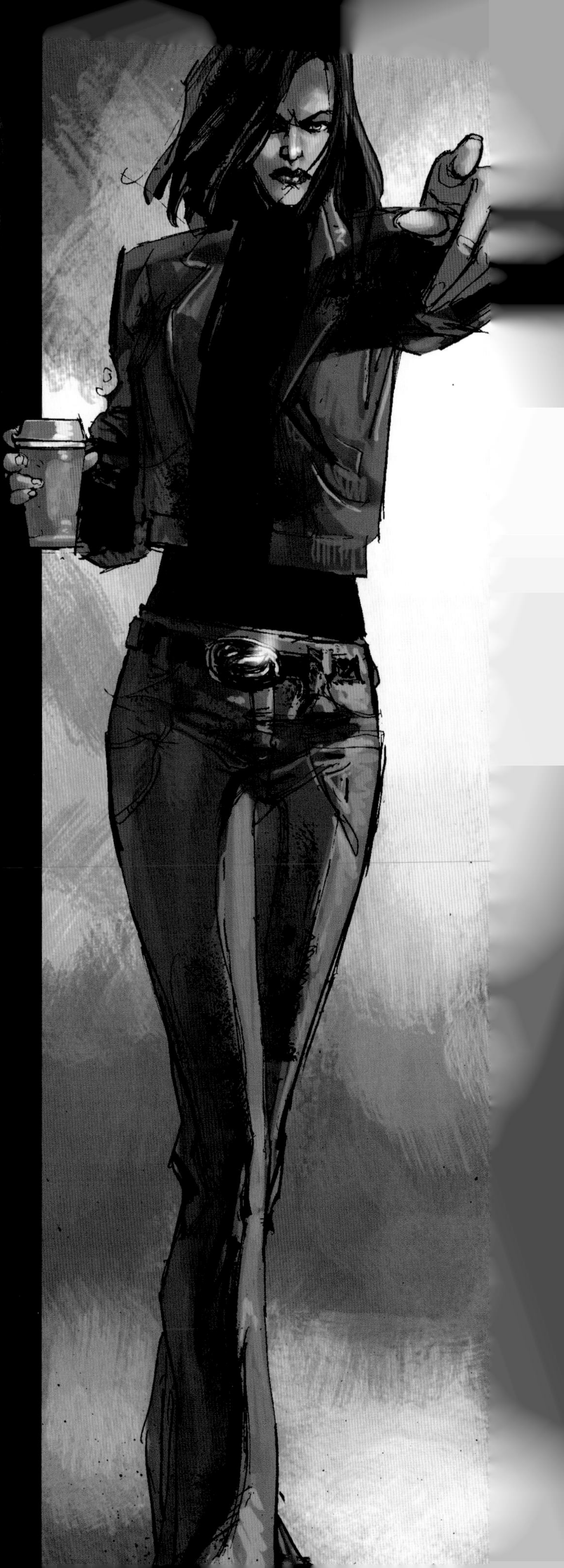

"I promise you this. If you don't let her go right now, neither of you will ever walk again."

BLACK WIDOW

When the stranger attacked her, as she had known he would, she took him down and waited for answers. They never came. The man would rather bleed out than reveal anything to her. This told Natasha that she was dealing with an old-school agent.

Wanting to stay off the grid, Black Widow looked up one of her old contacts—a former S.H.I.E.L.D. agent called Phil Dexter—who owed her a favor. To help identify her attacker, she brought Dexter a grisly souvenir: one of the dead man's fingers, complete with an extremely distinctive ring. The two also discovered that a female ex-KGB operative had been killed in Alabama, so they set off cross-country to find out if it was linked to the attack on Natasha. En route they were distracted from their mission when they witnessed a young girl being threatened by two truckers. There was no way Black Widow was going to turn a blind eye to this male brutality, and she

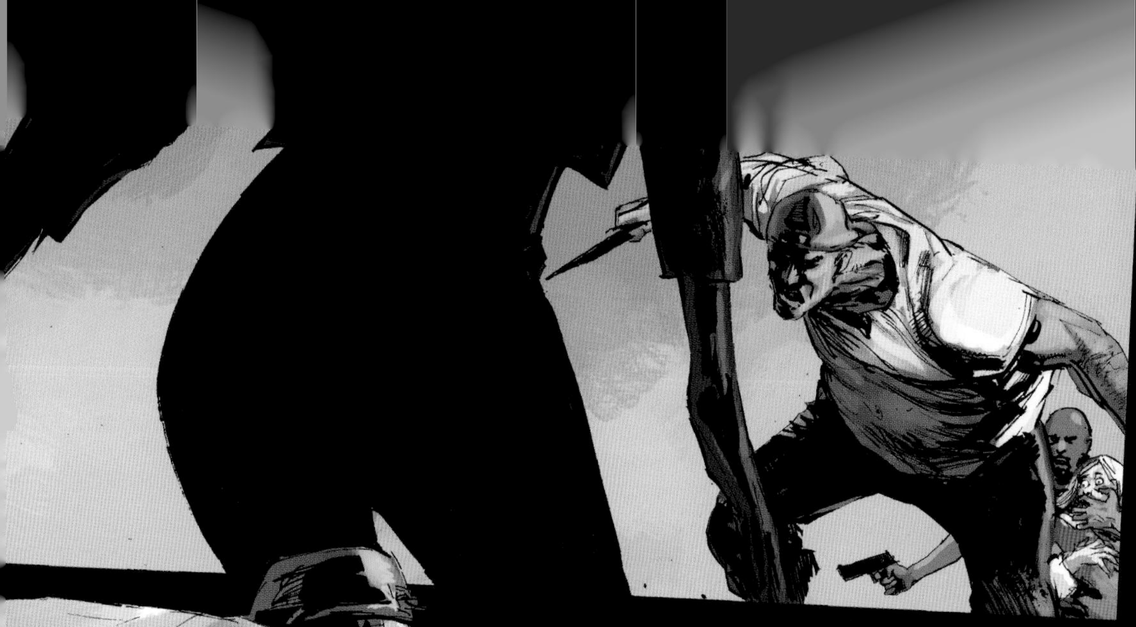

Opposite and left: **BLACK WIDOW #1 (NOV. 2004)** Despite the importance of her mission, Black Widow couldn't stand by and ignore a young girl in trouble, intervening with such brutality that it shocked the hardened secret agent who was accompanying her.

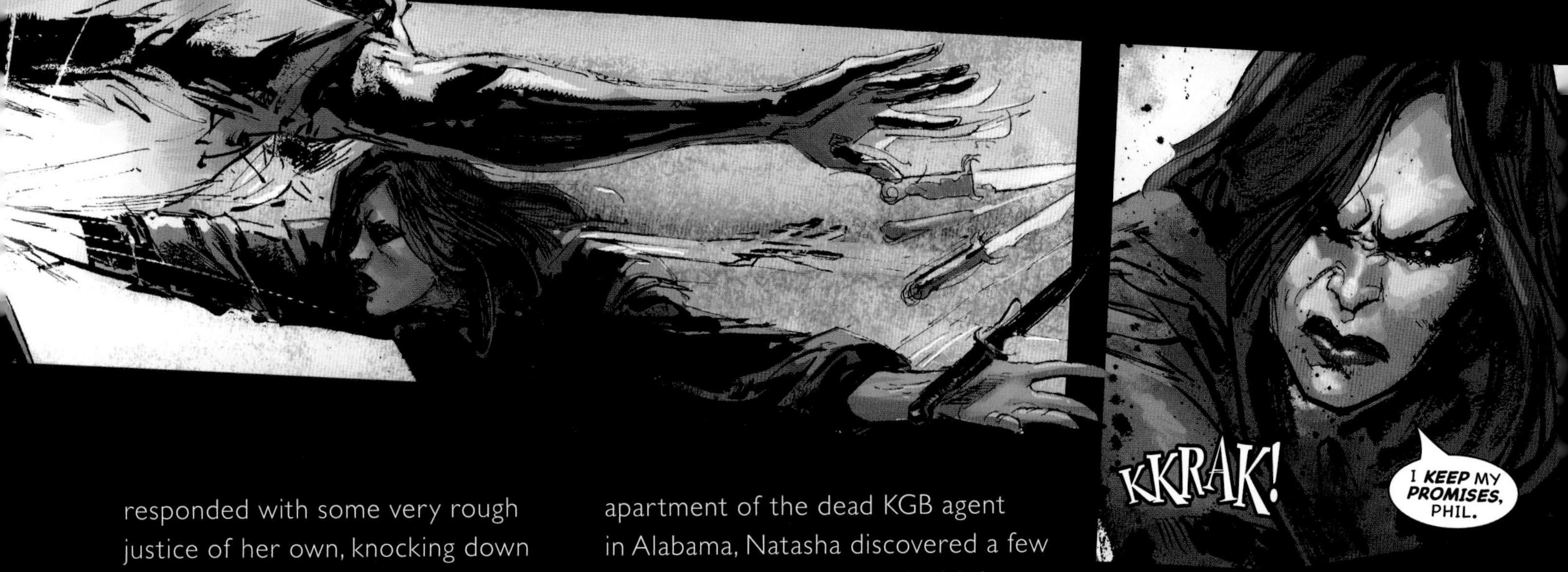

KKRAK!
I KEEP MY PROMISES, PHIL.

responded with some very rough justice of her own, knocking down and crippling both men. Natasha was no longer an Avenger or an agent of S.H.I.E.L.D.—the only rules she had were those she laid down for herself. She was out on her own, operating in a world where her enemies had no scruples about what they did to her, and she would play the game accordingly.

Natasha had shed her old gauntlets, declaring that they were too heavy and difficult to maintain. She now went on missions armed like most agents, with regular firearms—but augmented, of course, with her training, experience, and the serum with which she had been injected all those years ago. Searching the apartment of the dead KGB agent in Alabama, Natasha discovered a few mementos that resonated with her, particularly a coded letter from the KGB ordering the agent to return to the USSR. She, too, had received one of those, and had chosen to ignore it and take her chances in the West—just like the dead female Russian agent had done.

Right: BLACK WIDOW #2 (DEC. 2004) When Natasha found a coded Russian letter in a dead woman's home, she realized they were dealing with a murdered former spy.

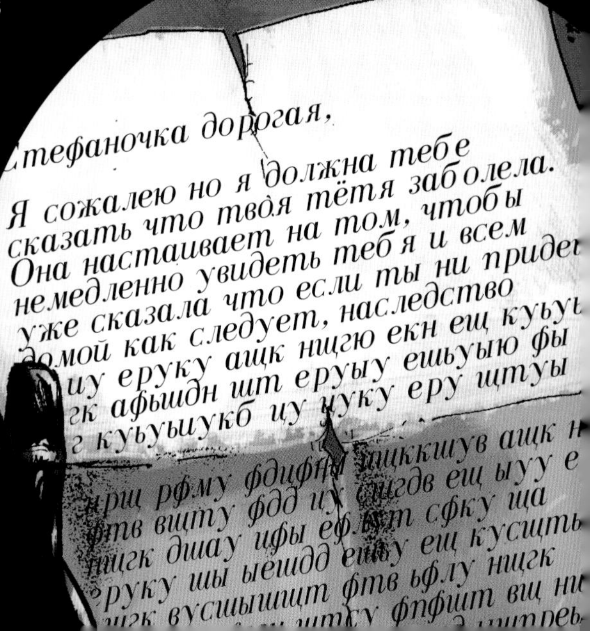

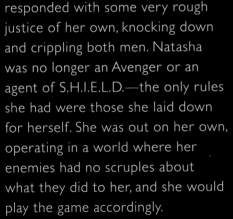

Стефаночка дорогая,
Я сожалею но я должна тебе
сказать что твоя тётя заболела.
Она настаивает на том, чтобы
немедленно увидеть тебя и всем
уже сказала что если ты ни придет
домой как следует, наследство

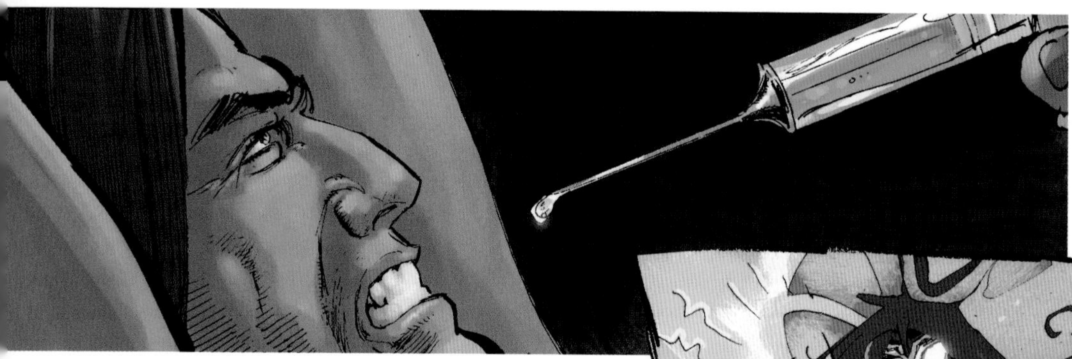

Left and below: BLACK WIDOW #3 (JAN. 2005) Using a mix of truth serum and hallucinogens, Black Widow extracted vital information from the new Red Room's US liaison.

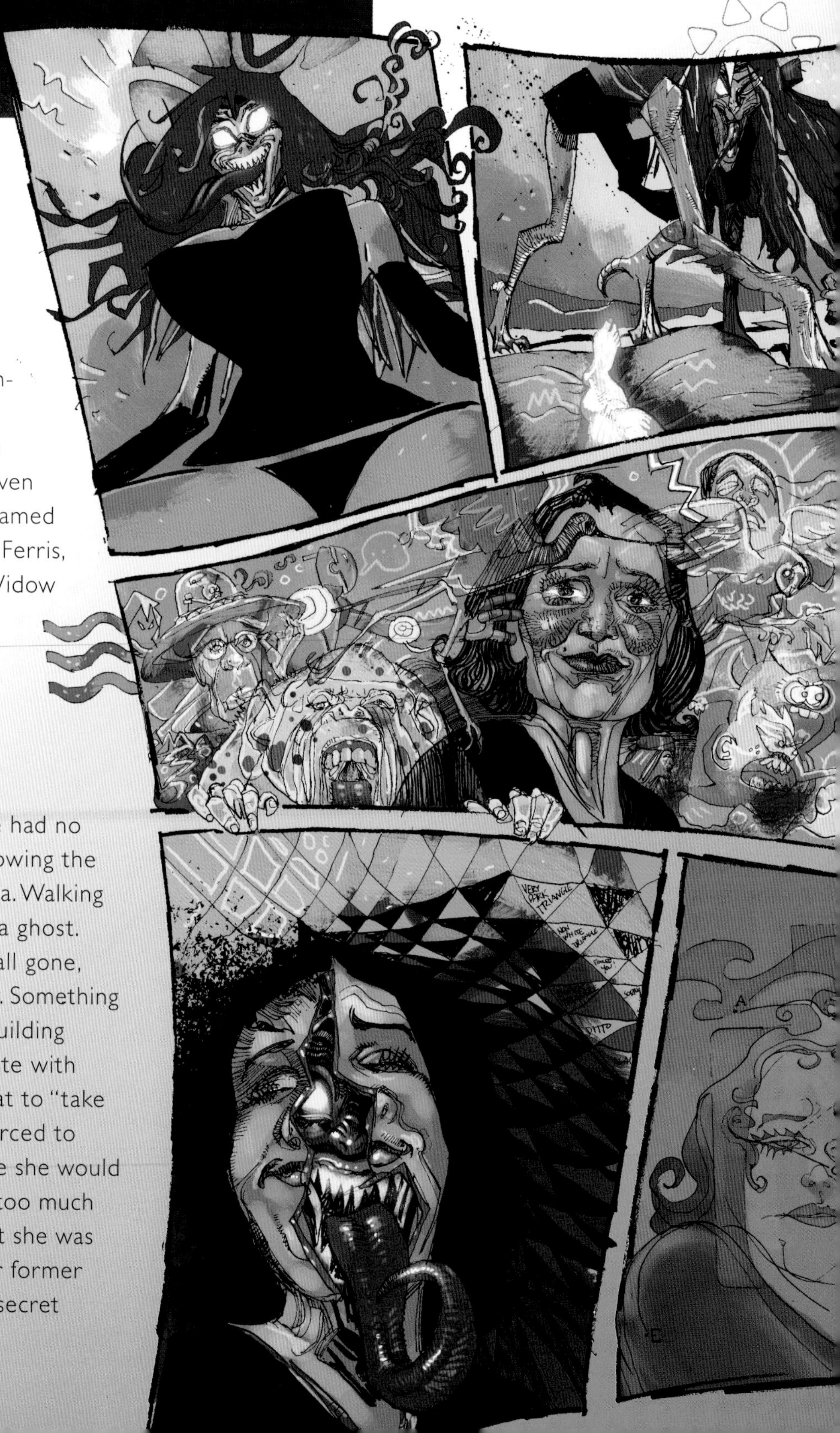

There were to be more unwanted reminders of home when Natasha discovered that the mysterious ring found on her would-be assassin confirmed him as an agent of the Red Room, an organization she had hoped was shut down. A truth-serum-fueled interrogation of a former US spy revealed that the Red Room was back in business, trading as 2R, and even had its own US government liaison named Martin Ferris. It was not long before Ferris, too, found himself telling the Black Widow everything he knew. Everything, it seemed, led back to a cosmetics corporation named Gynacon.

Breaking Point

Eventually, Natasha realized that she had no choice: if she was going to keep following the trail, she needed to go back to Russia. Walking Moscow's streets again, she felt like a ghost. The people she remembered were all gone, some, apparently, wiped from history. Something had remained, however: a derelict building where she had once trained, complete with a long-empty chair where she had sat to "take her medicine," all the while being forced to watch ballerinas on screen living a life she would never have. The recollection proved too much for Natasha, and she broke down. But she was not alone in the building—one of her former trainers had remained there, living a secret

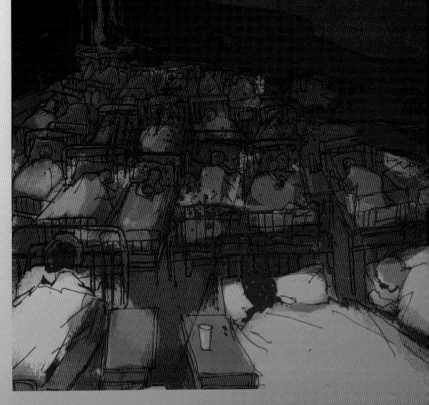

existence in an attic room. He explained that she was one of 27 original Black Widow agents deployed in China and the West. All of them had received the same conditioning. They had been implanted with false memories of training to be ballerinas, and cursed to be stricken with terrible headaches and nausea if they ever tried to think too deeply about the logic of what they believed to be their past.

While sorely tempted to kill her old trainer for what he had inflicted on her as a young girl, Natasha knew the mission was more important. She took him with her as she drove 2,000 miles east to a covert biochemical facility. On the journey there, she forced her unwilling accomplice to tell her everything he knew about her past, regardless of how nauseous it made her feel.

Once at the facility, Natasha met the Red Room's former chief biochemist, Dr. Lyudmila Kudrin. She told Natasha how the Black Widows had been created; how the serum had given them increased healing, slowed aging, and ramped-up immune and cell repair systems. However, one of the devastating side-effects of the serum was that Black Widows could never carry a pregnancy to full term, as their bodies would see it as a weakness to be overcome, and reject the fetus. The Black Widow program wanted warriors, not mothers. Natasha was furious to discover how the state had manipulated her life, and those of the other children in the program. She also found out that the Red Room had not been responsible for the recent hits on other Black Widows. The trail in Russia had gone cold, and it was time to head back to the West, taking Lyudmila Kudrin with her.

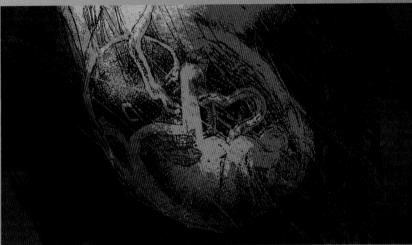

Right: BLACK WIDOW #5 (MAR. 2005) An anguished Lyudmila Kudrin revealed to Black Widow the whole truth about the effects of the serum that Natasha and all potential Black Widow agents were given as young girls.

EVERY TIME I TALK TO FURY I WANT TO BREAK HIS FACE. AND EVERY TIME I JUST LET HIM WALK AWAY.
YES, DEAR.
I'M AFRAID IT'S PHEROMONAL.

After touching down in the US, Black Widow was informed by Nick Fury that Phil Dexter and Sally Anne—the girl whom Natasha had rescued from the truckers and who had ended up tagging along with them—had both been shot by two unknown attackers. Dexter was in critical condition in the hospital and Sally Anne was missing. Fury believed the attack had been carried out by North Institute: private sector spooks carrying out espionage for high-paying corporate clients. As Fury walked away, Natasha wondered aloud why she always had the urge to hit Fury in the face, but every time she just let him leave. What followed was a revelation that shook her to the core.

Lyudmila told her that many years ago Nick Fury had stolen samples of an aftershave created by the Red Room to keep its female operatives compliant. The smell of the aftershave compelled the women not to hurt the man who wore it, to treat him as if he was the most beloved of family members. Fury had used the power of coercion the aftershave gave him when he first recruited Natasha for S.H.I.E.L.D., and had been using it ever since to keep her onside. Natasha's entire relationship with him had been dependent on her unknowing subjugation to his will.

However, Natasha was pragmatic enough to let Fury tell her where she might be able to find the two North agents who had injured her friends. Threatening the girlfriend of one agent to get information, she killed the other in cold blood.

The intel so brutally won led Black Widow to a yacht off the coast of Florida. Here she found an ex-KGB agent named Vassily Ulyanov protecting the Gynacon CEO, Ian McMasters. Gynacon had paid 2R—the former Red Room—for the biotech they had used to create the Black Widows. But Gynacon could not patent the biotech if it was already in existence inside the Black Widow agents. As a consequence, Gynacon had ordered them all to be killed to protect its investment. Natasha was now officially the last of the original Black Widows (Yelena Belova having emerged from an unsanctioned Red Room offshoot).

Taking on Vassily, Natasha was dismayed to detect the scent of the aftershave that had been formulated to stop her hurting its wearer. All she could do was take the savage beating from Vassily… until he broke her nose. Now unable to smell the aftershave, she was free to fight back. The exchange did not last long, and Black Widow claimed two further victims—including the Gynacon CEO. However, she was still no closer to learning where Sally Anne was being held.

"You broke my nose, Vassily. I can't smell anything anymore."

BLACK WIDOW

Left and opposite: BLACK WIDOW #6 (APR. 2005)
For years, Natasha had been under the influence of a powerful pheromone, disguised in an aftershave, that rendered her powerless against anyone wearing the scent—until her nose was broken in a fight.

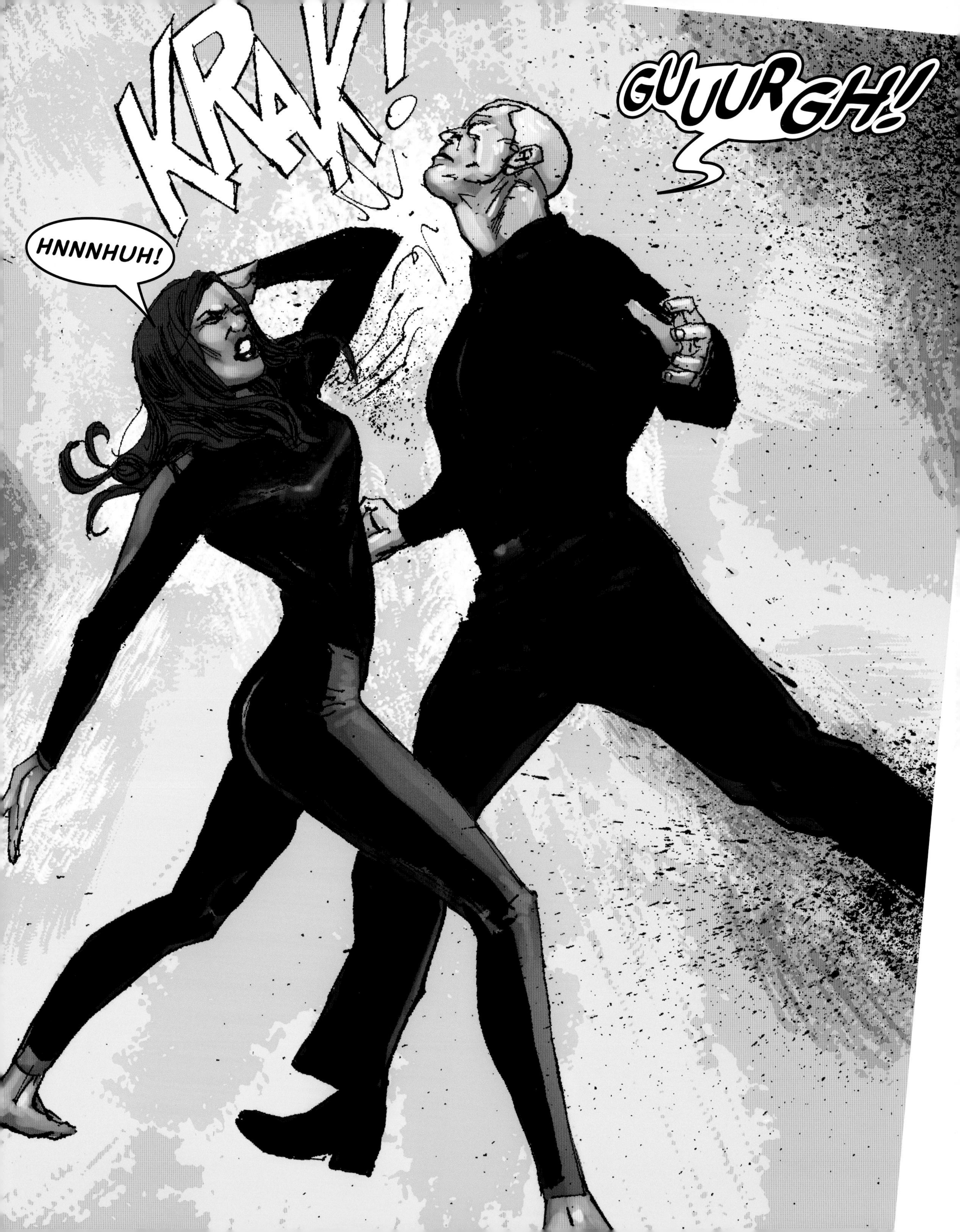
KRAK!
HNNNHUH!
GUUURGH!

A Deadly Path

BLACK WIDOW #1 (NOV. 2005) Exiled to Cuba, Black Widow found an unlikely protector and benefactor in her former antagonist, Yelena Belova.

Natasha's chance encounter on that desert road with Sally Anne had led both of them down a dangerous path. However, Black Widow now felt responsible for the young girl and would stop at nothing to find her. Perhaps Sally Anne had come to symbolize the vulnerable people that Natasha had always felt the need to defend against predators. More than missions for some country's flag or for some political ideology, Black Widow now valued fighting for those people who could not, or would not, fight for themselves.

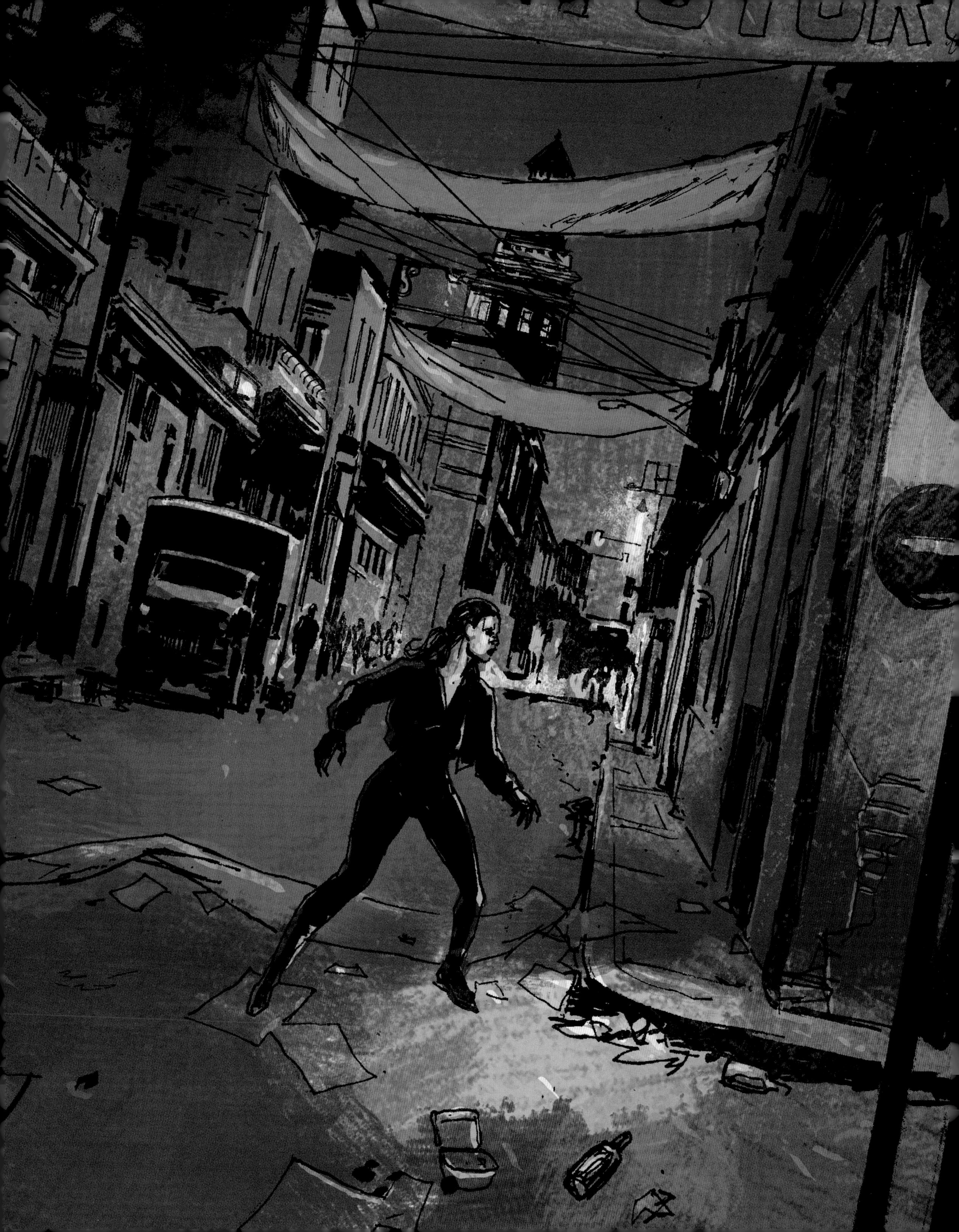

However, her recent run of violent means to achieve her ends was making her a whole host of new enemies. And top of the pile was no less than the President of the United States, who upbraided Nick Fury for allowing Natasha to get out of control, and placed her at the top of America's Most Wanted list. It seemed that Black Widow had outstayed her welcome in her adopted country. She fled to Cuba, where she was protected by an unlikely new ally—Yelena Belova. The "other" Black Widow had taken Natasha's earlier advice and chosen being Yelena above being a Black Widow. Being Yelena this involved power-broking in Havana, multimillion-dollar modeling contracts, and trying to rescue vulnerable young girls from the street. Finally Yelena had achieved exactly what she wanted out of life—could Natasha say the same of herself?

The two trained together for a while, and Yelena asked a favor of Natasha. She was trying to obtain vital medication for people who were living on the street, but her black-market supplier in the US had just put a huge price hike on the drugs she needed.

BLACK WIDOW #1 (NOV. 2005) A chance discovery on a mission for Yelena gave Natasha a lead in her search for the missing girl, Sally Anne, for whom she felt responsible.

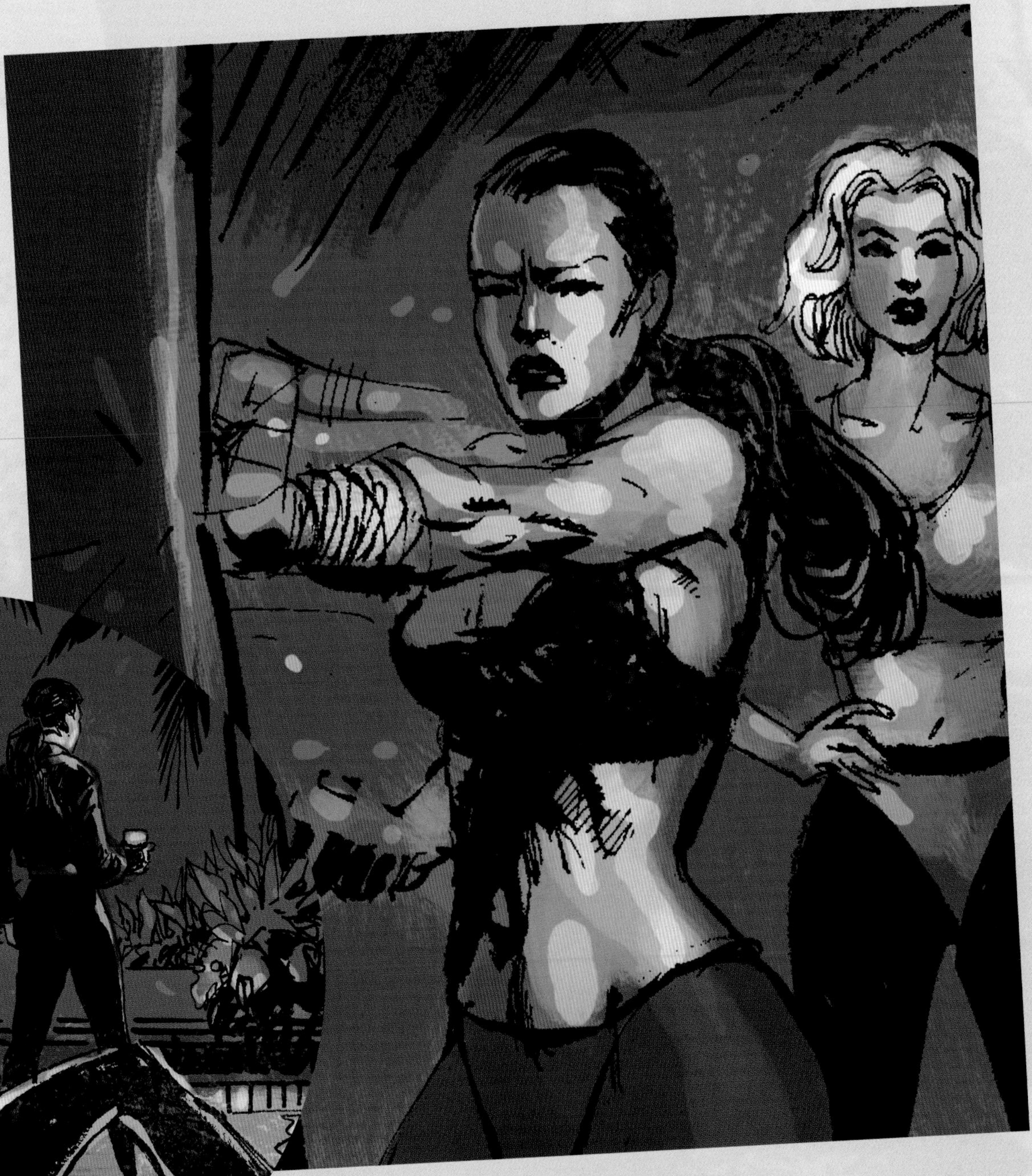

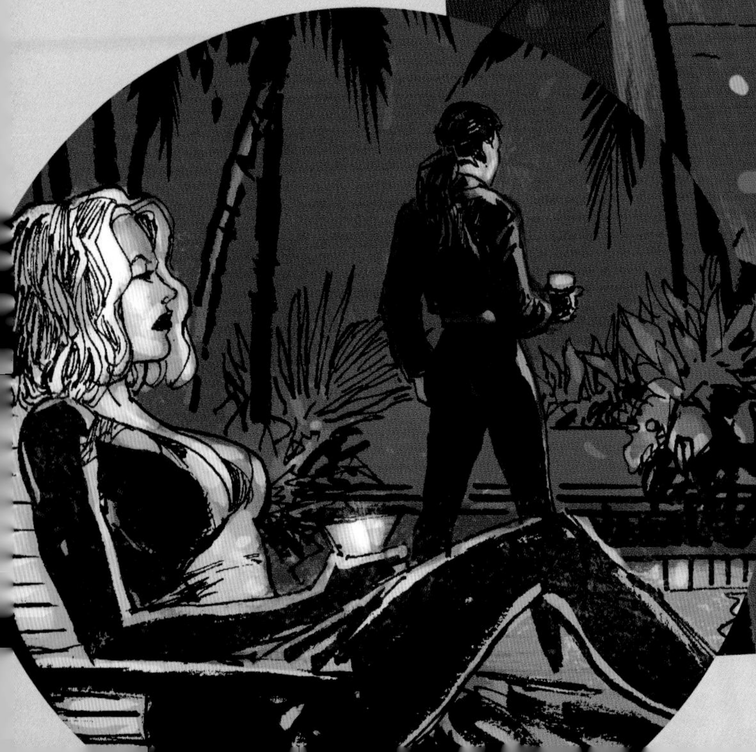

Yelena wanted Natasha to travel to Florida, liberate the medicine from the warehouse, and use her highly specialized talents to "renegotiate" the price. The former Black Widow finally admitted that Natasha was better at that sort of thing than her.

Leading a Cuban covert ops team onto a Florida beach, Black Widow quickly and efficiently carried out her mission. But when she found a possible Gynacon lead in the supplier's office, she sent her team back to Cuba and decided to stay in the country where she was now a wanted fugitive—it was worth the risk if it led her to Sally Anne.

Natasha's investigation took her to the house of a shady doctor, whom she discovered had operated on Sally Anne to save her life after the North agents shot her. The physician was unsure who Natasha was, so Black Widow enjoined him to think of her as one of the bad guys, because, as far as he was concerned, that was what she was. She was now a long way from super heroics.

Having learned that Sally Anne's disappearance could be linked to the Miami underworld, Black Widow set about cutting a swathe through the local gangsters and their lines of business. She shared her feelings about her one-woman war on crime with her old flame Daredevil, leaving him a voice message telling him that she now understood why he gained so much satisfaction from fighting criminals. For her, they just weren't at the level of the spooks and political operators she was used to dealing with—battling these thugs and mobsters was like playing tag with children. Her antics were causing serious disruption, and the mob bosses were in agreement that it needed to stop. Either someone needed to tell her where Sally Anne was… or Black Widow had to be eliminated.

Point of No Return

The mob members were not the only ones trying to stop Natasha. The surviving North agent was hell-bent on revenge for the murder of her partner, while 2R liaison Martin Ferris and the son of one of the crippled truckers who had attacked Sally Anne were also hunting the Widow. Natasha's enemies seemed far more numerous than her allies at this point. Daredevil had traveled south to stand with her, but she told him to go away. Her battles were in a completely different moral gradient from what he was used to, and she knew that Matt would disapprove of her more extreme methods. Nick Fury was unable to help— it was a measure of how far he had fallen in the eyes of the US government that North were able to arrest Fury, and have him confined in Cuba's Guantanamo Bay.

With a captured mobster as her guide, Natasha pressed on alone to the Darién Gap between Central and South America, where she finally succeeded in finding Sally Anne. The girl was being drugged and held in a sweatshop by the Cutting Corporation that had bought out Gynacon in the aftermath of the CEO's murder at the hands of Black Widow. Natasha dragged Sally Anne out and told her to get away as best she could, while she turned to face their pursuers. Despite, as always, fighting with everything she had, Black Widow was captured and restrained. But she did not allow her captors the satisfaction of breaking her. When the North agent visited Natasha in her cell, she accused her of the cold-blooded murder of her partner. Natasha retorted that she was playing in the sewers now and that's the way things went down there. The agent left, determined to find a way to make Black Widow feel *something*. Then it was Ferris' turn with the prisoner. He gave Natasha a hallucinogenic drug similar to the one that she had given him to extract the truth, but her willpower and training were able to overcome its effects with an ease that surprised and disappointed her enemies. But then they played their trump card: they had recaptured Sally Anne.

Black Widow had long accepted that in her line of work, luck and skill could only get her so far before death caught up. She had always thought she would die alone, but now it seemed Sally Anne would die with her. She apologized to the young girl for getting her involved, but Sally Anne would not accept it.

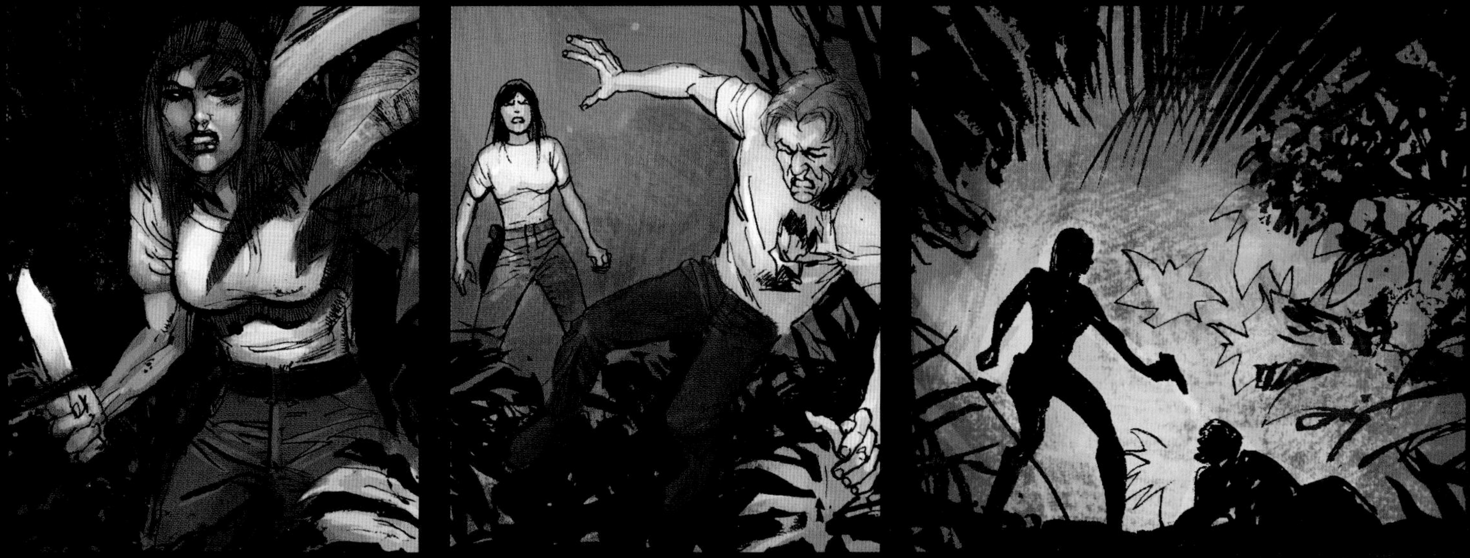

To her, Natasha had done more for her than her own mother ever had—she had saved her. Fortunately, former Black Widow Yelena Belova arrived with her Cuban agents and freed them both. However, Natasha Romanoff had two loose ends to clear up, which she did in her now customary fashion: eliminating Ferris and the North agent before they could escape.

There was no doubt that, unlike her battles alongside the Champions or the Avengers during her younger years, Black Widow now had little compunction about killing when the mission demanded it. It was, after all, part of her Red Room conditioning. As she herself had pointed out, when you faced such remorseless opponents, you had to be ruthless, or you wouldn't live very long. But her actions had pushed her outside the law, and she was now a wanted criminal in the country that she had been calling home for so long.

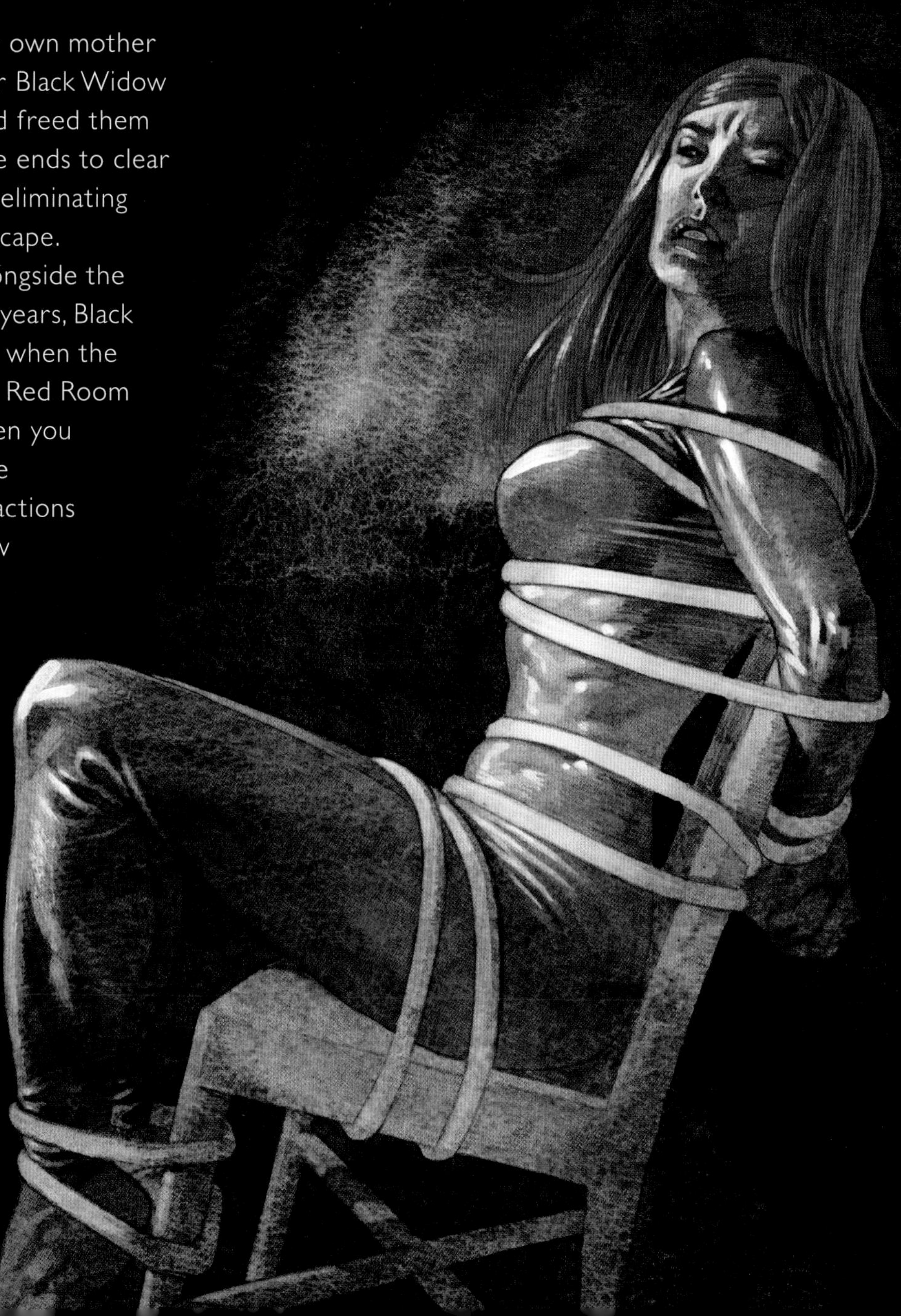

Opposite and right: BLACK WIDOW #5 (MAR. 2006) Natasha believed death had finally caught up with her, but her willpower enabled her to overcome the drugs that had been forced on her.

Above: BLACK WIDOW #6 (APR. 2006) Free again, Black Widow tied up the loose ends of the investigation—in uncompromising fashion.

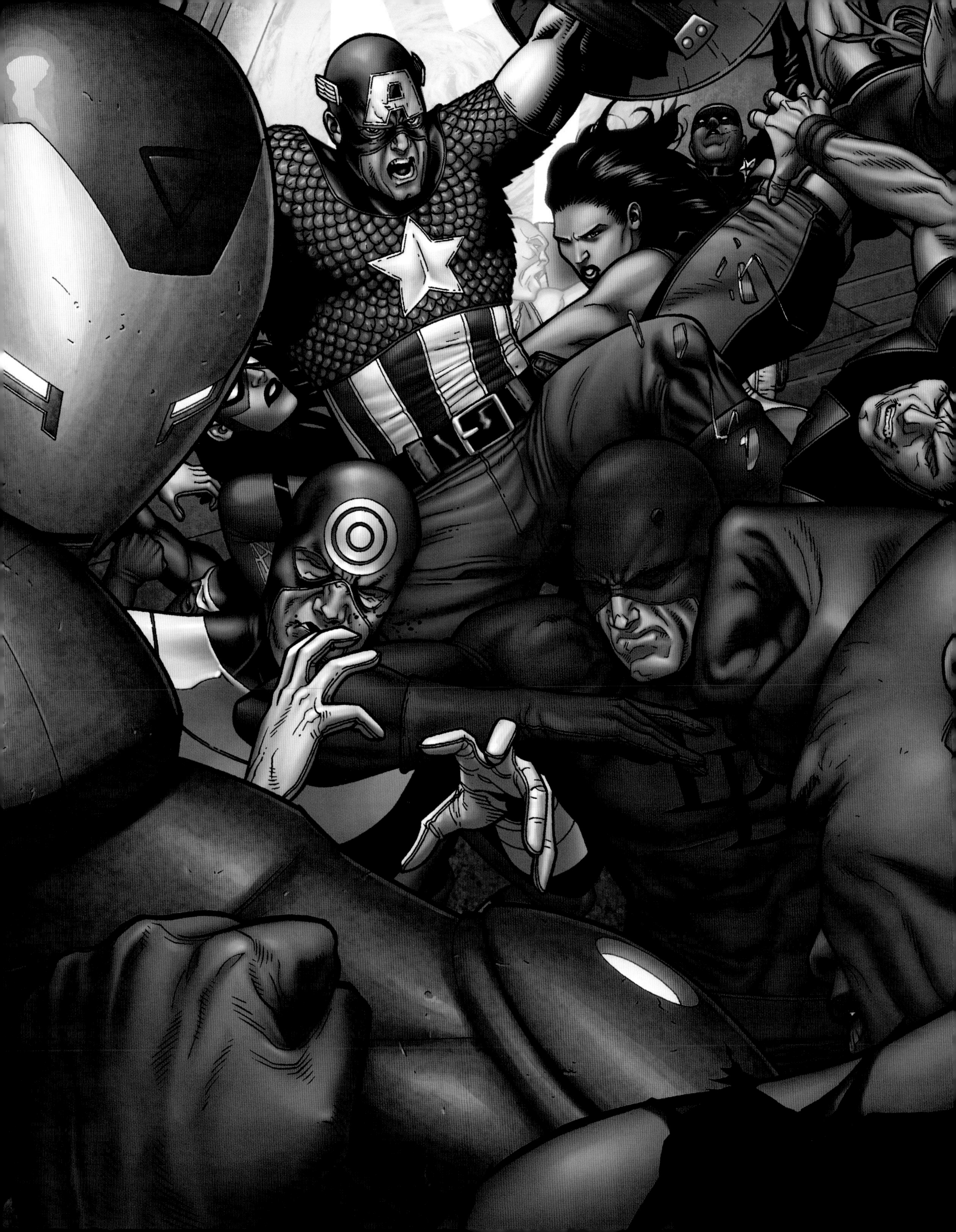

Picking Sides

CIVIL WAR #7 (JAN. 2007) As the Super Hero community tore itself apart fighting about whether to register with the government or not, Black Widow found herself opposing Captain America.

Back in the US, the Super Hero community was experiencing seismic shifts: changes that would fracture the bonds between old allies and even split teams apart. When a standoff between a group of young heroes and Super Villains ended with a massive explosion that claimed many innocent lives, it prompted a public demand for Super Heroes to be officially registered and licensed. Iron Man and his allies agreed with the registration movement, but Captain America, when told by S.H.I.E.L.D. that he would be expected to bring in unwilling comrades, refused and went on the run. Those heroes who steadfastly resisted registration joined the Sentinel of Liberty, thus triggering the first superhuman civil war.

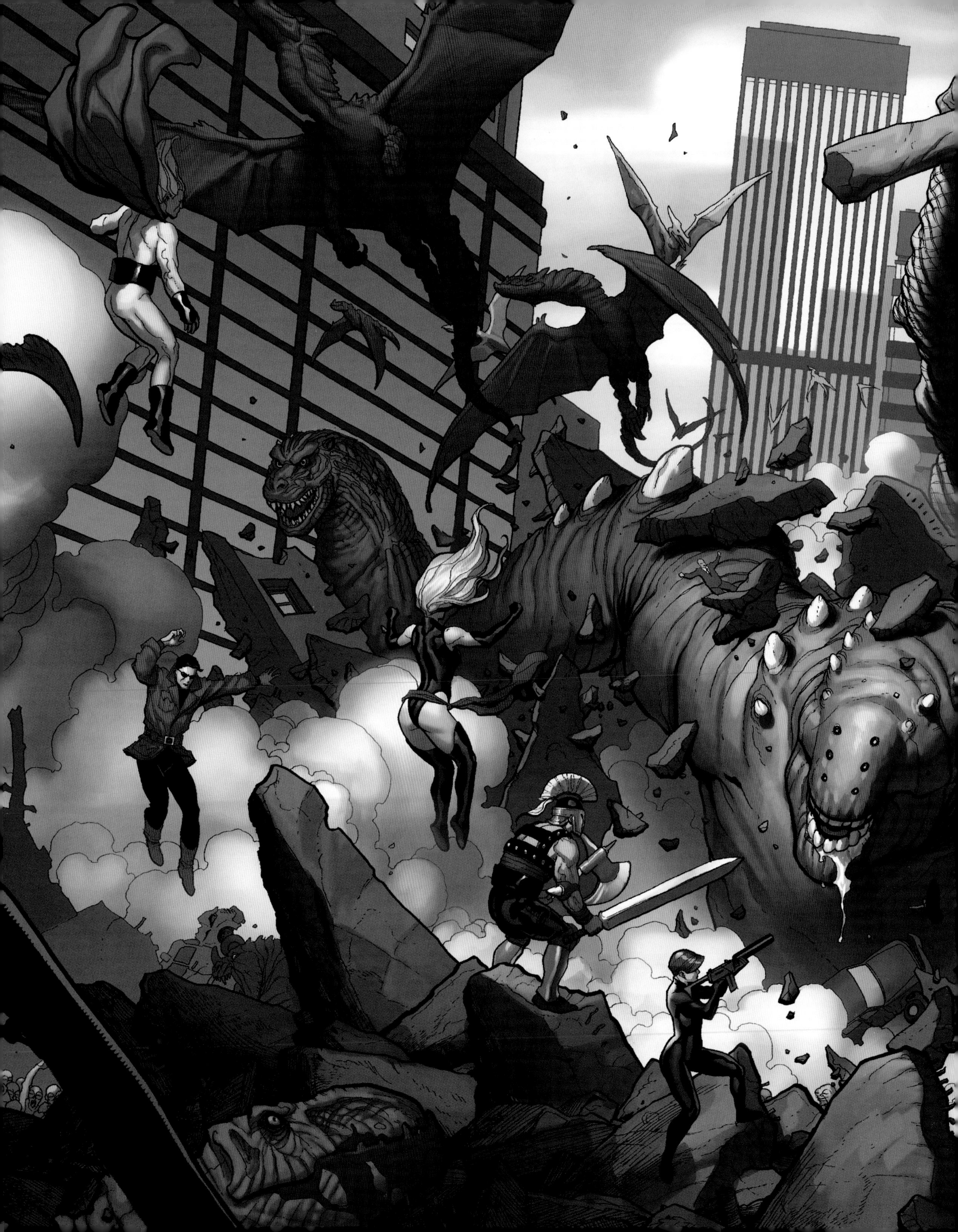

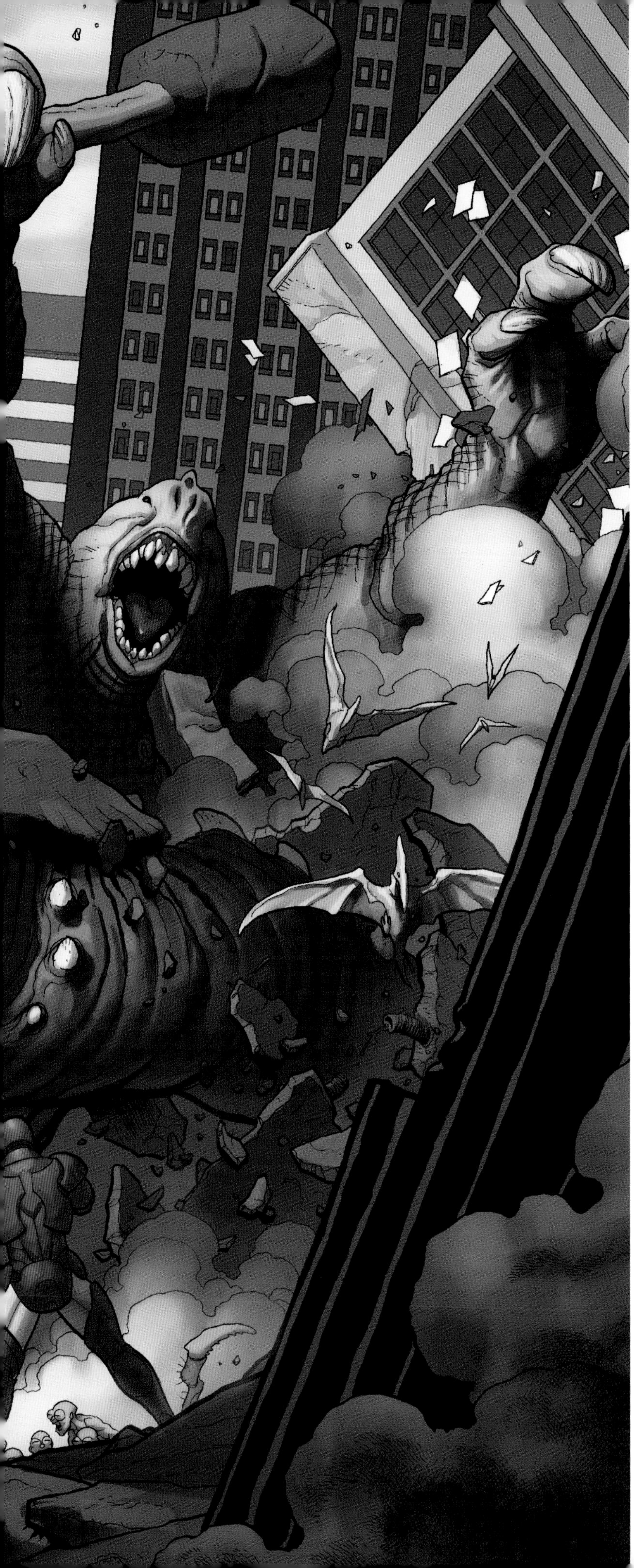

THE MIGHTY AVENGERS #1 (MAY 2007) Exactly 14 minutes after joining a new Avengers lineup, Natasha found herself fighting gigantic subterranean beasts sent by villain Mole Man.

Black Widow returned to the US to stand with the pro-registration side. Her stance gave her a platform to rehabilitate herself as a mainstream Super Hero and S.H.I.E.L.D. agent. Following Iron Man's victory in the superhuman civil war he became Director of S.H.I.E.L.D. and leader of a new Avengers Initiative. As well as placing a team of heroes in every US state, Iron Man chose a prime Avengers lineup to be based in New York City.

For the first time ever, the Avengers roster would be assembled not through fate or happenstance, but would be selected like a sports team. Rather than just pick the most powerful beings he could call upon, Iron Man wanted a mix of skills, and Black Widow was chosen as the "ninja team member." Natasha's stealth, strategic expertise, and hand-to-hand combat skills were the perfect foil for the other, more high-powered Avengers.

Early in her career with the Avengers Initiative, Natasha found herself getting a swift battlefield promotion. Iron Man was believed to be missing in action, and at the S.H.I.E.L.D. command post aboard a helicarrier, Deputy Director Maria Hill had been incapacitated. As the only ranking S.H.I.E.L.D. agent present, Black Widow was now in charge of the entire organization. She acquitted herself with distinction in the role, stepping up to assess the state of play and provide quick, decisive orders before Agent Hill recovered.

Back with Bucky

CAPTAIN AMERICA #27 (AUG. 2007) When Black Widow saw the Winter Soldier after decades apart, the two came to blows over who should have custody of Captain America's famous shield.

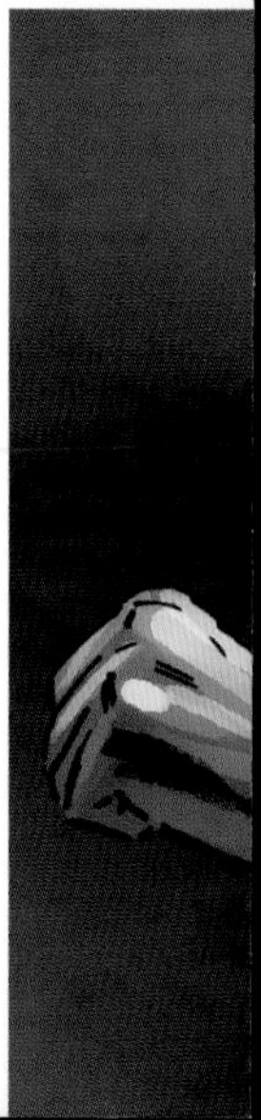

The world was shocked when Captain America was seemingly assassinated on the steps of a New York City courthouse. Iron Man—who had returned to his role as Director of S.H.I.E.L.D.—took custody of Cap's iconic shield, keeping it under lock and key. When he thought that someone was planning to steal it, Tony Stark gave Black Widow the task of moving it to a safe location. En route, Natasha was accosted by the would-be thief. It was the Winter Soldier, James Buchanan "Bucky" Barnes, Cap's WWII partner, former brainwashed Soviet super-agent, and her ex-boyfriend. Having not seen one another for decades, the two were astonished to run into each other. However, Natasha would not abandon her mission, and fought Barnes to stop him stealing the shield.

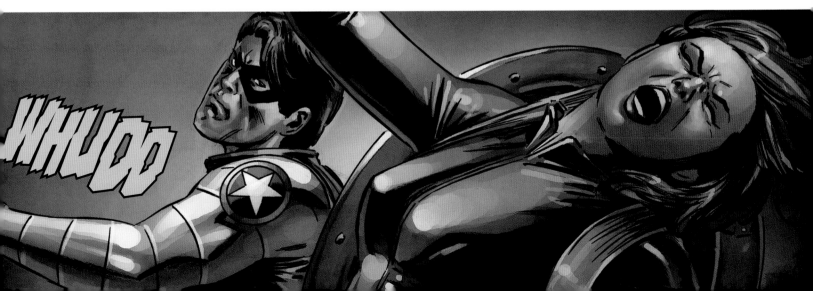

WHUDD

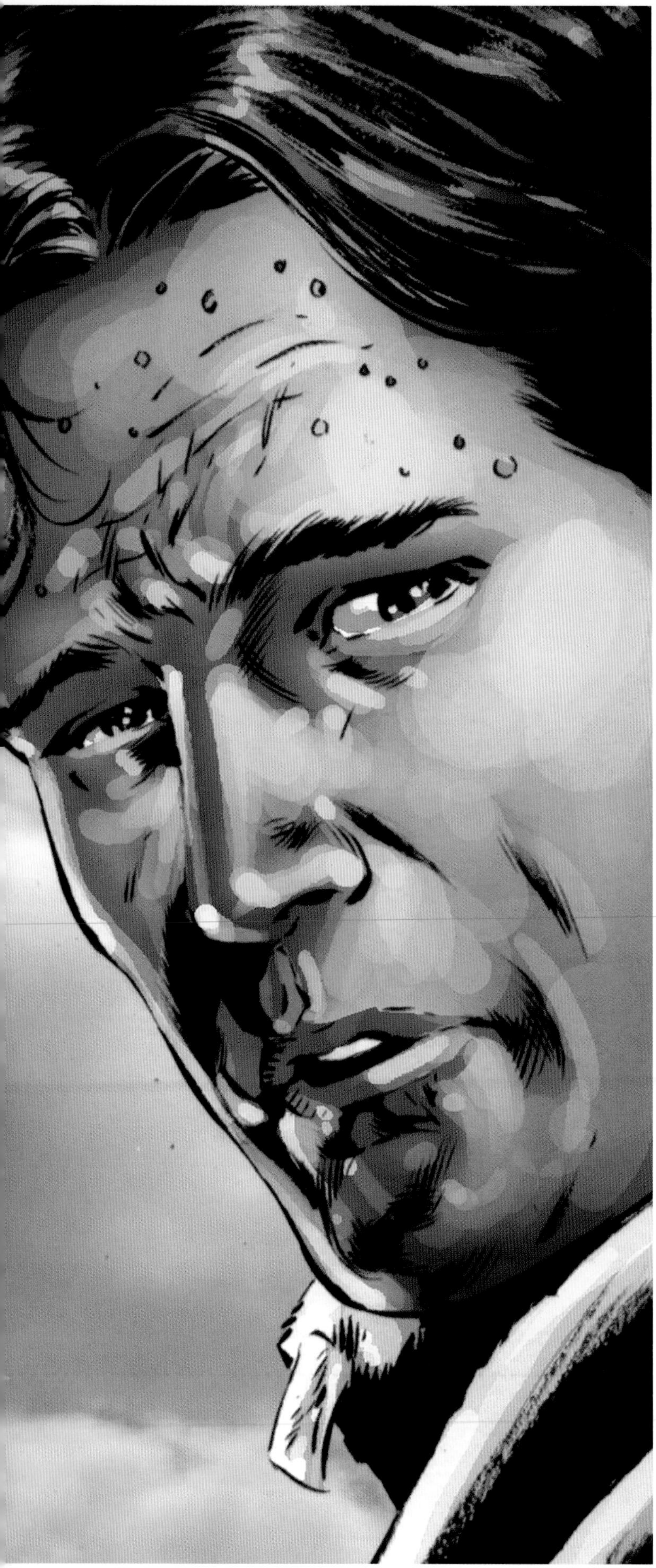

"No... It's not like that. I know how (Bucky) thinks. We were both weapons once... to be used."

BLACK WIDOW

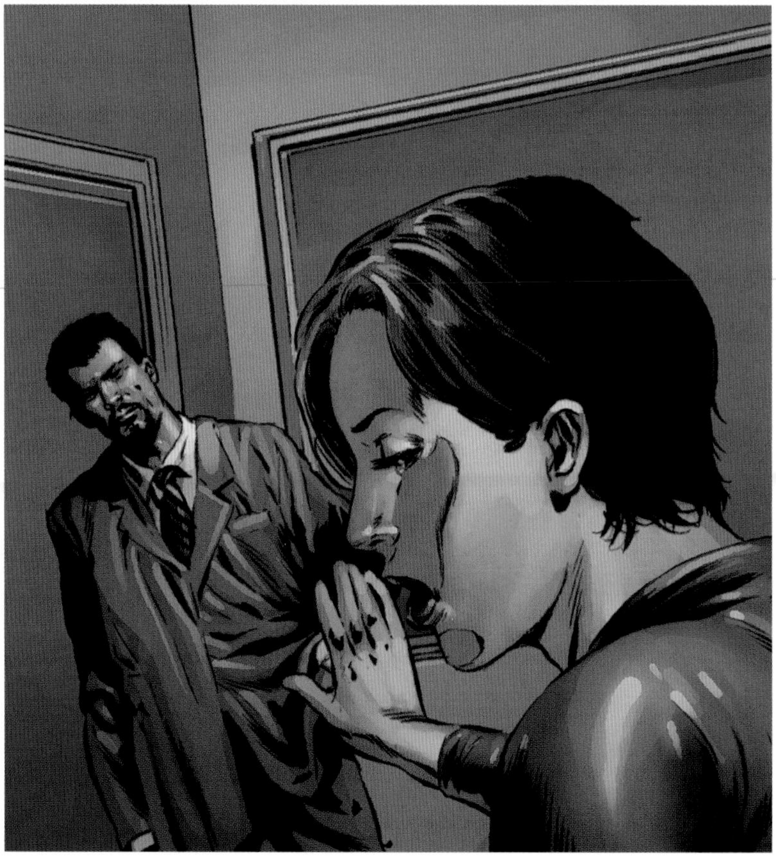

Above: CAPTAIN AMERICA #27 (AUG. 2007) Her knowledge of the Winter Soldier's methods and mindset convinced Natasha that Bucky's next target would be Tony Stark.

Opposite and right: CAPTAIN AMERICA #36 (MAY 2008) Natasha and Bucky shared a shadowy past, but both recalled that their time together had also brought them happiness.

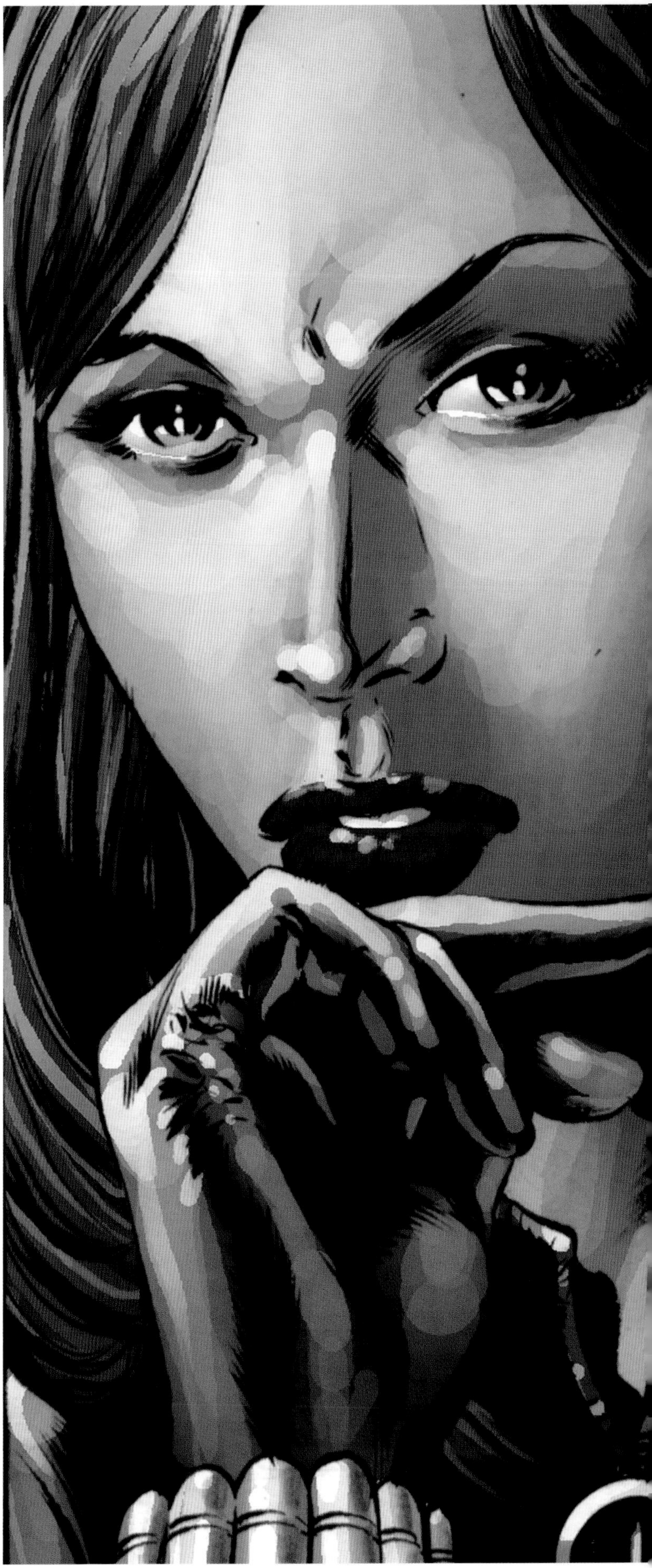

Unfortunately for Natasha, Bucky had trained her, knew her moves, and was able to best her. After he made off with Cap's shield, Black Widow—now feeling nostalgic for the relationship that had been stamped out so cruelly by the Soviet authorities all those years ago—reported back to Tony Stark.

Black Widow's next mission was to find the Winter Soldier. Teaming up with Falcon, she caught Barnes and placed him under arrest, bringing him back to Iron Man's helicarrier. Iron Man, knowing that Steve Rogers' last request to him was to look after his former partner, offered Bucky the chance to be the new Captain America. Although both Barnes and Natasha had their doubts about his readiness to take on that burden, he nevertheless donned the stars and stripes. Black Widow took on the role of his S.H.I.E.L.D. contact and frequent ally in his early missions. On one occasion, she even wielded the famous shield to assist him. Natasha and Bucky were frequently thrown together in life-and-death situations and would often reminisce about the happy times they had shared—among the only happy times of those years for both of them—and it was not long before they were a couple again.

In her role as an Avenger, Natasha was the only one to be suspicious about the return of Spider-Woman (Jessica Drew), who had previously refused to work with Iron Man after the superhuman civil war. Natasha's instincts were proved correct when it was revealed that "Spider-Woman" was really the shape-shifting Skrull Queen Veranke. As the Skrull Invasion of Earth unfolded, Black Widow came into her own, teaming up with old friend Wolverine to get a compromised Iron Man—poisoned and disoriented by a Skrull-administered alien cyber virus—ready for battle.

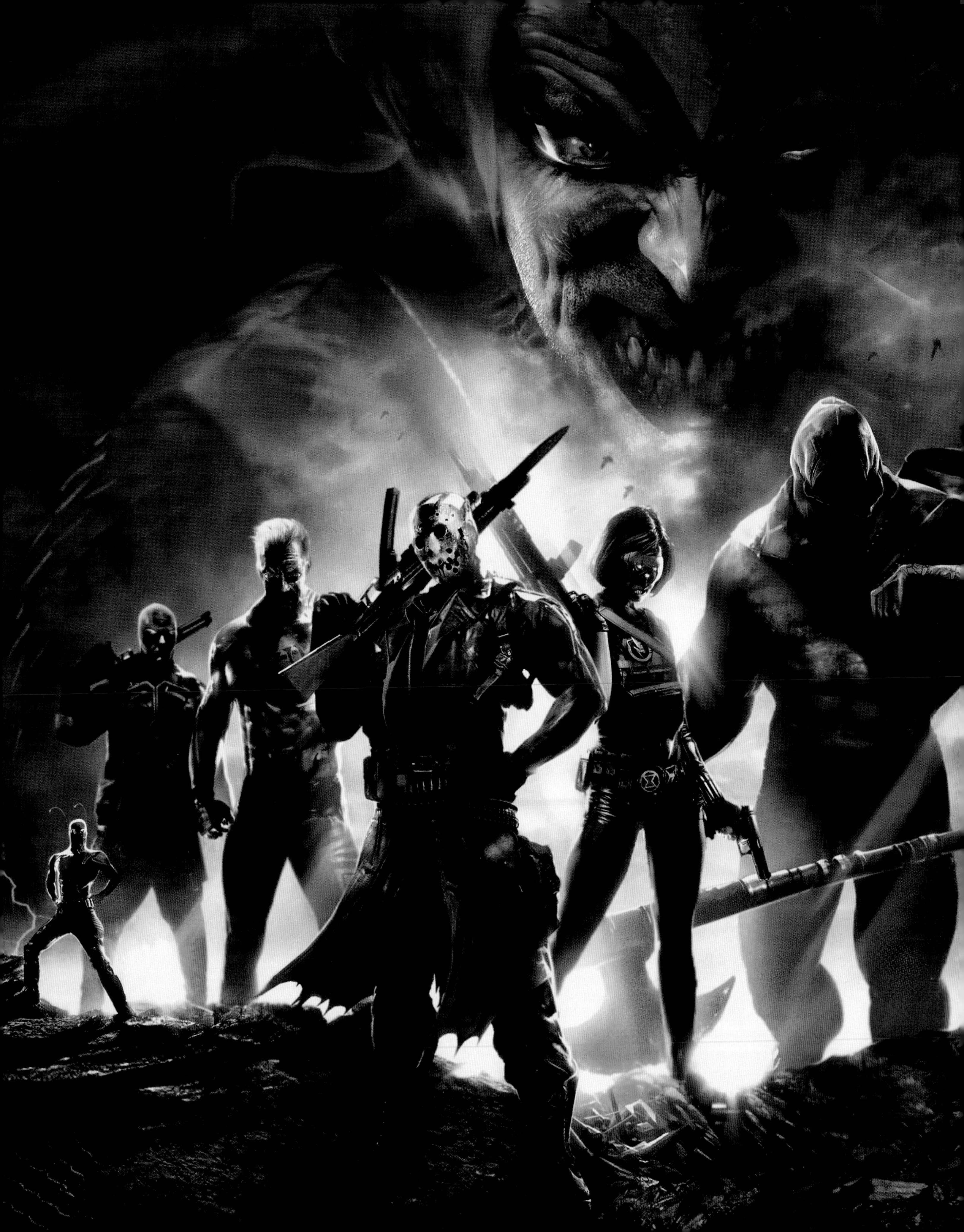

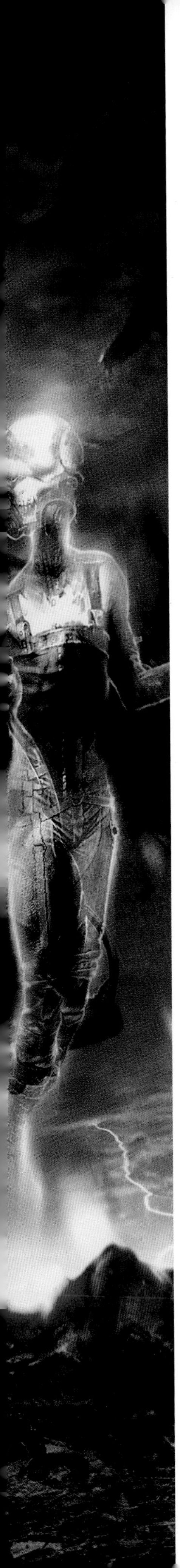

In Her Name

THUNDERBOLTS #128 (MAR. 2009) **Natasha (third from right) went into deep cover as Black Widow Yelena Belova to infiltrate Norman Osborn's Thunderbolts.**

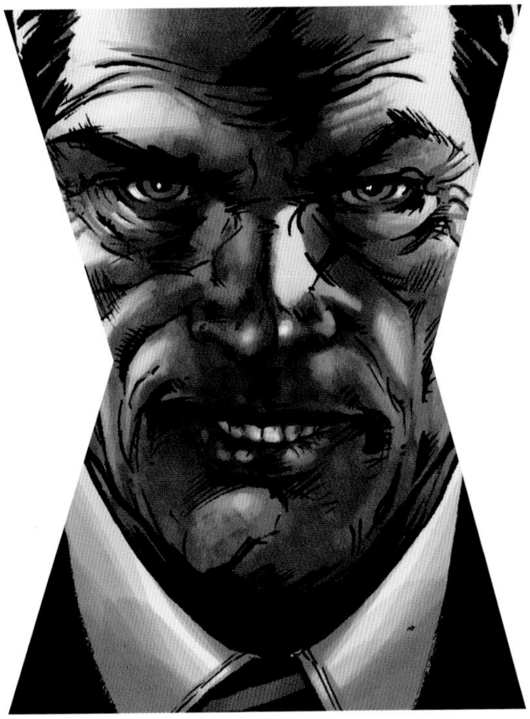

Billionaire businessman Norman Osborn brought about the end of the Skrull invasion by shooting dead the Skrull queen. Meanwhile, Tony Stark had fallen so far out of favor for failing to protect the planet—as he had sworn he would—that he was replaced as Director of S.H.I.E.L.D. by Osborn himself. Osborn immediately set about dismantling the agencies and teams of the past and creating new ones more in tune with his way of thinking. S.H.I.E.L.D. was replaced by H.A.M.M.E.R., a new Avengers team was created, and a covert ops squad, known as the Thunderbolts, was also founded. The latter team's chosen field leader was Black Widow, but she was not as she appeared...

THUNDERBOLTS #128 (MAR. 2009) Disguised as Yelena Belova, Natasha knew that breaking into a former S.H.I.E.L.D. facility would get Norman Osborn's attention and a route into his inner circle.

Natasha had genetically reconfigured herself to look like Yelena Belova so that Osborn would be more inclined to employ her. Once ensconced in the team, Black Widow secretly reported back to Nick Fury. This was the kind of mission she had been trained for all those years ago, but she had changed since then. Although still an expert in the art of espionage, Natasha could not countenance the killing of innocents, and had to carefully maneuver the Thunderbolts' missions to prevent the loss of life, and maintain her cover.

However, for all her efforts to maintain her Yelena persona, Osborn had been playing Natasha all along. He had been impersonating Fury on their calls from the start, using her reports to find out which of his Thunderbolts were truly loyal to him. He also had a long game: to capture the real Nick Fury. Following Natasha as she went to rendezvous with Fury, Osborn captured them both when they were knocked off their feet by an explosion. It turned out that "Nick Fury" was a Life Model Decoy. When her Thunderbolts teammates were ordered by Osborn

to kill Black Widow, some of them did not feel comfortable executing her, and they turned on each other. Natasha saw her chance, and escaped.

Black Widow was then free to take the fight to Osborn. She assisted Maria Hill—still on the run after S.H.I.E.L.D.'s reinvention as H.A.M.M.E.R.—and Pepper Potts—who was heading up Stark Industries —keep a message from the fugitive Tony Stark out of Osborn's hands. The message contained vital intel to help restore Iron Man to full strength.

Later, Black Widow helped Bucky decide what to do after the return of Steve Rogers. She told her boyfriend that he had distinguished himself as Captain America, and she backed him to continue in the role. After watching Bucky in action with Natasha at his side, Rogers agreed—the two were an exemplary partnership, like a well-oiled machine.

Following Norman Osborn's eventual fall, Rogers commissioned a number of super-teams to take the place of H.A.M.M.E.R. and S.H.I.E.L.D. One of them specifically focused on covert ops, and so Black Widow was asked to join the Secret Avengers.

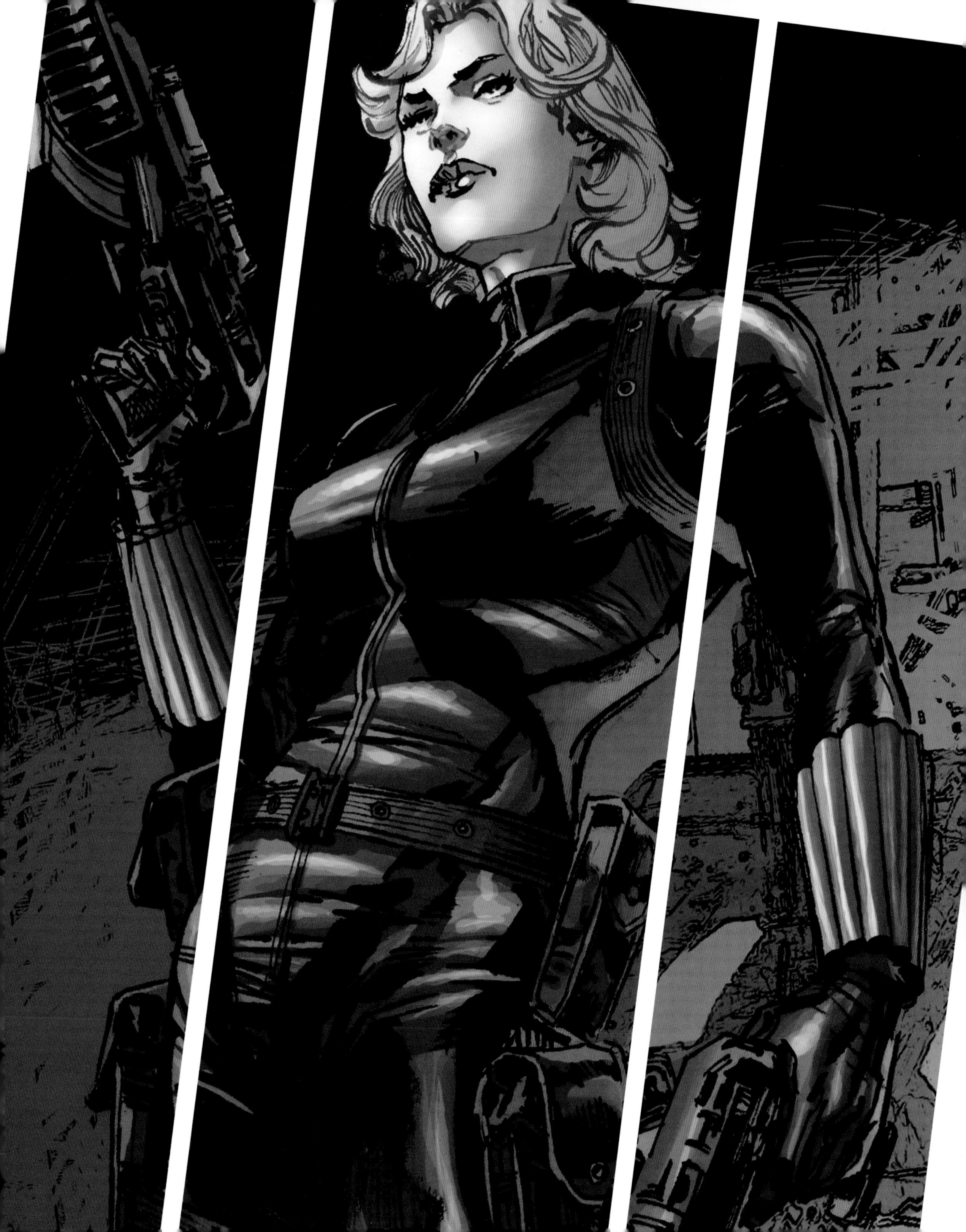

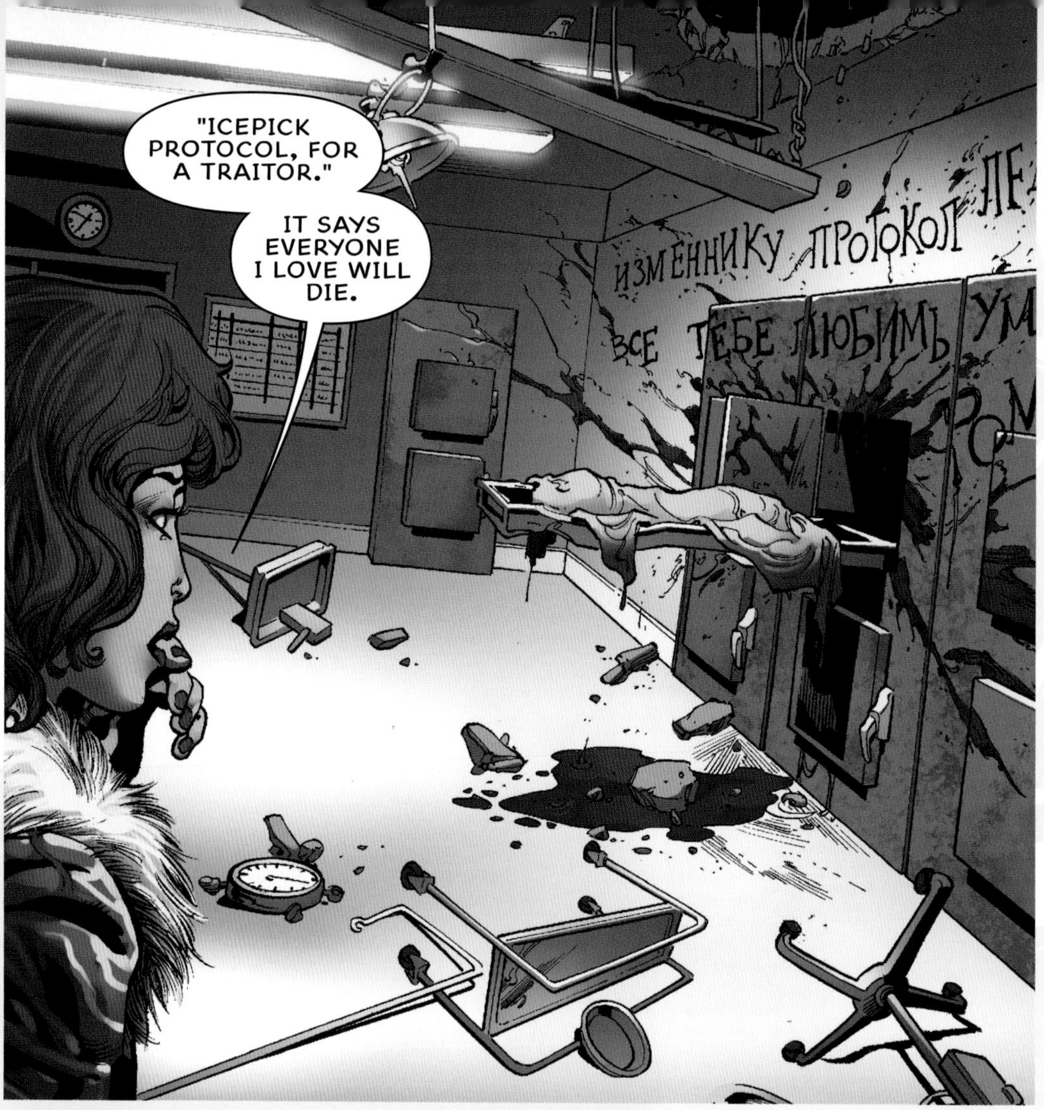
"ICEPICK PROTOCOL, FOR A TRAITOR."
IT SAYS EVERYONE I LOVE WILL DIE.
ИЗМЕННИКУ ПРОТОКОЛ
ВСЕ ТЕБЕ ЛЮБИМЬ

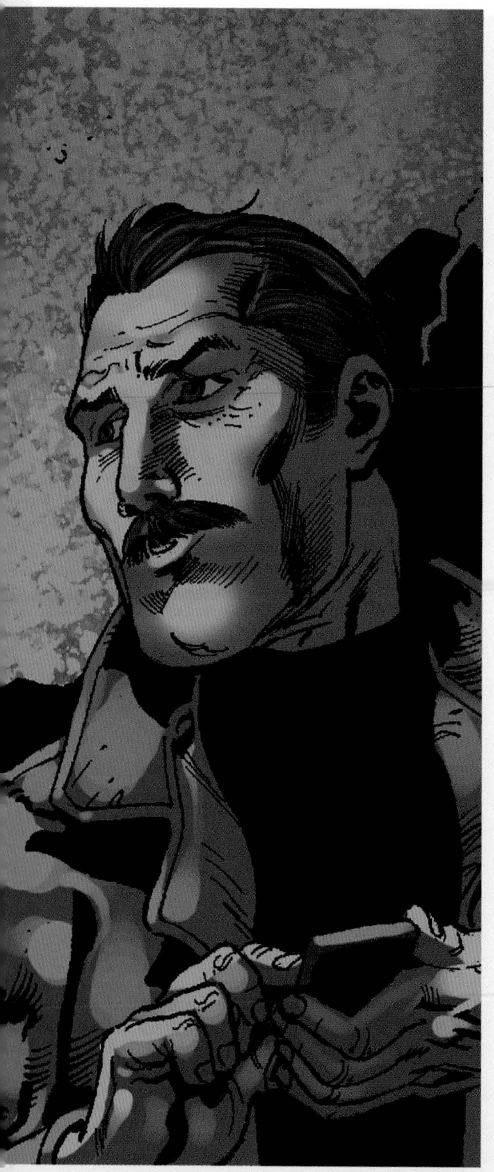

The Past Never Dies

Natasha still freelanced on her own missions where necessary. One night, she was awoken by a phone call from Ivan Petrovitch in Volgograd, formerly Stalingrad. Although she was delighted to hear from him again, her joy was short-lived. He only had time to warn her that the Icepick Protocol had been initiated, before he was killed. A devastated Natasha traveled straight to Russia to investigate, the former Winter Soldier at her side. He was ready to help her with anything she needed, but a message in blood on the wall of the morgue told her that everyone she loved was in danger.

As Natasha always put her friends first, the stark warning was enough to convince her that she alone should set out to avenge Ivan's death.

Managing to infiltrate a military installation, Black Widow found the truth about the Icepick Protocol, which filled her with horror. Her body had been infested with nanites many years before, and so she had unknowingly transferred them to anyone she had been close to: like a virus. When Icepick was activated, anyone with those nanites could be transformed remotely into a fanatical assassin. Rushing back to the US to check on those with whom she'd once been close, Natasha arrived just in time to stop the former Hawkeye's wife from killing him in a homicidal frenzy—a frenzy caused

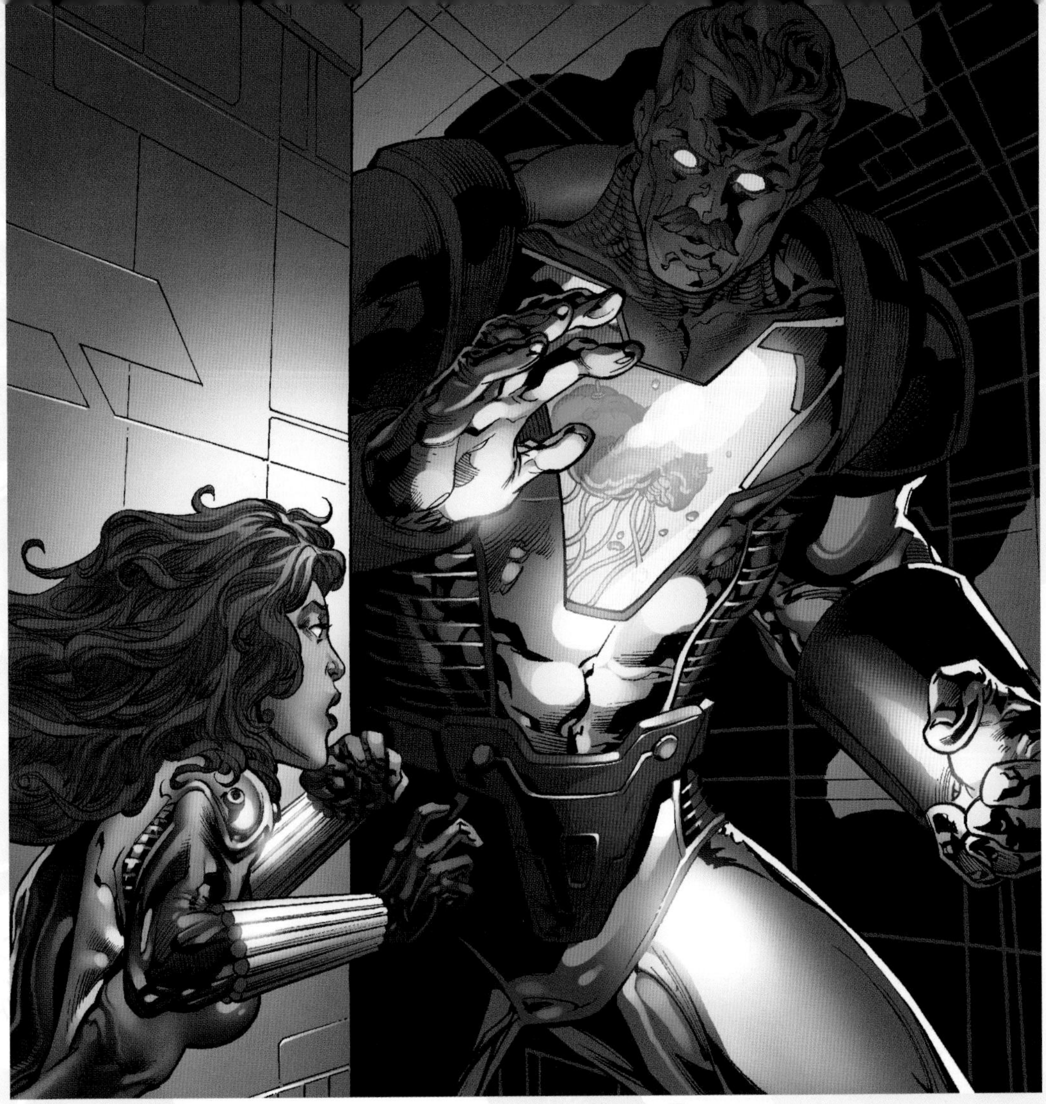

Opposite: BLACK WIDOW: DEADLY ORIGIN #1 (JAN. 2010) Natasha was devastated by Ivan Petrovitch's death and determined to avenge him and protect her loved ones from the same fate.

Left and below: BLACK WIDOW: DEADLY ORIGIN #4 (APR. 2010) Confronting and vanquishing the monster that Ivan had been "reborn" as, made Black Widow realize that she should no longer be defined by her past.

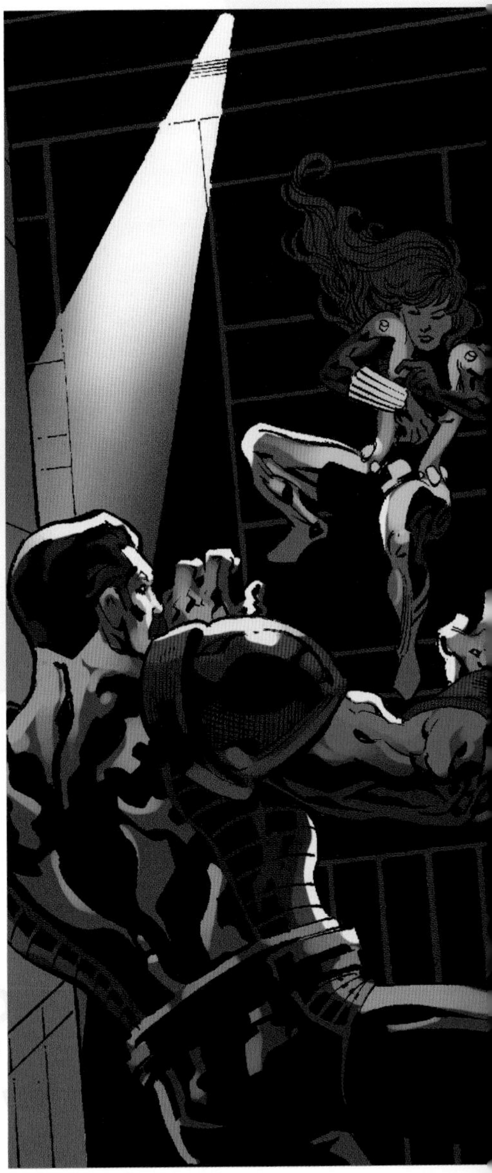

by the nanites. Black Widow had managed to obtain counter-nanites from Nick Fury to deactivate the originals, passing them on with a touch. Meeting up with Daredevil and Hercules to pass on the cure to them, Natasha's search for the perpetrator ultimately led her into Earth's orbit aboard a stolen H.A.M.M.E.R. shuttle. Here she was stunned to find the Dreadnought, a Soviet-designed space station bearing the flag of the old czars.

In a startling twist, it transpired that the person behind Icepick had been her old faithful Ivan. He had been in love with her for years, but since she did not see him that way, he had been forced to remain in the role of father figure and mentor. He had orchestrated his own death, arranging to have his brain and spinal column transferred to a robot body, with which he commanded the Dreadnought. Black Widow confronted Ivan, telling him that the serum he had taken all those years ago had driven him insane. Her Ivan really was dead, and this robot was a twisted abomination of what he had been. After defeating the deranged droid, Natasha departed in an escape pod as the space station was destroyed, toasting her old friend as she was propelled to safety.

Icepick had led her to reexamine her past, to meet up with everyone she had been close to over the years. Natasha accepted that in every choice she had made, she had just been trying to do the right thing and choose the right side. It was not until Ivan had gone, that she had truly become a whole person.

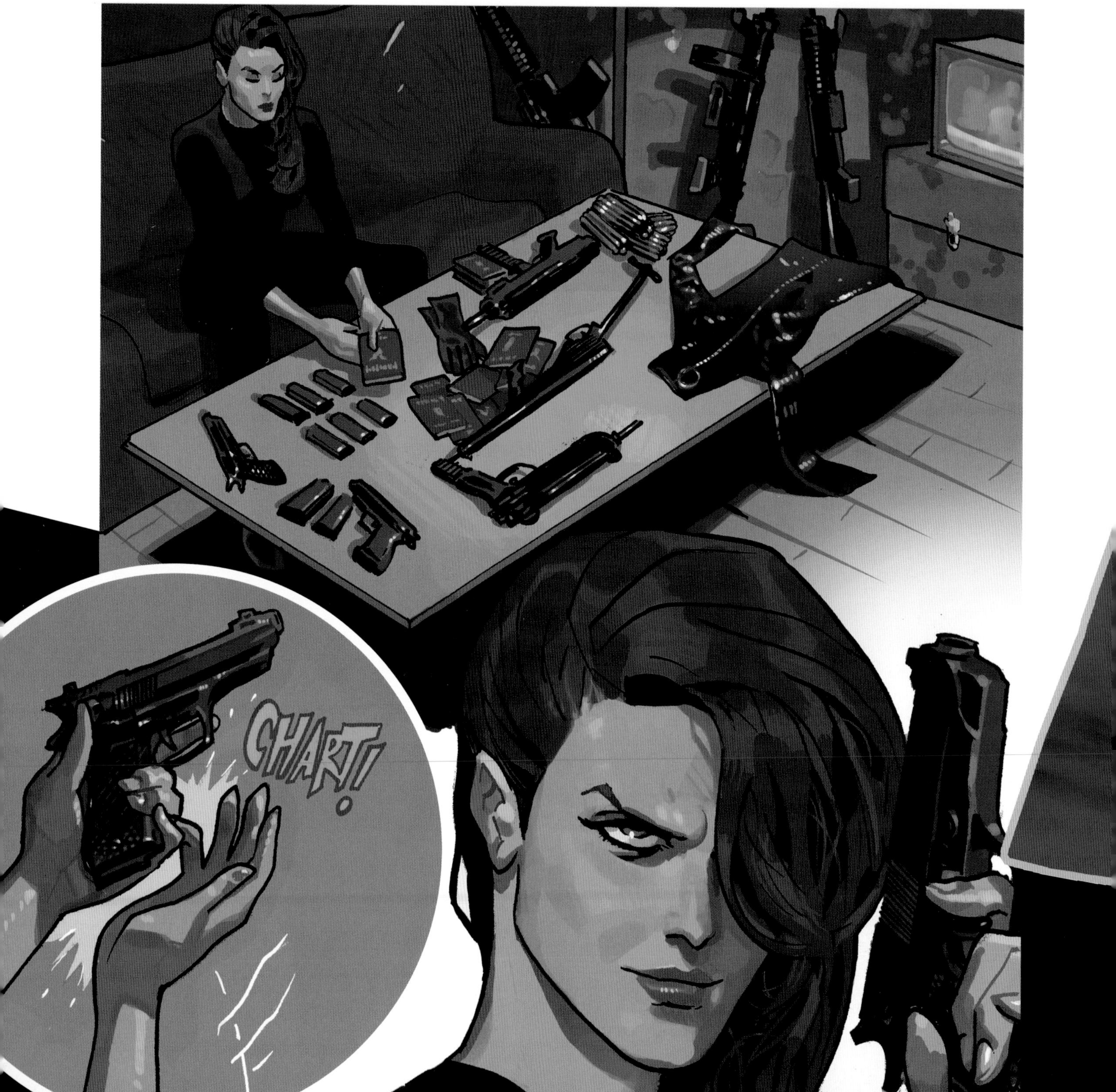
CHART!

ABOVE: BLACK WIDOW #2 (JUL. 2010) No matter what was going on in her life, Natasha could rely on a network of safe houses where she could retreat

OPPOSITE: BLACK WIDOW #5 (OCT. 2010) Fighting Imus Champion, Black Widow managed to convincingly best her much larger opponent

Although Natasha appeared to have come to terms with her past, it was not done with her yet. A black rose tied with a black ribbon had been sent to her—Natasha knew that it signified her lost baby and her wartime relationship with the long-dead soldier called Nikolai. The question was, who else knew and why were they using this knowledge now?

Then she was brutally attacked in the street, and a data chip extracted from her body. Natasha had been storing information on the chip about all her Super Hero colleagues. As Black Widow lay in the hospital, a government representative told Bucky, Hawkeye, and Tony Stark that Natasha was selling their secrets to the highest bidder. Although they did not believe it, she had to try and prove her innocence. Black Widow fled the hospital before anyone could stop her and headed for one of her safe houses to arm herself and plan her next move.

The trail led Natasha back to Europe, where she had deduced that her opponent was Imus Champion, a corrupt businessman and former Avengers enemy. He had been using robots to remotely carry out his orders. As soon as Black Widow had managed to extract and record a confession from a government official confirming that she had been framed, she went after Champion. He had managed to obtain Ivan Petrovitch's brain and used it to extract all Black Widow's secrets. Champion told her that they were alike, two lone killers, but she retorted that *she* would not be the one to die alone. They fought fiercely, with Natasha emerging victorious and ultimately destroying all of the villain's tech.

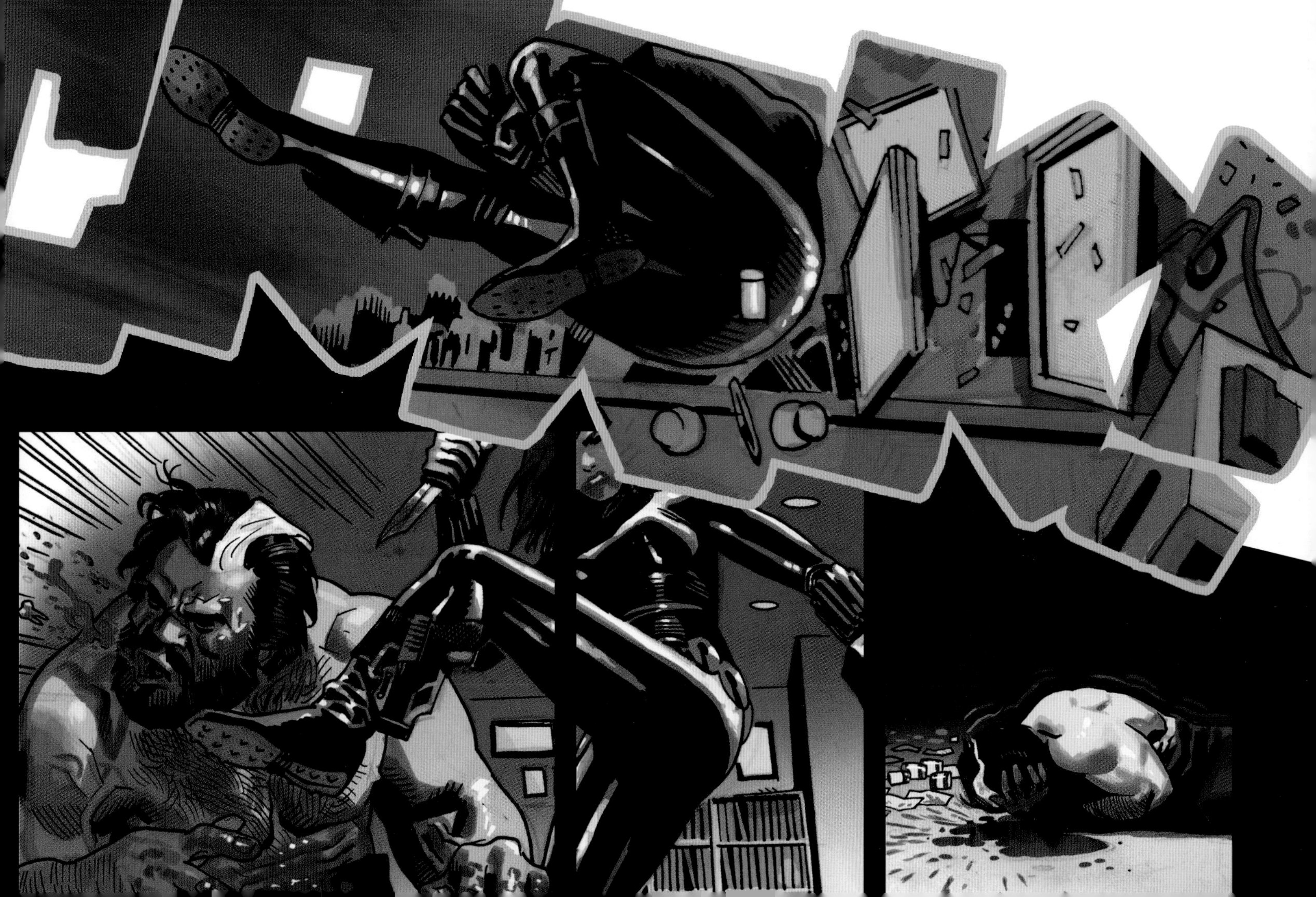

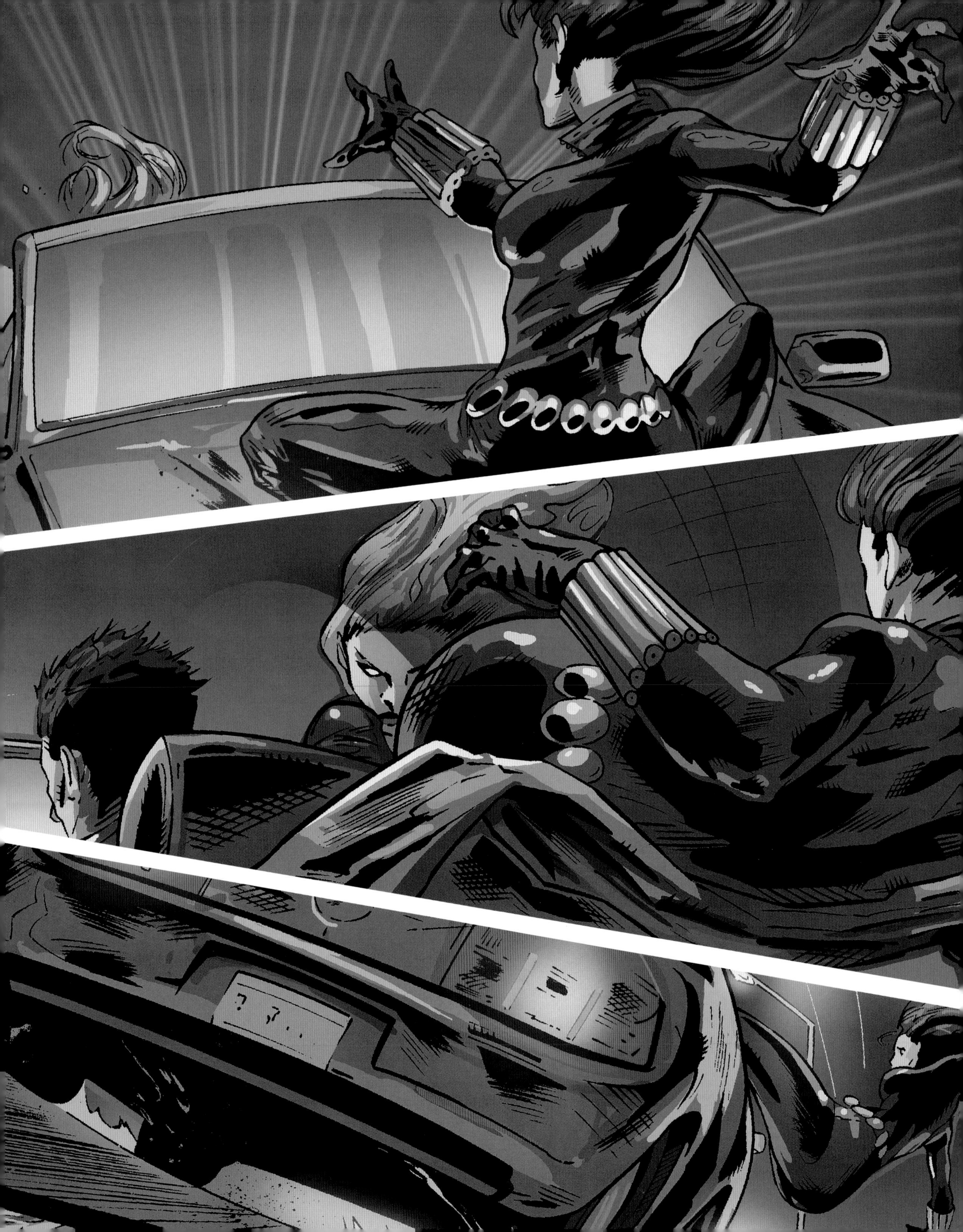

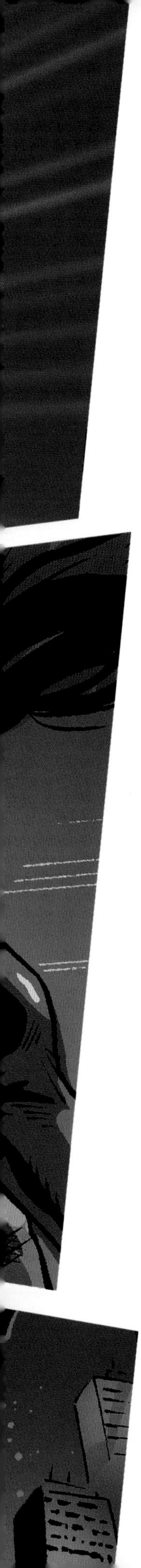

Heat of Battle

**BLACK WIDOW #6
(NOV. 2010)** After a Black
Widow doppelgänger
committed a series of
political killings, Natasha
Romanoff had to fight
to clear her name.

No sooner had Natasha defeated Imus Champion, than a formidable new enemy arose to plague her. Someone had been using a doppelgänger of Black Widow to murder political players and money men. The trail, once again, led her back to Russia, and a top-secret Red Room facility. Here she ran into Hawkeye, Mockingbird, the World Counterterrorism Agency chief, and the slow-aging mercenary Dominic Fortune, who were investigating the deaths of several spies. All the trainees in this Red Room had been executed, and evidence indicated that the ninja Ronin was the perpetrator. Since this had been one of Hawkeye's former identities, he was immediately arrested by the Russian heroes known as the Supreme Soviets.

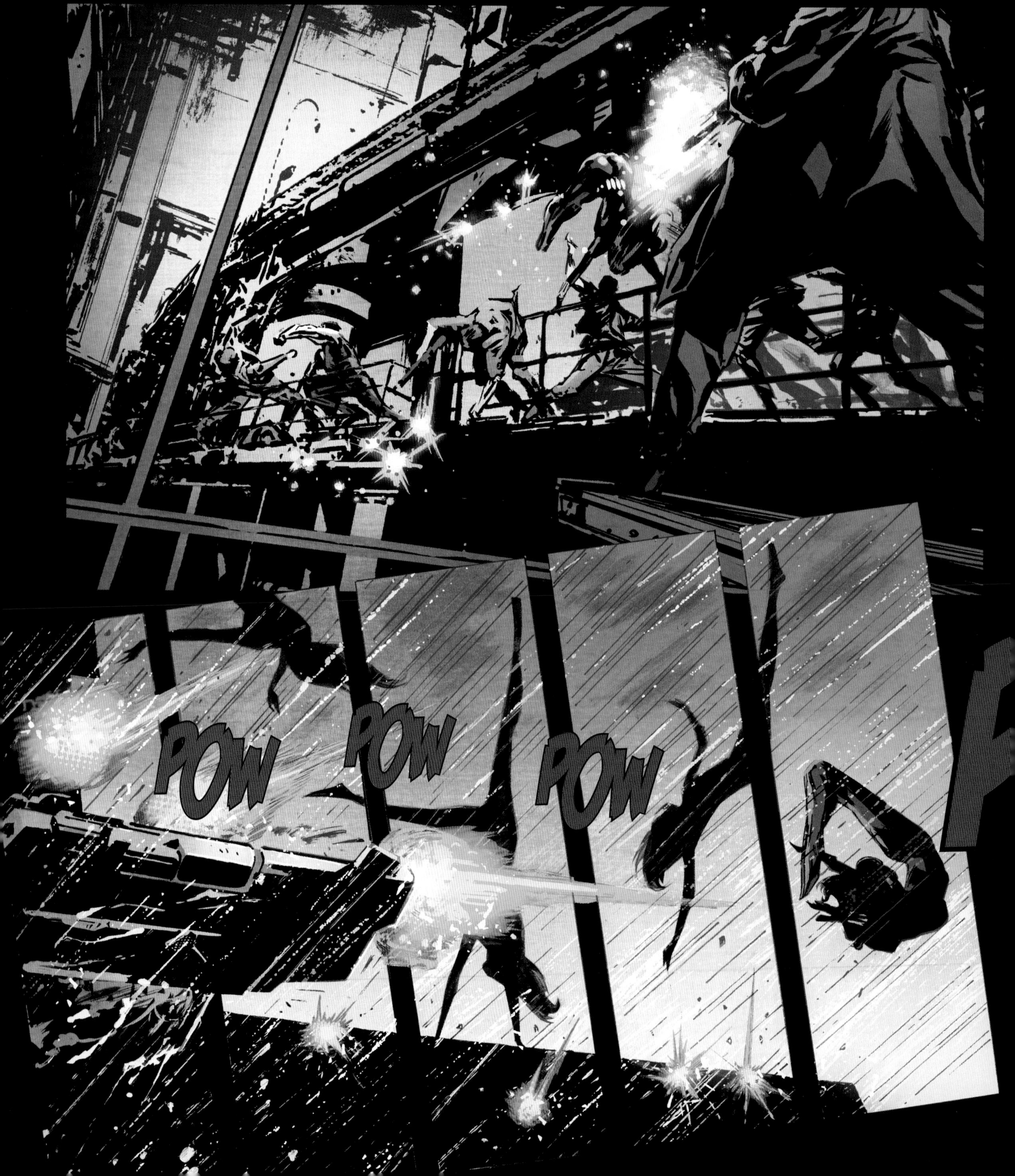
POW
POW
POW

Black Widow, Hawkeye, Fortune, and Mockingbird fought the Supreme Soviets to stop them leaving with Hawkeye. With her knowledge of the team, Black Widow knew that the key to defeating the Soviets was to take out the youngest team member, Fantasma, whose hallucinations caused fear and confusion in her enemies. Separated from Mockingbird and Fortune, Black Widow and Hawkeye set out to investigate the identity of the new Ronin.

Arriving at the disputed Kuril Islands in the Pacific Ocean, the duo came face-to-face with Ronin. Natasha attacked, having deduced that he was none other than her former husband, Alexei Shostakov. Having survived incarceration in Bulgaria, Alexei had come to despise Russia's transition to democracy, and became Ronin

to destroy the Kuril Islands and, ultimately, Russia and Japan. And he had lured Black Widow there to witness it all. She prepared to fight him again, but Alexei knew all her moves, so Natasha resorted to wilier methods to defeat him. Using Fantasma's hallucinatory powers to trick him into thinking he had defeated and even beheaded her, the real Black Widow shot Alexei. She kept him alive, much as she may have wished to do otherwise, so that he could answer for his crimes.

Natasha's close relationship with Bucky Barnes continued, although his role as Captain America was faltering. When the public found out that a former Soviet assassin was now wearing the stars and stripes, and claiming to fight the good fight, opinion turned against him. He was even extradited to Russia to face

charges of alleged off-the-books murders carried out during his time as the Winter Soldier. Natasha helped him escape the Siberian gulag where he was held, using her contacts and knowledge of the terrain as only she could.

Bucky's troubles with being in the public eye led Nick Fury, with Black Widow's support, to concoct a drastic plan. They faked Bucky's death as Captain America, with the intention of motivating Steve Rogers to resume his old role. This gave Bucky another chance at a life that would work for him. Although the scheme involved lying to almost everyone she knew, Natasha accepted it—after all, the art of deception had been part of her Red Room training. As the Winter Soldier, Barnes took on those covert missions that he was so suited to, with Black Widow alongside him.

Opposite: WINTER SOLDIER #1 (APR. 2012) Having both been trained as Soviet agents at the height of the Cold War, Black Widow and the Winter Soldier made a perfectly harmonized fighting team.

Hard Choices

Black Widow also continued to fight alongside the Avengers. Surviving an attack by the villainous gang Sinister Six, Natasha, Spider-Man, and Silver Sable were the only heroes left fit to fight on. It seemed they were too late when Sinister Six leader Doctor Octopus activated weaponized satellites to burn half the world. Silver Sable was in shock, and Black Widow told Spider-Man that she was no use to them now, but that they still had work to do. Spider-Man was taken aback by Natasha's apparent cold-heartedness, but he could see the sense in her decision. But when Spider-Man tried to help people close by, Black Widow exhorted him to stop. She had not meant that they should help the people in that part of the world that was already burning, but those in the as-yet undamaged hemisphere, by finding and stopping Doc Ock before he activated his remaining devices.

When it turned out that the destruction around them was an illusion created by Mysterio—intended to distract them—the heroes tracked down Doc Ock to a secret base in Guatemala. To their horror, they saw that somehow the villain had managed to revive the Avengers and turn them into his puppets. Black Widow was knocked out cold by an Octavius-controlled Iron Man, but luckily Spider-Man and a recovered Silver Sable were able to restore Earth's Mightiest Heroes to themselves and defeat the evil genius.

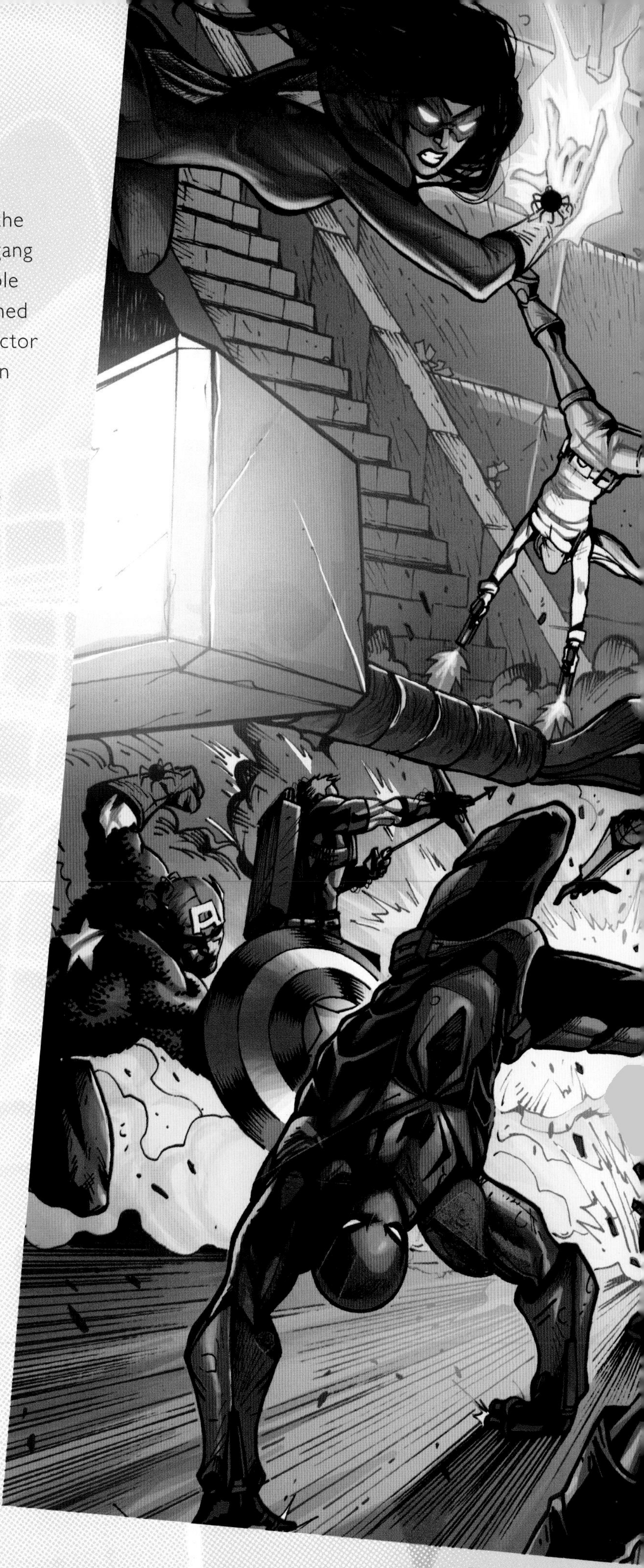

AMAZING SPIDER-MAN #686 (AUG. 2012) When Black Widow was the only Avenger to survive an attack by the Sinister Six unscathed, she was forced to fight her teammates alongside Spider-Man.

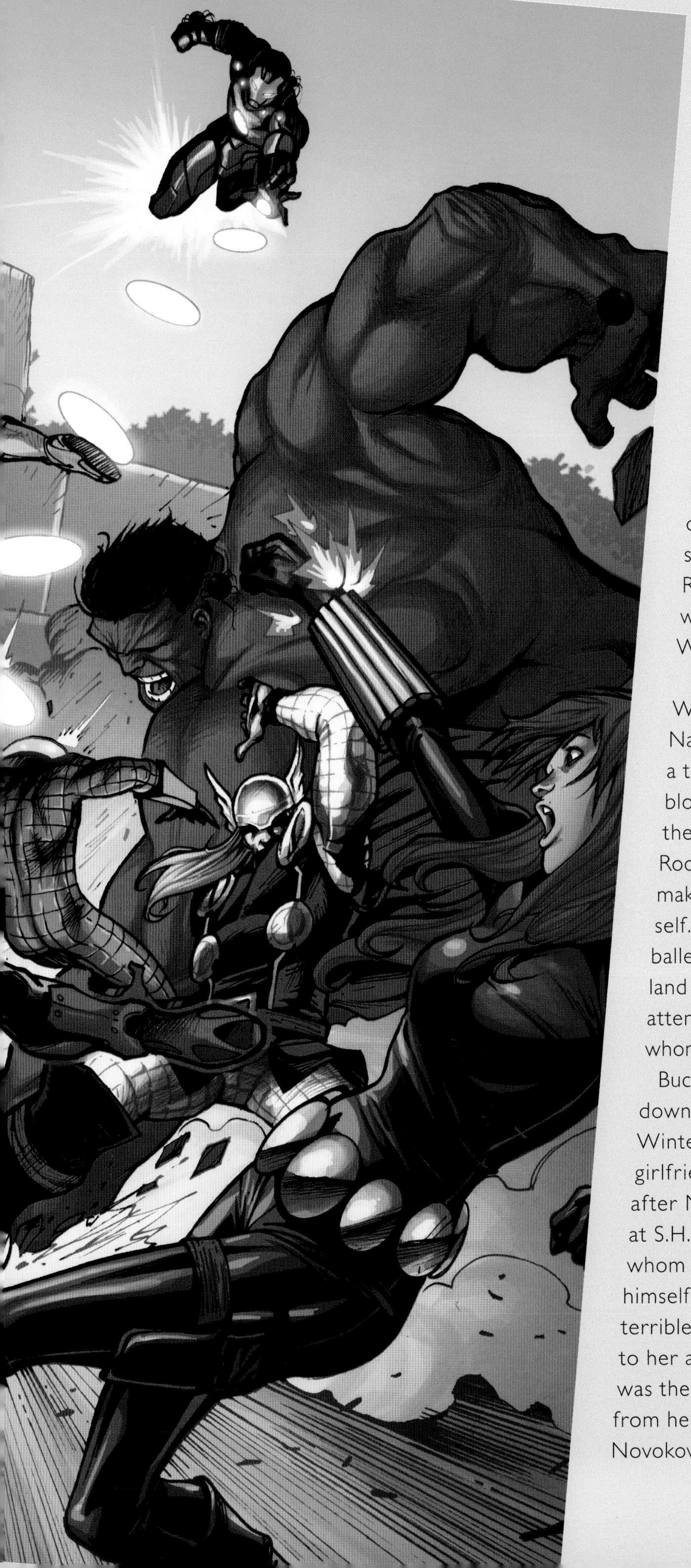

The Novokov Stratagem

On another mission with the Winter Soldier, Natasha was on the trail of missing Soviet agent Leo Novokov. Like Bucky, he was placed in stasis between missions, but was hidden in the US. Novokov had been unexpectedly woken by an earthquake, and was furious to discover that his mentor, the Winter Soldier, was now an American hero, albeit presumed dead. Further connections to the past surfaced when Novokov kidnapped Professor Rodchenko, a former Red Room scientist who had taken part in brainwashing Black Widow many years before.

As they pursued the Russian agent, Black Widow and Bucky became separated, and Natasha was captured by Novokov. He left a taunting note to Bucky written in Natasha's blood. Novokov had built a machine based on the one used to brainwash Natasha in the Red Room, and he kidnapped Rodchenko to help him make Black Widow revert to her old, anti-West self. She was given the cover persona of a ballerina, and Novokov manipulated events to land her a starring role in a show that would be attended by the first lady of the United States—whom Black Widow was tasked with assassinating. Bucky and S.H.I.E.L.D. tracked Black Widow down and removed her target, but then the Winter Soldier had to face his brainwashed girlfriend in combat. As he broke off to go after Novokov, Black Widow leveled her gun at S.H.I.E.L.D. agent Jasper Sitwell, an agent with whom Natasha had been close. Bucky hurled himself at her to save her from committing this terrible crime. Taking off his mask, he appealed to her as "James," knowing that the real Natasha was there somewhere. Tearfully, she broke away from her brainwashing and helped Bucky go after Novokov, who had escaped in the confusion.

However, Natasha's recovery was a ruse, engineered by Novokov as part of an elaborate and devious plot. Having been taken to the helicarrier, the appearance of Nick Fury seemed to activate something in Black Widow, and she rampaged through the ship, leaving a trail of broken bodies in her wake. Tragically, one of her victims was Jasper Sitwell, who the brainwashed Natasha had killed as he tried to protect Fury from her. Then Black Widow escaped.

As Bucky questioned Rodchenko, he was devastated to find out that all Natasha's memories of their relationship had been wiped. She now believed herself to be a double agent, with all her actions since she had come to the United States a sham. S.H.I.E.L.D. assembled a team of her old friends—Captain America, Hawkeye, Wolverine, and the Winter Soldier—to find her before she could do any more damage. Novokov's price for Black Widow's safety was a dire one: Bucky had to agree to being brainwashed and take on a new, unknown assignment.

The mission turned out to strike at the heart of Natasha's past, with the Winter Soldier's target being her former flame, Daredevil. Captain America helped Daredevil, Hawkeye, and Wolverine stop Bucky before he could do anything terrible, and later managed to cleanse him of Novokov's brainwashing.

Eventually, Bucky tracked Natasha to Arlington National Cemetery, where she and Novokov had gone to detonate a massive bomb. He managed to take down Novokov, but the rogue agent grabbed Natasha and held a gun to her head. The rest of Bucky's allies arrived in time to distract Novokov so that the Winter Soldier could shoot him. With Black Widow safely back on the helicarrier, S.H.I.E.L.D. doctors worked to restore her mind. Natasha remembered her past with the Avengers and S.H.I.E.L.D., but was unable to recall anything about her relationship with the Winter Soldier. Heartbroken, Bucky declared that she was better off without him, and told everyone to stop messing with her head—she'd had enough of that in her life.

WINTER SOLDIER #13 (FEB. 2013)
A reawakened Soviet sleeper agent, Novokov, managed to kidnap **Black Widow** and brainwash her into believing her whole life in the US had been one big undercover mission.

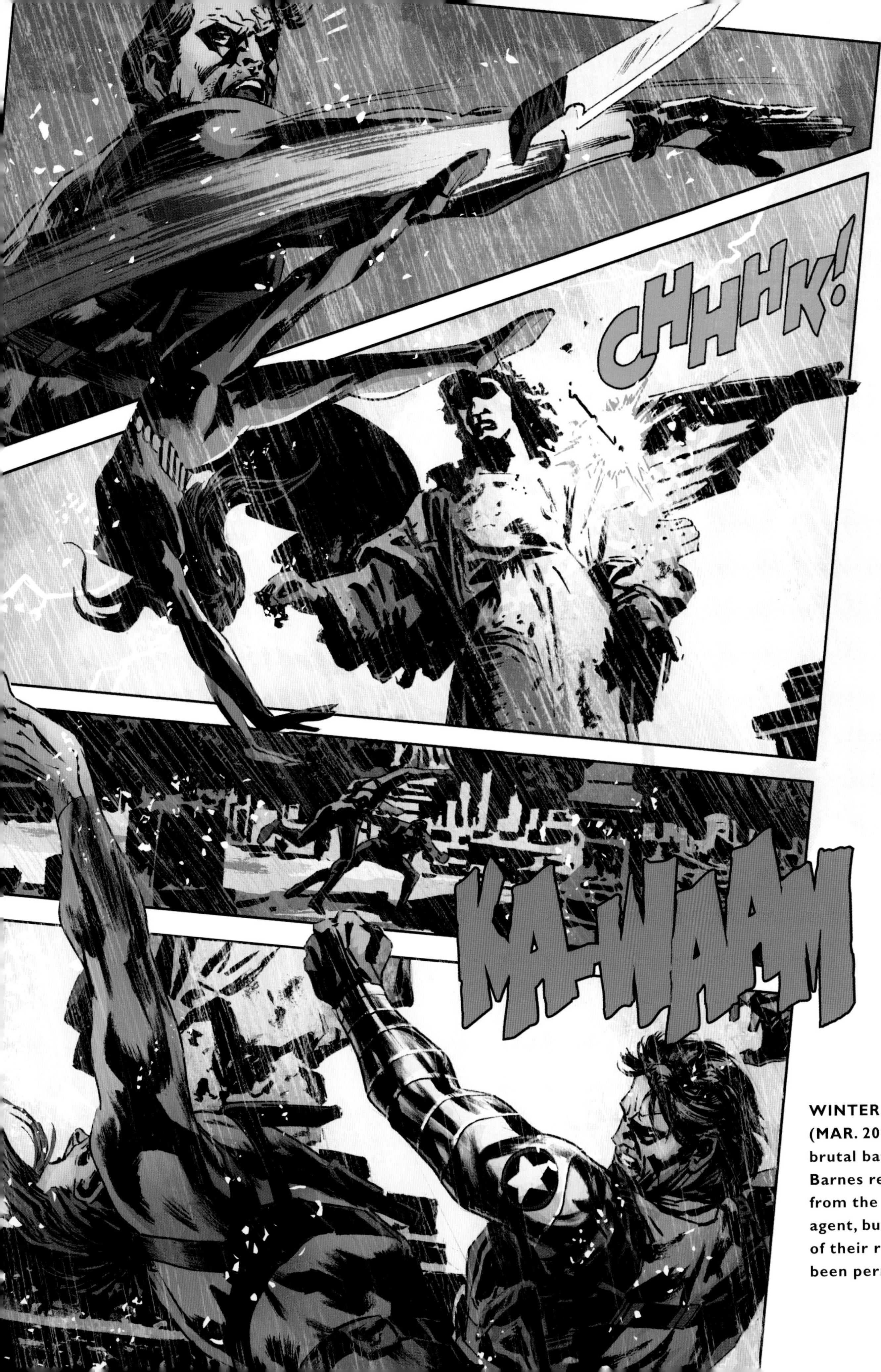
CHHHK!
KA-WHAAM

WINTER SOLDIER #14 (MAR. 2013) After a brutal battle, Bucky Barnes rescued Natasha from the Soviet sleeper agent, but her memories of their relationship had been permanently wiped.

Atonement

BLACK WIDOW #1 (FEB. 2014) Going freelance gave Black Widow the chance to atone for past misdeeds and put money into the trusts she had set up.

Outside of her work for S.H.I.E.L.D. and the Avengers, Natasha decided to start dealing with her guilt over the past in a practical way. She employed a manager—a lawyer named Isaiah Ross—to help her find freelance contracts. As well as bringing to justice some highly unpleasant people, she would also earn money to funnel into trusts created to benefit others in need. Natasha felt it was her way of atoning. As might be expected from the world's best spy, Black Widow also used her work-for-hire funds to build herself a "web": a network of safe houses in key locations around the world. It meant that she could go to ground when needed, and communicate with Isaiah back home in the United States.

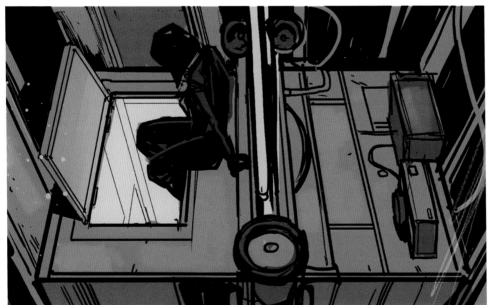

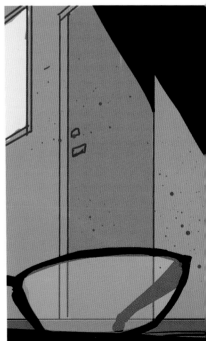

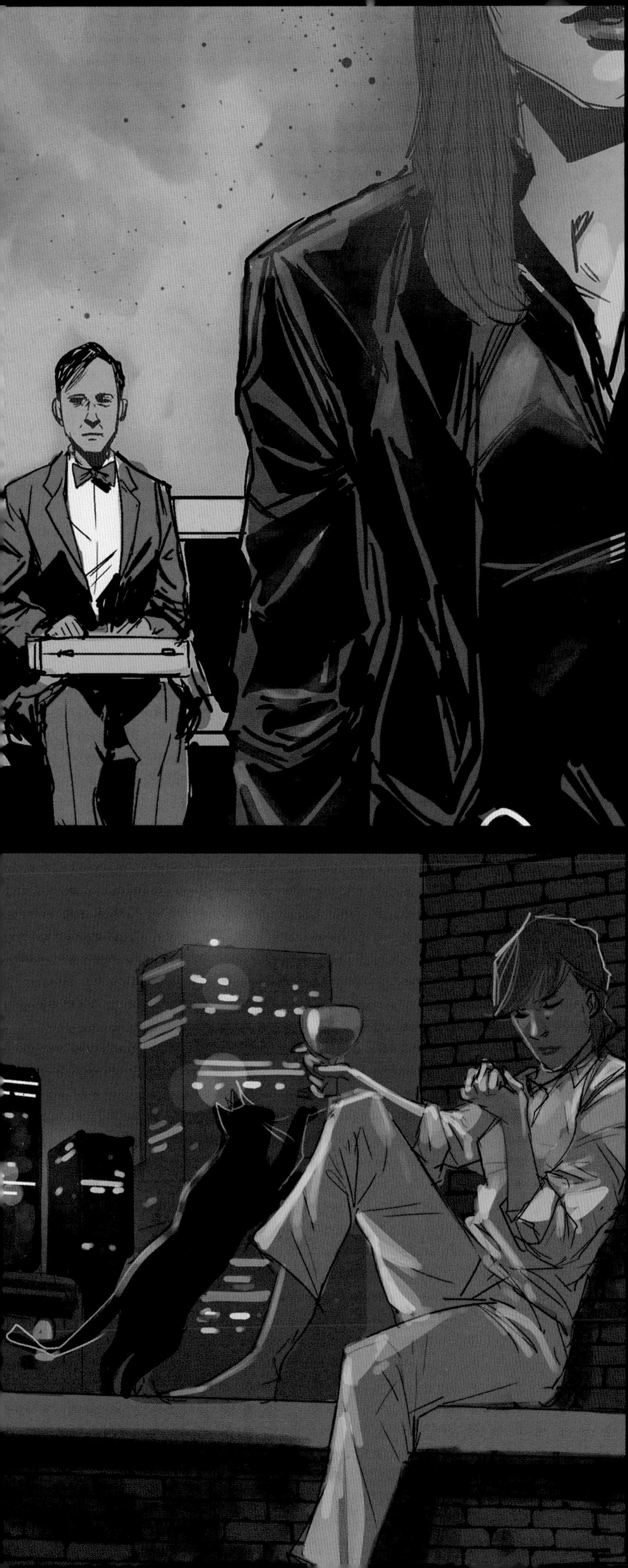

The world in which Natasha was operating was delineated in various shades of gray—the idea of bad guys and good guys seemed to belong to another life. She worked in the shadows, as she had been trained to do, making judgment calls about which jobs were morally acceptable and which crossed a line. On one occasion, she helped a man break out of prison after he was incarcerated for a crime he did not commit. However, Natasha soon realized that although he may not have committed that particular crime, her client was still a brutal gangster. Black Widow decided to forego her large fee for the job, pushing the man out of a helicopter into deadly caiman lizard-infested waters below. Later, she stopped by her neighbor's apartment to threaten him with extreme violence if he did not stop beating his wife and grant her a generous divorce settlement.

Although she was still working with S.H.I.E.L.D. and the Avengers, Black Widow was trying not to form close personal relationships. Thinking like a spy, she believed that having a life outside of work just weighed her down and made her vulnerable. Yet despite her determination to be alone, a stray cat managed to find a chink in Natasha's armor, and a space in her heart. She named it Liho, meaning "bad luck" in Russian. Although she had no memory of her relationship with Bucky, the Winter Soldier, perhaps that loss was driving her actions at a subconscious level, putting a shell around her to protect her from further heartbreak.

BLACK WIDOW #1 (FEB. 2014) Natasha took a step back from her former allies to pursue personal missions, only confiding in her lawyer Isaiah and a stray cat she named Liho.

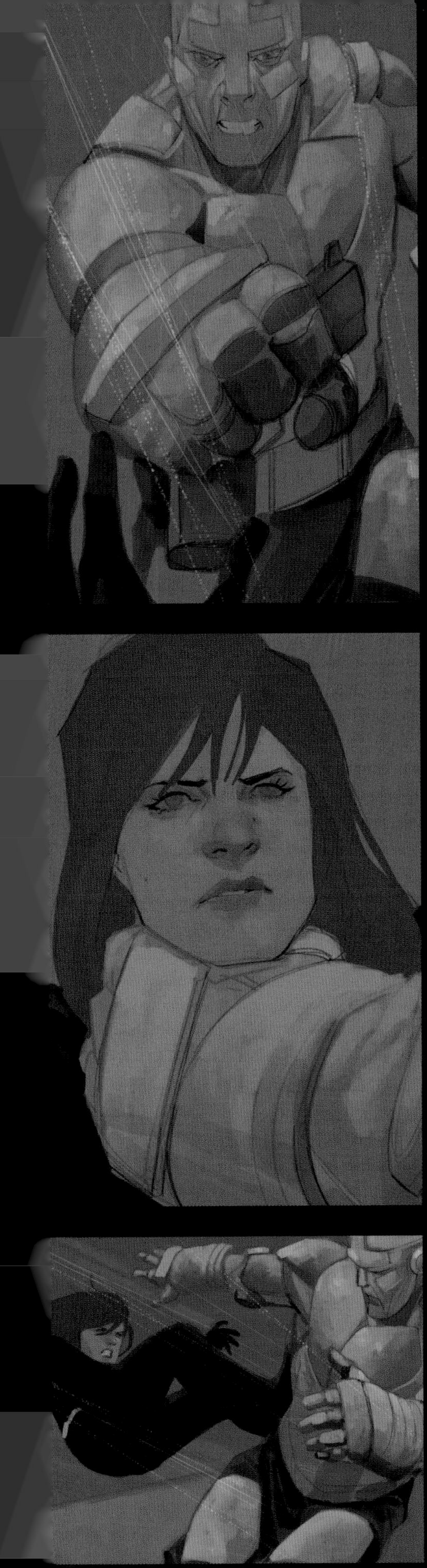

Trail of Terror

Her ability to operate in the murky underworld of crime and espionage continued to make Black Widow one of S.H.I.E.L.D.'s best assets. Tasked with investigating threats made to ambassadors in Paris and Cape Town, Natasha discovered that the trail led back to her old enemy, paranoid businessman Damon Dran, whom she had last seen on an island close to Hong Kong. Dran was no longer working for himself. Captured and taken into S.H.I.E.L.D. custody, he was killed by a rogue agent, and died rambling about "Chaos." Natasha seemed to have stumbled onto the fringes of a clandestine organization with a seemingly limitless reach.

Black Widow's next job was to infiltrate a ring of cyberterrorists. She returned to the streets of San Francisco where she realized a sniper was on her tail. Coincidentally, Daredevil had also returned to the city, but their reunion only emphasized the distance that now lay between the former lovers. Murdock disapproved of Natasha's methods of extracting information from people—usually at the point of a firearm—and he asked her to leave the city.

BLACK WIDOW #6 (JUL. 2014) Her travels through the criminal underworld brought Black Widow into the orbit of a menacing organization known only as Chaos.

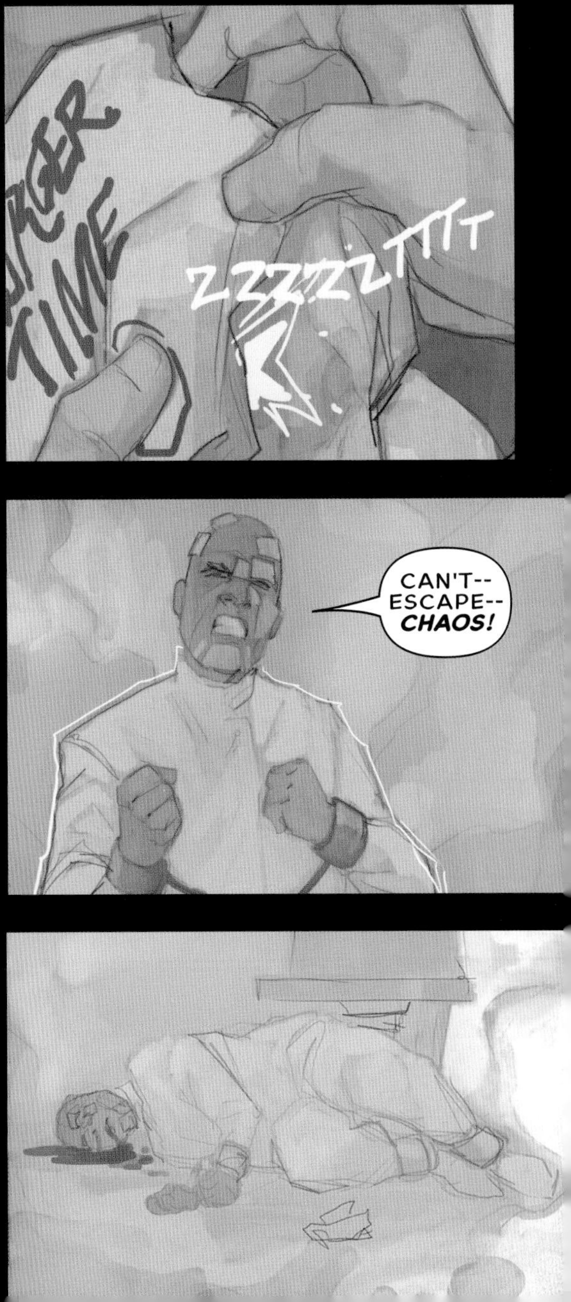
CAN'T--
ESCAPE--
CHAOS!

"They said 'Chaos would fall like rain.'"

BLACK WIDOW

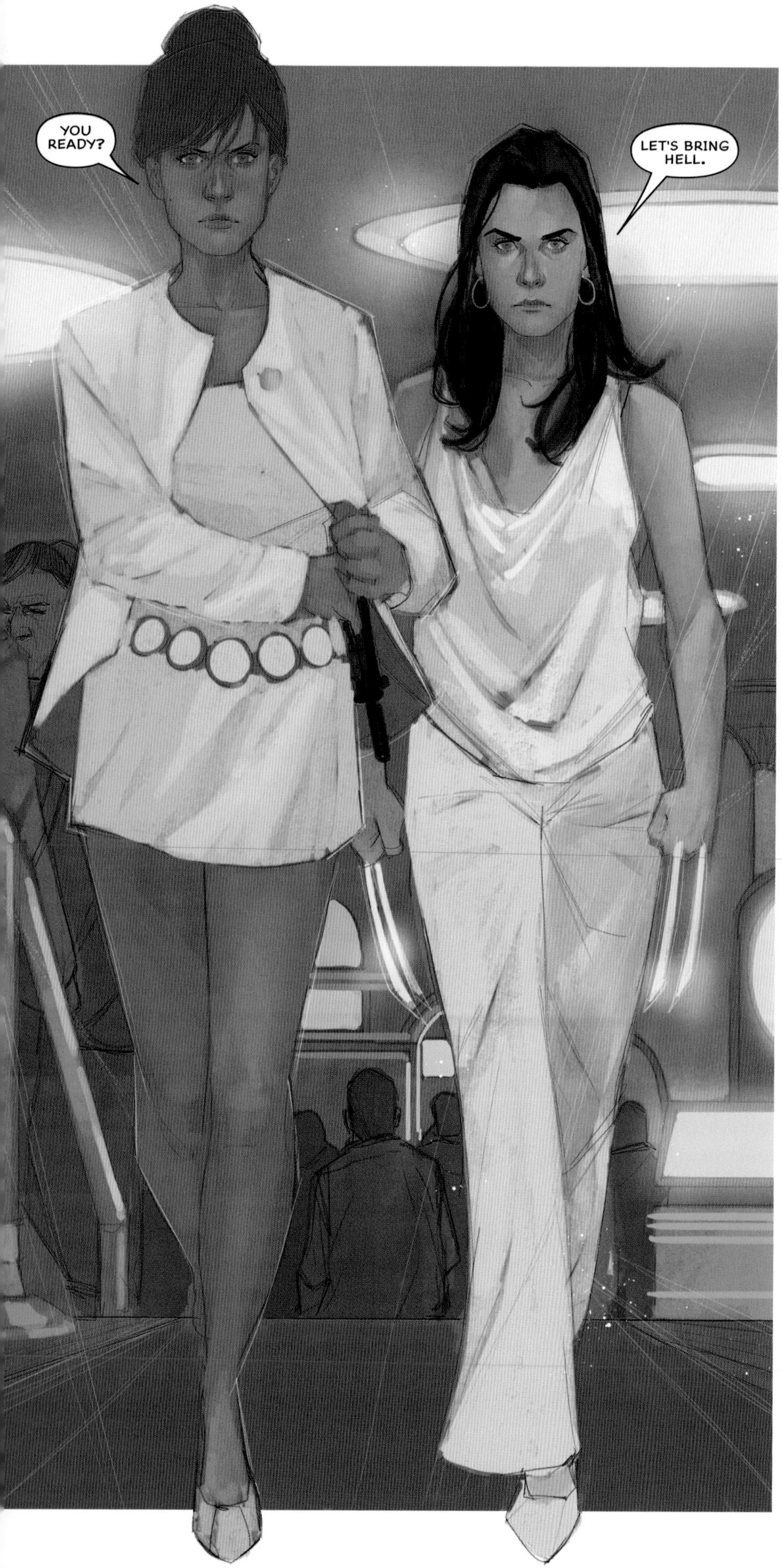
YOU READY?
LET'S BRING HELL.

Another, more poignant encounter came in Prague, when an assignment brought Black Widow and the Winter Soldier together again. Bucky helped Natasha, but managed to stop himself mentioning anything about their past relationship. She was still oblivious to it, aware of him as a good guy who was there for her, but not as anything more.

Trying to find out who had sent the sniper that had failed to kill her in San Francisco, Natasha journeyed to a remotely operated tanker that had rerouted calls to a cell phone belonging to the shooter. Here she made a few unpleasant discoveries—the ship was rigged to explode, the mercenary Crossbones and his henchmen were on it, and so was the vigilante the Punisher—but nothing that brought her any closer to finding out who was trying to eliminate her. Escaping the tanker, Natasha had one more nasty shock: someone had kidnapped Isaiah.

Her lawyer and manager was being held, at the orders of Chaos, in the Asian gambling capital, Macau. Black Widow decided that for this mission, a team-up might work better for her, and she took X-23 (Laura Kinney) along with her, whom she knew through her old friend Wolverine. The gambit was a success, and they managed to extricate a rather battered and bruised Isaiah. However, just like so many before them, her lawyer's kidnappers were prepared to die, rather than give up any intel on Chaos.

Black Widow found that she was taking part in as many street fights as covert intelligence activities. Back in the US, news networks were starting to ask questions about her methods, even wondering if she herself could be a terror threat. The American President himself called S.H.I.E.L.D.'s Director at the time, Maria Hill, questioning whether the agency should be associating itself with the notorious Black Widow. Hill, for her part, knew that Natasha was vital—she was willing and able to do all the dirty work that other heroes would not know how to handle.

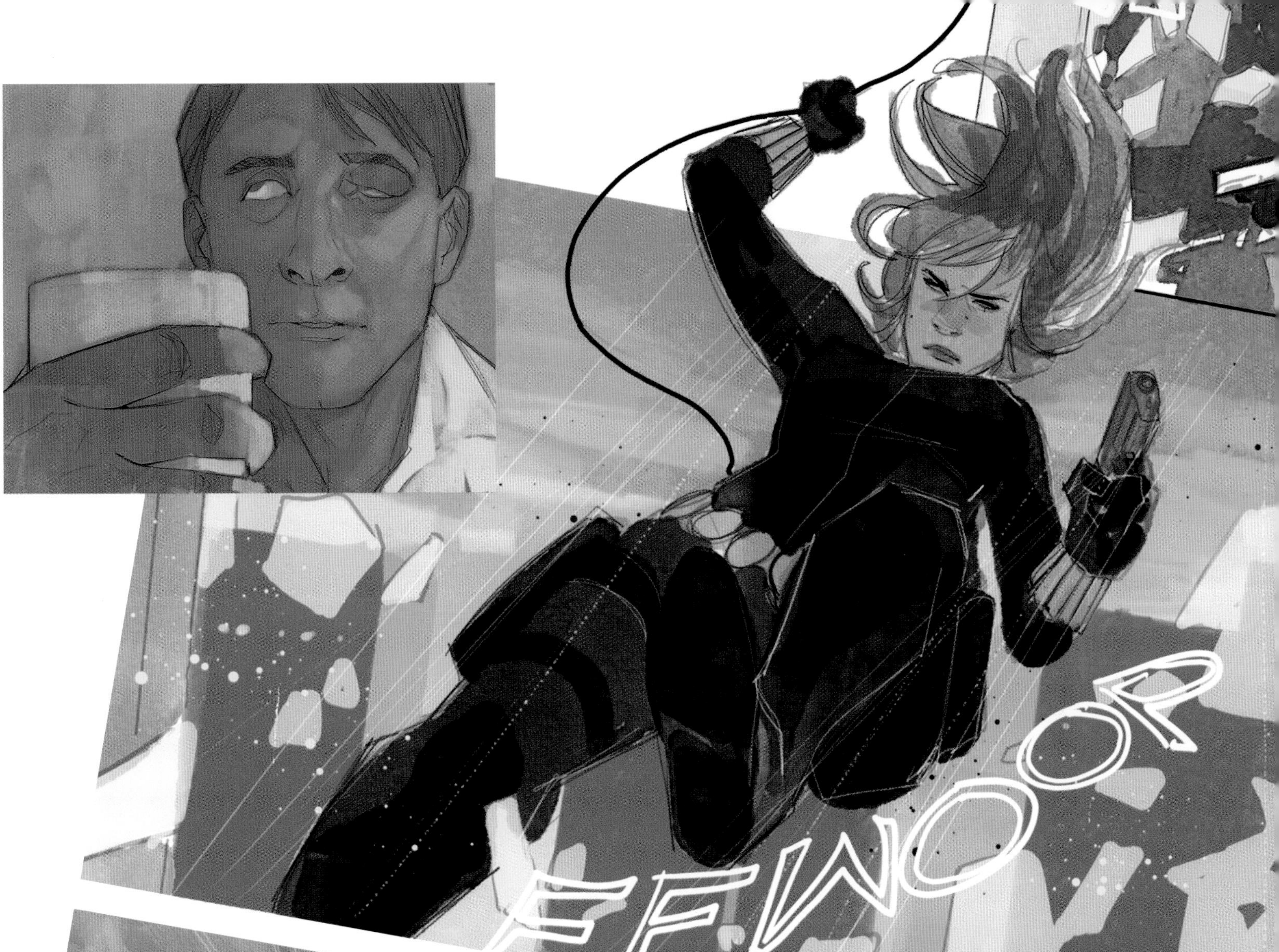
FFWOOP

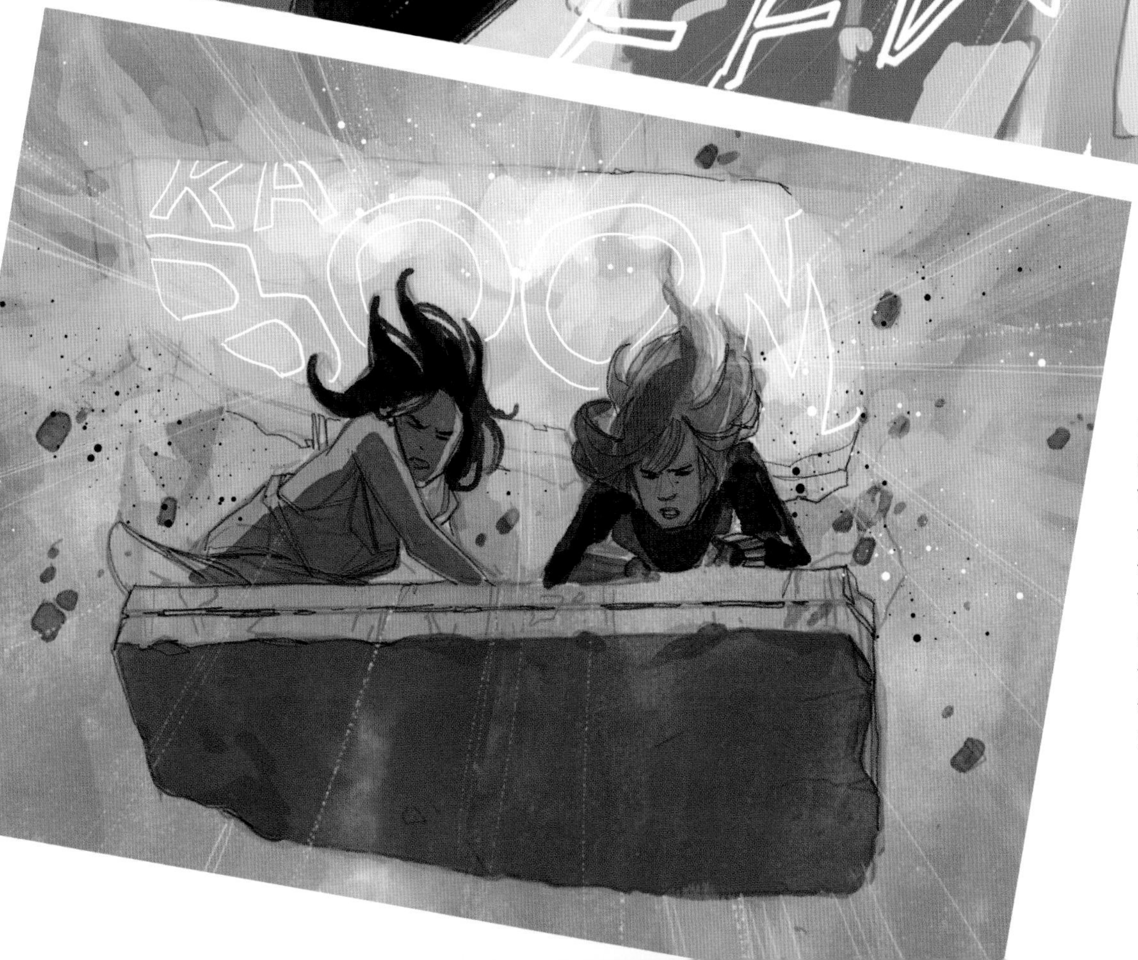
KA-BOOM

BLACK WIDOW #11 (DEC. 2014) After Black Widow's lawyer Isaiah was kidnapped, Natasha teamed up with X-23—Wolverine's female clone Laura Kinney—to rescue him from the clutches of Chaos in a Macau casino.

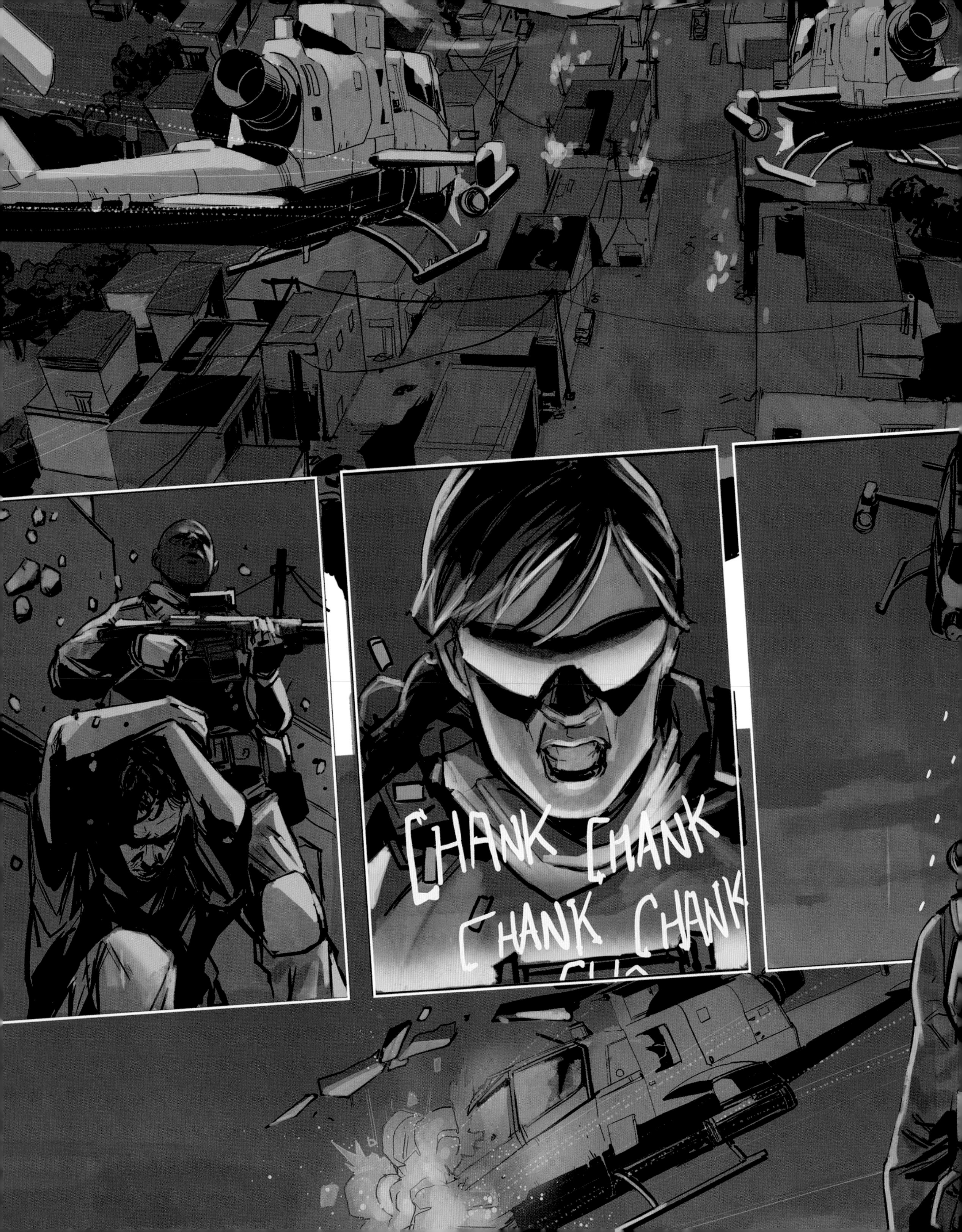
CHANK CHANK
CHANK CHANK

Chaos and Destruction

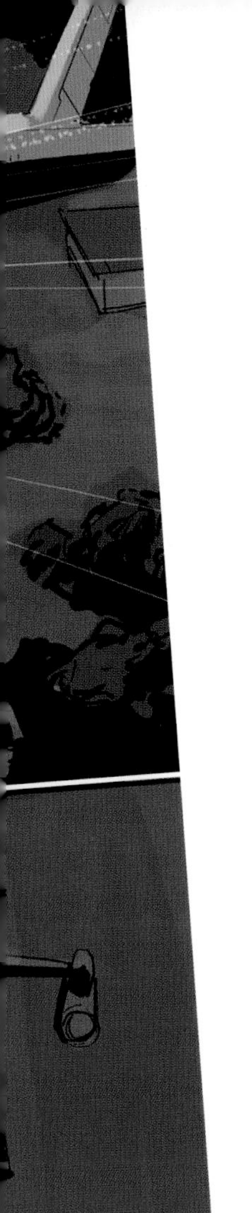

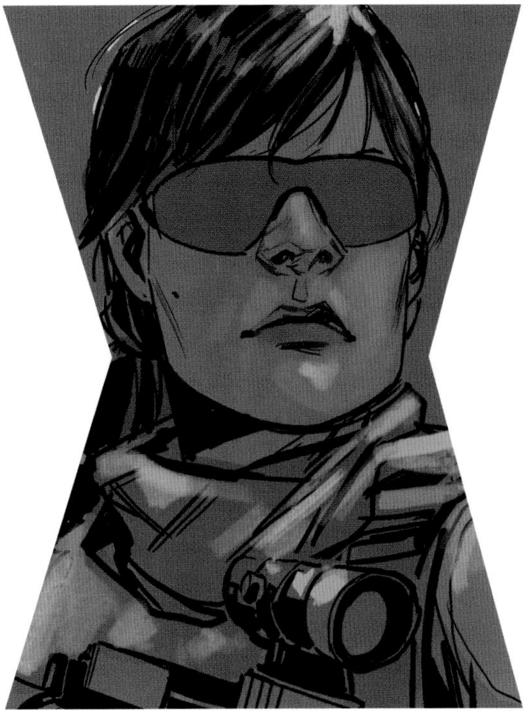

BLACK WIDOW #12 (JAN. 2015) On a black ops mission in Somalia, Black Widow was unaware that back home there were discussions on the TV news about whether or not she was a terrorist.

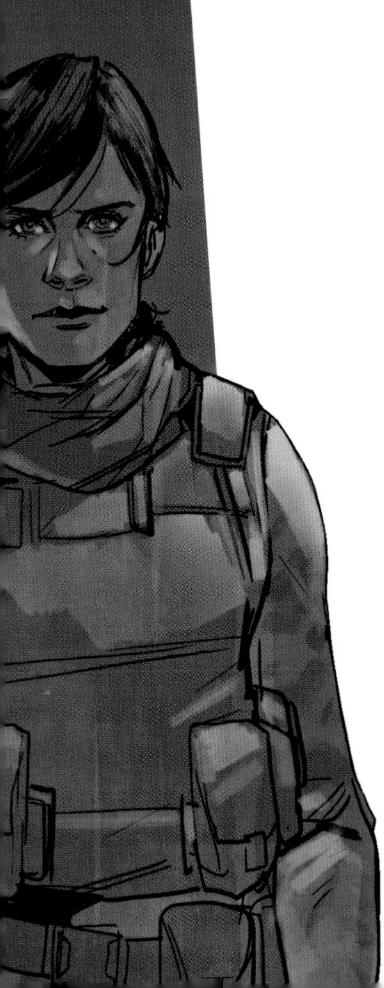

Slurs on her reputation and her loyalty were nothing new for Black Widow, and she took them in stride. However, what she could not bear was when her activities brought pain to those close to her, and so she was devastated when Isaiah was shot coming out of her apartment. Hospitalized, Isaiah begged Natasha to lie low for a while. But that wasn't her style. She used her contacts to get her hands on a list of Chaos' main money-launderers, and tricked them into meeting her on a cruise ship moored off the Spanish city of Barcelona.

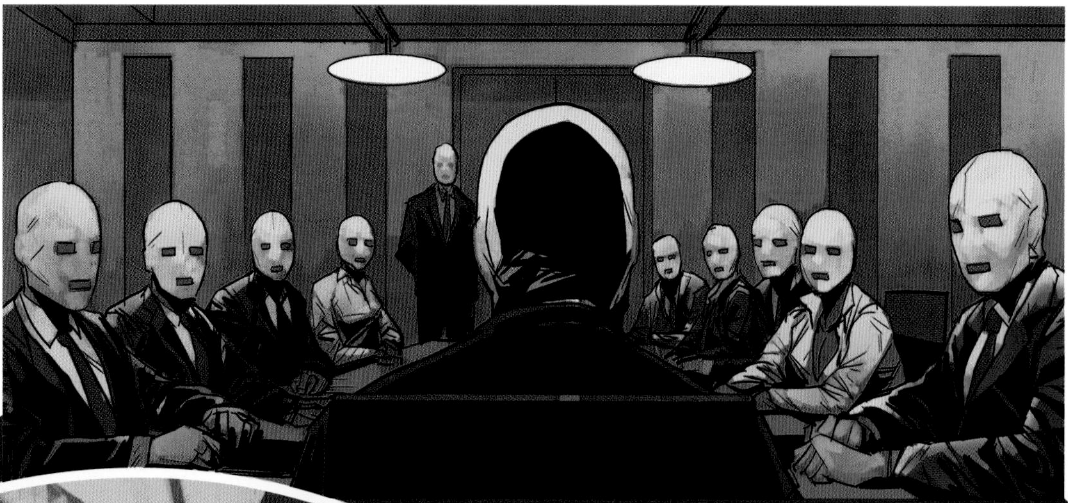

Right and below: BLACK WIDOW #14 (MAR. 2015) Black Widow struck right to the heart of the clandestine Chaos organization by infiltrating its ranks and luring all its members to a single, vulnerable location.

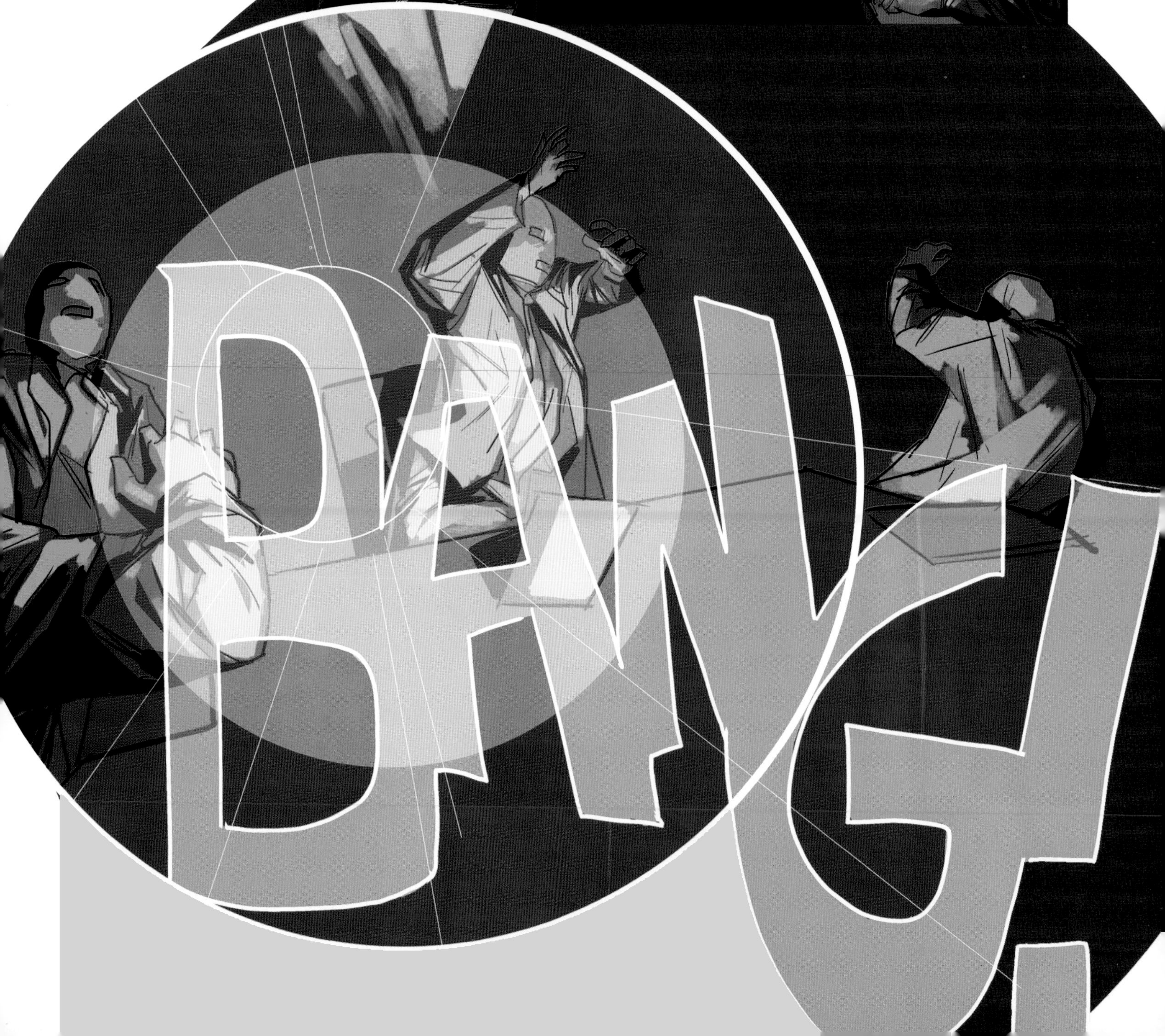
BANG!

Although they managed to escape her, Natasha pursued them with the help of the Winter Soldier, who had been watching over her since their chance meeting in Prague. As she closed in on her quarry, Black Widow was suddenly snatched from the scene by persons unknown.

Waking in the desert, Black Widow found herself finally facing her captor, a super-powered being calling himself the Prophet who was the leader of the Chaos organization. He asked her to join them, knowing that her unique skills would help them deal with their enemies. To tempt her, he showed her the future she could have if she agreed—a future where she was finally truly content, with Matt Murdock. Natasha turned him down. Annoyed, the Prophet teleported her to Russia and sent his invisible minions to dispatch her. But like so many of Black Widow's foes, he had underestimated her. Dealing with the henchmen in short order, Natasha killed the Prophet and signaled Bucky to extract her. Back at S.H.I.E.L.D., Maria Hill told Black Widow that she was a vital part of the organization, but Natasha had already made up her mind to quit. Taking her cat, she went sailing, telling the Avengers she would be there whenever they needed her.

Sadly, her blissful days on the water with Liho were numbered. With the imminent incursion of the Earth-1610 universe into her world of Earth-616, Natasha was summoned by the Avengers for a rescue mission, picking up specially selected scientists and engineers who would be boarding an escape vessel to help rebuild humanity after the cataclysm. Still troubled by guilt—especially over assassinating her friend Marina in Cuba all those years before—Black Widow leapt at the chance to erase a little more of the red in her ledger.

Tragically, she was killed in New York as she tried to pilot her craft away from the incursion site. Natasha had long accepted that death was inevitable in her line of work, and for it to happen while she was trying to save people, to do good for humanity, was the best end she could have hoped for.

**Above and left:
BLACK WIDOW #18
(JUL. 2015)** With the
Prophet and Chaos now
destroyed, for a brief
time, Natasha found
her happy place: out
on the open water with
her beloved cat Liho.

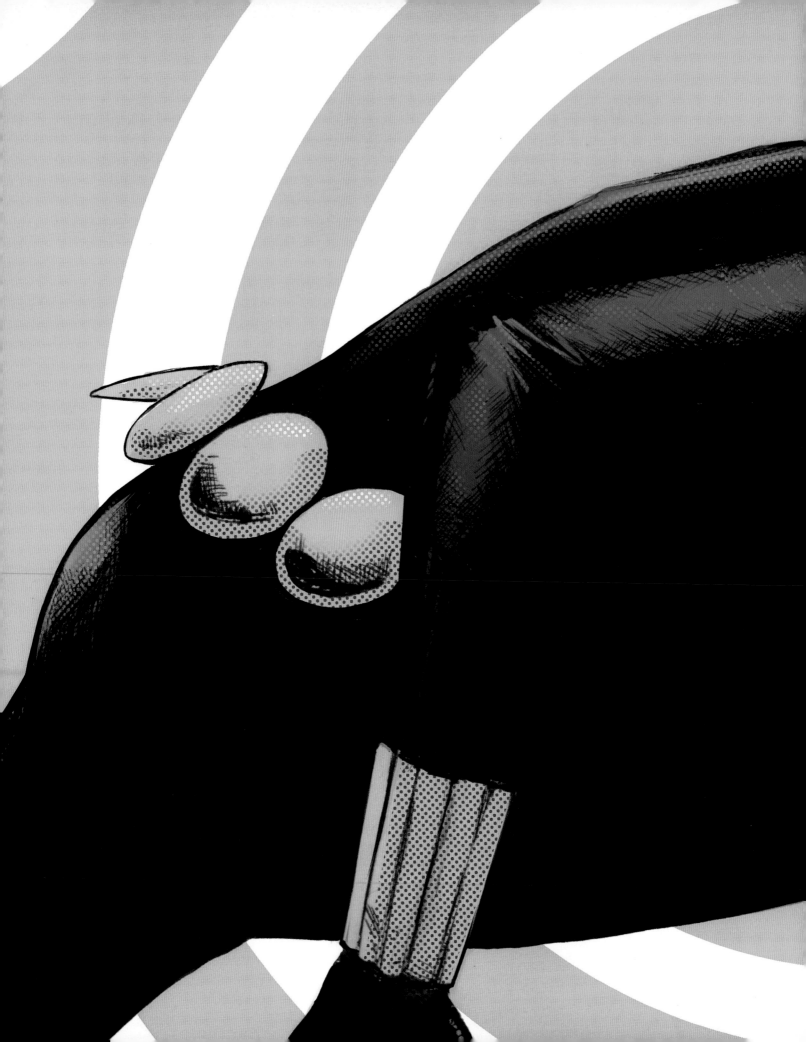

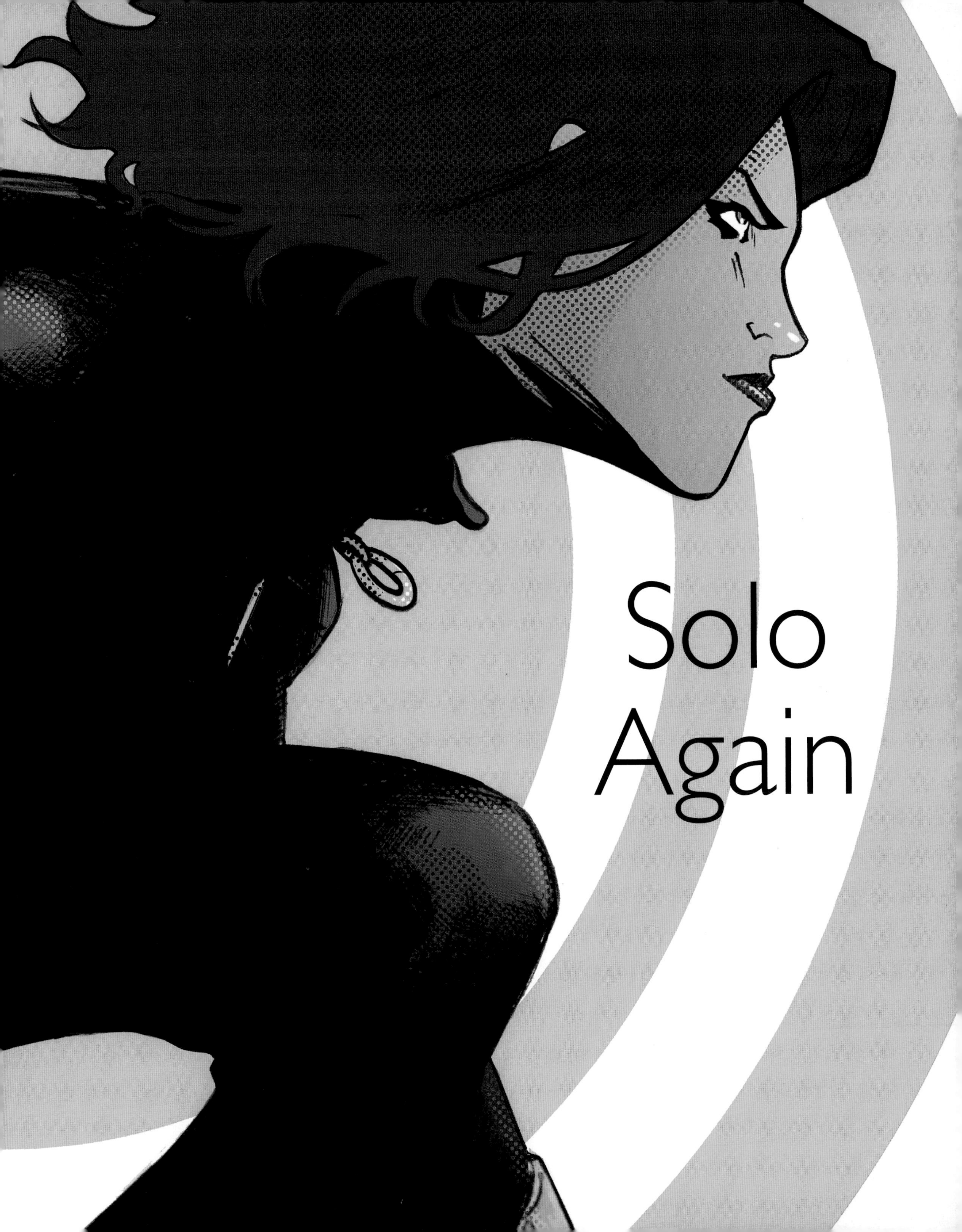

Solo Again

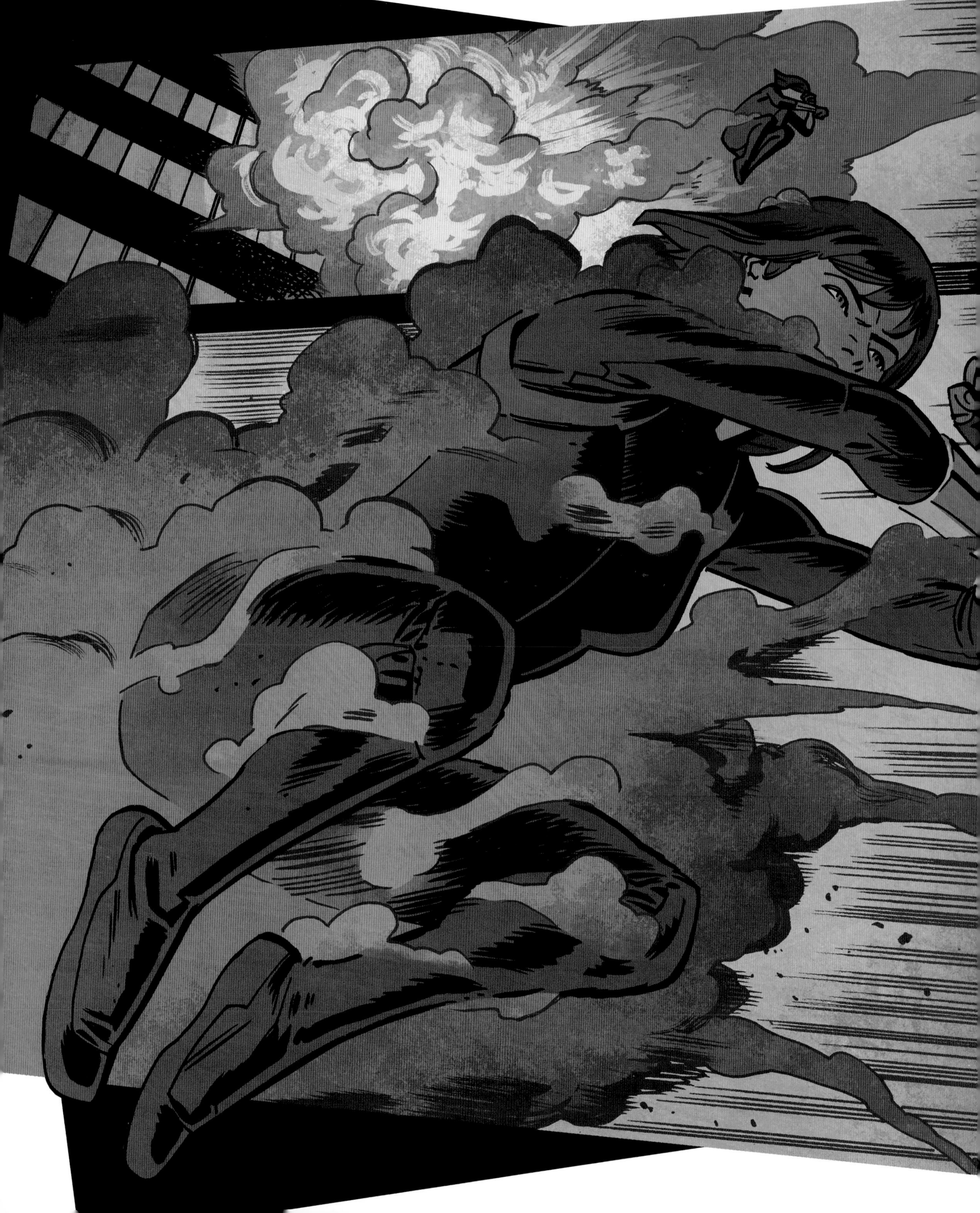

Dark Room

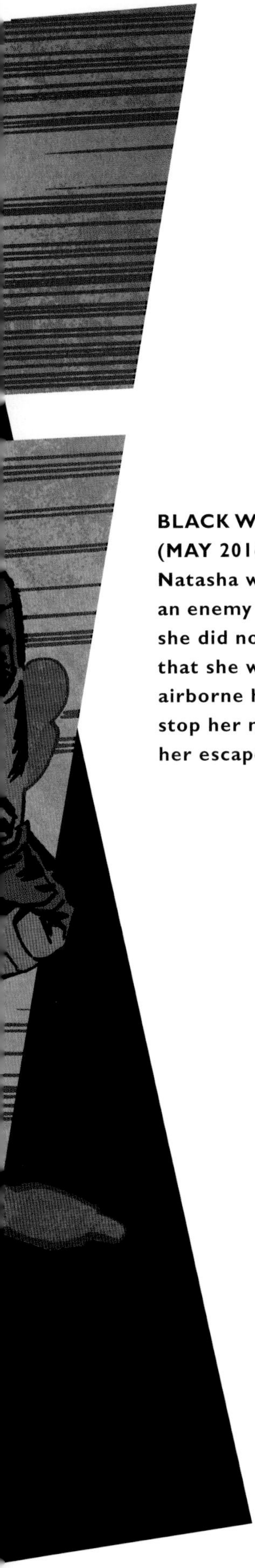

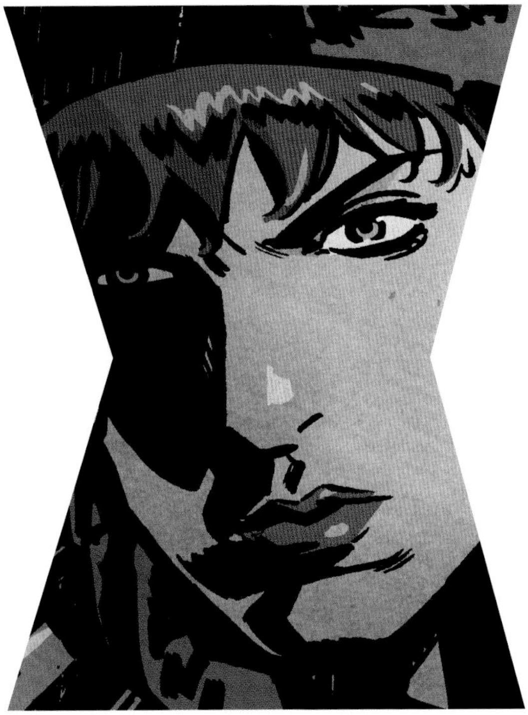

BLACK WIDOW #1 (MAY 2016) When Natasha was declared an enemy of S.H.I.E.L.D., she did not let the fact that she was in an airborne helicarrier stop her making good her escape.

After the restoration of Earth-616, Black Widow returned to existence along with all the other heroes from her universe. She soon got back to life as she knew it, which for Natasha Romanoff meant fleeing from an airborne helicarrier after being declared an enemy of S.H.I.E.L.D.

She had ended up in this perilous predicament a week previously, after being captured by a hulking, brutal, silent villain known as the Weeping Lion. Having fooled Black Widow into thinking he was sending assassins after S.H.I.E.L.D.'s Maria Hill, Weeping Lion set about the task of securing his real objective—Natasha herself.

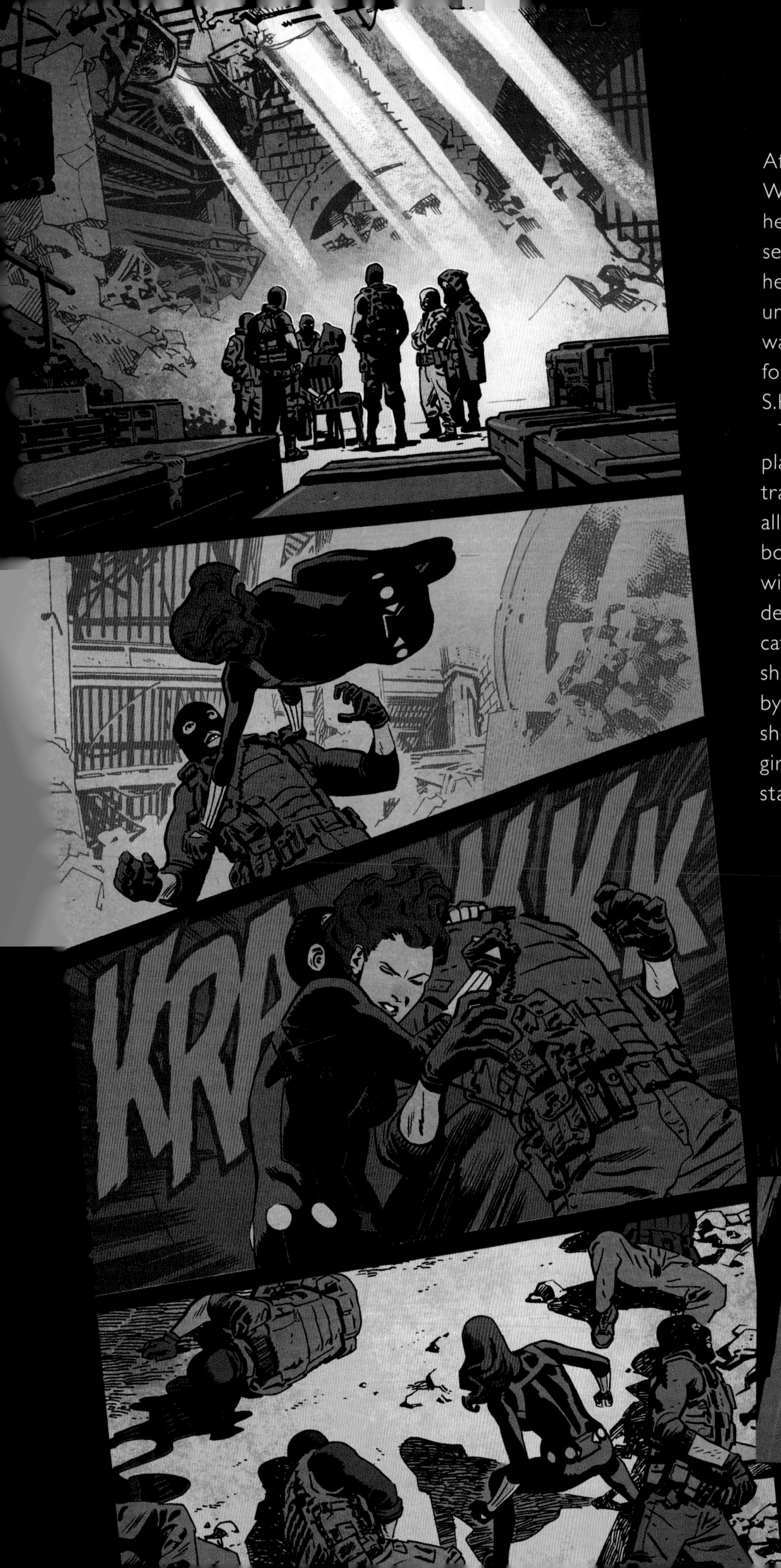

After capturing the famous Black Widow, Weeping Lion revealed that he had files containing her darkest secrets from her Soviet days, and that he would make their contents public unless she did what he asked. Natasha was compelled to agree, and thus found herself stealing a key from S.H.I.E.L.D. and going on the run.

The next part of Weeping Lion's plans for Natasha required her to travel to Russia and retrieve files on all known associates of the Red Room, both students and teachers. Starting with a visit to her old school, now derelict, she descended to the catacombs, where she walked in the shadows of her memories. Distracted by thoughts of the bloody missions she had undertaken while still a young girl, Natasha was ambushed and stabbed by a child assassin.

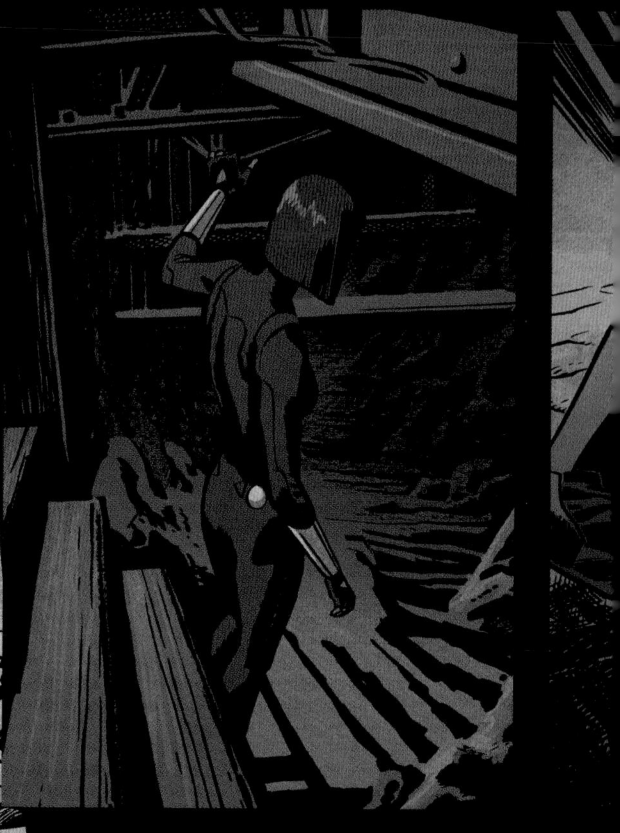

Black Widow woke to find herself in a cabin owned by a man named Iosef, who had known her when she was training at the Red Room. He told Natasha that the daughter of her old Headmistress had created a new version of the program, called the Dark Room. The girl who had attacked Black Widow was its first recruit. The Dark Room's first order of business was to wipe out everyone who had anything to do with the Red Room: a purge of the old so that the new could flourish. Natasha told Iosef that she was only playing along with Weeping Lion until she could find out his endgame—she knew that this knowledge was vital. Once she was in possession of all the facts, she would know who would be threatened by the villain's plot and what she could do to stop it from happening. Her own Red Room training had taught her that, where possible, intelligence-gathering should come before taking action.

Tracking down the Dark Room facility, she discovered her old Headmistress was alive, although apparently now dominated by her daughter Anya, who had given herself the codename Recluse. Although keen to test her mettle against Black Widow—about whom she had been nursing an unhealthy envy since childhood—Recluse agreed to wait until Natasha was fully healed after the assassin's attack: victory over a wounded opponent held no honor. Having obtained all they needed from the files, the Headmistress and Recluse were happy to hand them over to Black Widow.

Far left: BLACK WIDOW #2 (JUN. 2016) The villainous Weeping Lion's henchmen were no match for Black Widow, who escaped her bonds and took them all down in short order.

Below left, center, and right: BLACK WIDOW #3 and #4 (JUL.–AUG. 2016) A visit to her old Red Room school left Natasha Romanoff wounded and reunited her with her old Headmistress.

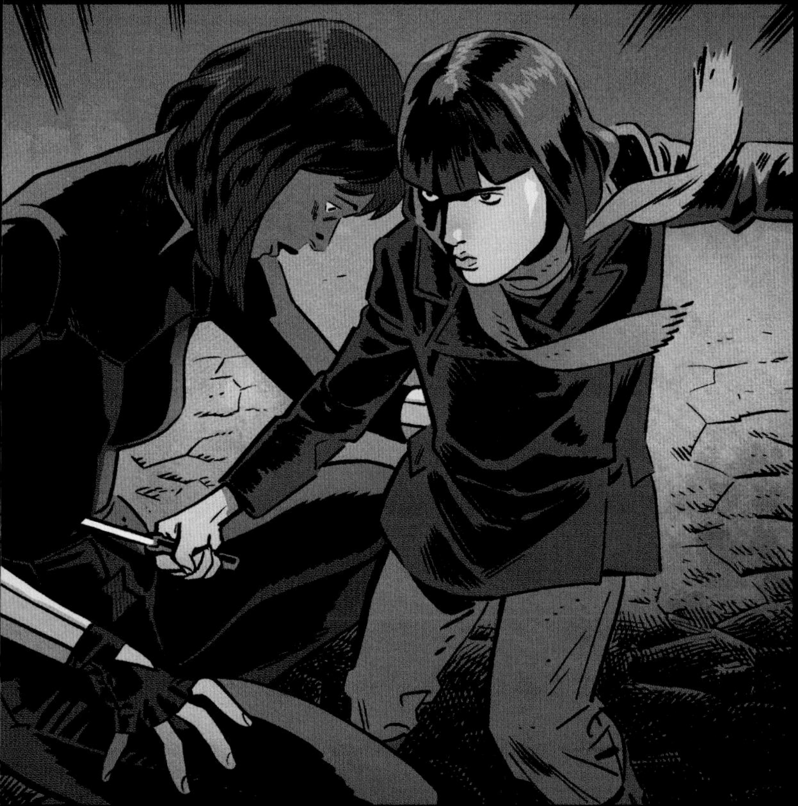

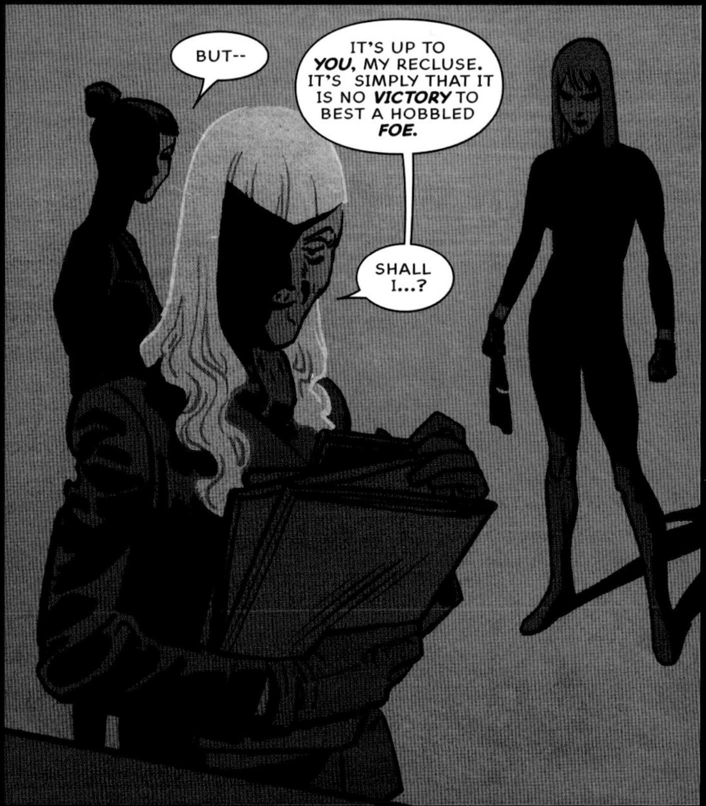
BUT--
IT'S UP TO *YOU*, MY RECLUSE. IT'S SIMPLY THAT IT IS NO *VICTORY* TO BEST A HOBBLED *FOE.*
SHALL I...?

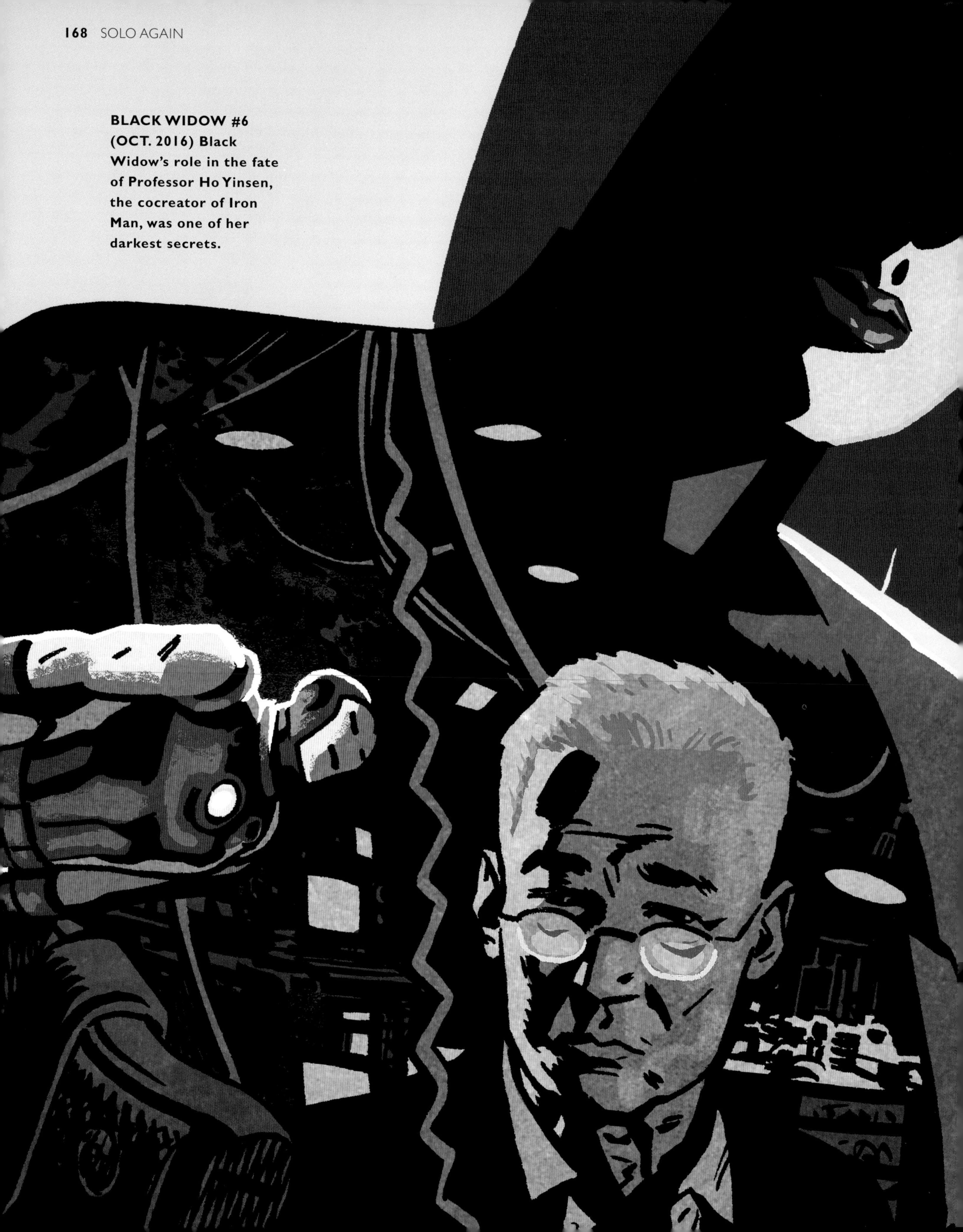

BLACK WIDOW #6 (OCT. 2016) Black Widow's role in the fate of Professor Ho Yinsen, the cocreator of Iron Man, was one of her darkest secrets.

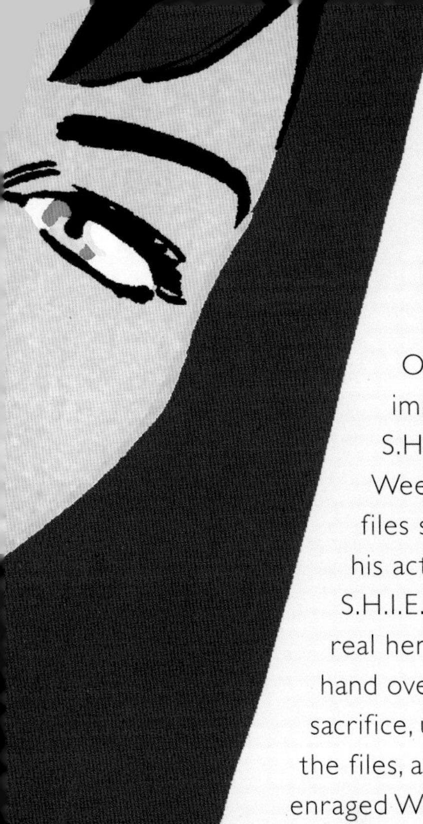

No more Secrets

On her return to the US, Natasha was immediately put under surveillance by S.H.I.E.L.D. When one agent posing as Weeping Lion's courier tried to obtain the files she was carrying, Natasha saw through his act right away. She attempted to get the S.H.I.E.L.D. agent to safety, but Weeping Lion's real henchmen seized him and forced her to hand over the files. The agent made the ultimate sacrifice, using a grenade to destroy his assailants, the files, and himself. The loss of the documents enraged Weeping Lion and, as he had threatened, he released all the information he had on Black Widow's missions as a Soviet agent.

The most explosive of these secrets was the fact that Black Widow had been responsible for the capture and imprisonment of Professor Ho Yinsen, the scientist who had helped Tony Stark create the first Iron Man suit before dying in captivity. This was something that Natasha had never shared with Stark, despite their closeness over the years, and he angrily tracked her down to Paris, where she had apparently fled to escape the heat following the revelations.

Iron Man found Black Widow wounded and exhausted, so offered to take her to his Paris office to rest while they talked. However, it seemed that Stark had learned little from their early encounters—she was faking her physical discomfort and had tricked him into allowing her access to his office. Back when she was captured by Weeping Lion, Black Widow's observed every detail about the place in which she was being held, including a crate stamped with a Stark Enterprises logo and a shipment number. Looking up the number on Tony Stark's computer, Natasha found Weeping Lion's address and went to take him on.

Below: BLACK WIDOW #5 (SEP. 2016) Weeping Lion's revenge on Black Widow had been decades in the planning. Her past was the weapon he would use against her.

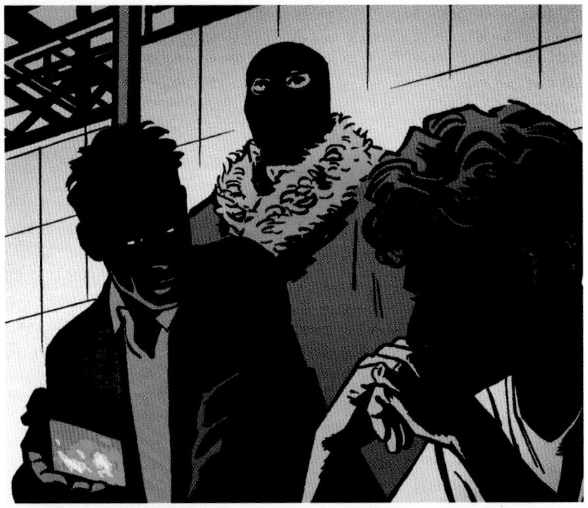

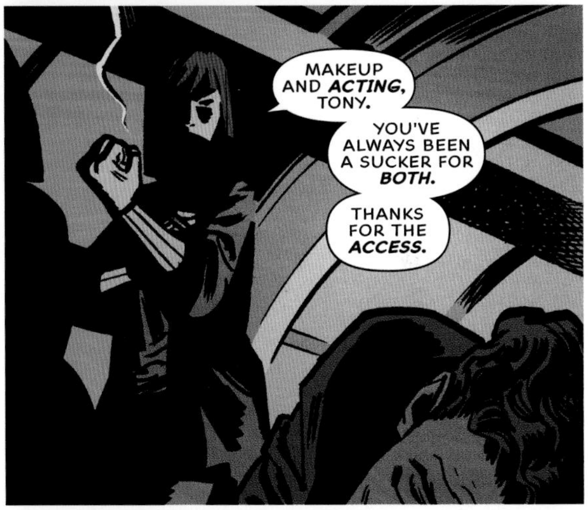
MAKEUP AND ACTING, TONY.
YOU'VE ALWAYS BEEN A SUCKER FOR BOTH.
THANKS FOR THE ACCESS.

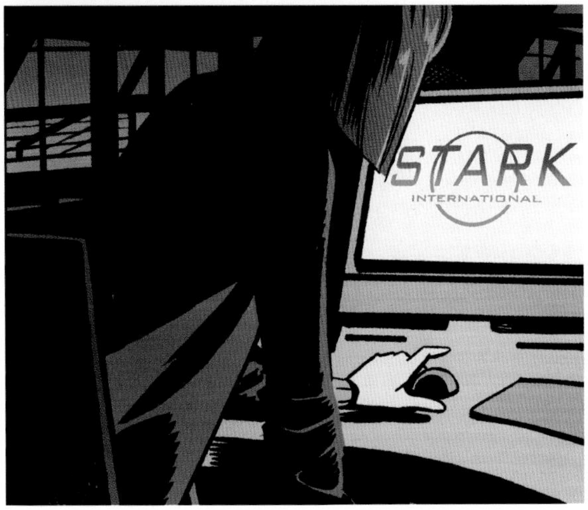
STARK
INTERNATIONAL

Center right and below right: BLACK WIDOW #6 (OCT. 2016) Natasha used her connections and espionage expertise to track the Weeping Lion to his hideout.

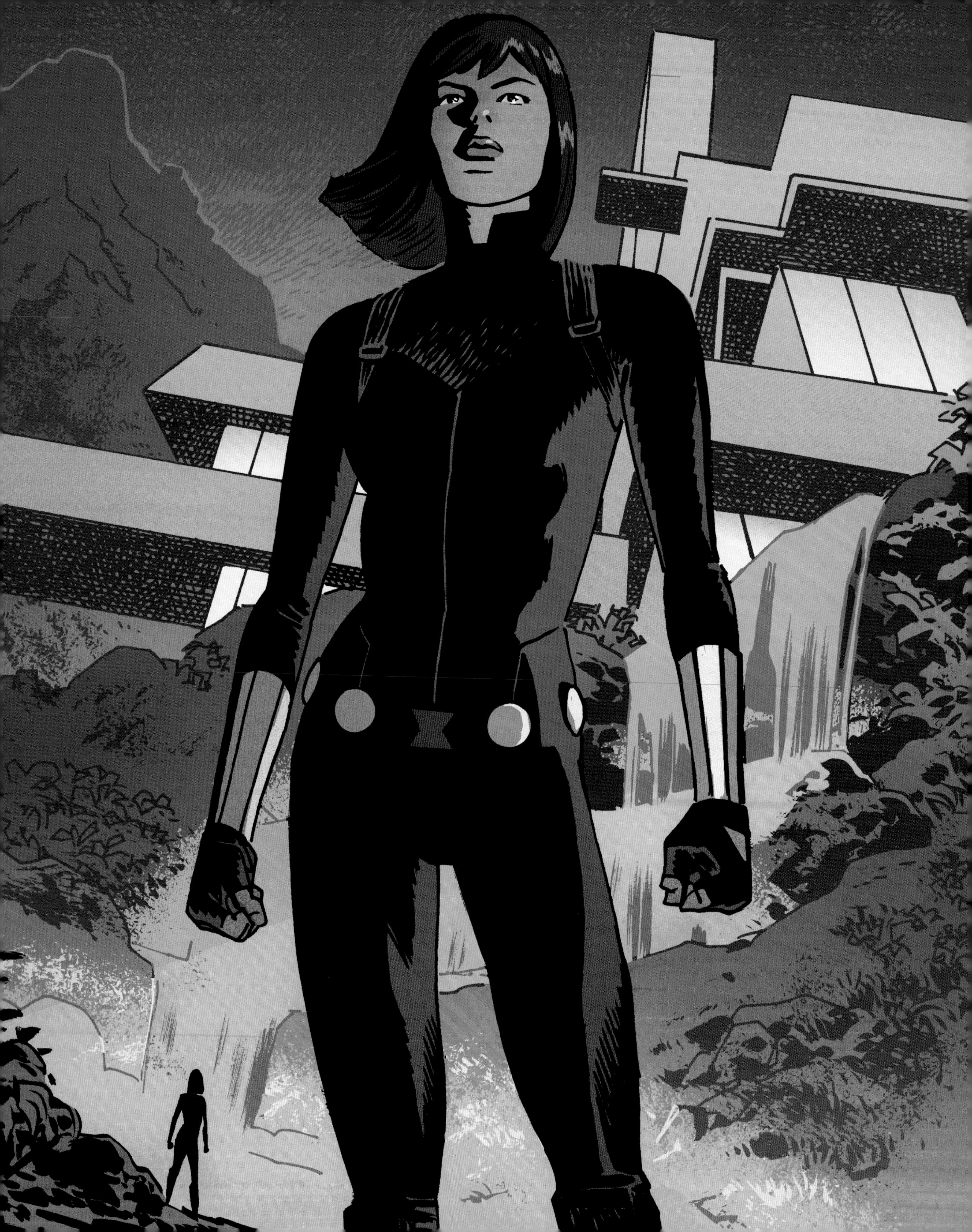

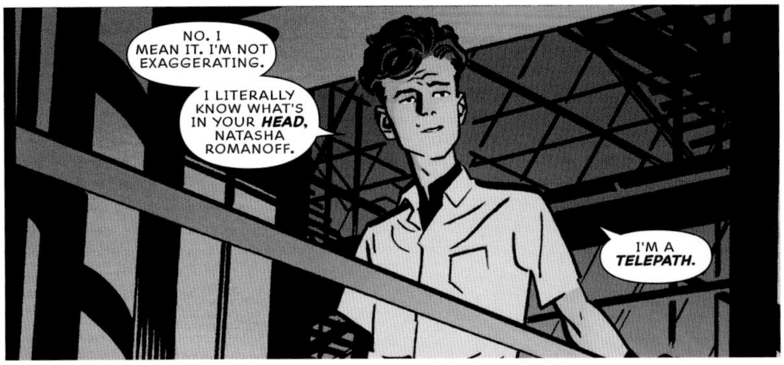
NO. I MEAN IT. I'M NOT EXAGGERATING.
I LITERALLY KNOW WHAT'S IN YOUR HEAD, NATASHA ROMANOFF.
I'M A TELEPATH.

Opposite, left, and below: BLACK WIDOW #6 (OCT. 2016) Weeping Lion believed his psionic powers gave him the upper hand over Black Widow, but she was more than ready for him.

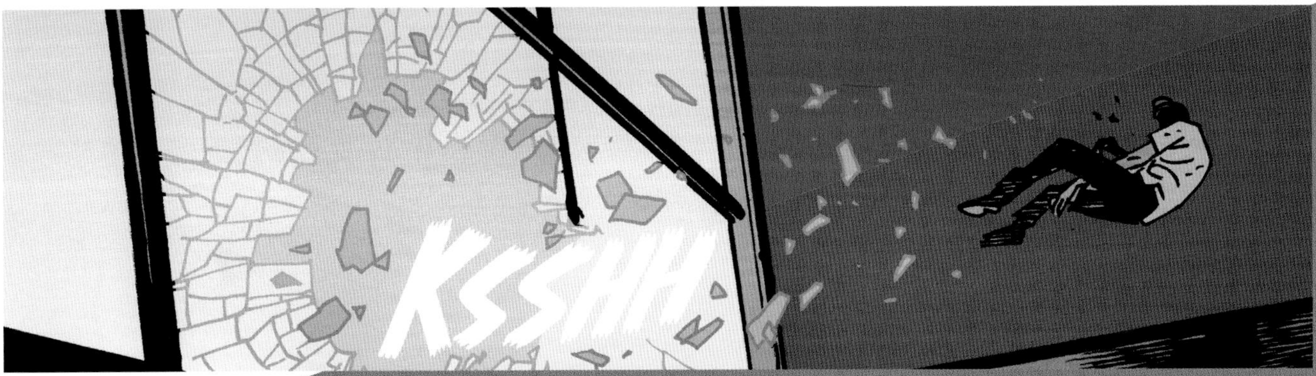
KSSHH

The imposing opponent who Natasha had thought to be Weeping Lion was, in fact, not the true villain. The real Weeping Lion was his physically unprepossessing, but telepathic cousin. His psionic abilities meant that he should have been able to read all Black Widow's darkest secrets straight from her own mind, but Natasha had prepared for such an eventuality. While at Stark Enterprises, she had discovered an earpiece that prevented invasions of the mind, and a handheld repulsor. Using these devices, she shut Weeping Lion out of her head, and blasted him out of a window. Knowing the value of a telepath, Black Widow used her new power over a recovering Weeping Lion to recruit him for her real mission: to find and rescue all the girls who were being trained by the Dark Room.

Weeping Lion had good reason to stop the Dark Room girls from embarking on new lives as killers. His path in life had been set many years before, when, as a boy, he survived the attack by a young Natasha that killed his uncle, the Yugoslavian, and left his cousin wounded and mute. Weeping Lion—back then just plain Ilija Knezevic—was physically unhurt, but the trauma of being in the car where the brutal assault occurred, which left him drenched in his family's blood, had ruined his life. The fact that Black Widow was later lauded as a hero was deeply offensive to Weeping Lion. He agreed to help her, but remained unconvinced by her claim that she wasn't a monster.

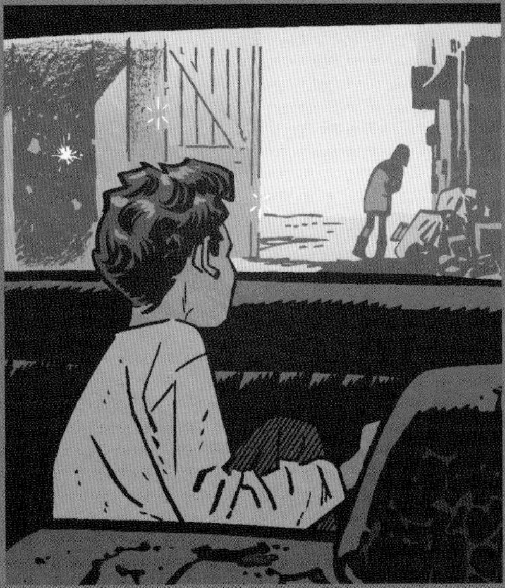

Above: BLACK WIDOW #7 (DEC. 2016) A botched assassination from many years before set Natasha and the boy who would become Weeping Lion on a collision course.

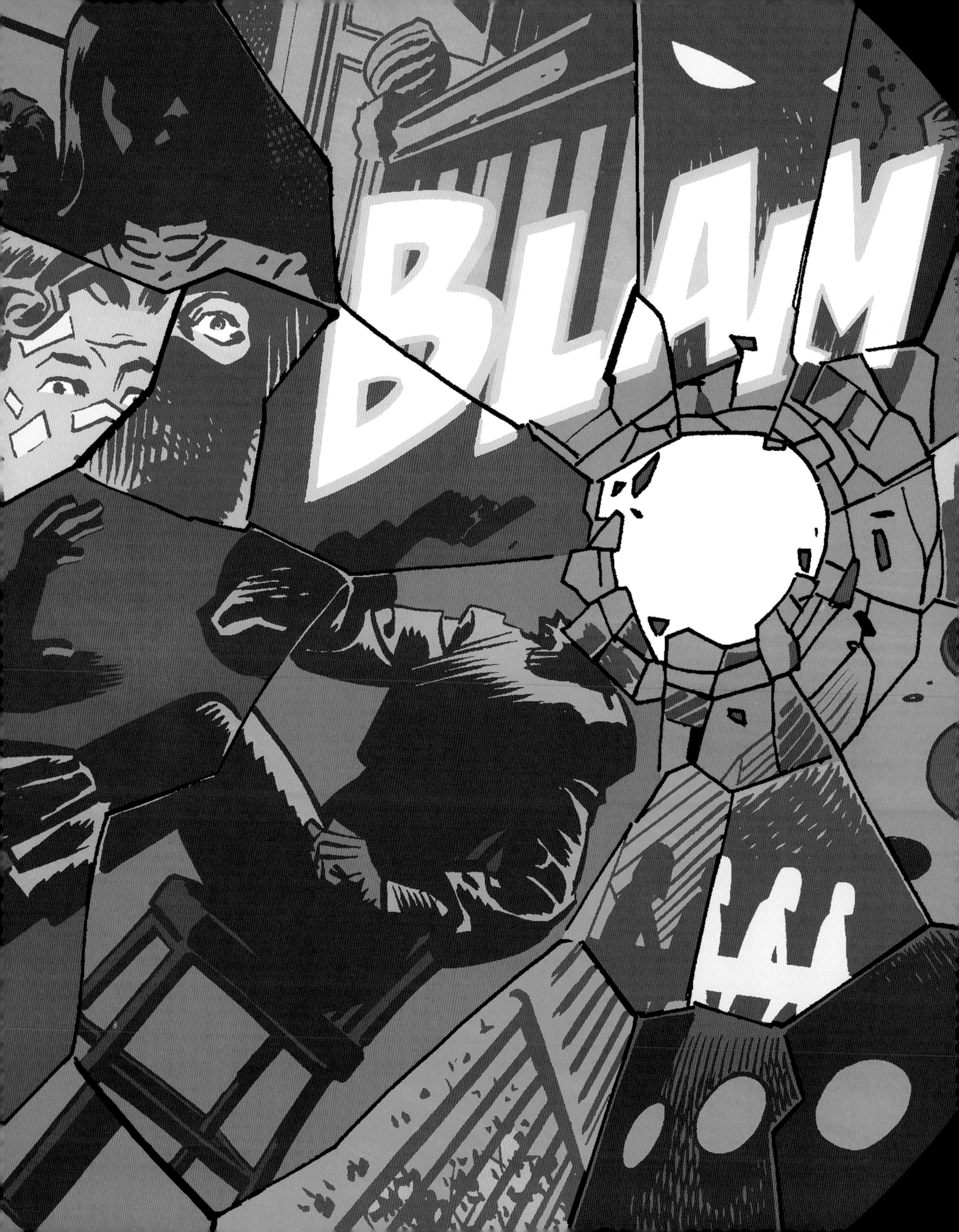
BLAM

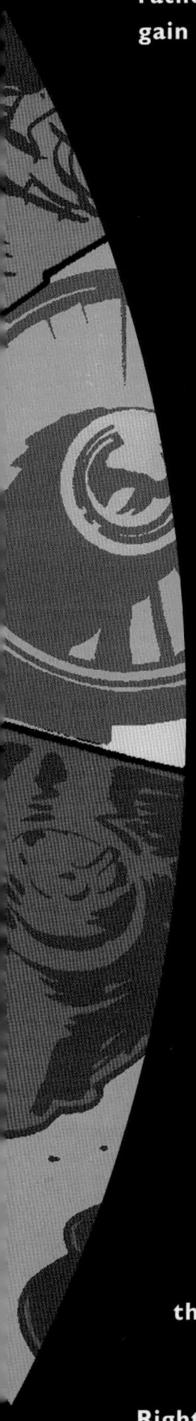

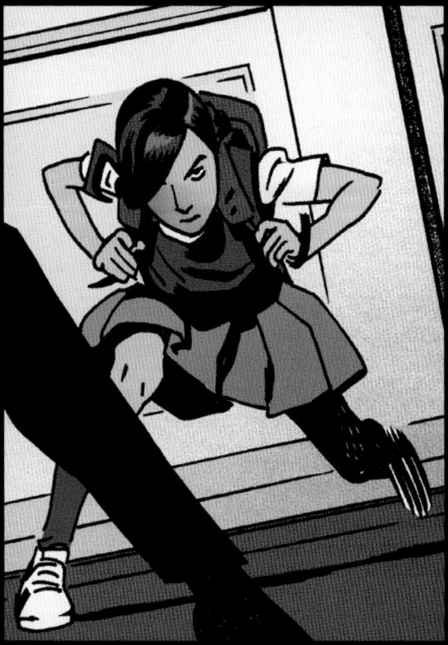

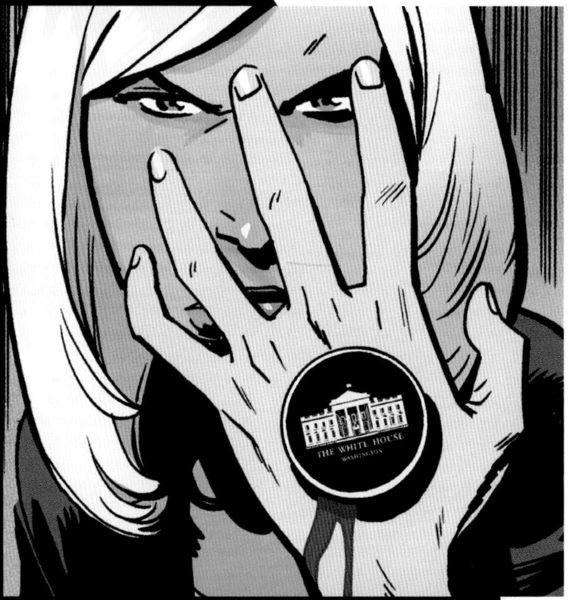
THE WHITE HOUSE

LEFT: BLACK WIDOW #7 (DEC.2016) The former Red Room Headmistress opted to take her own life rather than let Natasha gain access to her secrets.

The uneasy allies tracked down the Headmistress to a Dark Room facility in Greenland. Weeping Lion used his power to read her mind, but before he could extract information about the girls' location, the Headmistress shot herself rather than give up her secrets. Despite the setback, Black Widow and Lion managed to trace the first of the missing assassins to the White House, where they had been sent to kill the Vice President. Widow informed them that the Headmistress was dead, and that a new life awaited if they came with her. Happy to have given the girls the opportunity to lead something like a normal childhood, Natasha handed them over to S.H.I.E.L.D. for deprogramming, before setting off to find the rest of their classmates.

Returning to Iosef in Russia, Black Widow was shocked to find him dying after an attack by a vengeful Recluse. She had also captured and restrained the Winter Soldier, who had been watching over Natasha. He still remembered their relationship, even if she did not. Natasha's knowledge of Iosef's cabin meant that she knew Recluse had placed Bucky on a trapdoor. Pulling a lever, they both dropped into the basement where she set him free and they went after Recluse. Although they still worked well as a team, Recluse got away, and Bucky revealed that he had another motive for finding Natasha—Nick Fury had requested to see her.

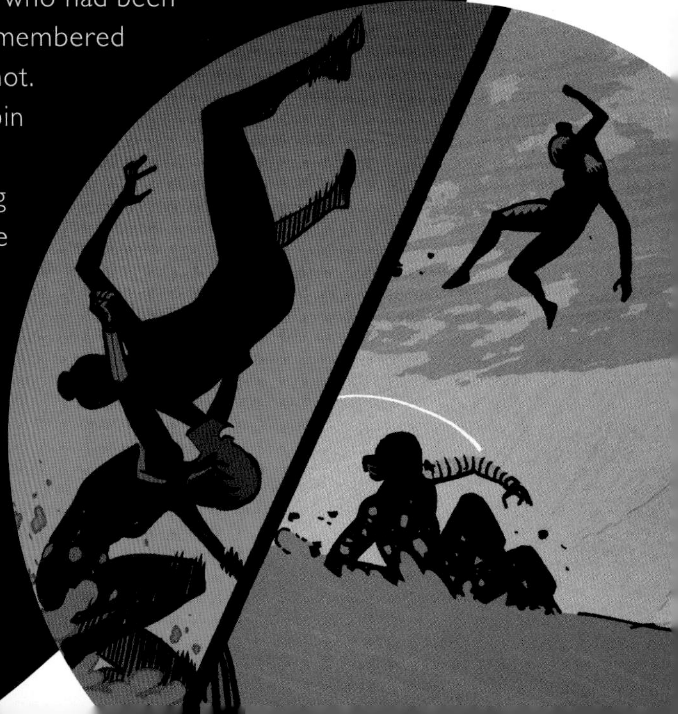

Above right: BLACK WIDOW #8 (JAN. 2017) Black Widow's quest to track down the child assassins of the Dark Room led her to the White House.

Right: BLACK WIDOW #9 (FEB. 2017) Black Widow and the Winter Soldier joined forces against Recluse, one of her jealous former classmates from the Red Room.

Unseen Assistance

Nick Fury was not the man he used to be. As punishment for all the sins he had committed over his long life, he had been transformed into a being called the Unseen by the ancient species known as the Watchers. Trapped in the Blue Area of the Moon, he was condemned to see everything happen on Earth, but remain silent.

Black Widow used her extensive connections to commandeer a spaceship that wasn't monitored by S.H.I.E.L.D. When she arrived on the Moon with Bucky and Weeping Lion, the telepath tried to read Fury's mind. The level of knowledge he found was so great that it caused his head to explode. What Natasha hadn't known until that point was that Weeping Lion was still her enemy. It was he who had been hiding the Dark Room assassins. One had stowed away on the spaceship and, having seen Weeping Lion's death, decided to hijack the ship and leave Natasha and Bucky stranded. Lion had earlier used his psionic powers to trick Black Widow and Winter Soldier into believing their breathing tanks were full when they were almost empty.

Natasha seized the chance to pay Bucky back for helping her, and to balance her ledger a little, giving him nearly all her remaining air. He rushed to stop the spaceship from taking off, then returned for his former girlfriend, who appeared lifeless. In desperation, he managed to resuscitate her, and they shared an affectionate embrace. Natasha told him that she knew what they must have once shared from the way he behaved around her, but she couldn't let their former romance get in the way of her mission: to rescue the girls.

BLACK WIDOW #10 (MAR. 2017)
Natasha, Bucky, and Weeping Lion flew to the Moon to meet a dramatically changed Nick Fury, unaware they'd been carrying a dangerous stowaway, and unprepared for the devastating impact the Unseen's infinite knowledge would have on Weeping Lion.

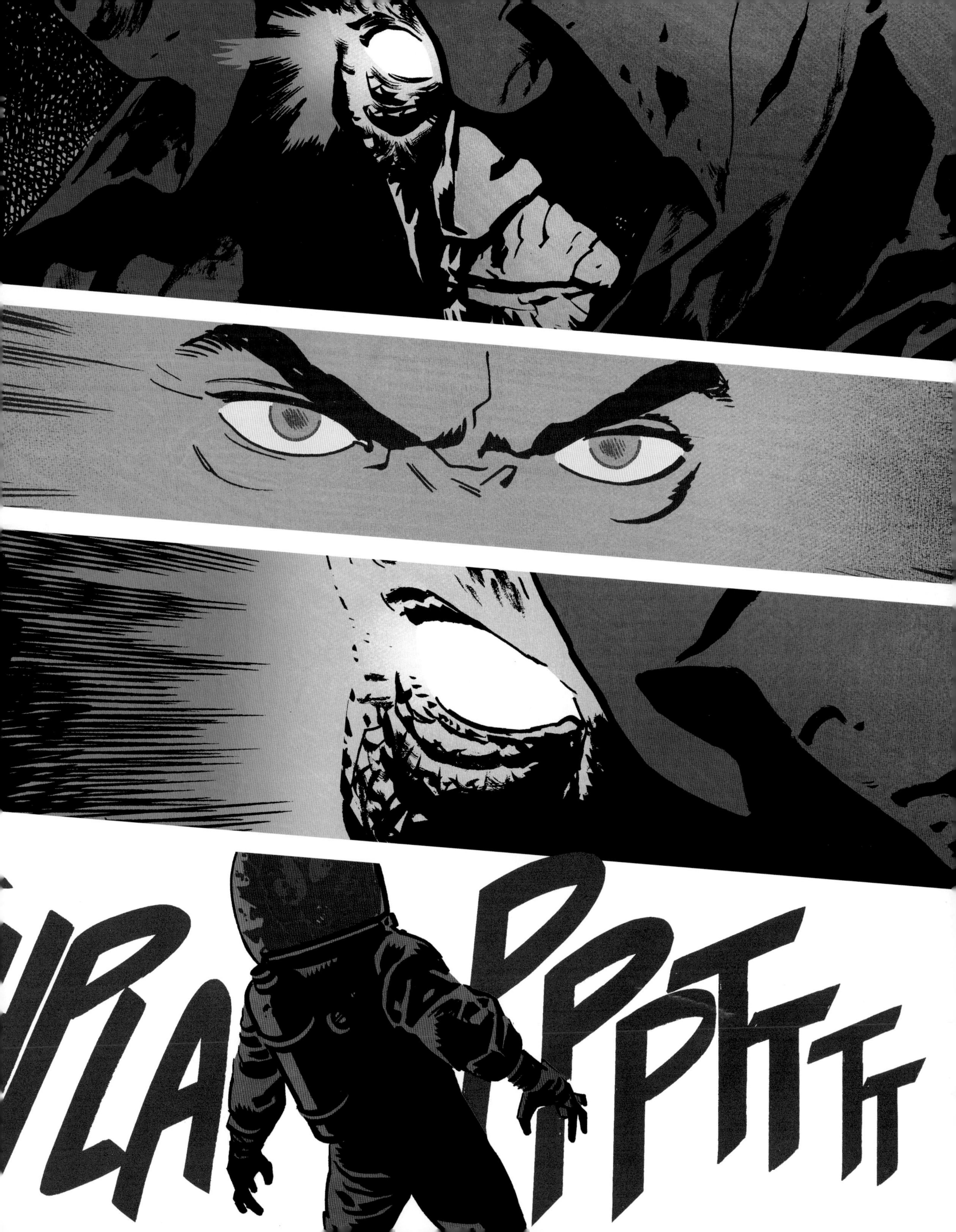
PLA
PPPTTTT

BLACK WIDOW #12 (MAY 2017) Black Widow rescued the remaining Dark Room child assassins, saving them from the life of killing that she had been forced into.

Despite his lack of verbal communication, Nick Fury had engraved a single word in the Moon's surface as a message to Black Widow. It was the Russian word for "friendship," a clue that took her to a secret facility in Antarctica originally built in the 1960s for the joint use of the US and USSR. S.H.I.E.L.D. later repurposed it as the top-secret site of a self-destruct mechanism for their entire organization. It was here that Recluse had taken the last remaining child assassins, to bring down S.H.I.E.L.D. in the most spectacular way.

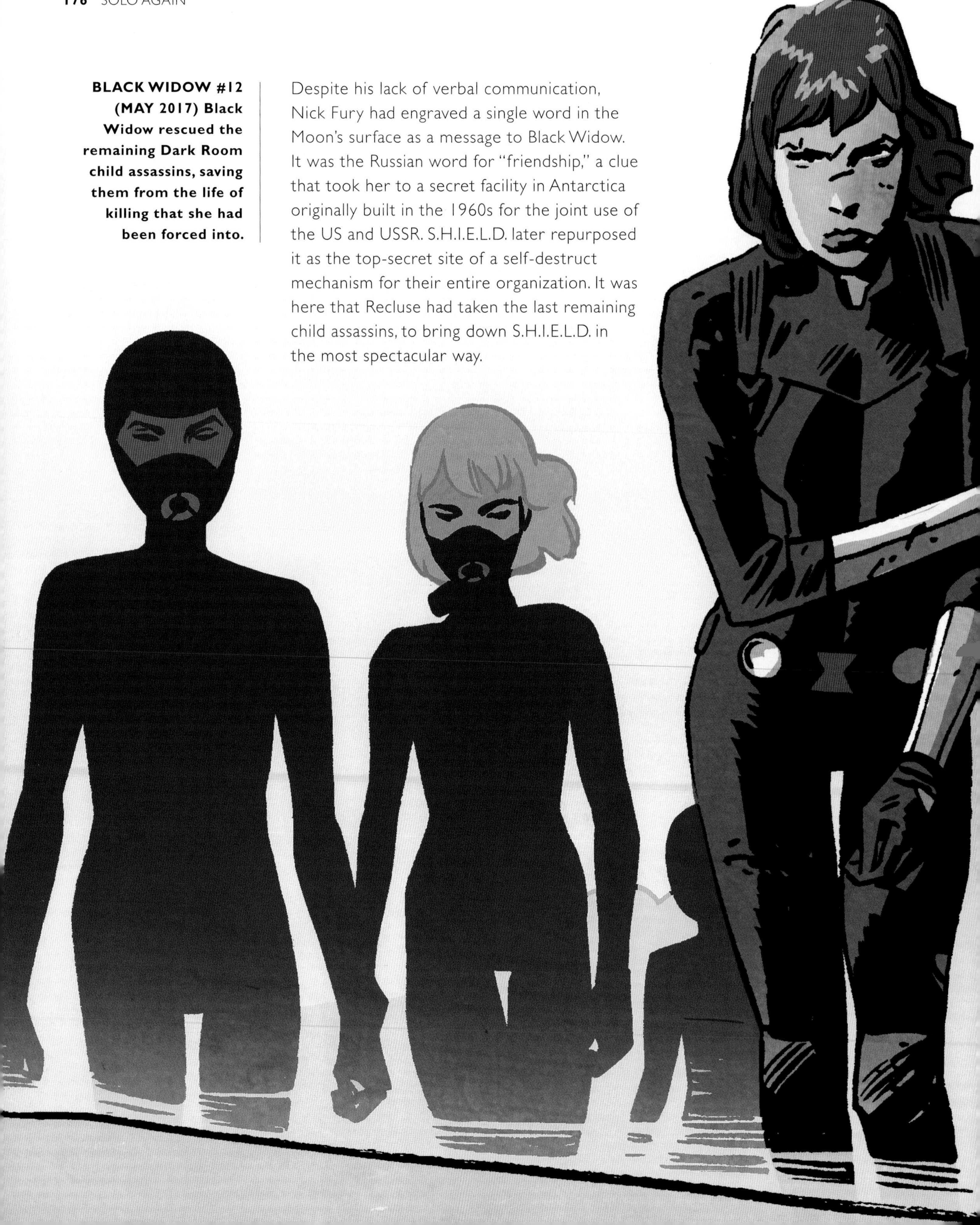

Drawing on all her knowledge of Black Widow's personality, and what would cause her the most pain, Recluse told Natasha that the only way to save S.H.I.E.L.D.—to stop helicarriers falling from the sky and all its active agents dying in the field—was to kill one of the Dark Room girls. Black Widow chose not to play this game, however, and managed to avert disaster by flooding the chamber and preventing the girls from starting the self-destruct process. Climbing out of the water, Natasha reasoned with the young assassins, telling them that Recluse was just using them as puppets, her living weapons. Rather than be exploited, they could choose their own path. With Recluse's control over them now broken, they attacked their former leader. Natasha led the girls outside where they found a S.H.I.E.L.D. team waiting for them. Maria Hill had realized that Black Widow had been working for the good of the organization all along. It was time for her to return to the fold.

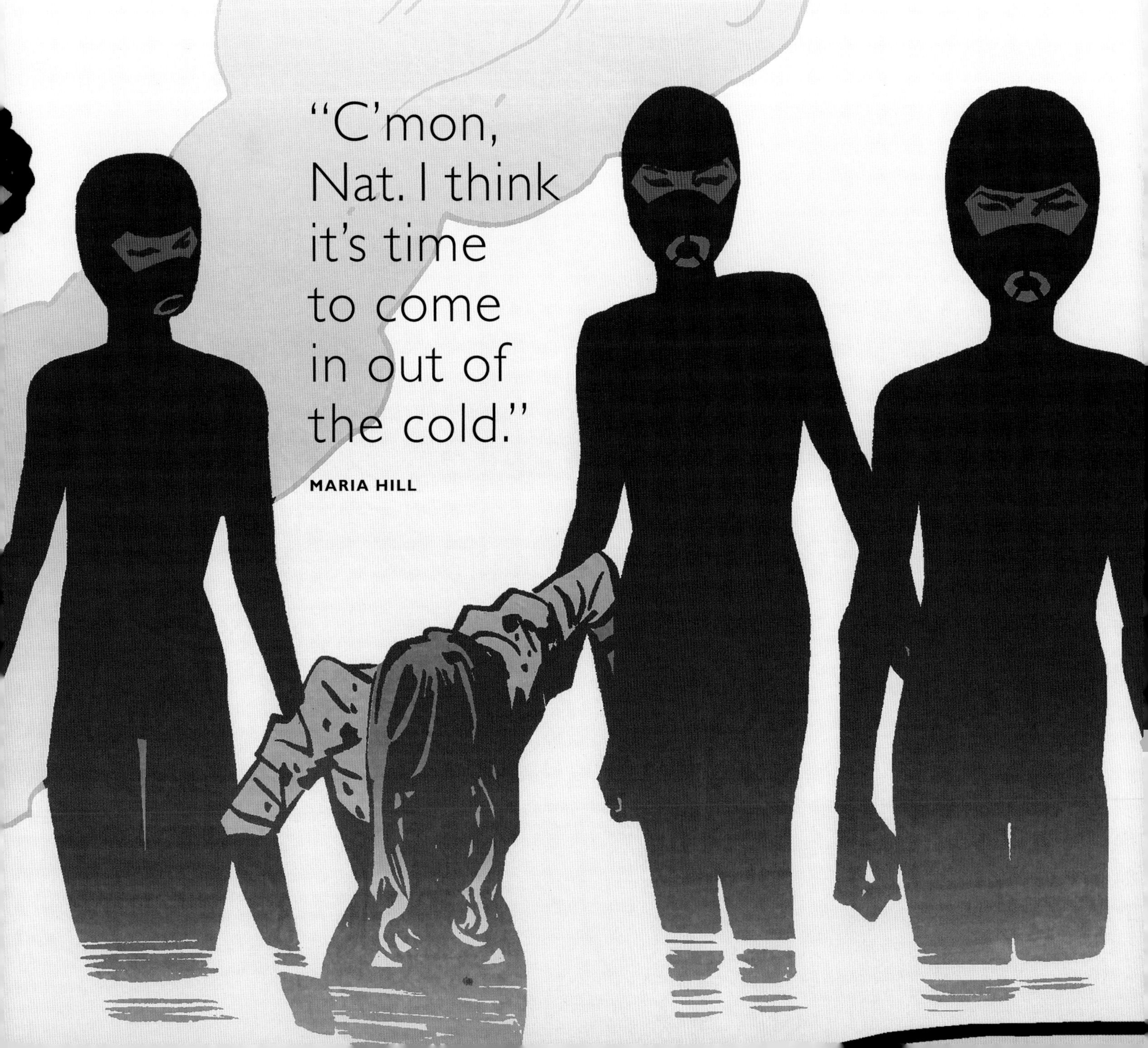

"C'mon, Nat. I think it's time to come in out of the cold."

MARIA HILL

Resistance

SECRET EMPIRE: FCBD #1 (JUL. 2017) When a malign version of Captain America led a Hydra takeover of the US, Black Widow instinctively knew that the right thing to do would be to resist—at any cost.

Natasha fought alongside Hawkeye during the invasion of the US by Hydra, led by an evil doppelgänger of Captain America created by a reality-altering, sentient Cosmic Cube. Following their defeat, the heroes retreated to a secret base to plan how they would resist the new regime. But Hydra's Captain America struck back against the Underground—as the resistance became known—by bombing Las Vegas, the nearest city to their headquarters, and executing Cap's former sidekick Rick Jones. While the Underground differed as to what to do next, Black Widow was in no doubt whatsoever: Captain America had to die.

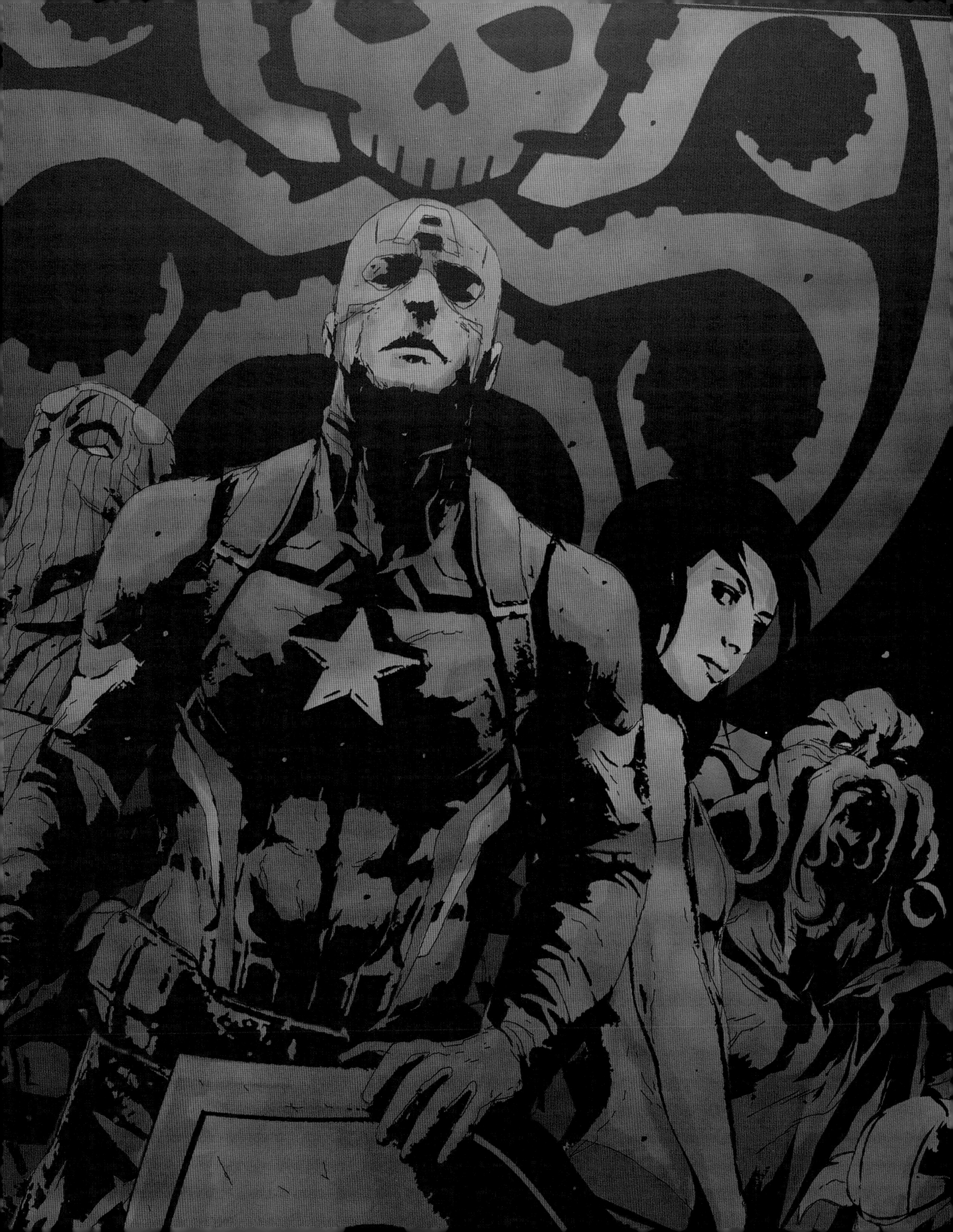

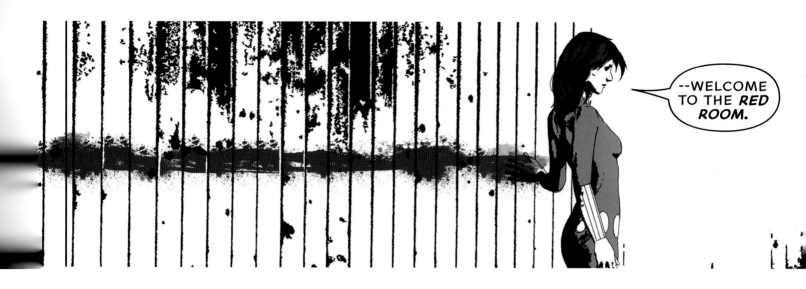

Hawkeye tried to persuade her to find another way, telling her she was more than just a trained killer, but Natasha was adamant. It was war. She had become more hardened since finding out that the Winter Soldier had apparently been killed by Baron Zemo in the buildup to the invasion.

Black Widow's plan to assassinate Captain America was not just motivated by a desire for revenge or to topple his corrupt regime. It was also to save another hero from having to carry out the terrible deed. Ulysses Cain, an Inhuman with the ability to see the future, had experienced a vision of Captain America being killed by a young Spider-Man (Miles Morales), and Natasha wanted to take that burden on herself. She had already done so many terrible things, it would be easier for her to carry the guilt than Spider-Man. Morales joined her at a safe house in Colorado to help plan the attack, along with a group of other young heroes. Black Widow declared their refuge to be the new Red Room, cutting her hand and smearing her blood along the wall to anoint it.

The Ultimate Sacrifice

Natasha used her contacts to find out when Captain America would be at his most vulnerable, picking a date when he was making a speech outside the US Capitol. In the meantime, she was training her new team, going at them hard to

Above: SECRET EMPIRE #2 (JUL. 2017) Natasha knew she had to be tough on the group of young heroes under her command if they were to successfully take on the cruel forces of Hydra.

prepare them for the tough choices they might need to make in a world ruled by Hydra. Captain America knew that the Widow was on his tail, describing her as the most dangerous of all the threats that his regime was currently facing. In response, he sent his own most ruthless operative—the Punisher—to stop Natasha by any means necessary.

When the day of the assassination attempt arrived, Black Widow drove to the scene with Spider-Man, but instead of allowing him to take part in the operation, she locked him in the van. The awful responsibility should fall to her alone. She was preparing to fire her sniper rifle from an elevated position when the Punisher finally caught up to her. Although she managed to take him down, by the time she returned to her vantage point, Black Widow saw that Spider-Man had escaped from the van and was confronting Captain America. Natasha rushed to the scene, determined to prevent Miles from becoming a killer. As she flung herself between them, she was struck by a glancing blow from Captain America's shield. Black Widow fell to the ground, killed instantly. And though the enraged Spider-Man overwhelmed the evil Cap and had him at his mercy, he did not kill him. Miles Morales understood that Natasha did not want him to become a killer. As Wasp (Nadia Pym) reminded him, Spider-Man had a choice, but Black Widow and Wasp—both Red Room graduates—had been trained since they were little girls to be killers, and were denied any such choices.

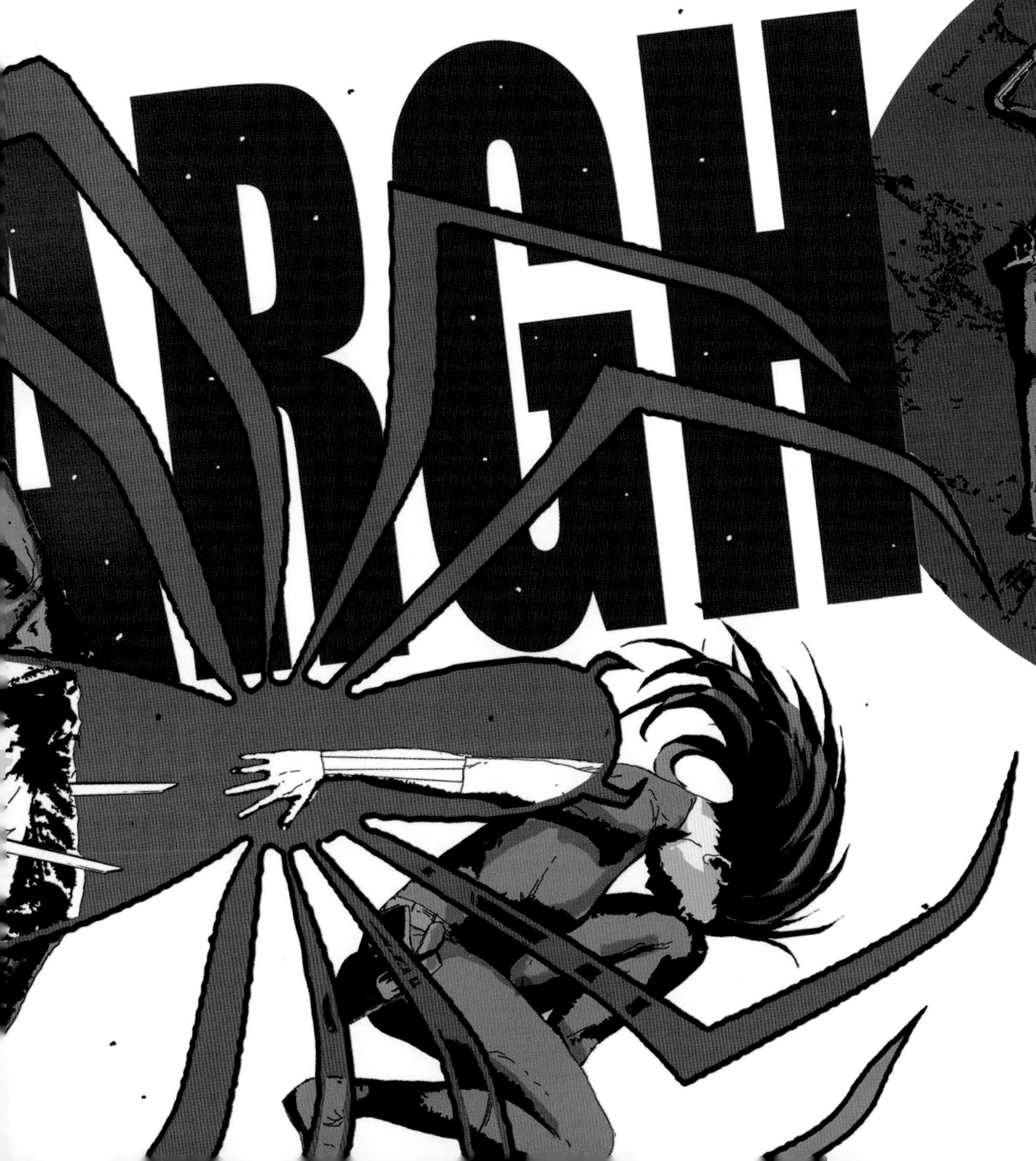
ARGH

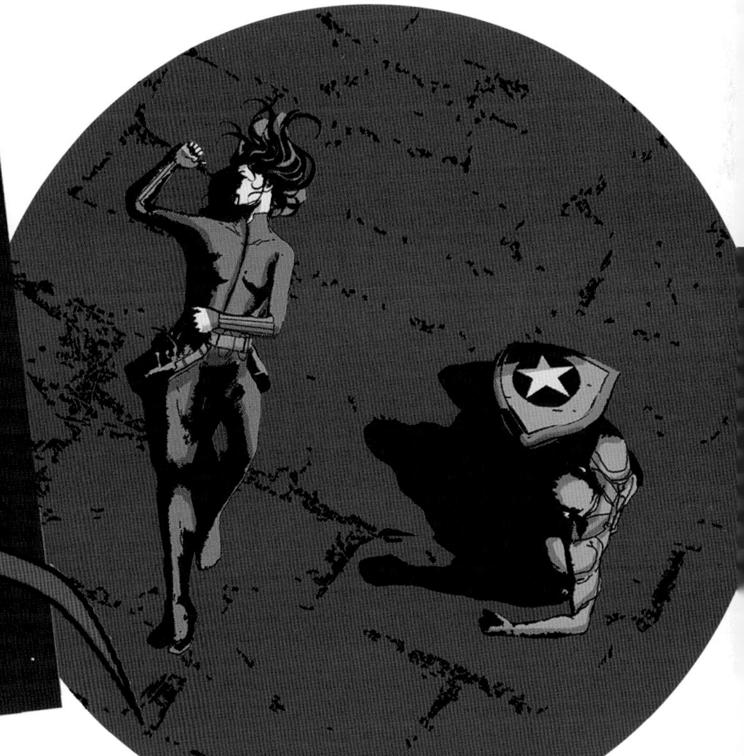

Left and above: SECRET EMPIRE #7 (SEP. 2017) After defeating the Punisher, Black Widow's long life ended in tragedy when she was killed by a blow from the shield of the Hydra-controlled Captain America.

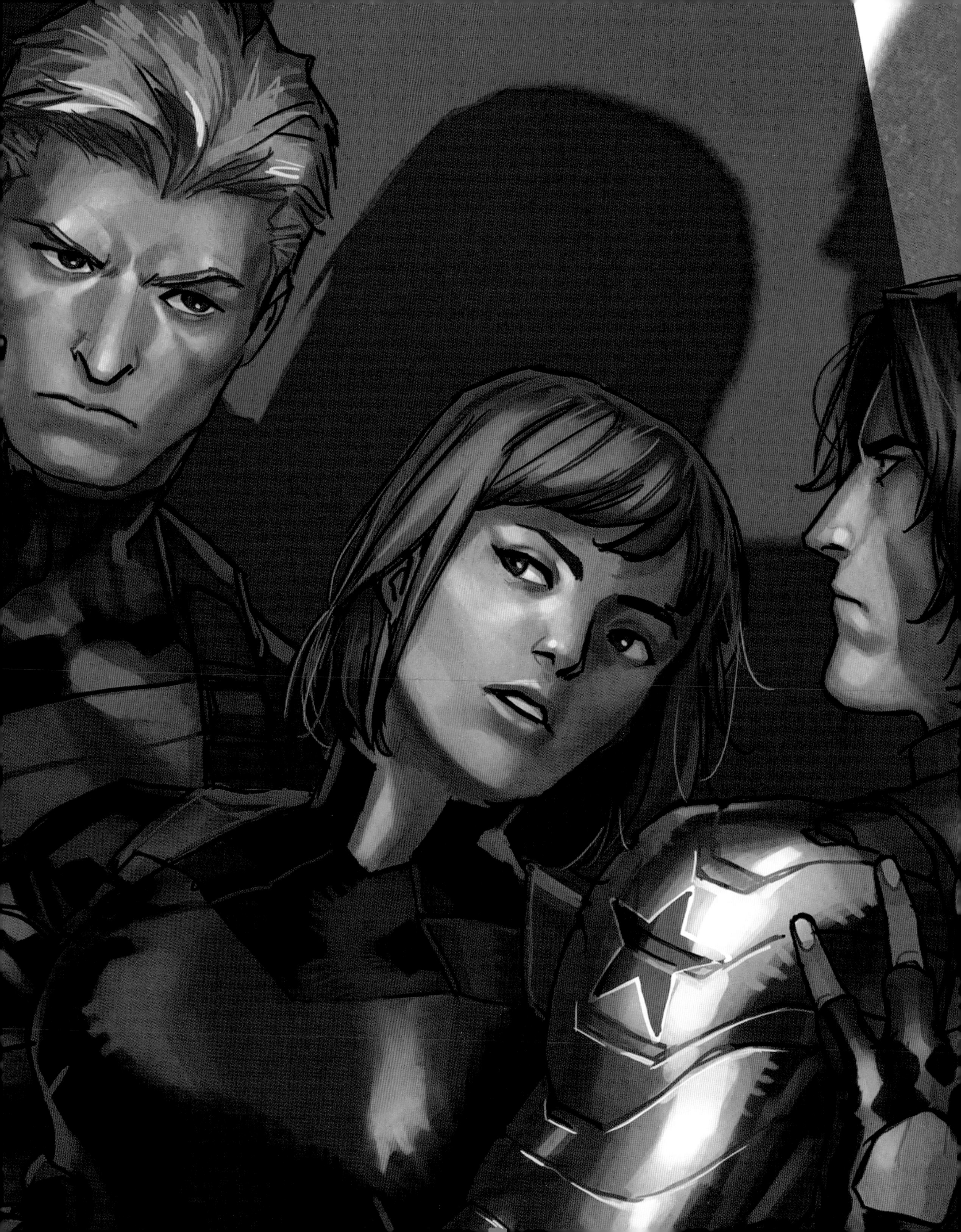

Born Again

TALES OF SUSPENSE #101 (MAR. 2018) A series of assassinations of former Hydra agents led the Winter Soldier and Hawkeye to believe that Black Widow was still alive.

After the evil Captain America had been defeated by the true Steve Rogers, who had been recreated from the Cosmic Cube, Hawkeye noticed a pattern of assassinations of former Hydra operatives. The archer believed that the killings bore all Natasha's hallmarks and, desperately hoping that she wasn't dead after all, traveled to Eastern Europe to investigate. Here Hawkeye bumped into the Winter Soldier, who, it turned out, had not been killed by Zemo and was also looking into the Hydra deaths. Although Bucky confirmed that Natasha's calling card—the Black Widow symbol—was found at the scene of the latest assassination, he refused to believe that it was really her.

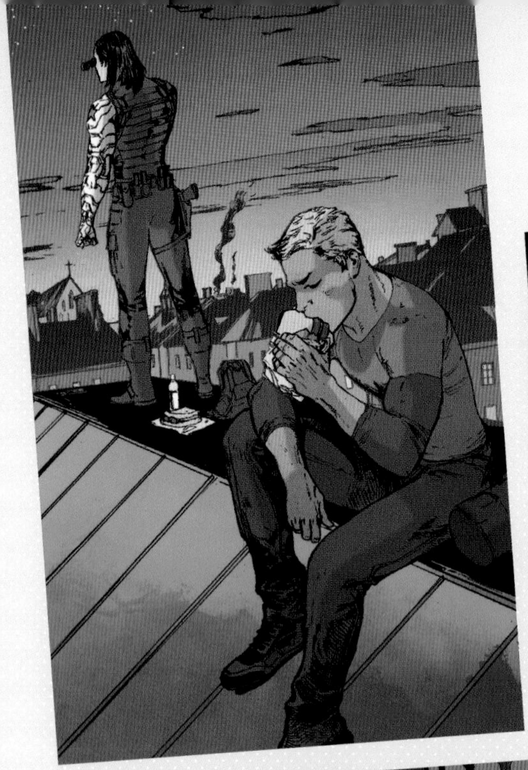

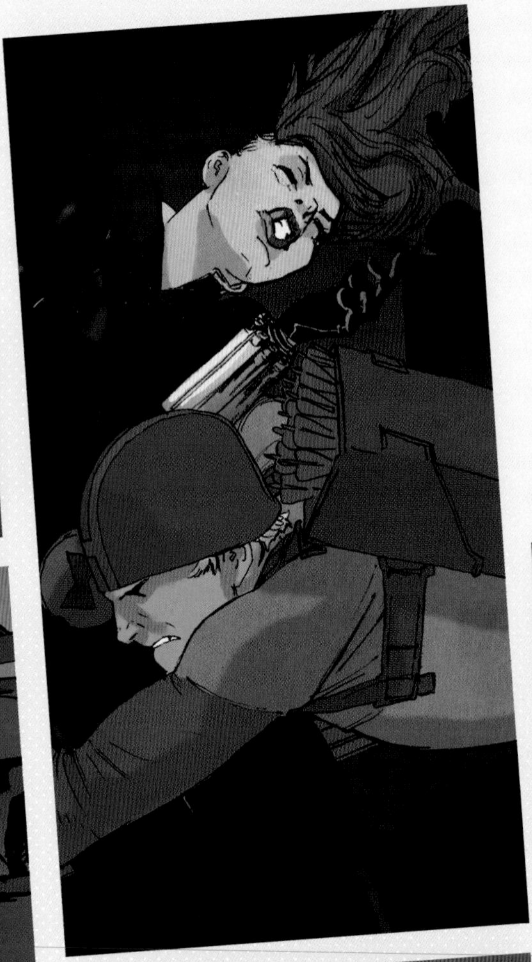

“I don’t think Nat’s on our team anymore.”

HAWKEYE

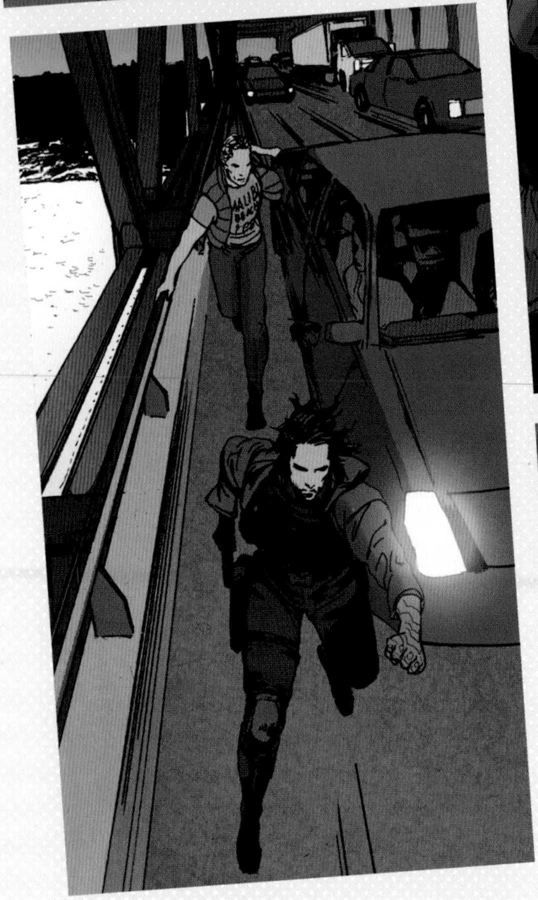

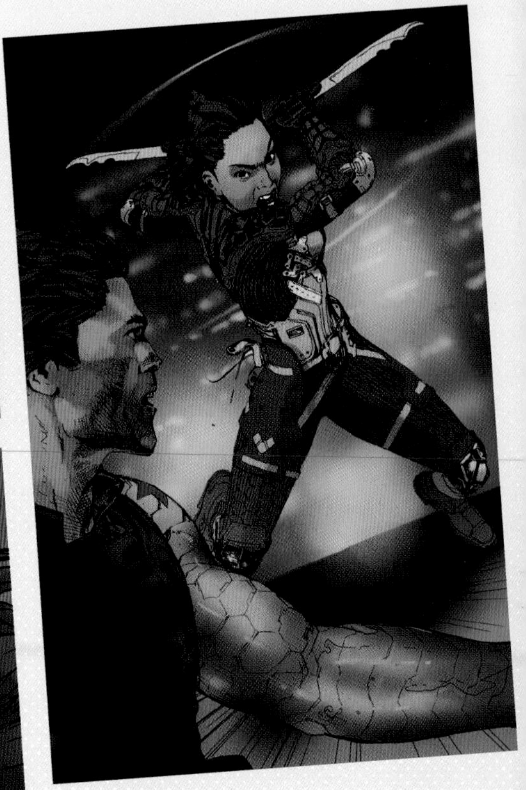

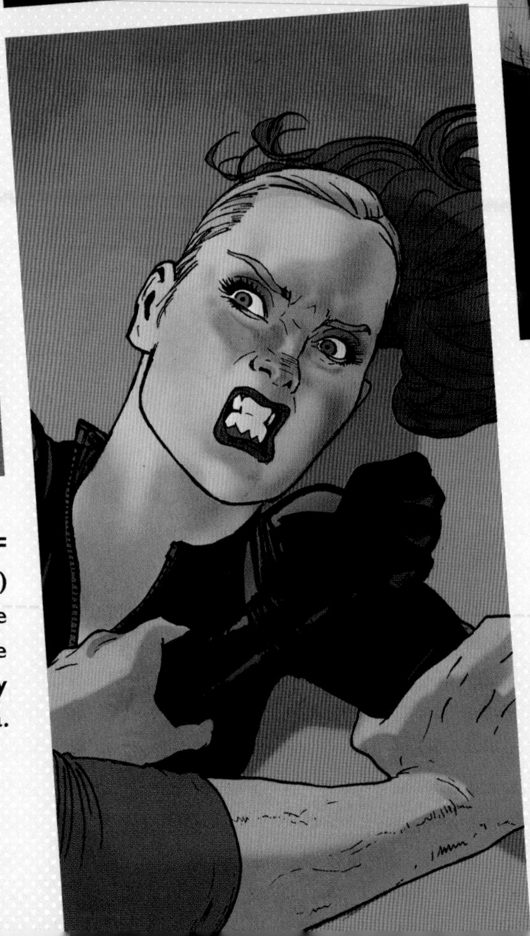

Above and center: TALES OF SUSPENSE #101 (MAR. 2018) In pursuit of Black Widow, the Winter Soldier and Hawkeye discovered that their quarry was actually Yelena Belova.

Above and right: TALES OF SUSPENSE #102 (APR. 2018) After fighting another Red Room graduate named Orphan Maker, Clint and Bucky finally appeared to be facing the real thing: Natasha Romanoff, resurrected.

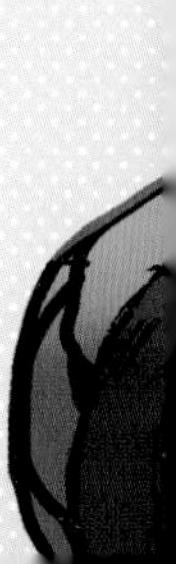

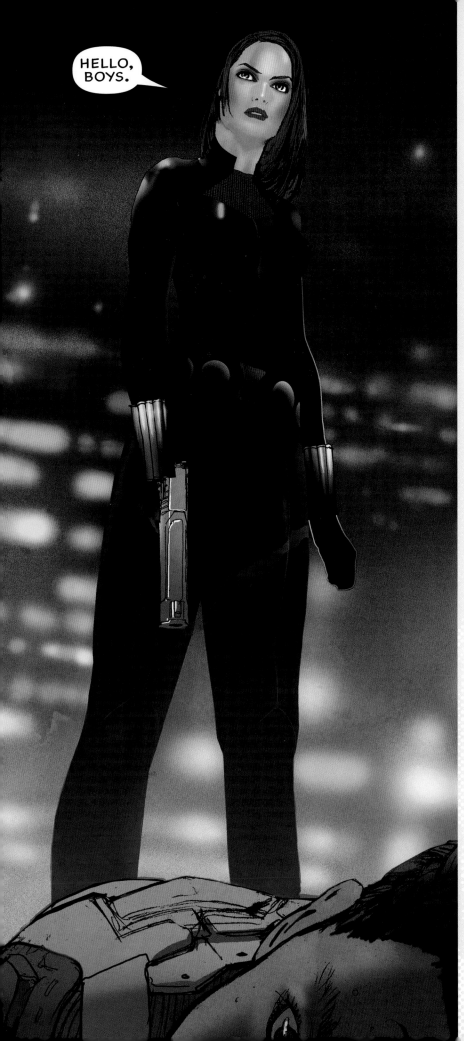

Hawkeye and the Winter Soldier returned to the US to speak to a former S.H.I.E.L.D. agent about what they had found. As they were talking, the heroes noticed a familiar-looking figure watching them and gave chase. Following her to a Westchester, NY, mansion, the Winter Soldier managed to shoot the mysterious woman in the leg. When they tackled her, they discovered that it was indeed Black Widow: Yelena Belova. Bucky decided to let her go so that they could find out who she was working for, but Yelena was killed shortly afterwards by an unknown assailant.

Managing to track down another former Red Room operative known as Orphan Maker, Hawkeye and Bucky discovered that the Red Room was collecting its debts, wiping out its former agents as well the competition: S.H.I.E.L.D. and Hydra. Its principal assassin in these missions was Natasha Romanoff, the late Black Widow.

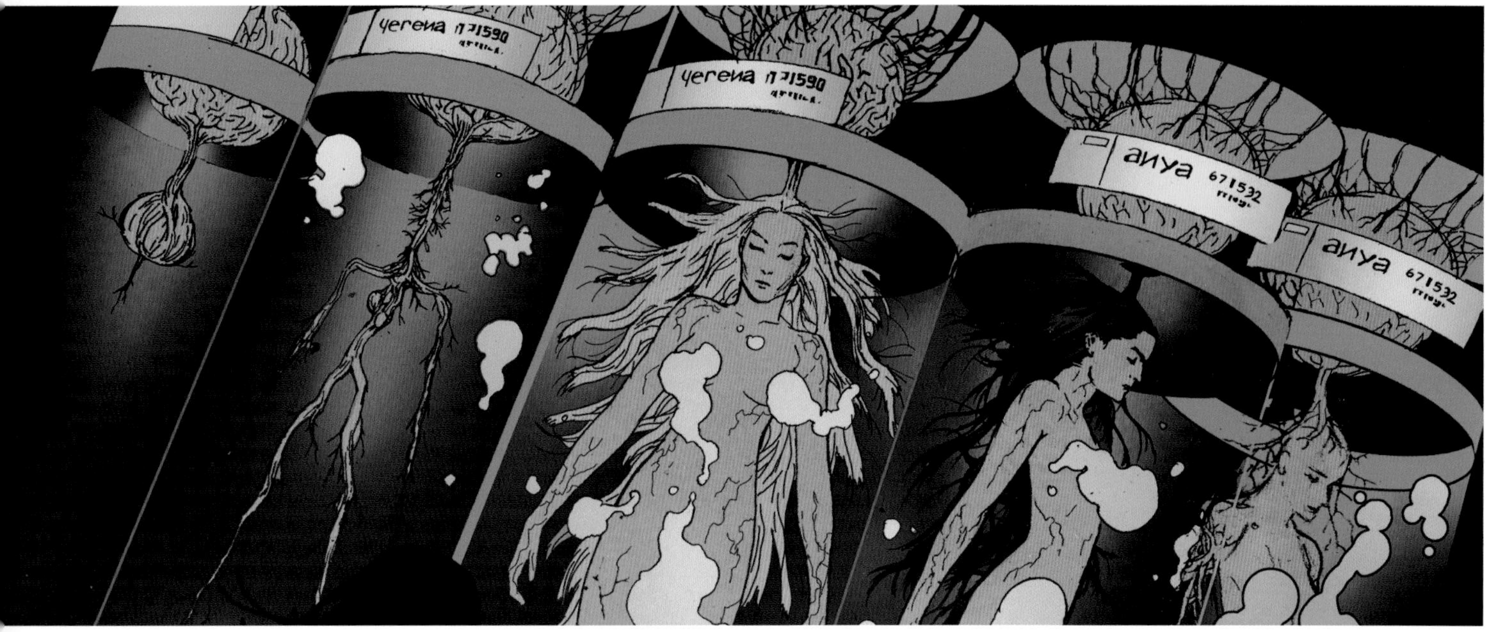
аиуа 671532
аиуа 671532

Above: TALES OF SUSPENSE #103 (MAY 2018) Black Widow woke in a Red Room facility to discover that clone bodies of all its top agents were kept ready in case of their deaths.

Opposite: TALES OF SUSPENSE #104 (JUN. 2018) Acting as a double agent within the Red Room itself, the resurrected Black Widow took over and freed all those under its thrall.

Not long before this revelation, Natasha had woken on a beach next to a talking bear. She soon realized that the beach was a hologram, while the talking bear was mutant and former Soviet agent Ursa Major. She was back in the Red Room. Instinctively she adopted one of her favorite tactics, appearing to play along while gathering intelligence about her situation. Sneaking around the facility, Natasha discovered something that shook her to her core. There was a room dedicated to growing new clone bodies of herself and other significant Red Room agents. She was not the original Natasha Romanoff, but one of these clones implanted with her personality and memories to make her essentially Black Widow, reborn.

After consulting with Ursa Major, this resurrected Natasha proved herself to be a true Black Widow by plotting to destroy the Red Room once and for all and forge her own destiny. She used clones to carry out the assassinations that had so confused Hawkeye and the Winter Soldier. Confronting the heroes in the US, Natasha tricked the pair into a panic room and blew up the surrounding building. While her former paramours were safe, but trapped, she took Hawkeye's bow and the Winter Soldier's arm to the Red Room as "proof" she had killed them.

Fully gaining the trust of the Red Room commanders, Black Widow took down the whole operation, with no quarter given. When Hawkeye arrived on the scene—after escaping from the panic room—he made it clear he disliked Natasha's brutal methods, but death had given her a new perspective; her unforgiving stance was further underscored when she and Bucky helped the Punisher hunt down other former Hydra agents with deadly force.

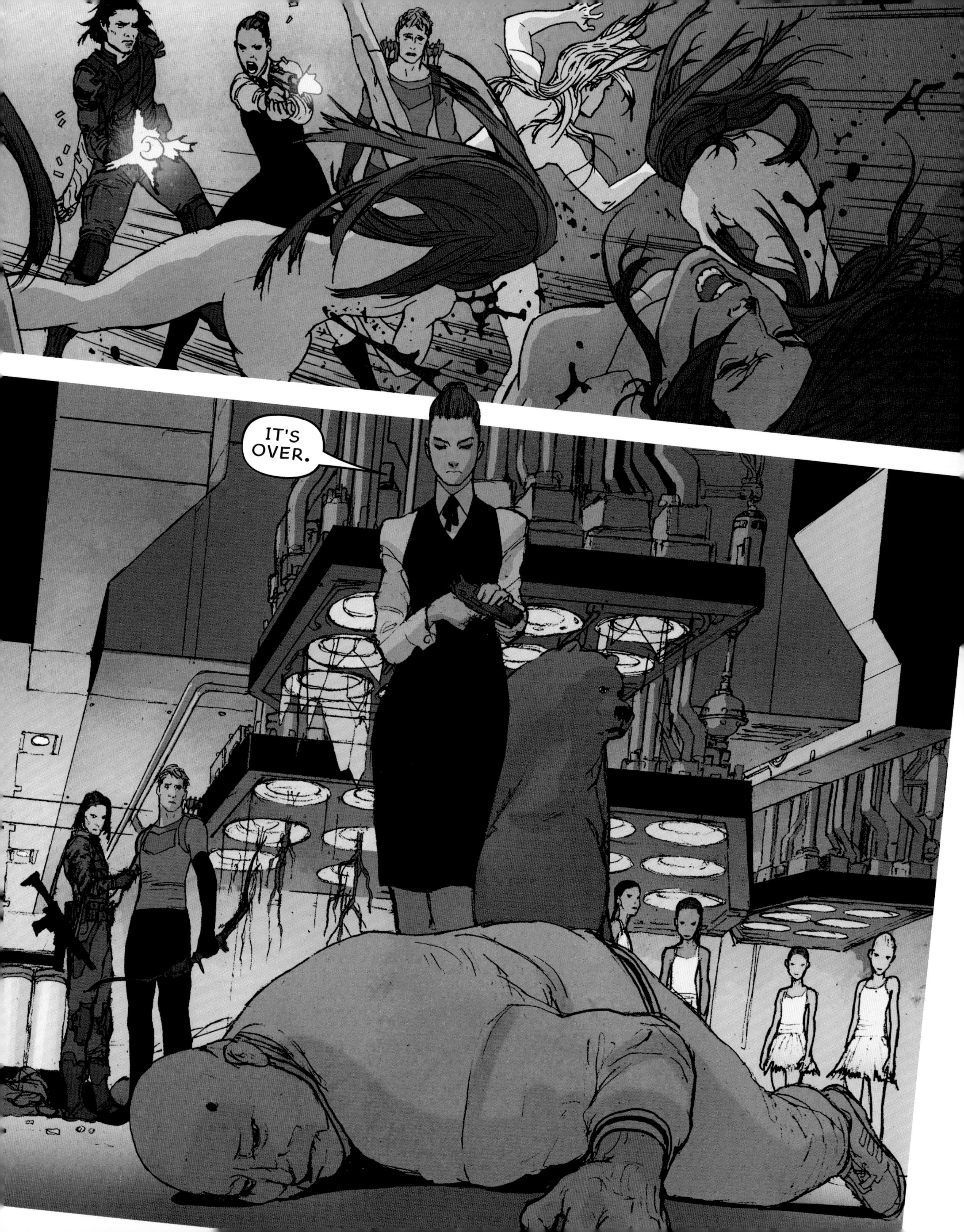
IT'S OVER.

Web of Horror

BLACK WIDOW #1 (MAR. 2019) Death had left Natasha feeling the need to take down some seriously bad guys—and she found exactly what she was looking for in Madripoor.

Natasha Romanoff was coming to find that being dead, or thought to be dead by most of the world, meant that she could act with a newfound freedom. Black Widow was also finding that she had come back changed, with rage and violence always simmering just below the surface and threatening to spill over. She needed to find a mission where she could let herself go against the worst of humanity without worrying about the consequences, and she found it in the southeast Asian island of Madripoor.

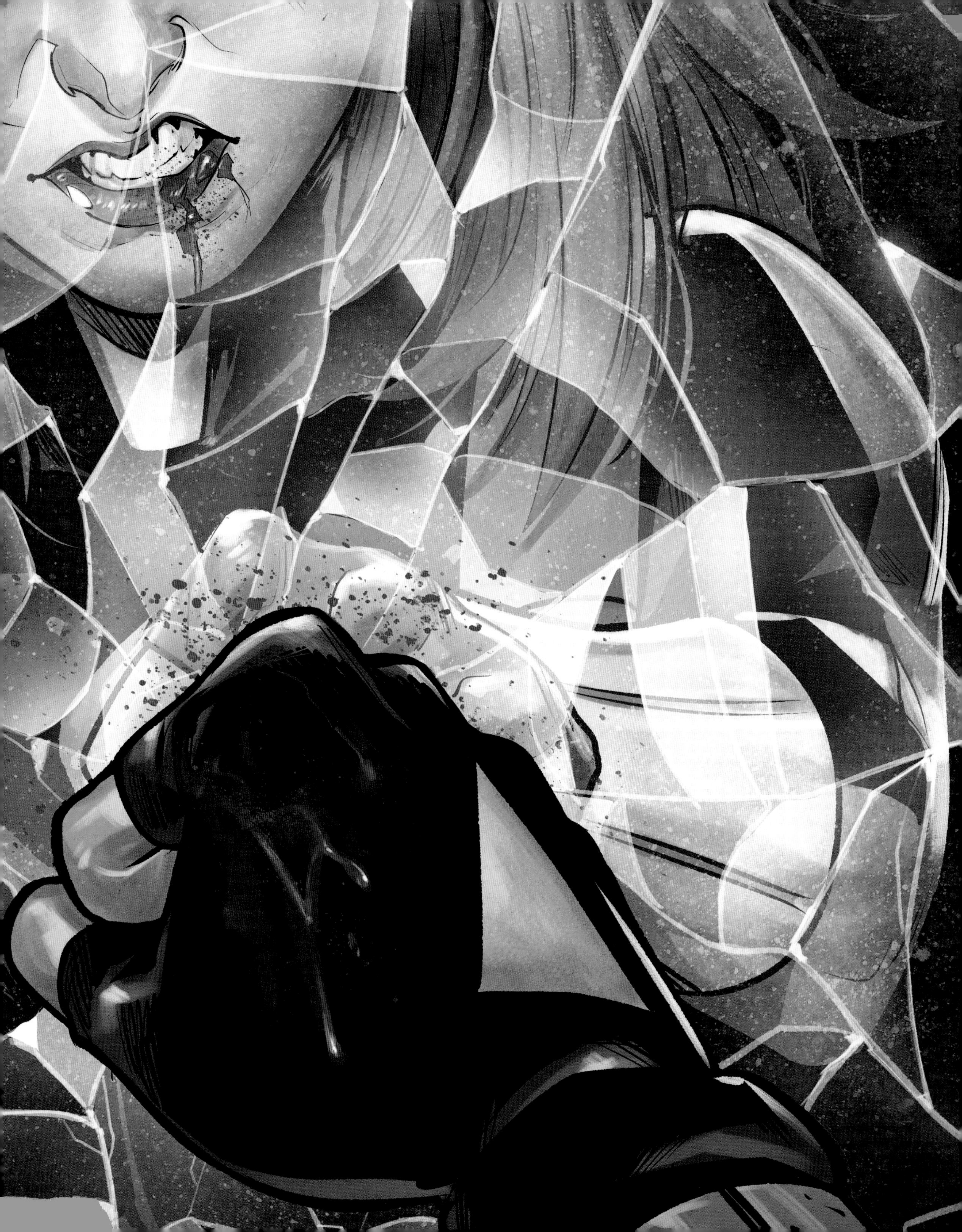

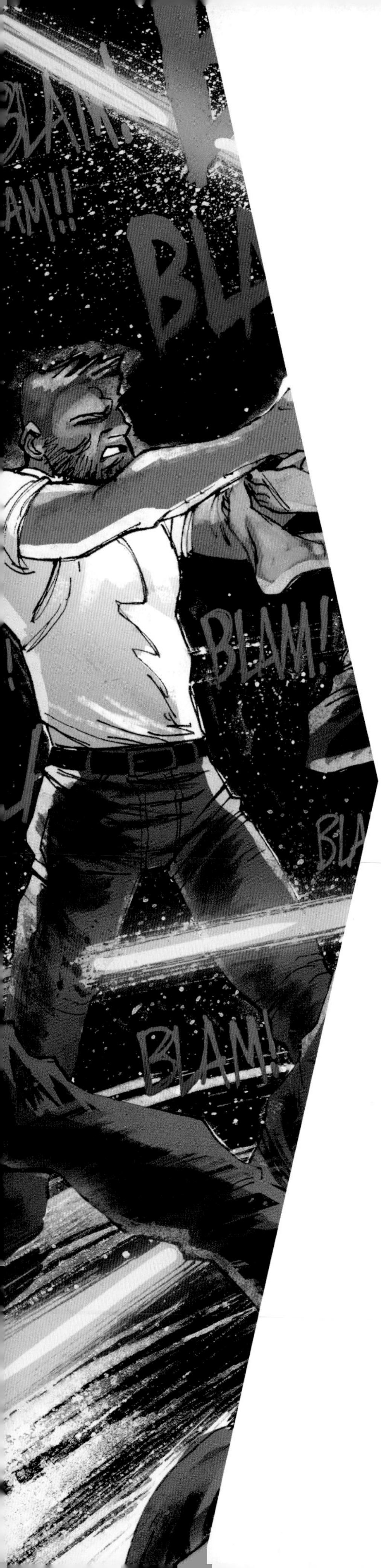
BLAM!
BLAM!

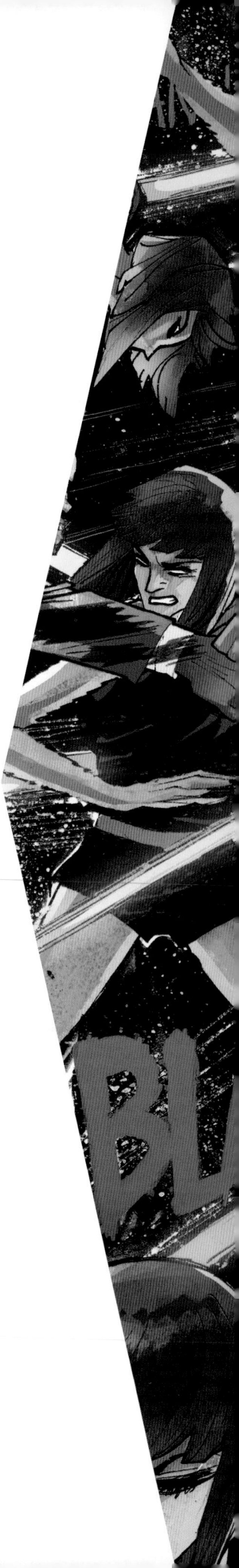

"Playtime's over."

BLACK WIDOW

Former banker and crime lord Tyger Tiger enlisted Black Widow's help to rescue some missing children. She believed they had been captured to feed the twisted pleasures of subscribers to a website known as "No Restraints Play," where young, defenseless victims were tortured for the amusement of the highest bidder, who would get to decide their fate. Natasha brutalized a succession of low-level connections to the dark web until she found the answers she was looking for. It was a mission tailor-made for unleashing the remorseless killer Black Widow was created to be. She was a lethal weapon who had found a fitting target.

Infiltrating a party for its customers disguised as the villain Madame Masque, Black Widow was captured by the people behind No Restraints Play, and set up to star in their latest depraved upload. However, they had failed to appreciate their captive's close-combat skills and her own lack of restraint. Natasha easily escaped her bonds and took down the whole gang, while Tyger Tiger rescued the captive children. Safely back in Madripoor, Tyger revealed that the children admired the Black Widow so much that they had started training to try and be like her, and were calling themselves the Widow Warriors.

Her mission accomplished, Black Widow returned to the US, where she had a heart-to-heart with Captain America, who was still harboring a lot of guilt for the appalling actions of his evil Hydra counterpart. She told him that the past could be an ugly place, and he should not dwell there. No matter how their stories started, they were the only ones who could determine how they would end.

BLACK WIDOW #4 (JUN. 2019) Captured so that she could be tortured for the entertainment of dark web users, Natasha fought her way out in typically lethal fashion.

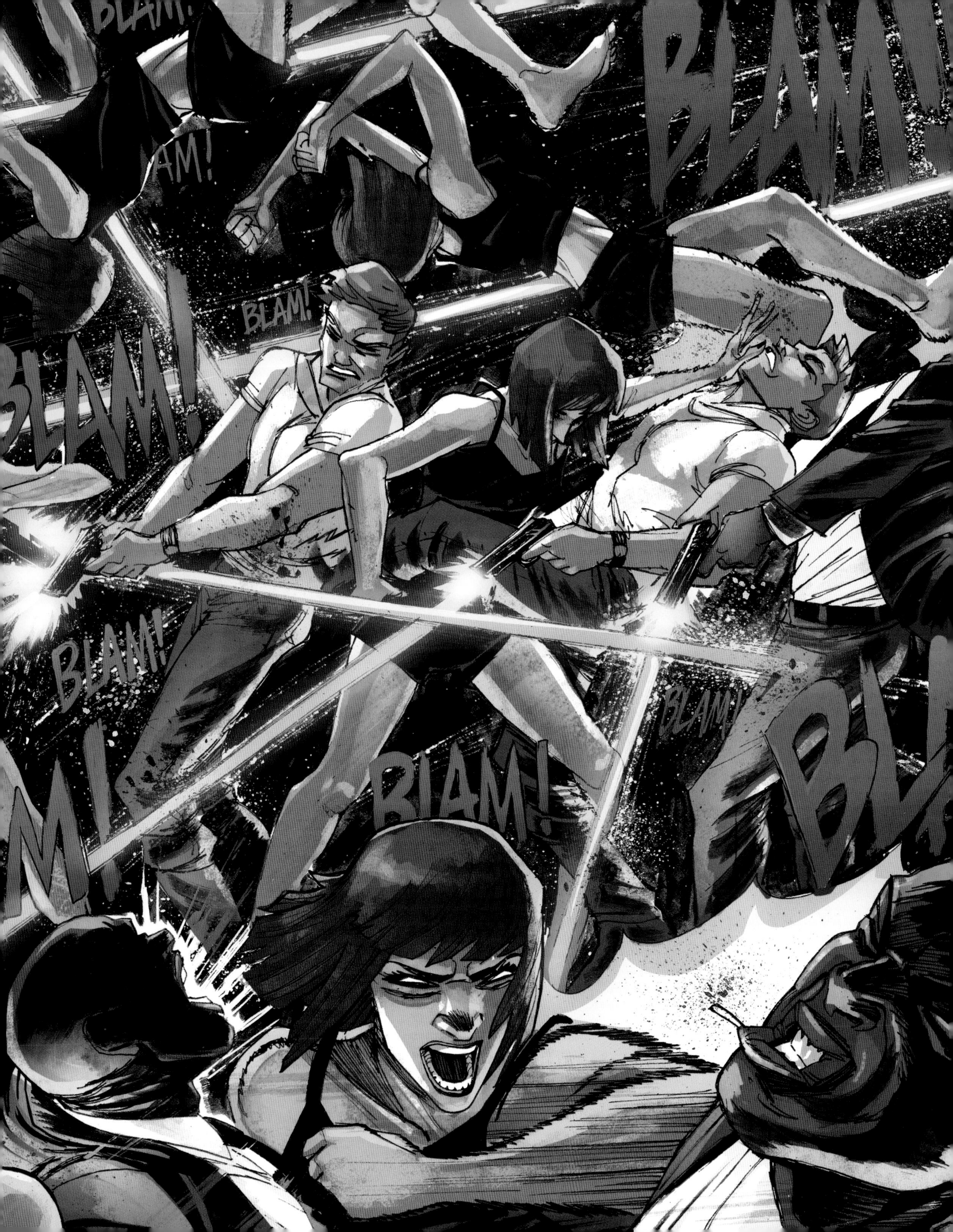
BLAM!
AM!
BLAM!
BLAM!
BLAM!
BLAM!
BLAM!
BLAM!

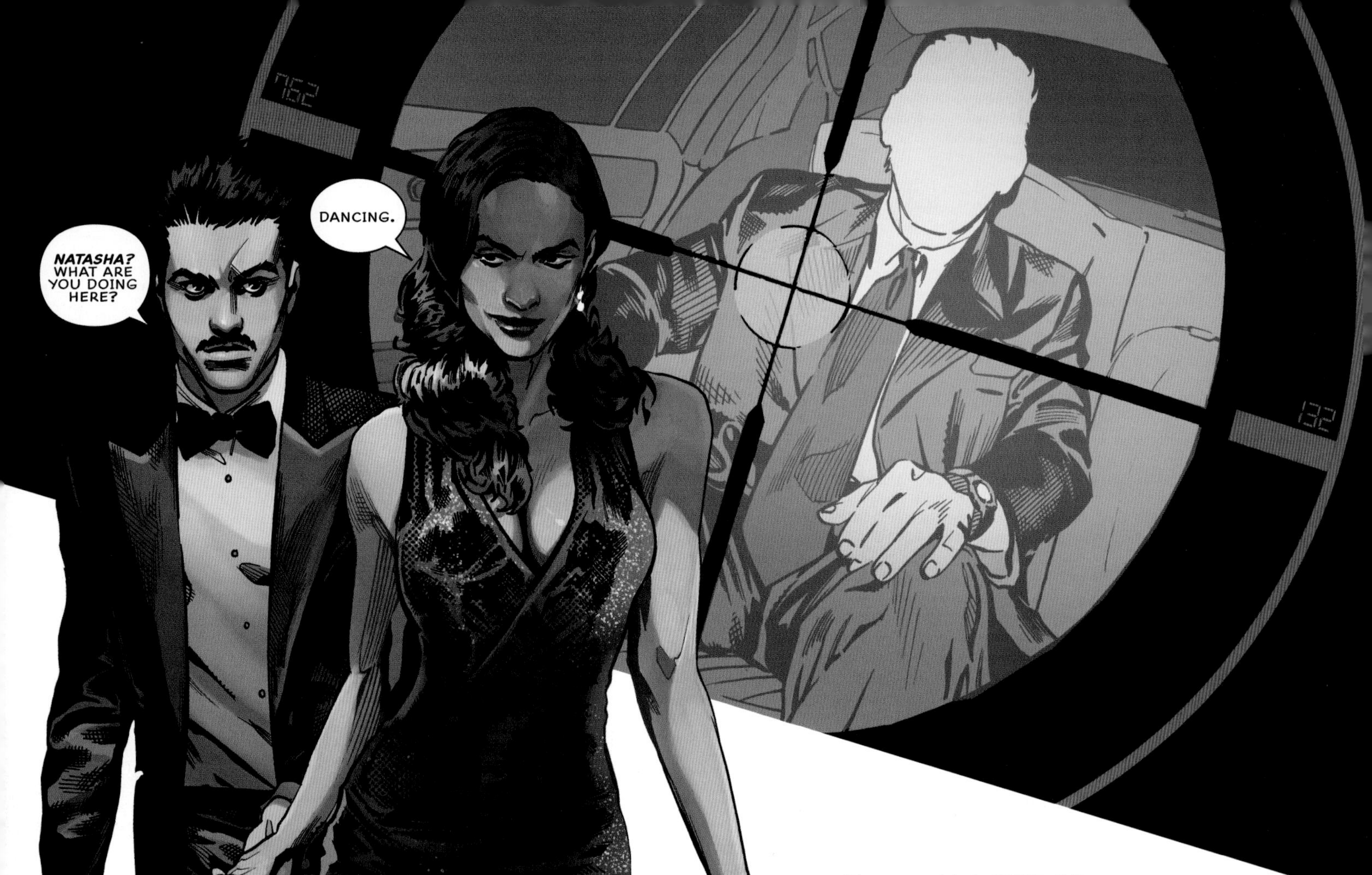
NATASHA? WHAT ARE YOU DOING HERE?
DANCING.

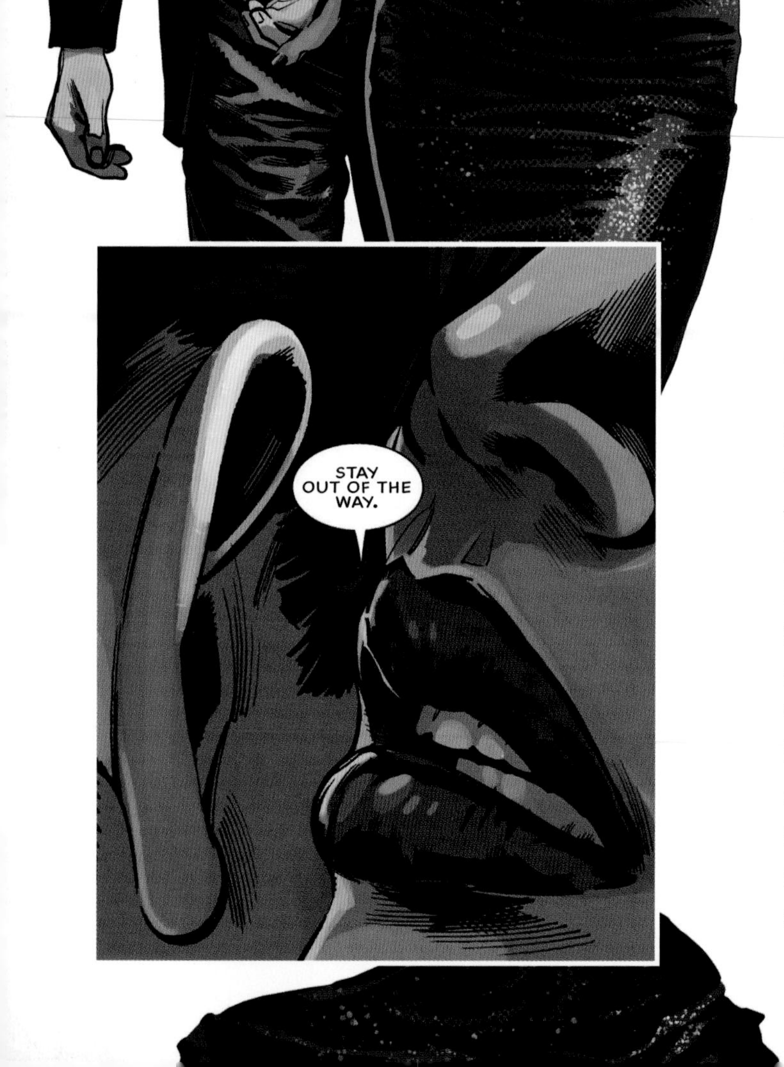
STAY OUT OF THE WAY.

Above and left: WEB OF BLACK WIDOW #1 (NOV. 2019) When Tony Stark ran into an undercover Black Widow at a corporate gala, he was instantly concerned for her, but he could not stop Natasha carrying out her mission.

Sins of the Fathers

Struggling to reconcile her memories of Red Room missions with her supposed heroic role, Black Widow went off-grid to expose those who had benefited from her terrible acts. First on her list was Walter Sobol, of Sobol Technologies. Many years earlier, a young Natasha had been employed by Sobol's grandfather to assassinate a business rival. This crime resulted in his firm becoming hugely successful, but Black Widow now wanted the world to know how this success had been won. She infiltrated a charity event held by the company and broadcast information relating to the assassination on a big screen. Iron Man, attending the event as Tony Stark, tried to reach out to Natasha to make sure she was okay, but she shrugged him off—she didn't want allies this time.

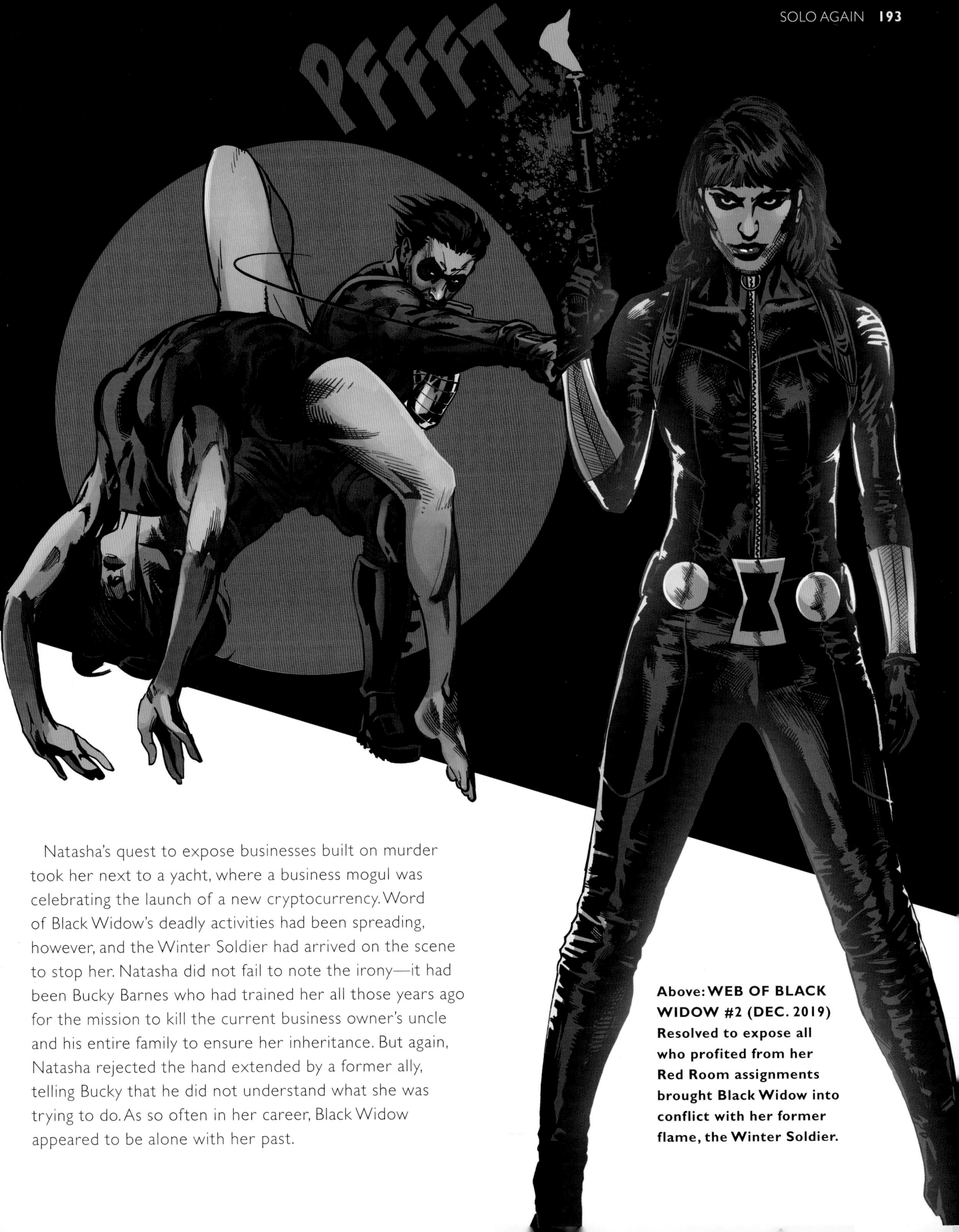
PFFFT

Natasha's quest to expose businesses built on murder took her next to a yacht, where a business mogul was celebrating the launch of a new cryptocurrency. Word of Black Widow's deadly activities had been spreading, however, and the Winter Soldier had arrived on the scene to stop her. Natasha did not fail to note the irony—it had been Bucky Barnes who had trained her all those years ago for the mission to kill the current business owner's uncle and his entire family to ensure her inheritance. But again, Natasha rejected the hand extended by a former ally, telling Bucky that he did not understand what she was trying to do. As so often in her career, Black Widow appeared to be alone with her past.

Above: WEB OF BLACK WIDOW #2 (DEC. 2019) Resolved to expose all who profited from her Red Room assignments brought Black Widow into conflict with her former flame, the Winter Soldier.

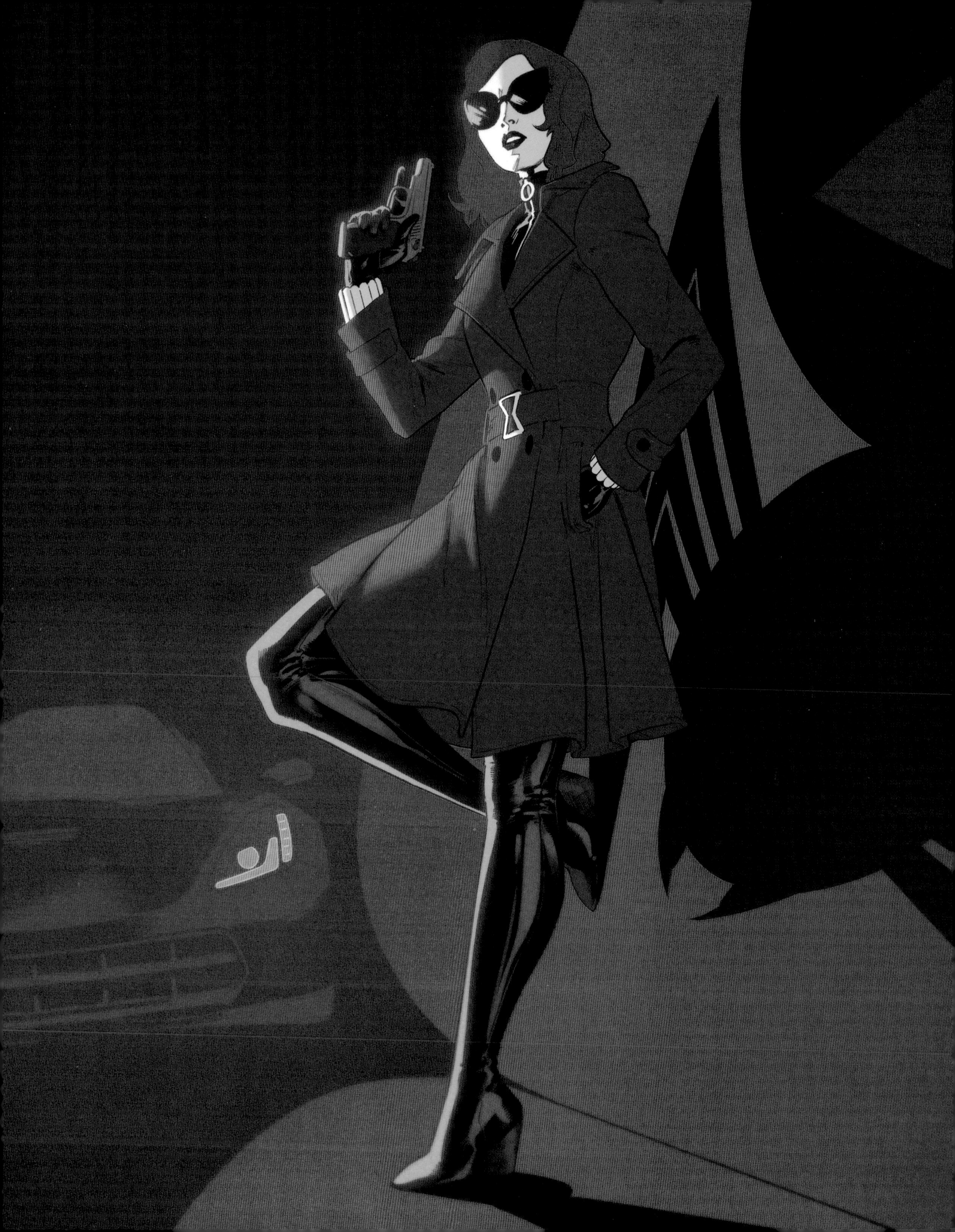

Widow's Way

With a life entangled in a web of duty and deceit, Black Widow is a hero like no other. She does not shrink from any challenge and backs herself against any opponent— no more so than when her mission involves protecting society's most vulnerable. This is when she is at her most passionate and driven. Natasha Romanoff's skills were forced upon her at a young age, when she was groomed to be one of the world's deadliest secret agents. But as she came into her own, she found a way to use those skills for missions that she chose, not as someone else's weapon.

While most at home in the shadowy world of espionage, Natasha has also fought immortals, aliens, and demons. They all underestimated her abilities, resolve, and courage. However, for all the good deeds she has done and the lives she has saved, her past just keeps coming back. The guilt of her early years as the Red Room's deadliest operative drives her to keep going, never to rest until she can balance out the red in her ledger. She believes that her quest for redemption is something she must do alone, but Natasha has amassed many loyal allies and frequently demonstrated strong leadership qualities that have inspired many to follow and respect her. But not even those closest to her will ever know her full story—Black Widow's secrets are legion, and some are buried so deep that even she does not know them. What she does know is that, whatever the truth about her past, she is in control of the present, and she alone can shape her future.

WEB OF BLACK WIDOW #1 (NOV. 2019) Raised to be an ideological weapon, Black Widow had turned herself into a weapon of atonement, using her skills to protect the vulnerable.

Index

N

O

P

R

S

T

U

V

W

X

Y

Z

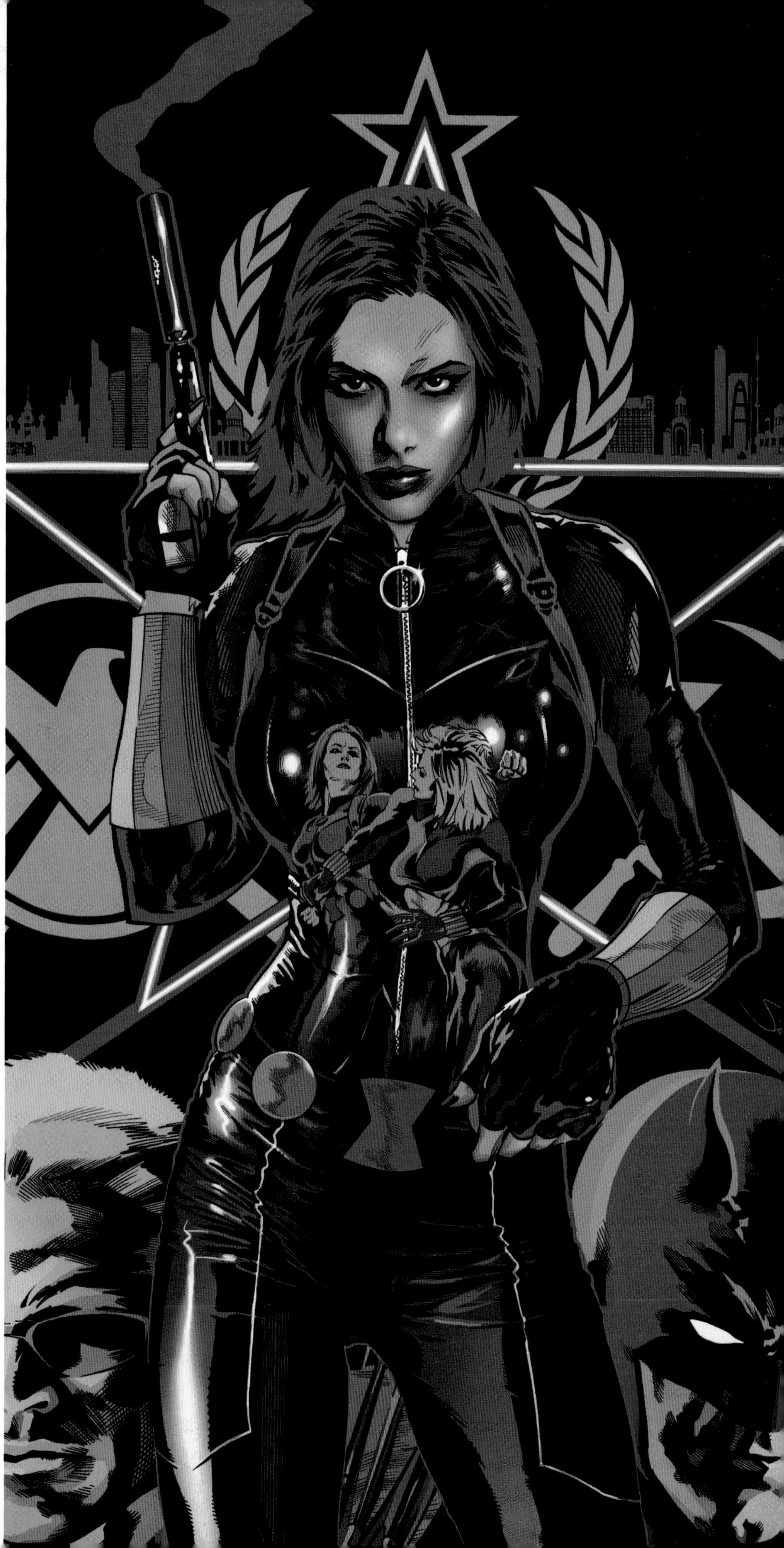

DK | Penguin Random House

Senior Editor Cefn Ridout
Senior Designer Anne Sharples
Copy Editor Kathryn Hill
Pre-Production Producer Mary Slater
Producer Siu Yin Chan
Managing Editor Sarah Harland
Managing Art Editor Vicky Short
Publisher Julie Ferris
Art Director Lisa Lanzarini

Cover artwork Jen Bartel
Cover design Clive Savage

Dorling Kindersley would like to thank:
Brian Overton, Caitlin O'Connell, Jeff Youngquist,
and Joe Hochstein at Marvel for vital help and advice;
Matt Jones for editorial assistance; Megan Douglass
for proofreading; and Vanessa Bird for the index.

First American Edition, 2020
Published in the United States by DK Publishing
1450 Broadway, Suite 801, New York, NY 10018
20 21 22 23 24   10 9 8 7 6 5 4 3 2 1
001–317737–Apr/2020

© 2020 MARVEL

A catalog record for this book is available from the Library of Congress.
ISBN: 978-1-4654-9692-8

DK books are available at special discounts when purchased in bulk
for sales promotions, premiums, fund-raising, or educational use.
For details, contact: DK Publishing Special Markets,
1450 Broadway, Suite 801, New York, NY 10018
SpecialSales@dk.com

Printed and bound in China.

A WORLD OF IDEAS:
SEE ALL THERE IS TO KNOW
www.dk.com

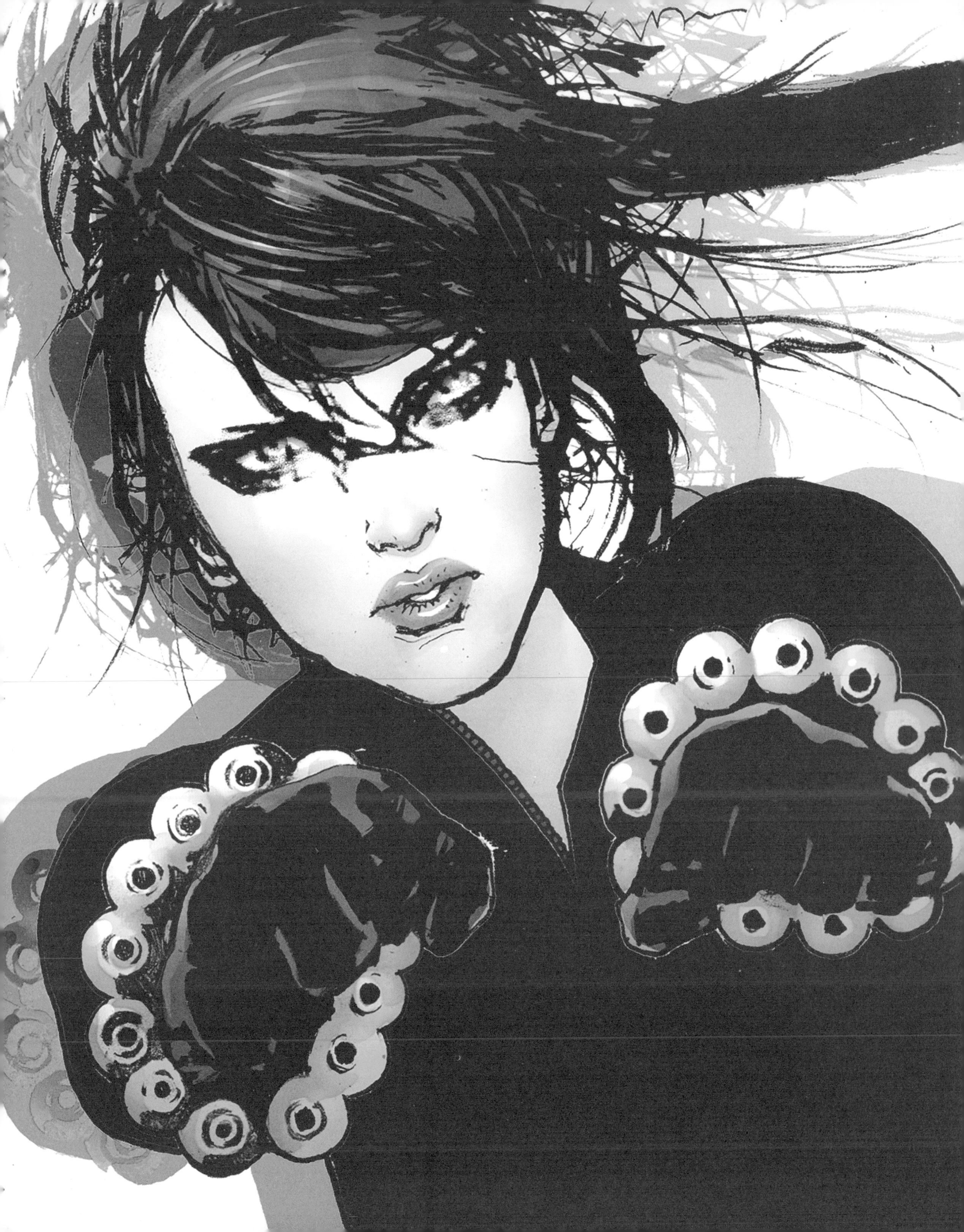